CW00857492

The American History and Encyclopedia of Music

Operas (Volume II)

W. L. Hubbard

Alpha Editions

This edition published in 2020

ISBN : 9789354016004

Design and Setting By
Alpha Editions
email - alphaedis@gmail.com

THE AMERICAN HISTORY AND ENCYCLOPEDIA OF MUSIC

W. L. HUBBARD
EDITOR IN CHIEF

EMIL LIEBLING GEO. W. ANDREWS
ARTHUR FOOTE EDWARD DICKINSON
ASSOCIATE EDITORS

EDITORIAL CONTRIBUTORS

G. W. CHADWICK FRANK DAMROSCH FREDERICK STOCK CARL FAELTEN
W. J. HENDERSON H. E. KREHBIEL FREDERICK STARR
CLARENCE DICKINSON THEODORE SPIERING FRANZ KNEISEL
EDWARD M. BOWMAN OSCAR SAENGER GEORGE C. GOW
FREDERIC W. ROOT W. S. B. MATHEWS
BERNHARD LISTEMANN HARRISON M. WILD
ARNOLD DOLMETSCH

IRVING SQUIRE
NEW YORK

LA SCALA, MILAN.

This is next in importance to the Paris Opera House. It is more historic but far less magnificent. It is called Teatro della Scalla from its having been built in 1778 on the site of a church raised by Beatrice Scala, wife of Barnabo Viscontex. Piermarini was the architect. It has always been admired for the excellence of its internal arrangements. Its cost was only $200,000. Until 1857 its principal entrance was from a side street, but it now opens upon a square in the center of which stands the famous statue of Leonardo da Vinci.

The interior is in the shape of a horseshoe and has five tiers of boxes, two hundred in number. There is a royal box above the entrance to the stalls. The curtain represents Parnassus and is the work of Riccardi. It was restored in 1878. It is the property of the city of Milan whose council grants an annual sum for its support.

Countless Italian masterpieces from Bellini's "Norma" to Verdi's "Falstaff" have been produced upon its boards. The training school attached to it has graduated probably more famous singers and ballerinas than has any other.

LA SCALA, MILAN.

This is next in importance to the Paris Opera House. It is more historic but far less magnificent. It is called Teatro della Scalla from its having been built in 1778 on the site of a church raised by Beatrice Scala, wife of Barnabo Visconti. Piermarini was the architect. It has always been admired for the excellence of its internal arrangements. Its cost was only $200,000. Until 1857 its principal entrance was from a side street, but it now opens upon a square in the center of which stands the famous statue of Leonardo da Vinci.

The interior is in the shape of a horseshoe and has five tiers of boxes, two hundred in number. There is a royal box above the entrance to the stalls. The curtain represents Parnassus and is the work of Riccardi. It was restored in 1878. It is the property of the city of Milan whose council grants an annual sum for its support.

Countless Italian masterpieces from Bellini's "Norma" to Verdi's "Falstaff" have been produced upon its boards. The training school attached to it has graduated probably more famous singers and ballerinas than has any other.

THE AMERICAN HISTORY AND ENCYCLOPEDIA OF MUSIC

OPERAS

WITH

INTRODUCTION

BY

H. E. KREHBIEL

W. L. HUBBARD

EDITOR

VOLUME II

IRVING SQUIRE
Toledo
New York Chicago

OPERAS, VOL. 2

LIST OF ILLUSTRATIONS.

THE TAMING OF THE SHREW

"The Taming of the Shrew," a comic opera in four acts, its libretto freely arranged by Joseph Widmann from the Shakespearian comedy of the same name, and with music by Hermann Goetz, was produced at Mannheim in 1872.

CHARACTERS.

Baptista, a rich gentleman of Padua.
Katherine, } his daughters.
Bianca, }
Hortensio, } suitors to Bianca.
Lucentio, }
Petruchio, a gentleman of Verona.
Grumio, his servant.
A tailor.
A steward.
A housekeeper.

As in Shakespeare's play, Baptista has two daughters, one of them Katherine, the shrew, and the other the gentle Bianca. When the curtain rises before Baptista's house, the love-sick Lucentio is discovered, addressing a serenade to Bianca's window. His dulcet tones are rudely drowned by a tumult in the house, caused by the vixenish Katherine. The servants coming out, thoroughly tired of her berating, declare that surely the fiend himself inhabits the house. When the storm has subsided, Lucentio, coming back to finish his serenade, has a delightful interview with his lady-love in which he is assured that she is not indifferent. They are interrupted by the arrival of an ancient beau, Hortensio, and his hired musicians, who play a serenade of his own composing. Lucentio is about actively to oppose the rival concert, when Baptista comes out of the house, very cross about having his rest disturbed with continual serenading, and reminds the suitors that there can be no hope for them until Katherine is safely wedded. Could any situation be more hopeless?

They depart in dejection and Hortensio meets the wealthy and gallant Petruchio of Verona, who has recently arrived in Padua. The two are old acquaintances and, in the course of the conversation, Petruchio laments the fact that he is rich and surrounded by sycophants and expresses a longing for the piquancy of having his will opposed.

Hortensio is at once reminded of Katherine, and recommends her for the purpose. Petruchio, drawing upon his memory, recalls her as a froward little girl he once met, who angrily escaped his kiss and ran away. His is a soul which loves to conquer opposition and he vows to wed this recalcitrant young lady. They are before her window, and looking up at it, he laughs quietly to himself and bids her,

> Sleep soft, for but one short and passing season,
> For thee a battle waits.

The second act takes place on the next morning and introduces to us Katherine in her own boudoir. Reports of her shrewishness are found to be entirely correct. Petruchio secures Baptista's all-too-willing consent and goes bravely about the formidable business of wooing. He has up-hill work of it, especially as Katherine has that very morning renewed her resolution never by any act to merit being called "the weaker vessel" like the rest of her sex. She fairly rages against his terms of endearment, but he meets all her scorn with honeyed irony. It finally occurs to her that, for the first time, she has met a man whose will is as unbending as her own. He insists that by Monday they will be wedded and in her fury she bethinks herself that perhaps she can best subdue him by marrying him and having him conveniently at hand. Promising to return to claim his gentle bride, he gaily departs for Venice.

In the third act, the taming process is seen to have begun even before the wedding. Petruchio makes Katherine submit to the humiliation of having to wait for her bridegroom. In fact, he is so long delayed that the guests depart thinking her a deserted bride and no one can really find heart to blame him for having repented his bargain. When tardy Petruchio does comes, it is without the promised finery and gifts for the bride. He bustles through the ceremony and despite the pleas of everybody, the bride not excepted, he will not stay for the wedding-feast but hurries Katherine away to the country with him.

In the fourth act, Petruchio and Katherine are seen at their country home with the taming process being continued. They attempt to dine but Petruchio snatches away each dish before his hungry bride can taste it, under the pretext that the waiting-people have not well served them. A tailor comes from Paris with fascinating gowns and bonnets and Kate for a moment forgets that she is half-famished as she inspects them with true feminine delight. She buys and eagerly waits to try the effect upon Petruchio but he declares her choice ridiculous and bids her discard the garments at once. But a strange thing has happened to Katherine. She does not want to fight with this Petruchio. She wants to love him and have him love her and she so confesses. The opera ends as Baptista arrives with Bianca and Lucentio, who just have been married, to find Kate and Petruchio not scratching each other's eyes out, but making love in the conventional way.

The opera, which is truly charming, was the only product of the genius of a composer, whose early death cut short a career full of promise.

Among the numbers are Lucentio's serenade, "Haste ye, tones of love and longing;" Petruchio's song, "She is a wife for such a man created;" Katherine's song in the second act, "I'll give myself to no man" and the quintet which closes the act.

In the third act are the love-songs of Lucentio and Hortensio, skilfully mingled with the giving of lessons to Bianca, and the music greeting the belated arrival of Petruchio. In the fourth act occur Katherine's confession "Of fighting I am wearying," and the love-duet of Katherine and Petruchio, "The silver moon invites."

GIROFLE-GIROFLA

"Giroflé-Girofla" is an opera bouffe in three acts, its music by Charles Lecocq and text by Van Loo and Aterrier. It was first produced at the Théâtre des Fantaisies Parisiennes, Brussels, March 21, 1874.

CHARACTERS.

Don Bolero D'Alcarazas, a Spanish nobleman, father of the twin sisters.
Marasquin, son of Marasquin & Co.; betrothed to Giroflé.
Aurora, wife of Don Bolero.
Giroflé, } twin sisters.
Girofla, }
Pedro.
Paquita.
The Pirate Chief.
The Godfather.
The Notary.
The Uncle.
The Page.
The Godmother.
Fernand.
Gusman.
A Lawyer.
Servants, pirates, bridesmaids, cousins, Moors.

The scene is laid in Spain in the last century. The story relates the pecuniary difficulties of Don Bolero, who is governor of the province and possesses a variety of titles but no money. He is, in fact, badly in debt, owing 4,000,-000 francs to Marasquin & Co., with no prospect of being able to pay it. His available assets consist of two daughters, twins, and so remarkably similar in appearance that they can be distinguished only by wearing scarfs of different color, one of blue and one of rose. These young ladies are of marriageable age and just when the family fortunes are at lowest ebb, their mother, Donna Aurora, who is a bit of a match-maker, betroths Giroflé to the heir of the house of Marasquin, and Girofla to Mourzouk, the Moorish chief, to whom Don Bolero is also in debt and who emphasizes his demands for payment with threats of death.

The curtain rises on the wedding-day of the twins. Marasquin comes first and is duly married to Giroflé, but before the arrival of the Moor a dreadful thing happens. Girofla is carried off by pirates and the parents are in despair at the thought of trying to appease her bridegroom. The mother again rises equal to the occasion and dispatches Admiral Matamoras in pursuit of the pirates. Giroflé then impersonates her sister and is married again, this time to the Moor. As they are waiting for the restoration of the stolen bride, Matamoras, who has been promised 10,000 piasters for his deed but who is doubtful of the paternal word in money matters, sends a message saying that he will proceed with the battle on receipt of cash. The cash is speedily collected and sent but the incident causes delay and Giroflé has a lively time posing as bride of two husbands during the interval. The situation is further complicated by the fact that she becomes intoxicated. The ingenious inventions of Don Bolero to account for the absence of the proper number of brides are remarkably amusing. Ultimately, everything is settled peaceably by the return of Giroflé's twin sister.

This merry opera, with its light and lively melodies of a rather higher standard than those of the usual opera bouffe, contains several favorites, among them being Paquita's ballad, " When the day's finished and evening has come;" the pirates' chorus, " The neatest and completest;" the drinking song, " The Glistening Wine;" the duet, " O Pretty Girofla" and the chorus of wedding-guests, " It is the cannon."

DIE FLEDERMAUS

"Die Fledermaus" or "The Bat," a comic operetta in three acts, the book by Haffner and Genée and music by Johann Strauss, was first performed in Vienna in July, 1874. It is founded on "Le Revillon," by Meilhac and Halévy.

CHARACTERS.

Von Eisenstein, a Baron.
Alfred, a singing-master.
Frosch, a court-usher.
Frank, a prison director.
Dr. Blind, an attorney.
Dr. Falke, a notary.
Ivan, Prince Chamberlain.
Ali Bey, an Egyptian.
Murray, an American.
Cancorney, a Marquis.
Rosalinde, wife of Eisenstein.
Prince Orlofsky.
Adèle, Rosalinde's maid.
Lord Middleton.
Dancers and masqueraders.

Happy he, who can see
Life is all a comedy.

sing the characters consistently in "The Bat," and they are faithful to their creed. The scene of this gay little adventure is laid in Germany in the last century. In Act I, we are grieved to find that Herr von Eisenstein has been sentenced to eight days' imprisonment for contempt of court. His friend, Doctor Falke, who has been the victim of one of Von Eisenstein's practical jokes whereby after a masked ball he has had to walk home through the streets in broad daylight in the unusual guise of a bat or flittermouse, decides to settle the score. Accordingly, he persuades Von Eisenstein to ignore his sentence and attend with him the ball given by Prince Orlofsky, an eccentric young Russian with a penchant for ladies of the ballet. Falke also invites to the festivity Rosalinde, the Baron's wife and Adèle, her maid. After the departure of Von Eisenstein and Doctor Falke, Rosalinde receives a visit from a former admirer, Alfred, a music teacher. So much does he make himself at home that when the warden of the jail, which is fairly yawning for Von Eisenstein, calls for his prisoner, Alfred is mistaken for the husband. To put the matter in the best light possible, Alfred allows himself to be arrested, and is led off attired in Von Eisenstein's dressing-gown.

In Act II, the ball is in progress at Prince Orlofsky's house. Here are assembled all the dramatis personæ, except, for obvious reasons, Alfred. Von Eisenstein, Falke, Rosalinde, who is masked, Adèle and Frank, are all posing as others than themselves. Rosalinde has a desperate flirtation with her own husband and succeeds in relieving him of his watch. The ball is a great success but it comes to an untimely end when Rosalinde, whose identity is about to be discovered by her husband, makes the clock strike six and the revelers run away thinking the dawn has surprised them. In the morning, all the guests go to visit Frank at the jail and find that instead of being the Chevalier, as he has represented himself, he is a warden. Adèle, thinking him an important personage, has come to beg his influence in securing her master's forgiveness for having worn her mistress' dress at the ball. Frank unfortunately is still under the influence of the champagne he drank the night before, and his jailor, Frosch, also is intoxicated.

Von Eisenstein, coming to give himself up as a prisoner, is astonished to find that another, arrested at his residence as Rosalinde's husband, is serving his term. Alfred, who does not recognize him, confides the whole story to him and affairs become greatly complicated. Rosalinde's arrival further entangles matters until she confronts her husband with damaging evidence against him in the shape of his own watch and he is forced to be forgiving and so is forgiven.

While the libretto of "The Bat" may not be of remarkable value, the score is excellent. As usual, the waltz king indulges his love of dance-music and charming waltzes, czardas, polkas, romanzas and drinking songs abound.

IL DEMONIO

"Il Demonio" or "The Demon," a lyric play in three acts, with music by Anton Rubinstein and text by Wiskowatov, after the Russian of Lermantoff, was produced in St. Petersburg, Jan. 25, 1875.

CHARACTERS.

The Demon.
Prince Gudal.
Tamara, his daughter.
Prince Sinodal, Tamara's fiancé.
The Angel of Light.
Servant to Sinodal.
Tamara's Governess.
Good and bad spirits, angels.

The scene is laid in Grusia in the Caucasus. The Demon has left the nether world and wanders about on earth in search of prey, impelled by his hatred of the Creator and all his works. When the curtain rises, the Demon is seen in the flashes of the storm, leaping about in fury. The evil spirits and the voices of the wind taunt each other in the darkness and a chorus of created things speak in fervent praise of Heaven. The demon is complaining of his ennui and raving of unprecedented deeds of evil, when approached by the Angel of Light, who in vain begs him to repent and seek the forgiveness of heaven.

In vivid contrast is the second tableau, which discloses Tamara, daughter of Prince Gudal, a maiden of transcendent beauty, making merry with her attendants. She is observed by the Demon, who, enchanted by her appearance, resolves to secure her for himself, despite the fact that he hears her speak of the early return of her adored bridegroom, Prince Sinodal. She feels the baneful influence of his presence even before she sees him. When alone for a moment, she catches a glimpse of him and hears him whisper that she shall be his queen and that all the world shall bow to her. Overwhelmed by astonishment and dismay, she flies to the castle.

The next scene shows a pass in the mountains of the Caucasus. The tinkling of bells announces the approaching caravan of the Prince Sinodal and his suite, who encamp for the night. The former chafes at the delay, which keeps him from his bride-to-be, and his old servant attempts to comfort him. Nevertheless, the usually courageous old servant is weighted down with foreboding, and rebukes the retainers, who sing and jest around the fires. Sinodal sings of the absent Tamara and of the joy anticipated for the morrow, and then falls asleep with the rest. They are surrounded by a band of marauding Tartars and Sinodal, though resisting bravely, is wounded and dies in the old servant's arms, after catching a glimpse of the Demon, who had decreed his death.

The second act is played in the castle of Prince Gudal, where the nuptial preparations are complete. As the household waits in festive garments to receive the bridegroom, his dead body is brought in upon a bier. The bitter sorrow of Tamara cannot be appeased, although the pitying father bids her seek consolation in Heaven. While frantic with grief, she hears the familiar seductive voice of the Demon assuring her that Sinodal, as the guest of heaven, has now forgotten her. The fiend's presence makes her fearful that she will not be strong enough to resist him and she begs to be allowed to enter a convent. Her father reluctantly consents and prepares to seek vengeance in war upon the Tartars, the slayers of the prince and destroyer of his daughter's happiness.

In Act III, the interior of Tamara's cloister is seen. The old servant of Sinodal sits outside singing a Christian hymn and the Angel of Light guards the threshold. The Demon appears seeking Tamara and struggles with the Angel, who disputes his right to enter. At last he gains entrance and becomes visible to the maiden, whose dreams have been haunted with glimpses of him. He declares his overwhelming passion and invokes Tamara's love which alone can redeem him from his curse, promising to end his struggle with Heaven and tread in virtue's path forevermore. He argues in a score of ways and paints vividly the glories he can offer her as his queen. Tamara implores aid from on high but finally her strength gives out and she finds herself powerless to resist the Demon's embrace. At this the Angel of Light appears and she seeks refuge in his arms and sinks to death. There is a mighty clap of thunder and the nunnery falls in ruins, from the midst of which Tamara is seen carried by angels to Heaven.

In "The Demon," the most successful of Rubinstein's operas, a number of passages are notable. In the first act are the opening chorus of evil spirits and voices of nature; the Demon's aria, "Verhasste, Verfluchte Welt" ("Despised, accursed World"); Tamara's aria, "Ach! liebe Mädchen!" ("Ah! lovely maiden"); the Tartar chorus, "Stille, Stille, schleichet näher" ("Softly, softly"). In the second act are found the ballet music and the Demon's romanza, "Süsses Kind, du weinst vergebens" ("Dearest child, 'tis vain thy weeping"); while the third act contains the long duet between the Demon and Tamara.

Copyright
by
A.Dupont

EMMA CALVE,

In the Title Role of Bizet's Carmen.

The latest and by far the greatest interpreter of the role of Carmen in Bizet's opera, was born in 1866 at Decazeville, France, and made her operatic debut at Brussels in 1881, as Marguerite in Faust. She originated the role of Santuzza in Cavalleria Rusticana, but her greatest triumphs followed her first appearance in Carmen at the Opera Comique, Paris, in 1894.

She first came to America, in 1893 and has since made yearly visits in grand opera and in recital. She is of a philanthropic nature and has built and endowed an orphanage for girls near her mountain home in France.

CARMEN

"Carmen," an opera in four acts with music by Georges Bizet and text by Meilhac and Halévy, was first produced at the Opéra Comique, Paris, March 3, 1875. It follows the story of Prosper Merimée, bearing the same title.

CHARACTERS.

Don Jose, a brigadier.
Escamillo, a toreador.
Il Dancairo, } smugglers.
Il Remendado, }
Zuniga, a captain.
Morales, a brigadier.
Carmen, a gypsy.
Michaela, a peasant girl.
Frasquita, } gypsies, friends of Carmen.
Mercedes, }
Lillas Pastia, an innkeeper.
A guide, officers, dragoons, lads, cigar girls, gypsies, smugglers.

The scene is laid in Seville, that favorite spot of opera writers. The date is 1820. The curtain rises upon the public square, where Don José and his soldiers are idly awaiting the coming, at the noon hour, of the girls employed in the cigar-factory near by. The most bewitching of them all is the gay, fickle, handsome, unprincipled Carmen, who with an acacia flower in her mouth and a bouquet in her bodice, strolls by apparently indifferent to her swarm of admirers. Seeing that Don José is thinking of another fair maid "with flowing hair and dress of blue," and is not mindful of her charms, she throws him a rose, and flits away. The coquetry is as effective as she hoped and it requires the appearance of the gentle Michaela, his own sweetheart, who comes to deliver a message and a kiss from his mother, to dispel the vision of her haunting eyes. Just as he is about to throw away the rose, he and his soldiers are summoned to the factory, where they find that Carmen, in a fit of passion, has stabbed one of the girls. She is arrested but opens up the battery of her charms again and Don José unties her hands and allows her to escape with the promise of meeting him that evening.

In the second act, she is found at the cabaret of Lillas Pastia near the ramparts, singing and dancing with gypsy friends and soldiers about her. Escamillo, a dashing toreador, comes in and Carmen at once finds in him a new admirer and one who especially appeals to her. Don José has been in prison for a month as punishment for having let her escape from arrest. His sentence ends tonight, however, and he comes direct to her. He grows jealous when she tells him of having danced for others but is content when she sings and dances for him alone. She tries to lure him to abandon his soldier life and to become a smuggler but he will not listen to her. His captain surprises him with Carmen, swords are drawn and there is nothing left for José to do but to join Carmen and her companions.

The third act opens in the haunt of the gypsies, who are also smugglers. Carmen has wearied of Don José, with his high ideas and his tiresome sensibility of conscience. She therefore welcomes the arrival of Escamillo with undisguised delight. Just as the rival suitors have been prevented from a duel by the gypsies, the gentle, forgiving Michaela comes with a message that Don José's mother is dying and, reluctant even then, he leaves the field to Escamillo.

The action of the last act takes place on the day of a bull-fight at Seville of which Escamillo, the toreador, is to be the hero. Carmen and all the gypsies have accepted his invitation to be present. Don José has come and hopes to make an effort to regain Carmen. In her festal attire she meets him but his prayers and his anguish do not move her and, with characteristic bravado, she tells him that it is only Escamillo who is lord of her affections. Maddened, he tries to seize her, but she escapes, throws his ring at him and rushes to the arena to greet his rival. Don José overtakes her and just as the people acclaim Escamillo the hero of the bull-fight he stabs her through the heart.

"Carmen's" predecessors from the hand of Bizet were all more or less failures and even with "Carmen" the composer did not live to taste the satisfaction of success, for the great favor into which the work came was only gradual and Bizet died three months after the initial presentation. Today, however, the opera has but few equals in popularity throughout the entire music world.

Among the most admired numbers are the overture; the cigarette girls' chorus; Carmen's Habanera (a genuine Spanish tune), "L'amour est une oiseau rebelle" ("Love like a wild bird"); the duet of Michaela and Don José, "Ma mère, je la vois" ("My mother now I see"); the seguidilla, "Près des ramparts" ("Down by the walls"), sung by Carmen; the stirring toreador song; the famed romanza for José, "La fleur que tu m'avais jettée" ("The flower which thou didst give me"); Carmen's "card-scene" aria which she sings, following the fortune-telling duet for Frasquita and Mercedes and Michaela's aria, "Je dis que rien" ("I say that nothing shall deter me").

One recalls many melodies when this opera is brought to mind. The overture contains the most characteristic themes. It opens with a burst of rhythmic fanfare which we hear again at the bull-fight—the motiv of the bully Escamillo. We also hear the theme of passion, which is Carmen's motiv. Throughout the opera the music is passionate and original, and though the story is very sombre, the Spanish atmosphere in music and libretto, as well as the attractive stage settings, draw to its performances large audiences. Carmen is rightly called Bizet's most popular as well as his best operatic work.

THE QUEEN OF SHEBA

"The Queen of Sheba," a grand opera in four acts, was first presented in Vienna, March 10, 1875. Its text is by Mosenthal, and its music by Karl Goldmark.

CHARACTERS.

King Solomon.
Baal-Hanan, steward of the palace.
Assad, Solomon's favorite.
High Priest.
Sulamith, the High Priest's daughter.
The Queen of Sheba.
Astaroth, slave of the Queen of Sheba.
Priests, Levites, singers, harpists, body-guards, women of the harem, dancers, people.

The libretto is founded on the Biblical mention of the visit of the Queen of Sheba to Solomon but it must be added that the Old Testament account has been much embellished by the librettist. When the opera opens, a marriage is about to be splendidly celebrated in Solomon's palace in Jerusalem. It is that of Sulamith, the High Priest's daughter, who is to be united to Assad, favorite courtier of the King. Assad had been sent to conduct to the court the Queen of Sheba, who now with her retinue waits at the city's gate. Assad, however, is much dejected, for though he would be faithful, his thoughts constantly recur to a woman of transcendent beauty whom he had seen while escorting the Queen. This woman, who was bathing in a pool in the forest, was a glorious creature, who discovering his presence, had come out of the water like a nymph, to wind her snowy arms about his neck. In his distress, he seeks the counsel of the King whose wisdom is indisputable and Solomon bids him marry his affianced one at once and then to pray to Heaven for peace.

Meantime, the Queen of Sheba appears with her attendants. She enters veiled, and followed by a procession of slaves and lovers, with Astaroth, her chief slave, next to her. When she frees her face from its covering, and stands forth in all her beauty, Assad sees again the goddess of the pool. The Queen makes no sign of his presence but his agitation is only too apparent. Solomon, noting it, reminds him that the morrow is his wedding-day. The Queen overhears these words and Assad discovers that her indifference is assumed, for she flashes a look at him eloquent with passion and yearning.

At night Astaroth summons Assad to the fountain in the courtyard, where the Queen meets him and completes his captivation. In the morning — his bridal morning — the priests come to conduct him to the altar and the Queen follows in dazzling apparel, bringing a golden cup filled with pearls for a wedding present. Assad, as he stands by Sulamith's side, while the voice of the High Priest is lifted to chant the nuptial ceremony, sees the Queen, and can no longer restrain himself. Casting away the marriage ring, he falls at her feet, crying aloud that she is his divinity. He is seized and condemned to death for profaning the temple.

The honor of the Queen's visit is now celebrated with a ballet and feast. Sulamith has pleaded for Assad's life and now the Queen tries with all her arts to influence Solomon to release him but the King is unmoved. In his wisdom, however, he realizes the Queen's baseness; his heart is softened to Assad and he lightens his sentence to exile in the desert. Thence the Queen follows him, but Assad only repulses her. Sulamith also seeks him in his desolation, forgiving and ready to die with him. A simoom sweeps over the desert and they perish in each other's arms, while a mirage shows the Queen and her retinue journeying homeward.

"The Queen of Sheba," which established Goldmark's fame throughout the musical world, is particularly notable for the rich Oriental coloring of both its instrumental and vocal scores. The composer has made use of Hebrew melodies in the great Temple scenes and in many portions of the work has had recourse to intervals and progressions essentially Eastern. The result is a beauty in color and an unusualness in effect, which lend the opera distinctly original qualities and place its creator among the notable composers of the present time.

The chief numbers are the brilliant chorus with which the opera opens; Sulamith's bridal aria, "My Assad Returns;" Assad's recital of his seeing the nymph in the forest; the gorgeously colored music which accompanies the entrance of the Queen and her retinue; the Queen's aria, "Let me from the festal splendor," in which she voices her love for Assad and her jealous hatred of Sulamith; the remarkable song for Astaroth, one of the most strikingly Oriental and beautiful numbers in the entire score, with which she lures Assad to the garden; the duet of Assad and the Queen; the music accompanying the great scene in the Temple; the ballet music and the lament of Assad in the desert.

THE GOLDEN CROSS

"The Golden Cross," an opera in two acts with music by Ignaz Brüll and text by H. S. Mosenthal, after the French comedy "La Croix d'Or," by Brazier and Melville, was first produced in Berlin, Dec. 22, 1875.

CHARACTERS.

Gontran de L'Ancre, a young French nobleman.
Nicholas Pariset, owner of the mill and the inn.
Christina, his sister.
Theresa, his cousin and betrothed.
Bombardon, a sergeant.
Soldiers, peasants, village youths and maidens.

The story is laid in the little village of Melun, situated not far from Paris. It begins in 1812, at the time when Napoleon is preparing to lead his armies into Russia. Nicholas the innkeeper, or Colas as his friends call him, is about to be married to his pretty cousin Theresa. All arrangements have been made; the bride's friends have come to present the customary bouquets of rosemary and Christina has smothered a natural sisterly jealousy, roused by the thought of giving her brother to another woman. For, left orphans at an early age, and growing up in each other's care, they have meant much to each other and Christina has dismissed all lovers, preferring to stay with Colas. Even now she swears, quite as other maidens have done, that her heart shall ever be proof against the little god of the bow and arrows. When everything is looking quite auspicious for the lovers, Bombardon, the recruiting officer, appears in the village and announces that a conscription is to be made among the young men available for military service. Colas' about-to-be-acquired responsibility as a husband unfortunately does not exempt him and the little circle is in despair.

Soon after Christina has made her ill-advised remarks about single blessedness, Bombardon and his military friend, Gontran de L'Ancre, approach the inn, singing of the wine with which they hope soon to refresh themselves. This leading to the kindred subject, woman, Gontran voices his conviction that any one who puts his trust in them will rue it. Theresa, left alone at the inn, finds an opportunity to rehearse her future role as landlady. The gallant Bombardon is openly enchanted by her bright eyes. Warmed by the wine she brings them, Gontran tells of his betrayal by a woman, who had sworn to be faithful to him, thus explaining his cynical attitude toward the sex. His first glimpse of Christina stirs him remarkably but he reminds himself to be on his guard.

Meantime, Christina is enduring agonies of mind, induced by visions of her dear brother Colas buried under the snow and ice of Russia. She hopes to contrive a way to save him from danger and the only possible solution seems to be a substitute, an alternative which money cannot buy. She remembers many rejected suitors who have given expression to their unbounded friendship and, meeting a number upon whom the conscription has not fallen, she promises to marry whomever will take her brother's place in the ranks and bring back to her, at the end of his service, the cross of gold which hangs on a ribbon about her neck. But the prize is not sufficient to tempt them into real danger and no one comes forward to claim the pledge. Colas is about to march away, perforce, when Bombardon announces that a substitute has offered himself and Christina promises solemnly to be true to the unknown.

A period of three years elapses before the second act. The curtain rises again on the mill and inn of Colas. A number of things have happened in this time, during all of which Christina has been true to her vow. Colas, upon a later conscription, has been forced to go to war. and has barely escaped with his life. His captain has found him wounded and has been carrying him off the field, when he himself is hit by a bullet, Colas being by this time able to return the compliment by saving him. This same young captain has been taken to the inn and nursed to convalescence by Christina, and, as frequently happens, patient and nurse have lost their hearts to each other. Nevertheless, believing it to be her duty to remain faithful to the possessor of the golden cross, Christina daily watches for his return. At last the captain declares his love for her and assures her that she may have no hesitation in accepting him, as it was he who was her brother's substitute. He explains that he has delayed his avowal, hoping to win her heart as well as her hand. The delighted Christina asks to see the pledge, but Gontran tells her that once when he thought himself fatally wounded he entrusted it to a comrade to bring back to her. Christina fancies it to be a ruse instigated by Colas and Theresa to make her accept the happiness within her reach and she sends the captain away hurt by her suspicions.

At this crisis, there comes down the hill by the inn as jauntily as a man may who has a wooden leg, a person whom no one recognizes as the one-time fine recruiting officer. His uniform is worn and ragged, his face is scarred and weather-beaten, his leg is gone at the knee, but the Cross of the Legion of Honor gleams brightly upon his breast. "Yes, children, thus it is that the Grand Army returns to France," he says gaily, but nevertheless he wipes a furtive tear from his eye. He talks jokingly with Colas and his wife and asks for Christina. It is he who has the golden cross and he reminds her of her promise. Her heart sinks but she resolves to keep her word and places her hand in his.

Then Bombardon hears Gontran's familiar but disconsolate voice and fairly falls upon him in his joy. In fact, he is a great deal happier to find an old friend than to win a bride. The matter is cleared to Christina's satisfaction and Bombardon gaily takes the couple, one on each arm, and followed by the rest sings joyously:

Rataplan! Tarara!
Now peace reigns in the land.
Capitulate the Grand Armée
In hymen's sacred band.

"The Golden Cross" which is very popular in Germany and is an excellent example of the German comic opera, or singspiel, has among its most interesting numbers Christina's romanza, "Die Eltern starben frühe" ("My parents died long years ago"); a duet for Theresa and Christina, "Man soll's nicht verschworen" ("One never should declare"); a duet for Bombardon and Gontran, "Halt, Front, Gewehr bei Fuss" ("Halt! Front! Attention give!"); Gontran's song, "Jugendgluck, Jugendtraum" ("Joy of youth, Dream of Youth"); the delightfully stirring rataplan song of Bombardon; the duet of Theresa and Nicholas, "Schau, schau, mein Männchen" ("See, see, my hubby"); Gontran's romanza, "Nein, nein ich will ihr Herz nicht zwingen" ("No, no, not force can make her love me"); the supper-table quartet; the love duet for Christina and Gontran, "Darf ich's glauben" ("Dare I think then") and Bombardon's song, "Wie anders war es" ("How different then").

FATINITZA

Fatinitza, a comic opera in three acts with music by Franz von Suppé and text by Zell and Genée, was first produced in Vienna, Jan. 5, 1876.

CHARACTERS.

Count Timofey Gavrilovitch Kantchukoff, a Russian general.

Princess Lydia Imanovna, his niece.

Izzet Pasha, Governor of the Turkish fortress at Rustchuk.

Captain Vasil Staravieff.

Lieutenant Osipp Safonoff.

Ivan,
Nikiphar,
Fedor,
Dimitri,
Wasili,
Michaloff,
Casimir,
Gregor, } cadets.

Steipann, a sergeant.

Vladimir Samoiloff, a lieutenant of a Circassian cavalry regiment.

Julian Hardy, the special war correspondent of the "New York Herald."

Hassan Bey, leader of a squad of Bashi-Bazouks.

Besika,
Diona,
Zuleika,
Nursidah, } wives of the Pasha.

Mustapha, guardian of the harem.
Vuika, a Bulgarian.
Hanna, his wife.
A Cossack, a military cook.

The opera opens in a Russian camp on the lower Danube. Vladimir, a Circassian cavalry lieutenant, is wakened from his dream of Lydia, a girl whom he has met but whose surname he does not know, and is ordered to act as the officer of the day. He is young, good-looking and very popular with the regiment and the men are soon chaffing him about his conquests. The story comes out that while recently masquerading as a girl and calling himself Fatinitza he has met Count Timofey Kantchukoff, the Russian general, who has fallen violently in love with him. As the soldiers make merry, there is brought into the camp, as a spy, one Julian Hardy, an American war correspondent, in whom is combined newspaper enterprise, much fun and good nature and a gift for extricating his friends from dilemmas.

The monotony of camp life is beginning to pall upon the lively fellows and Vladimir's recountal of his success in feminine attire suggests amateur theatricals, which are speedily arranged, with the fair Fatinitza as leading lady. While the company has retired to dress for rehearsal, General Kantchukoff arrives unexpectedly and the first object of his displeasure is the journalist, who escapes punishment by means of his passport and his ready tongue. Other actors stroll in fantastically dressed but the appearance of Fatinitza, the old bachelor's first and only love, diverts his wrath from them. In order to be left alone with her, the General orders the men off to drill but Vladimir, who has been drinking allash, is coy about receiving the kiss of betrothal. The love-making is interrupted by the arrival of the General's niece, the Princess Lydia, whose incipient affair with Vladimir has caused him to be transferred to the outposts by her wary relative. Vladimir, who learns his sweetheart's rank for the first time is fearful lest the lady may penetrate his disguise but the resourceful Hardy smooths over the remarkable resemblance by explaining that Fatinitza is the sister of the young man Lydia has seen and loved. Lydia naturally is much interested in the girl and when the General commends his sweetheart to her, she offers to share her sleigh with her. Scarcely has the General left to inspect his troops when the camp is surprised by a band of Bashi-Bazouks, who capture the Princess, Vladimir and Hardy, the last being left to arrange a ransom. The doting General will not allow the troops to be fired upon lest they hit Fatinitza.

The second act shifts to the harem of Izzet Pasha, where his four wives are discovered deftly applying cosmetics. When the lord and master arrives, they quarrel for his kiss, but he insists that "order must be maintained even in a harem." His information that he is about to increase their number to five, by the addition of a beautiful Christian maiden captured by Hassan Bey, is received with disapproval. As he is cleverly reconciling his boasted reform sentiments with this course, Vladimir, still in woman's attire, is brought in with Lydia. The captives soon are cheered by the arrival of Hardy and the Russian sergeant Steipann to arrange for their release. The Pasha announces himself as ready to give up the lovely Fatinitza, but is determined to keep Lydia. Steipann is despatched to carry the Pasha's terms to the General and is also intrusted with a secret message from Julian telling him how he can surprise the Turks with his army. Vladimir reveals the secret of his true sex to the quartet of wives and they are happy to aid in his escape and especially in that of their rival, Lydia. Meantime, the Pasha and Hardy are "getting on" famously and the host provides elaborate entertainment, which includes a Turkish shadow pantomime. While this is in progress, the Russian army comes successfully to the rescue.

The third act takes places in the General's summer palace at Odessa, where Lydia and the four wives of her former captor are discovered. Lydia declares spiritedly that she will not marry a certain "ancient ruin," i. e., a crippled old friend that her uncle has picked out for her. Hardy brings in the favored Vladimir and so adroitly smooths matters over, that the testy old General himself directs the wedding procession into the church. The old fellow, who has been ever in quest of his lost Fatinitza, is overjoyed to hear that his agents have at last found her but his joy is changed to disgust when a veiled negress bearing that name is brought in. The conspirators terminate his only love-affair by having conveyed to him a letter which leads him to believe that the real Fatinitza has died of grief over her separation from him. The General blesses the union of his niece and the brother of his faithful love and all ends as comfortably as possible.

The principal numbers of this popular light opera are in the first act, called "At the Outposts." They are Vladimir's song, "Lost is the dream that bound me;" the reporter's descriptive song, "With my note-book in my hands;" the General's pompous expression as he enters, "Thousand fifes! and drums and cannon!" Lydia's sleighing-song; the chorus of Bashi-Bazouks "Now up, away, no sound betray." In the second or "Kismet" act the principal numbers are the primping chorus in the harem; the duet of Vladimir and Lydia, "I fear to think what is her destiny;" the Kismet duet, by Pasha and the reporter; Hardy's song, "My Native Land" and the effective bell sextet. In the last act, called "Chimes of Peace" the most conspicuous numbers are Lydia's "Bell aria" and the trio of Vladimir, Lydia and Hardy.

LA GIOCONDA

"La Gioconda" is a grand opera in four acts, the words by Arrigo Boito and the music by Amilcare Ponchielli. It is an adaption of Victor Hugo's drama, "Angelo," and was first presented at La Scala, Milan, April 8, 1876.

CHARACTERS.

La Gioconda, a ballad singer.
La Cieca, her blind mother.
Laura, wife of Alvise.
Barnaba, a spy of the Inquisition.
Alvise Badoero, one of the heads of the State Inquisition.
Zuane, a boatman.
Enzo, a Genoese Noble.
Isepo, a public letter-writer.
A pilot, monks, senators, sailors, shipwrights, ladies, gentlemen, populace, masquers.

The action takes place in Venice in the Seventeenth Century. When the opera opens there is shown the court-yard of the ducal palace, decorated in honor of a regatta and filled with people in holiday attire. Among them is a gay, light-hearted street-singer, La Gioconda, who brings her blind mother, La Cieca, to her accustomed seat near the church. She is observed by Barnaba, who makes some advances and is repulsed by the girl. Undaunted, he plots to get the mother into his power, thereby securing the daughter. He tells Zuane, who has been unsuccessful in the boat-race, that his defeat has been caused by the evil influence of La Cieca, who is a witch. The report spreads and the populace demands her death. Enzo arrives opportunely to protect her, and to quiet the mob. The grateful daughter is already in love with Enzo, whom she believes to be a mercantile captain. Alvise and Laura now come upon the scene and La Cieca is freed by the intercession of the latter, who receives the rosary of the blind woman in token of her gratitude.

Laura, who still loves Enzo, her former lover, notwithstanding her recent marriage to Alvise, exchanges many eloquent glances and at last a word with him, watched by Barnaba. He manages to whisper to Enzo that Laura will be on board the ship Hecate at nightfall during her husband's visit to the Council but he is overheard by La Gioconda. Barnaba then hastens to send a message to Alvise warning him that his wife is about to elope.

We next meet the characters on Enzo's vessel. The sailors are carousing and Barnaba and his fellow spy, Isepo, the public letter-writer, are disguised as fishermen. Laura joins Enzo on board and they decide to sail during the night. When Enzo goes below to complete his preparations, La Gioconda creeps upon Laura to slay her but, when the latter holds up the crucifix in appeal, the ballad singer remembers that it was this woman who had aided her mother. She resolves on giving tangible proof of her gratitude. She gives her masque to Laura and, summoning a boat, sends her away before the arrival of her husband.

Alvise determines to kill Laura the following night. He gives her a vial of poison to drink but during his momentary absence from the room, La Gioconda, who is aware of his purpose, rushes in and administers to the wife a powerful narcotic, emptying the flask of the poison. When he returns Laura is unconscious and Alvise believes that his revenge is complete.

The scene then changes to a grand fête, where Alvise is among the revelers. Barnaba drags in his victim, La

Cieca, whom he has found in one of the reserved apartments, praying for "her who is just dead." The guests are horrified but Alvise laughs. Enzo, who has heard that Laura has been killed, denounces Alvise and is seized by the guard. Gioconda promises Barnaba to be his if he will save Enzo, and he agrees. Alvise opens the curtains of Laura's chamber and shows her stretched upon her bier, vowing that he has taken her life to avenge his outraged honor.

In the last act, Laura wakes at last to call Enzo's name. She and her freed lover escape in a boat provided by the street-singer. Left alone, La Gioconda remembers her compact with Barnaba and resolves to fly. As she is praying to the Virgin for deliverance from her fate, he overhears her from the half open door. When he confronts her, she smiles and tells him that she will keep her word but she must array herself to do him honor; and, while he waits, delighted, she seizes a dagger and stabs herself, saying, "I have sworn to be thine. Take me, I am thine."

"La Gioconda" met with success and had in Italy one of the greatest runs known in Italian opera history.

Among the famous numbers in the opera are La Cieca's song in the first act, "Voce di donna o d' angelo" ("Voice of Woman or of Angel fair"); Enzo's passionate romanza, "Cielo e mar" ("Heaven and Sea"); the finale to the third act, the widely-known ballet, "The Hours" and, in the fifth act, as Gioconda plans to escape from Barnaba by death, her song, "Per te voglio ornare" ("For thee fain I'd prepare").

DER RING DES NIBELUNGEN

"Der Ring des Nibelungen" or "The Ring of the Nibelung" is the vastest achievement in the history of opera. The composition of this mighty work covered a long period of time, a period which included the years of Richard Wagner's prime. The subject suggested itself in 1848, just after the completion of "Tannhäuser," and, as usual, the conflicting claims of history and legend presented themselves. As usual, however, legend won the decision, for the story of Frederick Barbarossa and his deeds, which long occupied Wagner's thought, was discarded in favor of that of Siegfried of the Nibelungen myths. The source from which the dramas were drawn may be traced back through devious ways to the old Norse Sagas, principally to that division known as the Eddas, which took a later form in the "Nibelungen Lied," the national epic of Germany. As in previous works, Wagner seized upon a somewhat chaotic substance and invested it with the form and life of his own genius.

Wagner's original idea was by no means the monumental affair which the "Ring of the Nibelung" ultimately proved to be, for the work grew in scope, and changed in design under his hands. He began with the "Death of Siegfried," incidents and material now contained in the "Dusk of the Gods," but soon discovered that to make clear and effective the dramatic conditions and events leading up to the passing of his hero, a single drama would not suffice. He therefore planned the play dealing with the birth and life of the young Siegfried of the trilogy and, finding that still further explanatory material was desirable, decided upon " The Valkyrie " and, as introduction to the whole, fashioned " The Rhinegold." The trilogy was written backwards, therefore, so far as sequence of its different parts is concerned. In 1853, the great dramatic poem was completed and ten years later it was published as a literary product.

The work on the score was interrupted in 1857, for the composition of " Tristan and Isolde," done both for pecuniary reasons and to preserve the composer's connection with the stage. Between the years of 1861 and 1867, he frequently turned from his main scheme for the composition of " The Mastersingers."

Prior to the completion of the trilogy and somewhat against Wagner's personal inclinations, there were presented in Munich two of its separate parts, " The Rhinegold," in 1869 and " The Valkyrie " in 1870. " Siegfried " and " The Dusk of the Gods," however, were not seen until the performance of the entire work in August, 1876, at the opening of the Bayreuth Theatre.

The Nibelung trilogy includes plays for three days and a prior evening. The four dramas are in order of sequence, " The Rhinegold," " The Valkyrie," " Siegfried " and " The Dusk of the Gods." Together, they form a single great tragedy. This mighty work illustrates Wagner's dramatic and musical theories, his principal dramatic theory being the delineation of the " universal and eternal aspects " of human life by means of prototypes, his leading musical theory being the employment of the guiding theme, a system by which each of the principal factors of the opera is represented by a musical equivalent. The leading characters, influences and situations each have their own accompanying musical phrase, expressing them as vividly and appropriately as it is possible for tone to do.

There are over eighty guiding motives of this kind in the Ring. Each one consists of a short musical phrase and in each instance the phrase is so individual and characteristic that it is instantly recognizable. Belonging as is does to a clearly defined person, emotion or object, the motive becomes a tonal guide and to hear it is to have that for which it stands instantly suggested to the mind. It is evident that to be familiar with the motives increases many fold the interest and clearness of the opera. For instance, a character may fawn upon a companion and under his blandishments is lurking a desire for the other's destruction. The guiding motives allow us to look beneath the hypocrisy and to recognize the evil that is in the heart as well as the smile that is on the lips. The motives do not necessarily appear at the introduction of the character or idea but may hint of them long before they enter actively into the drama and may reappear whenever thought of them is suggested by the situation. Neither do they always retain the same exact musical form. The general tonal sequence and outline are preserved, so that the motive is recognizable but by a wondrously skilful handling of the phrase, by changing the harmony or the rhythm, varying but related conditions and emotions are linked together musically so that the orchestra's utterance becomes a tonal commentary and explanation, making clear all that is taking place in the drama. The sword motive, which occurs repeatedly in the trilogy, may be mentioned as an example of the employment of the guiding phrase to express merely a thought. The sword does not come materially into the action until the last scene of the first act of "The Valkyrie," when Sieglinde draws Siegmund's attention to the weapon left in the ash-tree by Wotan, yet this motive or phrase of seven notes is heard in "The Rhinegold," when the gods pass in procession to Walhalla and when Wotan ponders on the strife which the Ring has begotten and on the need of defense arising therefrom. Into his mind flashes the thought of the sword, by the placing of which in the hand of some free-willed agent he hopes to avert the downfall of the gods which Erda has predicted. Energetically and hopefully there comes ringing out from the orchestra the motive of the sword and, to the informed listener, the thought that passes through the mind of the god is made instantly clear.

DAS RHEINGOLD

The action of "Das Rheingold" or "The Rhinegold" begins in the depths of the Rhine, the scene showing the rock caverns of the river and the entire stage seeming to be filled with water.

CHARACTERS.

Wotan, Donner, Froh, Loki, } gods.
Fafner, Fasolt, } giants.
Alberich, a Nibelung.
Mimi, a Nibelung.
Fricka, Freya, Erda, } goddesses.
Wellgunda, Woglinda, Flosshilda, } nymphs of the Rhine.
Nibelungs.

Upon a peak lifting its head from the river's bed gleams the Rhinegold, while about it gracefully swim its guardians, the three beautiful Rhine maidens, Wellgunda, Woglinda and Flosshilda, daughters of the god of the river. Soon there appears an unprepossessing spectator of their joyous play, Alberich, the Prince of the Nibelungs, a race of dwarfs sprung "from the womb of night and death" who have their dwelling in the caves of the earth. He feasts with greedy eyes upon the charms of the nymphs and, growing bold, tries to pursue them through the water. Thoroughly enjoying the sport, they mock him with smiles and blandishment but always evade the clasp of their misshapen admirer just as he thinks to catch one of them. At last, when impotent with rage from his fruitless clambering over the slimy rocks of the river bed, his attention suddenly is diverted by an illumination of the waters from the glow of the Rhinegold, now lighted by the rays of the rising sun. The maidens hail their golden treasure with rapturous delight, singing as they swim about it:

> Rhinegold;
> Glittering joy!
> Thou laughest in radiance rare!

Incautiously, they reveal the magic property of the gold, which their father has warned them a dwarf such as this will seek to wrest from their keeping. They tell Alberich that whoever shall shape a ring from the Rhinegold shall gain the kingdom of the whole world and shall possess measureless might. But to this dazzling information they add the condition that he who would gain this puissance must renounce forever the joys of love. Alberich after a moment's consideration of the price, clambers up the peak, exclaims

> Hear me, ye floods!
> Love I renounce forever

and, wrenching the gold from the pinnacle of rock, vanishes with it and its light to the underworld, while the Rhine maidens lament their loss in the darkness.

The gloom gradually is dissipated and instead of the river bed is seen a valley through which the Rhine is flowing. The stream is overlooked by a grassy plateau, whereon lie sleeping Wotan, king of the gods, and his consort Fricka. As they awake they turn to gaze at the stately walls of the new palace, Walhalla, which rises on a height on the opposite bank and which has been built by the giants Fafner and Fasolt to insure for Wotan the sovereignty of the world. Fricka's pride in its splendor is soon lost, however, for she remembers the fee the giants have exacted for their labor, nothing less than the beautiful goddess Freya, keeper of the golden apples, from which sustenance the gods derive their youth and strength. Upbraided by his wife for rashly having promised such a fee, Wotan expresses a hope that with the aid of Loki, the god of fire, who, like that flickering treacherous element, is a trickster, he may evade a payment which will deprive the world of its beauty, light, and sweetness. As they speak, the terror-stricken Freya rushes in, pursued by the giants. She implores Wotan to save her and summons to her protection her brothers, Donner and Froh, the gods of thunder and sunshine. But even their presence does not abash the giants, who are determined to obtain their reward.

The tense situation is relieved by the arrival of Loki, whose delay has been caused by his having wandered far throughout the world in his search for something sufficiently alluring to take the place of Freya. He has learned of nothing save the enchanted gold whose theft the Rhine daughters have reported to him. The giants listen eagerly to the tale of Alberich's possession and of the marvelous power he is able to exert through it, not only over his own race but over all the earth. They consent to accept this gold instead of Freya, if before nightfall Wotan and Loki can obtain it for them. They depart but carry with them the shrieking goddess as an hostage. The absence of the guardian of the sacred apples makes the gods grow visibly old and gray and Wotan, observing the appalling change in everyone about him, resolves to gain possession of the gold, be the price what it may.

Wotan and Loki start for the underworld. The scene gradually changes and they soon are discovered descending into the domain of the Nibelungs, ruled by Alberich.

Mimi, Alberich's slave-brother, has fashioned for him the ring and it has not disappointed in its endowment. With all vestiges of love now banished from his heart, he thinks only of oppressing his people and piling up gold for himself. Mimi has been forced also to make from the Rhinegold a Tarnhelm or helmet, which is to give either invisibility or any form desired to the wearer. This too has proven a success and, to thank the forger for his work, Alberich becomes invisible and lashes him with a whip. The gods find Mimi writhing in agony, and craftily draw from him the story of the ring. As they speak, the dwarf-ruler appears, driving before him hosts of serfs, who bear loads of gold plate and jewelry. The magic of the ring gives him insight into the real object of the visit of Wotan and Loki but he feels so secure in his new power that he defies even the gods. Finally, he is beguiled by Loki into displaying the qualities of the Tarnhelm and changes himself first into a huge serpent and then into a toad. While under the second transformation, Wotan places his foot upon him, Loki seizes the helmet and together they convey him, restored to human form, to the upper air. Having dragged their prisoner to the mountain top, Wotan commands him to summon his dwarfs and have them fetch the treasure from Nibelheim. Alberich reluctantly obeys but is furious to find himself compelled to add the Tarnhelm to the treasure that his serfs pile up. He hopes to keep the ring, however, but even this is demanded and forced to yield it up, he in his rage hurls with it a dreadful accompanying curse, declaring that destruction ever shall come to the one who wears it.

Alberich is released and Fricka, Donner and Froh appear, followed closely by Fasolt and Fafner and the weeping Freya. The giants declare that only gold enough entirely to screen the goddess can buy her back. When all the horde is piled about her and even the magic helmet has been added they discover still a chink through which can be caught a glimpse of Freya's golden hair and Wotan is forced to sacrifice the ring. This he refuses to do until Erda, the earth goddess and the mother of the fates, rises from the ground to tell him that to keep it means ruin.

> Three daughters, norns of fate,
> Were born to me, ere the world began;
> By these was I called to counsel thee;
> That direst danger, day of gloom,
> Dawns for all the gods;
> Hence I warn thee, beware the ring!

The released Freya embraces her kin, who now are dowered once more with the rose of youth. The inevitable evil of the ring begins to exert its power, however. The giants quarrel over the division of the gold and Fafner slays his brother and departs, carrying the whole treasure. As Wotan broods over the baleful curse which has entered the world, heavy haze and mist settle over the river and castle. Thor, the god of thunder, compels the storm elements to obey him and, when lightning and thunder-peals have cleared the air, a shimmering rainbow is seen bridging the space between the valley and Walhalla. Wotan giving his hand to Fricka, invites the gods and goddesses to follow him to their new home. As they advance, a celestial procession across the shining bridge, the lament of the Rhine daughters over the stolen gold rises to their ears from far below. Wotan questions Loki as to what means this sound and, on being told, commands that it cease. Loki mockingly calls to the Rhine maidens, bidding them forget the loss of their shining gold and sun themselves in the splendor of the gods. The lament continues as the gods enter Walhalla.

"The Rhinegold" is the prologue to the great Nibelungen trilogy and is the key to all which follows. Many of the characters which figure in the later action are introduced. In it, the sin of the king of the gods, i. e., the breaking of the contract with the giants and his coveting and securing by force the ring, which is the symbol of earthly power, is committed. The consequences of this sin make up the action of the ensuing dramas. Wotan, not Siegfried, is the true hero of the trilogy and the real plot is concerned with his efforts to escape the retribution which inevitably must follow wrong-doing. It must be remembered that the gods of Teutonic mythology are not immortal. Streatfield says, " Behind Walhalla towers the gigantic figure of Fate, whose reign is eternal. The gods rule for a limited time, subject to its decrees. This ever-present idea of inexorable doom is the guiding idea of Wagner's great tragedy. Against the inevitable the gods plot and scheme in vain."

As yet no human interest has been engendered, however, for the world to which we are introduced is one of mystery, dealing with naught save gods, giants, dwarfs and nixies.

DIE WALKÜRE

With "Die Walküre" or "The Valkyrie" the human interest of the cycle begins. As a spectacle, the drama is picturesque and splendid. The music is a wonderful fabric of guiding themes, so expressive that the auditor familiar with them could follow the complete development of the story, without reference to the libretto.

CHARACTERS.

Siegmund.
Hunding.
Wotan.
Sieglinde.
Brunnhilde.
Fricka.
The eight Valkyries.

There is much that happens between the close of "The Rhinegold" and the opening of the trilogy proper in "The Valkyrie." Wotan, dwelling in Walhalla, has brooded long over Erda's prophecy and his contact with the curse of the ring which has fallen upon the world has engendered in him the lust for power. As Fafner has secured the gold by just contract, Wotan himself cannot recover it. It must be regained by some independent agent acting of its own free will. Wotan descends into the domain of the earth goddess to consult her whose wisdom enables her to know everything and there he woos her so successfully that she accepts him as her spouse. To the union are born nine daughters, the Valkyries, who are to assist him in the work the mother predicts for him. He has waved his spear over the earth and unending war and strife have been kindled. It is the mission of the Valkyries to ride forth each day upon flying horses and to choose and carry to Walhalla the bravest of the slain. In their celestial dwelling-place, these revived heroes regale themselves upon boar heads and mead, drunk from the skulls of their enemies, and keep themselves ready to defend Walhalla from the Nibelungs should the need arise. Fafner, meantime, has changed himself into a dragon, the better to guard the ring. Wotan resolves to breed a race of heroes who shall be able to win it from the monster. To this end, he visits the earth in the guise of the man Volse and unites himself to a mortal woman, who bears him the splendid Volsung twins, Siegmund and Sieglinde.

While the children are still young, the savage hunter, Hunding, discovers their hut, which he burns, killing the mother and carrying off the daughter. Volse and Siegmund, returning to find this demolition, swear an oath of vengeance upon their enemy. When Siegmund has grown to manhood, his father suddenly disappears, leaving behind only a wolf skin, and the youth is forced to fight alone against the foes which surround him. While one day defending a maiden, he is overpowered by numbers and, losing his sword, is forced to take refuge in a hut. It is here that the action of "The Valkyrie" begins.

It is Hunding's hut where Sieglinde dwells, for much against her will the cruel hunter has forced her to become his wife. She is startled when, while the storm rages without, a disheveled stranger staggers in and falls exhausted before the fire.

Sieglinde brings the intruder food and drink and the two instantly are drawn toward each other by the power of some strange attraction. Hunding enters and, from

Siegmund's recital of his story, he discerns in him his mortal foe. Restrained by the sacred traditions of hospitality, he informs his guest that he will be safe until the morrow, but that at dawn he must be ready to fight for his life. Siegmund, left alone, bemoans the loss of his sword but finally remembers his father's promise that in the hour of greatest need a weapon would be found. Soon Sieglinde, who has drugged her husband's night draught, comes to urge the guest to fly. She points out to him the ash-tree which supports the dwelling and shows him a sword embedded in its trunk. She relates how, on the day that made her an unwilling bride, an unbidden guest strode in and, glancing at her, thrust a sword deep into the trunk of the tree saying that to him who could draw it forth, it should belong. Many guests had come and gone since then, many had tried to loosen the weapon and had failed. Siegmund, feeling his dire necessity for means of defense on the morrow, seizes the hilt and, with a mighty tug, draws forth the sword to which he gives the name of Nothung or Needful. The brother and sister, who now recognize their relationship, fall into each other's arms, knit by a closer and more passionate tie.

The storm has passed and the light of the springtime moon pours its benediction upon the two, who in rapture plight their strange troth, Siegmund singing

> Bride and sister
> Be to thy brother,
> Thereby to cherish the Volsung name.

The next act is laid in a wild mountainous pass where the armored Wotan is discovered conversing with his favorite Brunnhilde, the leader of the Valkyries. He tells her of the conflict which is soon to take place between Siegmund and Hunding and bids her, by means of her protection, throw the victory to Siegmund. As Brunnhilde departs on her errand, Fricka, the goddess of wedlock, whose feelings have been outraged by the unnatural union of the Volsung twins, appears in her chariot drawn by rams. There follows a long altercation but finally the lordly Wotan is compelled by the wifely remonstrances to reverse his decree of victory. Hunding, the wronged husband, shall triumph. Brunnhilde, whose warlike cry has been echoing in the mountains, is recalled and entrusted with the new orders, which the sorrowing Wotan gives though knowing that if Siegmund is destroyed he himself never shall be freed from the curse of the ring. To Brunnhilde he confides his sore distress over having his scheme to avert destruction thus foiled.

Siegmund and Sieglinde appear fleeing from the wrath of Hunding. Foreboding has entered into the soul of Sieglinde and, overcome with sorrow and exhaustion, she falls senseless into her brother-husband's arms. As Siegmund attempts to kiss her back to consciousness, the stern Brunnhilde appears to warn him that his hour is near and that soon he shall go to join the heroes in Walhalla. He protests that he will relinquish that joy rather than be separated from Sieglinde, at which the Valkyrie inquires

> So careless art thou
> Of heavenly rapture?
> One weak woman
> To thee is all.

Rather than leave Sieglinde to some unknown fate, he lifts his sword to slay her with his own hand, when Brunnhilde, deeply touched, relents and tells him that in defiance of her father's command, her shield shall be for his defense. Even now Hunding's horn is heard and Siegmund rushes to the encounter . The combatants meet in the midst of the din of thunder which announces the coming of Wotan. Brunnhilde hovers over Siegmund to ward off the force of Hunding's blows and, just as the victory is to be the Volsung's, Wotan, who has arrived in the fury of the storm, thrusts his spear between the two warriors. Siegmund's sword is splintered upon it and Hunding strikes him dead. But the hunter has not long to celebrate his triumph, for Wotan slays him with an accusing look. Brunnhilde collects the fragments of Siegmund's sword and escapes bearing the fainting Sieglinde with her upon her horse.

The third act is upon the summit of a rocky hill capped with fir-trees. Riding through the storm-clouds upon their winged steeds come, one by one, the eight Valkyries in full armor, some with dead warriors hanging from their saddles. The sound of their martial shouts fills the air. Last of all arrives Brunnhilde, carrying the wretched Sieglinde. The woman pleads for death but is entreated by her protector to live for the sake of Siegfried, the son that she is to bear, who shall be the greatest hero of the world.

Brunnhilde bestows upon her the fragments of Siegmund's sword and bids her escape to the tangled forest where Fafner the dragon watches over his Ring and whither Wotan dares not go. The voice of the angry god is heard even now in the midst of the thunder and, as he rushes in, he commands the trembling Brunnhilde to stand forth from among her sisters who try to conceal her. She is to hear the penalty imposed for her disobedience. For failing in her duty, she shall be banished from the valorous sisterhood, and may never hope to see Walhalla again. Nor is this all. She shall be changed from her high estate to mere mortality, shall be mastered by a man and be but a housewife. To this end she shall be thrown into a deep sleep and shall lie upon the mountain top, the prey of the first man who comes to waken her. Her tears and passionate entreaties wring from Wotan only the promise that in order that no one but a hero may win her she may be encircled while asleep by a wall of magic fire.

Wotan presses a tender kiss upon the eyes of his beloved daughter and, as her godhood slips away and slumber comes upon her, he places her gently upon the grassy slope, adjusts her helmet and spear and lays her shield over her for protection. Then calling upon Loki, he bids him surround her with fire. As the god disappears, the flames leap up about Brunnhilde who is to lie here in slumber until her hero shall come to waken her.

Among the great moments in this, the most popular of the four parts of the cycle, are the prelude, which depicts the tumult of the thunder-storm; Siegmund's spring song, one of the loveliest of the Wagnerian melodies, beginning

> No one went
> Yet some one came,
> See how the spring smiles in the hall,

and Sieglinde's rapturous response,

> Thou art the spring,
> For whom I lay longing
> And fasting through the winter's frost.

The ride of the Valkyries; Wotan's farewell to Brunnhilde; and the concluding magic fire scene are also well known numbers.

SIEGFRIED

"Siegfried" has been called the scherzo of the great Nibelungen symphony. To the tragedy and defeat of "The Valkyrie," with its thunder and war-cry and rushing flame, succeed peace and serenity with the young laughter of the innocent boy and the singing of the forest birds. It is a veritable pæan of youth and love and courage.

CHARACTERS.

Siegfried.
Mimi.
Wotan, The Wanderer.
Alberich.
Fafner.
Erda.
Brunnhilde.

After the close of the preceding drama, Sieglinde, to escape the heavy hand of Wotan, flees to the forest, where she wanders until, starving and exhausted, she finds herself in the cavern of Mimi, the dwarf-brother of Alberich. Here Siegfried is born and his mother, dying to give him life, entrusts him to the care of her misshapen host. Mimi brings him up in ignorance of his real parentage and plans to use him as the instrument for the recovery of the gold. In the depths of the untrodden wood, the boy grows to manhood strong as an oak and knowing no fear. The wild beasts are his companions and his diversion is to imitate the cries of the birds which circle about him and which merrily answer his call. But sometimes into the peace of his heart penetrate half-formed longings and aspirations which he cannot understand.

When the curtain rises, there is seen the grimy workshop of Mimi, a cave which opens towards the wood. Here the dwarf is at work before the forge, hammering a sword upon his anvil and voicing his chagrin that the "fiery stripling," with untutored strength, breaks every weapon made for him. Mimi is growing discouraged, for he long has striven to weld a blade with which his bold charge might slay the enemy Fafner, who, as a dragon watches over the ring, the helmet and the hoard.

While he is complaining, Siegfried rushes into the workshop, leading a huge bear which he has bridled and which he mischievously urges to the attack of the cringing dwarf. When Mimi has been thoroughly frightened, Siegfried finds that he has had enough of the sport and, sending Bruin back to the wood, he runs to the forge and with one blow shatters upon it the dwarf's latest achievement. Impatient with such worthless workmanship, he throws himself down in rage near the fire, while Mimi tries to regain his favor with offers of food and drink. These Siegfried thrusts from him in disgust, for he is heartily tired of the fawning dwarf and his treatment of him. In this mood, he demands some knowledge of what love means and of his own parentage. He inquires contemptuously

Where have you, Mimi,
Your minikin consort
That I may call her mother?

After many lies and evasions, Mimi reveals to him the facts concerning his birth, telling him his mother's name and that his father was slain. He then brings out the fragments of Siegmund's sword, the legacy left at Sieglinde's death. With troubled mind, the youth rushes to the forest to escape Mimi's hated presence and the dwarf begins to hammer on the pieces of the sword

Nothung. While he is thus engaged, Wotan, disguised as The Wanderer, with his hat drawn low to hide his missing eye, comes upon Mimi's cave and stops to interview him. Wotan proposes a contest of wit and each stakes his head upon successfully answering three riddles Wotan replies correctly to Mimi's questioning but Mimi fails on his part. The god refuses to take advantage of such a puny adversary and leaves the dwarf the gage. But he tells him that no one can forge Nothung anew, except he who knows not the meaning of fear.

Mimi, realizing his own limitations, does not attempt to resume the work and is upbraided for idleness when Siegfried returns. The dwarf explains the conditions of the task and as the youth does not know even the meaning of the word fear, he describes graphically many kinds and causes of terror even to that produced by sight of the "monstrous worm," Fafner. But Siegfried cannot recognize any of them. He springs up and seizes the fragments of the sword, blows the darkened coals to a glow, and fixing the pieces in a vise, files them to a powder which he puts in a crucible and reduces to molten metal over the heat. He then carefully casts the weapon and hammers the blade to shape, lustily singing

> Nothung! Nothung!
> Notable sword!

The blade is finished, is in the handle and Siegfried breaks forth in triumphal praise of his work. Then to test its power he smites with it the anvil, which splits in twain from top to bottom, falling asunder with a great noise, while Mimi, in terror, sinks prostrate upon the floor.

The scene now shifts to another part of the forest, where Mimi's brother Alberich, former master of the ring, keeps gloomy guard at the entrance to the cave where Fafner, the dragon, hugs his gold. Dense darkness reigns. A sudden gust of wind sweeps by, rustling all the leaves, and brings The Wanderer, Wotan, to warn the dwarf of the approach of a fearless one who shall wrest the treasure from the Nibelungs. The dragon, waked by Wotan, calls out that he is fairly starving for a hero, and then peacefully resumes his slumbers.

When the morning breaks, Siegfried approaches with Mimi, his guide, and as they wait for the coming forth of the foe, Mimi describes again its horrors, its yawning maw, its lashing tail, its noisome venom and its fiery breath. Siegfried does not quail but chatters gaily of his method of assault. Nothing disturbs the youth save Mimi's false protestations of great love which rouse in him such irritation that he summarily dismisses the dwarf, who hobbles off muttering, "Fafner and Siegfried, Siegfried and Fafner, would each the other might kill!"

While Siegfried sits alone under the lime-tree, waiting for the dragon to appear, the forest murmurs sound in his ears and he falls to musing upon his birth. He is sure that his sire bore no resemblance to Mimi and he wonders whether his mother's eyes were soft and tender. As he broods sadly upon the fact that he never shall know, the birds' songs attract his attention and he fashions a pipe from a reed and tries to imitate them. But after repeated trials, forced to acknowledge his failure, he throws the pipe away and blows a challenging call upon his hunting-horn. At this, there is an ominous stir in the cave and a huge, snarling, lizard-like thing comes forth from its lair. Siegfried laughs as he rushes to the fray. He eludes the flaming breath and horrid claws and, when his opportunity comes, thrusts his sword deep into the monster's breast. Before he dies in awful convulsions, the dragon warns his slayer of the curse of the Ring. As Siegfried draws the blade from the wound, a drop of fiery blood falls upon his hand and he seeks to alleviate the burn by touching it with his lips. To his amazement, the taste of the blood enables him to understand the song of the birds. From one of them he learns that the Nibelung hoard in the cave is now his by right of conquest and that while the Tarnhelm can tide him through wonderful tasks, the Ring can give him the ward of the world. Thanking his feathered friend, he descends into the cavern, and comes forth with his magic equipment to meet Mimi and Alberich who, deeply suspicious of each other, are hastening in. As they slink aside at sight of him, the bird speaks once more and warns the hero against the fawning Mimi, who soon approaches, proffering a poisonous draught. Siegfried, out of all patience with his deceit, draws his sword and kills Mimi with a single blow, the brother dwarf laughing in delight at the sight. The hero flings the dead body into the cave and again pauses to listen to the bird in the lime-tree. This time it tells of Brunnhilde, lying in fire-girdled slumber till he who knows no fear shall come to awaken and claim her. Eagerly Siegfried starts to his feet, for a strange new feeling has found place in his breast and, with the bird fluttering ahead to show the path, he starts joyfully out upon the quest.

When the curtain rises again, a wild mountainous region is revealed dimly through the shadows of night. Wotan, The Wanderer stands in the midst of thunder and lightning. The place is the foot of Brunnhilde's rock. Wotan conjures his witch-wife, Erda, from her earthly abyss and, pallid as with hoar-frost, she rises in bluish vapor from the depths, reluctant to break her long sleep. He questions her as to the future and whether the doom of the gods may be averted but she knows nothing more except that the time of Brunnhilde's awakening has arrived. As she sinks back into her chill abiding-place, the mellow light of the moon reveals and illumines the figure of Siegfried, who comes across the gorse led by the bird. Wotan attempts to bar the youth's passage, knowing that he who wakes and wins the sleeping Valkyrie shatters the power of the gods. Siegfried, brooking no interference, shivers to pieces Wotan's spear, the emblem of the god's authority, and, with a song on his lips, passes unfaltering and untouched toward the wall of magic fire. The scene changes and Brunnhilde is discovered lying at the foot of the fir-tree just as Wotan left her sleeping there. Near by lies Grane, her war-horse, waiting till his mistress wakes. Siegfried has passed the wall of magic fire and now finds the motionless maid. He thinks her a warrior but when he lifts the helmet and her long hair escaping its bondage, ripples about her in a golden flood, he starts back in surprise at the beauty revealed. She does not stir, he listens for her breathing, but in vain. Tenderly he cuts the iron corselet and greaves from her body, and she lies before him, throbbing with life, a beautiful woman in soft female garb. Trembling, he sinks down with his head upon Brunnhilde's bosom, for love has taught him the fear which Fafner could not inspire. Finally, with an ardent kiss he rouses her who went to sleep a goddess and awakes a woman, with a woman's reluctance to surrender to love. She resists him. She pleads with him but, at last, won by his wooing, although knowing that capitulation means the downfall of Walhalla, and the doom of the gods, she throws herself into the arms of the hero whose coming she herself has foretold. She deems all well lost for love and exclaims exultantly

Far hence, Walhall' lofty and vast,
Let fall thy structure of stately tow'rs;
Farewell, grandeur and pride of gods!
End in rapture, ye Æsir, your reign!
Go rend, ye Nornir,, your rope of runes!
Round us darken, dusk of the gods!
Night of annulment, now on us gain!
Here still is streaming Siegfried, my star.
He is forever, is, for aye
My own, my only and my all.
Love that illumines, laughing at death.

GÖTTERDAMMERUNG

The awakening of Brunnhilde marks the commencement of " Götterdämmerung " or " The Dusk of the Gods," for from that moment the dusk of the gods begins to lower. All the threads of the great mythical fabric now are brought together to form a sublime and transcendent conclusion. There is no depressing anti-climax, for the greatest single act in all opera is the last of the trilogy.

CHARACTERS.

Siegfried.
Gunther.
Hagen.
Alberich.
Brunnhilde.
Gutrune.
Waltraute.
Woglinde, }
Wellgunde, } Rhine Daughters.
Flosshilde, }
Vassals, women.

The action opens on the Valkyrie's rock, made familiar to us in the previous divisions of the music drama. The black of night, lighted only by the glow from the magic fire, serves for the setting of a scene weird in the extreme. Here about the great fir-tree sit the three Norns or goddesses of Fate, weaving the web of destiny.

As they weave, they sing of the rape of the Rhinegold, of Siegfried and his deeds and of the fiery doom which awaits Walhalla. Suddenly, the great cord of fate snaps under their fingers, and they vanish to join their mother Erda in her dank subterranean caverns.

When the day breaks, Siegfried and Brunnhilde emerge from their cave, the hero clad in shining armor, and his companion leading Grane, her horse, by the bridle. They take a loving farewell, exchanging vows of constancy, and Brunnhilde, no longer the stern martial Valkyrie, pleads with her hero not to forget her. Siegfried, as a pledge of his faith, gives her the magic ring. She gives him Grane and bravely sends him forth to fulfil his mission in the world, while she waits his return behind her wall of flame.

These two scenes have been but a prologue. When the curtain rises upon the first act, there is seen the hall of the Gibichungs on the Rhine. Here sits the mighty Rhenish chief, Gunther, his beautiful sister, Gutrune, and their half-brother Hagen. Hagen is the son of Alberich the dwarf and therefore his nature is evil. He has been charged by his father to win back the Nibelung gold. As the three speak, the horn of Siegfried is heard and before he has crossed the threshold, his ruin has been planned. He lands from his boat at the door of the hall, is greeted with fair words of hospitality and Gutrune advances to offer him the drink of welcome, in which a potion of forgetfulness has been mixed. As he partakes of it, he murmurs

> The goblet's quaffed,
> With quenchless passion
> Brunnhilde, my bride, to thee.

But even as the sound of her names dies away, so does his remembrance of her and he gazes with swiftly kindled infatuation at the girl who stands before him with downcast eyes. Gunther speaks of Brunnhilde, whom he covets for his wife, and Siegfried offers to pass the magic barrier to win her for him if, in return, he may have Gutrune as bride. The compact is made and the two men swear blood-brotherhood.

Meanwhile, Brunnhilde, faithfully watching for her husband's return, is sought by Waltraute, her sister Valkyrie, who comes to plead eloquently for the restoration of the ring of the Rhine Daughters. She has learned that by this means the gloom which weighs down Wotan in Walhalla may be lifted. Brunnhilde recoils with indignation from the suggestion of surrendering Siegfried's love-token. It is to her

> More than Walhalla's rapture,
> More than the god's renown.

In despair at the futility of her errand, Waltraute mounts her winged steed and flies away.

When evening has fallen, Brunnhilde listens with transport to the sound of Siegfried's horn and runs to meet him. It is indeed Siegfried but in Gunther's guise, for he has donned the Tarnhelm. The flames waver and yield as he boldly crosses their barrier. He announces to the terrified woman that she is to be his wife. With the strength the ring gives her, she repulses his rough wooing, until in the struggle he snatches the circlet from her finger. Then her power is gone and she is led to her chamber, where Siegfried, true to his oath to Gunther, lays his sword between himself and his blood-brother's bride that is to be.

In the second act, Hagen, left alone to guard the ancestral home of the Gibichungs on the banks of the Rhine, is seen sleeping outside the castle in the moonlight. A creature of sinister aspect crouches before him with its hands upon its knees. It is his father Alberich, the dwarf, who has come to him in a dream to incite him to further efforts to regain the ring. Hagen freely gives the assurance

> The ring I will ravish!
> Rest thou, nor rue,
> My soul swears it!
> Cease thou thy sorrow.

Alberich vanishes before the sun, and as its rays are mirrored in the Rhine, Siegfried appears to herald the coming of Gunther and Brunnhilde and to boast of his own prowess in winning the bride. He joyfully reminds Gutrune that she is pledged to wed. Then Hagen summons the vassals and tells them of their lord's approaching marriage. This news they welcome with delight and begin to deck the altars for the ceremony. Soon Gunther leads in the pale and dejected Brunnhilde, who raises her eyes only when she hears Siegfried's name. Dropping Gunther's hand, she is about to rush impetuously into her husband's arms but is repelled by the coldness of his glance, and the fact that Gutrune stands before him. She falters out an inquiry and Siegfried tells her that he is about to wed Gunther's sister as Gunther is to wed her. She persistently denies her troth with Gunther and asks Siegfried pathetically whether he does not know her. Half fainting, she staggers against him and with a wave of his hand he gives her over indifferently to Gunther. Then Brunnhilde notices the flash of the ring, and demands in indignation how he dares wear a pledge which Gunther wrested from her hand. At mention of the ring, Hagen is on the alert. Siegfried denies that Gunther gave it to him, and declares that he took it from the dragon Fafner. Hagen hastens to get from Brunnhilde the assurance that Siegfried could have secured it only by trickery and deceit and this being precisely the admission that he wishes, he proposes that the traitor shall straightway pay for his villainy. The misunderstanding deepens, for Brunnhilde, referring to their first meeting declares that she has been as a wife to Siegfried, while he, forgetful of all save his second love, insists staunchly that he has dealt honestly with his blood-brother and has not laid hands upon the bride. Brunnhilde's words half convince Gunther of Siegfried's treachery, and he gives way to indignation and distrust.

Siegfried affectionately draws Gutrune from the circle and all the company disperse save Brunnhilde, Gunther and Hagen. Gunther sits apart brooding over his dishonor and shame and Brunnhilde gives way to a tempest of rage and grief. While in this mood, Hagen approaches her with proposals to slay the man who has betrayed her and she agrees, with the eagerness of desperation. Even Gunther gives his sanction to a crime which will make his sister a widow and the murder, which is to be explained as a hunting accident, is set for the next day in the forest.

The next day Siegfried appears on the banks of the Rhine in merry search of game which has escaped him. The three Rhine Daughters, whilom guardians of the magic treasure, appear on the surface of the stream and playfully promise to restore the quarry, if, in reward, the hunter will give them his ring. To tease them, he at first refuses, little though he values the trinket. Quickly they banish the smiles from their faces and predict that this very day he will die unless he intrusts it to their keeping. This threat defeats their purpose for Siegfried is not to be moved through fear. Putting the ring back on his finger, he declares that now he will keep it. The water-nymphs swim away with ominous words, while Siegfried smilingly philosophizes:

Alike on land and water
Woman's ways now I learn,
And him who their smiles distrusts
They'd frighten with their threats;
And should they both be scorned,
They bait him with bitter words.

His meditations are interrupted by the merry music of hunting-horns. He responds to the call and Gunther, Hagen and their vassals join him. The drinking-horns and the mead are brought forth and as the men rest and drink, Siegfried, to entertain the company, begins relating incidents of his youth. As he is speaking, Hagen slyly squeezes into his drinking-cup the juice of an herb, which undoes the work of the magic draught. As he reaches that part of his recountal where Brunnhilde awakens at his kiss, and is telling joyously of how he made her his bride, Gunther starts up with a cry of surprise and anger. Two ravens, Wotan's messengers, fly across the scene and as Siegfried turns to see them Hagen smites him in the back with his spear. The hero falls dying and with his last breath murmurs the name of his beloved Brunnhilde. Hagen stalks moodily away and mournfully the vassals raise Siegfried's body on his shield and to strains of funeral music carry it back to the castle.

Here Gutrune awaits her lord, anxious at his long absence. Fearing Brunnhilde, she has listened at her door, and found the apartment empty, for the unhappy woman is watching for Siegfried on the river bank. Preceded by Hagen, the corpse is brought into the hall and Gutrune giving herself up to measureless grief, refuses credence to the story that her husband was killed by a boar. Then Hagen boldly acknowledges his dark deed and as Gunther moves to take the ring from Siegfried's finger, Hagen attacks him and kills him too. When he in turn snatches at the gold the dead man's hand is threateningly raised and Hagen falls back in dismay.

Now Brunnhilde advances. She understands at last that Siegfried would have been true but for the draught of forgetfulness. Half pitying, she bids Gutrune remember that none but she was Siegfried's lawful wife. Gutrune, filled with shame that she may not mourn over him who was another's husband, creeps over to the dead body of her brother and remains weeping there.

After a long contemplation of Siegfried's face, Brunnhilde gives command to the people to erect a funeral-pyre upon the river bank. As they engage in their gloomy task, she draws the ring from Siegfried's finger and places it upon her own. The body is borne to the pyre and she herself flings the brand into the pile, while Wotan's ravens circle above. Then leaping upon her horse, Grane, she rides with a bound into the fire. The flames tower high and threaten the hall but the swelling river rises mightily to quench them, and on the highest wave are seen the Rhine Daughters. Hagen plunges into the flood to seize the gold he covets, but Woglinde and Wellgunde drag him beneath the water, while Flosshilde, who has recovered the ring from the ashes of Brunnhilde on the pyre, holds it triumphantly aloft. Now a ruddy glow illumines the heavens and Walhalla is seen burning in the sky, while Wotan and his gods and heroes sit calmly waiting their annihilation. It is the passing of the old order and the coming of the new, for the world has been redeemed from its curse by self-sacrificing human love.

Some of the noblest of Wagner's music is contained in "The Dusk of the Gods." "Siegfried's Rhine Journey," an orchestral interlude between the prologue and Act I pictures the journey of the hero from the Valkyrie rock to the hall of the Gibichungs. The appeal of the Rhine Daughters to Siegfried is of supreme beauty, as is also the hero's story of his adventures, in which recur all the motives of the "Siegfried" division of the trilogy, i. e., the sword melody, the storm, the notes of the wood-bird, Mimi's blandishments, the rustle and snap of flames and the triumph of Brunnhilde's awakening. The magnificent funeral march telling in motives the story of Siegfried's life and forming the most impressive orchestral lament ever penned and the superb closing scene of Brunnhilde's immolation are among the mighty moments in this mightiest of music-drama creations.

THE BELLS OF CORNEVILLE

"The Bells of Corneville," frequently called "The Chimes of Normandy," is a comic opera in three acts, with text by Clairville and Gabet and music by Robert Planquette. It was first produced at the Folies Dramatiques, Paris, April 19, 1877.

CHARACTERS.

Serpolette, the good-for-nothing.
Germaine, the lost Marchioness.
Gertrude, Jeanne, Manette, Suzanne, } village maidens, belles of Corneville.
Henri, the Marquis of Corneville.
Jean Grenicheux, a fisherman.
Gaspard, a miser.
The bailiff.
Registrar.
Assessor.
Notary.
Villagers and attendants of the Marquis.

The time is the Seventeenth Century and the story opens in the forest near the Normandy village of Corneville. A tall post by the entrance of the adjacent fair bears the bill "Corneville Market, Grand Hiring of Maid Servants, Coachmen and Domestics," reminiscent of a similar scene in "Martha." This especial fair is to be notable from the fact that Henri, Marquis of Corneville, who, owing to the civil war, has been an exile since childhood, has returned to his ancestral home and will be in attendance. The primary action of the opera consists in some very energetic gossiping among the village women. Serpolette, known as the good-for-nothing, serves as subject for some of the scandal but arrives in time to turn the tables on the others. The young lady who early expresses the suspicion that she has royal blood in her veins has a lively tongue before which her detractors may well quail.

"What do you think of the grand wedding that is to come off soon?" inquires Serpolette airily, "Little Germaine, hardly out of her pinafores and that precious booby of a Baillie, who is as old as Methuselah and looks like a scarecrow."

Though not expressed very pleasantly, all this is true. Gaspard, the miser, wants to marry his niece, Germaine, to the principal magistrate of the district. This arrangement does not suit either the young lady or a young fisherman named Jean Grenicheux, who claims to have saved her from drowning, and therefore, according to all precedent, should have her hand. Gaspard dismisses his case in a word. "He was fishing. My niece fell off the rocks into the sea and he could not help catching something."

To escape from the distasteful marriage, Germaine takes advantage of the privileges of the fair and becomes the servant of the Marquis, while Serpolette and the sighing Grenicheux follow her example.

The Marquis immediately begins on the work of improving the ancestral estate and decides to inaugurate the work of reconstruction by laying the ghost which haunts the castle. He discovers that the supposed supernatural visitations are due to Gaspard, who has concealed his treasures in the castle and who has undertaken to protect them from discovery in this wise. When the old man hears the chimes of the castle ringing for the first time since the flight of the old Marquis and knows that the nature of the appearances has been discovered, he becomes crazy and babbles about the bells.

A great fête is given to celebrate the return of the young Marquis and Serpolette comes as Marchioness, for she maintains that some papers found in the château verify her claims of noble origin. Gaspard recovers his reason in time to show that Germaine instead is the real heiress and a general reconciliation is effected. The opera closes with a love-scene between Henri and Germaine, while the famous bells this time, in the words of the chorus,

> Ring, ring out! far and wide!
> For our lord, and for his bride!

Their message changes in import in the ears of the repentant old miser, who cries gladly,

> Ah, the bells ring! I am glad,
> They are my friends, nor drive me mad!

Admired in the score are Serpolette's song, "I may be princess;" Grenicheux's barcarole, "On Billow Rocking;" Germaine's solo with chorus, "Legend of the Bells;" Henri's waltz rondo, "With joy my heart has often bounded;" the taking "Cider song," sung by Serpolette and a chorus, and the final number, "Ah, love, the minstrel thou."

EUGEN ONEGIN

"Eugen Onégin," a grand opera in three acts, the text by M. Kashkin, after Pushkin's novel, and the music by Peter Ilyitch Tschaikowsky, was first produced in St. Petersburg in May, 1877.

CHARACTERS.

Larina, owner of a country estate.
Tatjana, } her daughters.
Olga, }
Filipjewna, a nurse.
Eugen Onégin.
Lenski.
Prince Gremin.
Head servant.
Saretzki.
Triquet, a Frenchman.
Gillot, a waiting-man (silent).
County people, ball guests, landed proprietors, officers.
The time is the second decade of the Nineteenth Century.

The opening act reveals Larina in the garden of her estate, attending to household affairs with the help of the old nurse, Filipjewna. Within the house Larina's daughters, Tatjana and Olga, are singing. Their songs arouse memories of her own early romance with a young officer, a romance ended by the marriage arranged for her by her parents against her own wishes. She has found relief from her woe in the routine of her country home.

The peasants flock upon the scene for the harvest dance and are graciously received and feasted by Larina. One feature of the merrymaking is the dancing of the maidens with a sheaf fantastically dressed as a person. The daughters of the house come out upon the terrace to enjoy the fun. Olga is gay and practical; Tatjana is a dreamer, who revels in books of romance. Her mother warns her that there are no heroes in real life.

Some excitement is aroused in the household by the arrival of Olga's lover, Lenski, and his friend and neighbor, Eugen Onégin. Larina welcomes the stranger and introduces her daughters. Tatjana at once falls in love with him and tells her sister that she has seen him in her dreams. Larina excuses herself to oversee the servants and Onégin and Tatjana are left together. Onégin treats the girl with cool courtliness. She tells him how she spends her time reading and dreaming in the garden and he admits that he, himself, was once like that.

When night falls the four young people are invited in to supper. Tatjana is in a waking dream. The nurse follows, solicitously, watching her.

The next scene is played in Tatjana's apartment. The girl stands at the mirror in deep thought. She complains of wakefulness and Filipjewna tries to entertain her with a story. After dismissing the nurse, Tatjana remains in deep meditation for a while and at last resolves to write a letter to Onégin declaring her love. Having written the letter several times, she seals it and throws back the curtains, letting in the daylight. The nurse enters to call her, and Tatjana with much telltale confusion bids her send her son to Onégin with the letter. Her agitation so frightens the nurse that she hesitates about leaving her alone.

In the next scene, another part of Larina's garden is shown, where girls are picking berries. Tatjana throws herself breathless upon a bench, her agitation arising from the approach of Onégin, whom she receives with drooping head. Onégin is cold and quiet. He tells her that he will be as frank as she was and that he loves her as a brother would. He adds that he was not born for happiness and that Hymen would bring them only sorrow.

The second act shows a brilliantly lighted apartment in Larina's house, where a ball is in progress. Onégin and Tatjana, Lenski and Olga dance. The older women comment upon Onégin, calling him uncouth, uneducated, a gambler and a freemason. He overhears and declares that to be misjudged serves him right for wasting his time at a ball. He blames Lenski for bringing him and decides to flirt with Olga. Lenski claims that she has promised a certain dance to him but Onégin carries her off and Lenski's jealousy is aroused. He reproaches Olga and, when Onégin asks for another dance, she grants it to punish her lover. A quarrel follows, then an insult and a challenge. The duel is fought the next morning, Onégin bringing his serving-man, Gillot, as his second. The terrified Gillot, from behind a tree, sees his master kill Lenski.

The third act discloses a hall in the palace of Prince Gremin, in St. Petersburg, where a fashionable company is assembled. The hostess, Princess Gremina, once Tatjana, is now a brilliant, distinguished woman of the world. Onégin is there after years of conscience-stricken wandering. He is presented to Tatjana, who meets him coldly and excuses herself on the plea of fatigue.

The second act shows the Princess in rich morning-dress in her apartments. Onégin enters and throws himself at her feet. Consumed with love, he beseeches her to give herself to him. But, although Tatjana cannot conceal the fact that she still loves him, she remains true to her husband, who has made her rich and distinguished and, saying "Farewell forever," leaves the scene.

NANON

"Nanon" is a comic opera in three acts, the music by Richard Genée and the text by F. Zell. It was first produced in Vienna in 1877.

CHARACTERS.

Nanon Patin, hostess of the Golden Lamb.
Ninon D'Enclos, the famous beauty.
Madame de Maintenon, mistress of the King.
Countess Houlières, } friends of Ninon.
Madame de Frontenac, } friends of Ninon.
Marquis de Marsillac.
Hector, his nephew.
Marquis D'Aubigne.
Louis XIV.
La Platre, the Abbé.

The scene of the opera is laid in Paris at the time of Louis XIV. In it a number of characters made famous by the history of that gilded reign make their bow.

The romance recounts how the handsome mistress of the Inn of the Golden Lamb became a countess. It much concerns itself with a song which is sung in the first scene and which is heard so often thereafter that it comes to bear the guise of an old friend.

Nanon is so renowned for her beauty and charm, that visitors come from a distance merely to see her. Among such is the Marquis de Marsillac and his nephew, Hector. Hither comes also the Marquis D'Aubigne, who is disguised as the drummer Grignan. He makes love to Nanon and sings to her the serenade, "Anna, thy beauty leads me to thee." Marsillac overhears it and makes note of it for future use.

Ninon D'Enclos claims D'Aubigne as her lover and her suspicions are aroused that he is paying his devotions to the pretty innkeeper. She is reassured to hear that Nanon is to marry a drummer named Grignan. Nanon bids the guests to the wedding and the bridegroom, to escape from this dilemma, causes his own arrest for dueling, an offense punishable by death. Nanon, in despair, decides to call on the influential Ninon for aid.

In the second act, D'Aubigne receives the reproaches of Ninon for remaining away from her side so long and he appeases her by singing "Anna, thy beauty leads me to thee." Nanon arrives on her mission to Ninon. Hector is present also and he and D'Aubigne quarrel over the two women and retire to the garden for a duel. While they are gone the Marquis announces that he will pay Ninon the compliment of addressing to her a little song of his own composition, and the familiar strains of "Anna, thy beauty leads me to thee" are heard. The company take his plagarism as a great joke. Hector, in the meantime, is brought in wounded and limping but D'Aubigne escapes.

The third act is laid in the sanctuary of Madame de Maintenon, where the pious Abbé sings the serenade to her in the guise of a hymn. Hector is released, his friends interceding with the Madame, who is D'Aubigne's aunt. To gain her influence, D'Aubigne and Marsillac both wish to compliment her on her birthday with an original song and the familiar strains of "Anna, thy beauty leads me to thee" are heard twice. A dispute over the authorship of the song ensues.

Nanon receives the pardon of the king for Grignan but she has recognized him as the Marquis D'Aubigne and presents the pardon to Ninon for him. He is touched by this evidence of Nanon's devotion and offers her his hand. Wishing to terminate the attentions of the king in the direction of Nanon, which attentions Madame de Maintenon fears are becoming dangerous, consent to the marriage is granted and the hostess of the Golden Lamb has become a countess.

Of its tuneful numbers may be mentioned the ever-recurring song of D'Aubigne, "What day is this," with the refrain, "Anna, thy beauty leads me to thee;" Pierre's song, "See Uncle Matthew;" Ninon's couplets, "I have been true to this idea;" the chorus of Nanon's country relations,

> Marshaling in troops of dozens
> Come your uncles, aunts and cousins.

Marsillac's song, "I'd e'er by Ninon be;" Nanon's song, "Tell me, sir" and Hector's song ," Always Fearing."

THE SORCERER

"The Sorcerer," a comic opera in two acts, by W. S. Gilbert and Sir Arthur Sullivan, was produced at the Opéra Comique, London, Nov. 18, 1877.

CHARACTERS.

Sir Marmaduke Pointdextre, an elderly baronet.
Alexis, his son, one of the Grenadier Guards.
Dr. Daly, Vicar of Ploverleigh.
Notary.
John Wellington Wells, of J. Wells and Co., Family Sorcerers.
Lady Sangazure, a lady of ancient lineage.
Aline, her daughter, betrothed to Alexis.
Mrs. Partlet, a pew-opener.
Constance, her daughter.
Chorus of peasantry.

The opera begins with a gay entertainment at which the villagers assemble to celebrate the betrothal of Alexis, heir of the great Sir Marmaduke Pointdextre, to Aline, daughter of Lady Sangazure. Mrs. Partlet, the pew-opener, arrives with her daughter Constance, who alone of all the company is out of spirits. The maiden confesses that it is because she is so hopelessly in love with the Reverend Dr. Daly, the vicar. That reverend gentleman indulges in some reminiscences of the time when he was a fair, pale young curate and all the feminine portion of the parish trembled at his slightest indisposition. Mrs. Partlet hints that a clergyman's wife would be a great acquisition to the village and that Constance is getting to be of marriageable age, but he is entirely oblivious to any relation between the ideas, and announcing that he shall live and die a solitary old bachelor, he leaves the maiden plunged in dark despair. Alexis appears, and is showered with congratulations. Sir Marmaduke and Lady Sangazure, who were in love fifty years before, hold ardent conversation, from which it is evident that the sentiment has withstood the test of time. The marriage contract is signed and the affianced are left to themselves for a while.

Alexis now refers to his pet theory that men and women should be coupled in matrimony without distinction of rank. It seems that his lecture delivered at the mechanics' institutes, the workhouses, beershops and lunatic asylums has been received with enthusiasm, although the aristocracy still holds aloof. He confides to Aline that he is about to take a desperate step in support of his principles. Calling Sir John Wellington Wells, of the firm of J. Wells and Co., old established Family Sorcerers, from the refreshment tent, he orders a large quantity of his love-at-first-sight philtre. This magic compound has the effect of making any single person who partakes of it fall in love with the first party upon whom his eyes alight. Rather against her will, Aline doctors the teapot, the vicar brews the beverage and everybody troops up for a cup. As the charm begins visibly to work, the curtain of the first act goes down.

The second act is played in the village market-place. All the villagers have paired off and a greater collection of ill-assorted couples it would be hard to find. Here an old man and a young girl gaze languishingly into each other's eyes; there a sallow youth and an ancient dame stroll by making violent love. The young affections of Constance have lighted upon a very old and very deaf notary It appears that

He's dry and snuffy, deaf and slow, ill-tempered, weak and poorly,
He's ugly and absurdly dressed and sixty-seven nearly.
He's everything that she detests, but yet she loves him dearly.

Aline and Alexis stand by and congratulate themselves on the happy way in which they have helped the whole village to pair off. Their enthusiasm is momentarily dampened when Sir Marmaduke presents Mrs. Partlet as his bride-to-be but Alexis, true to his theory, tries to make the best of it. Only Dr. Daly is thoroughly unhappy, for he has been a little slow and can find no one to love him, everybody being previously engaged. He is greatly at a loss to account for the epidemic of prospective matrimony in a village hitherto little addicted to the habit. To cap the climax, Lady Sangazure rushes up to Mr. Wells whose conscience is beginning to cause him much uneasiness and begins to adore him. He warns her that he drops his H's, eats peas with his knife, and is engaged to a "maiden fair with bright brown hair who waits for him by the sounding sea." At the latter falsehood, Lady Sangazure departs, threatening suicide.

Alexis has insisted that to make their love eternal Aline shall taste the philtre. She drinks, meets Dr. Daly and there is the usual result. Alexis is not prepared for such a test and is very wroth indeed. However, Dr. Daly assures him that he will be no man's rival but will quit the country at once and bury his sorrows in the gloom of a colonial bishopric. Mr. Wells volunteers the information that there is one way in which the spell may be removed — a victim must be offered to Ahrimanes, and he finally consents to be said victim. As he vanishes into the earth amid red fire there is a new and proper pairing off; Aline with Alexis, Lady Sangazure with Sir Marmaduke, Dr. Daly with Constance, and Mrs. Partlet with the notary.

Popular numbers in the first act are Dr. Daly's ballad, "Time was, when love and I were well acquainted;" the duet of Sir Marmaduke and Lady Sangazure, "Welcome Joy;" Alexis' ballad, "For Love Alone;" the amusing song of the sorcerer, "My name is John Wellington Wells," in the strain in which Mr. Gilbert is so happy; Mr. Wells' incantation, "Spirits of Earth and Air;" the country dance, "Happy are we," with which the second act begins; the song of Constance, "Dear friends, take pity;" the duet of Lady Sangazure and Mr. Wells, "Oh, I have wrought;" Aline's air, "Alexis, doubt me not" and Dr. Daly's song, "Oh my voice is sad and low."

SAMSON AND DELILAH

"Samson and Delilah," an opera in three acts, with music by C. Saint-Saëns, and text by Ferdinand Lemaire, was produced at the Court Theatre, Weimar, Dec. 2, 1877. It is founded on the Biblical narrative.

CHARACTERS.

Samson.
Abimelech, Satrap of Gaza.
High Priest of Dagon.
Delilah, his daughter.
Old Hebrew man.
A lad.
Messengers.
Chorus of Hebrews and Philistines, priestesses.

The curtain rises upon a public square in the city of Gaza in Palestine. Here is assembled a multitude of Hebrews in grief and prayer. Evil days have come upon them; their enemies, the Philistines, have triumphed over them, and they fear that the God of Israel has deserted their cause. Only Samson, the strong, brave Hebrew soldier, lifts his voice in expressions of hope and reassurance. The people, crying that his words are from the Lord and that he will save the nation, feel new courage inspire them.

Abimelech, Satrap of Gaza, enters followed by the Philistine warriors, who shout defiance at the Hebrews and drown their voices with praises of Dagon, the pagan deity. Samson interrupts their foolish taunts to cry, "Israel, break thy chains! Arise and conqueror be!" Abimelech brooks no symptom of independence from the Hebrews and, sword in hand, he attacks Samson, who turns and slays him. The Philistines, headed by the High Priest, swear to avenge the death of their prince.

In the morning, Delilah and the Philistine women come to Samson with garlands in their hands. Delilah, the high priest's daughter, is very beautiful. She hails Samson as hero and employs her subtle enticements to win his heart. Samson feels himself yielding to her spell and struggles manfully against it, but his soul is possessed by her grace. The old men see it and warn him.

In the second act, the High Priest tells his daughter that Samson has led the Hebrews against the Philistines and has been victorious. He urges her to attempt to ensnare the hero, promising her if successful, anything she may desire. He taunts her with the report that Samson now boasts that his love for her is dead and that he laughs at a passion that lasted but a day.

The strong man and the enchantress meet and Samson again is submitted to the test of Delilah's allurements. He is determined at first, confessing his love, but telling her that he believes the Lord has chosen him for greater things than loving; that his task is to deliver his nation out of the hand of the oppressor. But she pleads the cause of her great love with magnificent hypocrisy. The dramatic effect of the struggle between the two is intensified by the crashing of thunder and the play of lightning about them. At last the chagrined Delilah runs into her house, thinking that she has failed and casting imprecations behind her. But Samson, after another inward battle, follows her. Like a flash, Delilah gains her terrace, and calls upon the waiting Philistines, and Samson is betrayed into their hands.

In the third act, he is seen in the prison of the Philistines, Blinded and shorn, he is reduced to grinding at a mill. The Hebrew captives tell him of his people's subjugation and cry reproachfully that he sold them for a woman's charms. To make his humiliation complete, he is led into the temple of Dagon where the High Priest mockingly bids him call upon his Jehovah to restore his strength and cure his blindness. Delilah, too, adds her voice to her father's. The libation is poured upon the sacred flame, and the High Priest commands the prisoner to kneel and present offerings to Dagon, telling the child who leads the fallen hero to guide his steps to the middle of the temple "that all beholding may in scorn deride him." Praying fervently for a restoration of strength, Samson grasps the pillars between which he stands and the temple falls upon the shrieking multitude.

"Samson and Delilah" is the masterpiece of Saint-Saëns and has done more perhaps than any of his other works to bring him to world-wide fame. The first act is written in the oratorio style and for this reason the opera is most frequently given in concert form. Although the score was completed in 1872, not until two years later was any portion of the opera accorded performance and then only in private, when Mme. Viardot-Garcia gave the second act. The first act had a hearing at the Colonne concerts in Paris in 1875 and, two years later, Edouard Lassen produced the entire work in opera form in Weimar. In 1878, it received presentation in Brussels; in 1883, in Hamburg; in 1890, in France at Rouen and, at last, in 1892 it reached the Paris grand opera and was mounted in magnificent manner. The first hearing of the work in the United States was made possible by Walter Damrosch's production in New York, March 25, 1892, when it was given in oratorio form.

Notable passages are, in Act I, the chorus sung by the captive Hebrews and the choruses of the priestesses of Dagon; the trio in which Delilah begins to exert her spell over Samson, sung by Samson and Delilah and a remonstrating old Hebrew man and Delilah's lovely aria "Spring voices are singing." In Act II are Delilah's song, "O

Love! in my weakness give power;" the dramatic duet between the High Priest and Delilah, in which he urges her to ensnare the hero; the duet betwen Samson and Delilah sung in the tempest, "My heart at thy dear voice," an intensely passionate love song and the most widely known number in the entire work. In Act III are the prayer of Samson, mourning his lost sight and the ballet music in the temple of Dagon.

PINAFORE

"Her Majesty's Ship, Pinafore," or, "The Lass that Loved a Sailor," "an entirely original, nautical comic opera," written by W. S. Gilbert and composed by Sir Arthur Sullivan, was first presented May 28, 1878, at the Opéra Comique, London, and ran for seven hundred nights with an enthusiasm probably never before equaled.

CHARACTERS.

The Right Hon. Sir Joseph Porter, K. C. B., First Lord of the Admiralty.
Captain Corcoran, commanding H. M. S. Pinafore.
Dick Deadeye.
Ralph Rackstraw, an able seaman.
Bill Bobstay, a boatswain.
Bob Becket, a carpenter's mate.
Tom Tucker, a midshipmite.
Tom Bowlin.
Josephine, the Captain's daughter.
Little Buttercup (Mrs. Cripps), a Portsmouth bumboat woman.
Hebe, Sir Joseph's first cousin.
First Lord's sisters, his cousins and his aunts, sailors, etc.

The action begins on the quarter-deck of the "Pinafore," which is lying in the harbor of Portsmouth. The sailors are busily cleaning brass work, splicing ropes and engaging in other like tasks. The first important actor to appear is Little Buttercup, the fat, jolly bumboat woman, who suggests at once, in characteristic fashion, that under a round and rosy exterior may be lurking a canker-worm. Dick Deadeye, the villain, comes on board and is followed by the fine young sailor, Ralph Rackstraw, who is sighing over the fact that he loves a lass above his station, the lass in question being Josephine, the daughter of Captain Corcoran of the "Pinafore." The Captain has ambitions for his daughter and is deeply grieved that the young lady "does not tackle kindly" to the attentions of Sir Joseph Porter, K. C. B. The fair Josephine arrives to confess to her father that she loves a common sailor but assures him that her pride will prevent his ever knowing it. Sir Joseph accompanied by "all his sisters and his cousins and his aunts" comes to press his suit. An abundance of satire directed against the British navy, snobs, the national self-complacency and other important institutions is wrapped up in the character of Sir Joseph, who early explains that a British sailor is any man's equal, excepting his. Josephine, declaring that Sir Joseph's attentions nauseate her, smiles on Ralph until he is encouraged to make a declaration. She then conceals her real feelings and haughtily bids him seek some village maiden for a mate. He draws a pistol and is holding it to his head, when she prevents his taking off by the timely confession that he possesses her heart. They plan to elope and are overheard by Dick.

In the second act, the Captain is discovered singing to the moon and very much out of sorts. Little Buttercup, who has remained on board, offers to soothe his aching heart and becomes alarmingly sentimental. He tells her that owing to the difference in their stations, he can be only a friend and she, at once nettled, warns him that her gypsy blood enables her to see that a change is in store for him. Sir Joseph enters to complain of Josephine's indifference and her father hastily suggests that perhaps her modesty makes her feel unworthy of him. This tickles the suitor's vanity, and when Josephine appears, much worried over her approaching elopement, he bids her

> Never mind the why and wherefore,
> Love can level ranks, and therefore—

This is exactly the assurance she has been craving for her hesitating heart. She promises to follow his advice and her parent is delighted that he is to be the father-in-law to a Cabinet minister. As Josephine and Ralph are leaving the ship to seek a clergyman, Dick Deadeye discloses their plan and they are confronted by an angry papa. Ralph is interrupted in the midst of the pretty metaphors expressive of his love and ordered to be loaded with chains and sent to a dungeon cell. At this, Little Buttercup demands a hearing and confesses that "many years ago" she "practised baby-farming" and that, in her own words,

> Two tender babies I nussed—
> One was of low condition,
> The other upper crust,
> A regular patrician.

She further explains that they were Captain Corcoran and Ralph and that she purposely mixed them up. This highly probable explanation is at once accepted. Sir Joseph declares a union with Josephine impossible under the circumstances; her marriage with Ralph takes on a new aspect; and Corcoran, now a common seaman, gives his hand to Little Buttercup.

"Pinafore" is probably the most popular of all the Gilbert-Sullivan operas. It met with enormous success, not only at home but abroad. It was hummed; it was whistled; its catching phrases were heard on the street and in the home; contemporaneous literature teems with allusion to it. Its satire is keen but friendly and, in music as in text, it is gay and amusing. Sullivan, who has been called the English Offenbach was very fortunate in having Gilbert for a co-worker, for his librettos have distinct literary value. One critic claims that Sullivan has not quite succeeded in "writing down" to the popular taste, for the most of his music is "too graceful in melody and too refined in harmony to be appreciated by the absolutely uncultivated," but adds that it is "exactly adapted to the very large class which knows a little."

Among the many popular numbers are the recurring chorus "We sail the ocean blue and our saucy ship's a beauty;" the song "I'm called Little Buttercup;" Josephine's, "Sorry her lot, who loves too well;" Sir Joseph's "I am the monarch of the sea" and "When I was a lad I served a term;" the trio, "A British tar is a soaring soul;" Corcoran's song to the moon; the duet between the Captain and Little Buttercup, "Things are seldom what they seem;" Dick Deadeye's "The merry maiden and the tar;" the octet, "Farewell my own" and Buttercup's recountal "A many years ago."

BOCCACCIO

"Boccaccio, or the Prince of Palmero," a comic opera in three acts with music by Franz von Suppé and text by Zell and Genée, was first produced at the Carl Theatre, Vienna, Feb. 1, 1879.

CHARACTERS.

Boccaccio, a novelist and poet.
Leonetto, his student friend.
Pietro, Prince of Palmero.
Lotteringhi, a cooper.
Lambertuccio, a grocer.
Scalza, a barber.
Fiametta, Lambertuccio's adopted daughter.
Beatrice, Scalza's daughter.
Isabella, Lotteringhi's wife.
Peronella, Lambertuccio's sister.
Checco, a beggar.
Fratelli, a bookseller.
Fresco, the cooper's apprentice.
The unknown.
Florentine students, journeymen, girls, beggars, servants.

Boccaccio, the hero of this tale, is a novelist and poet whose virile pen deals with truth not romance, and who has brought down upon his head the hatred of many of the Florentines, who are portrayed in his novels with really embarrassing fidelity. They vow vengeance upon him and his life, or at least his safety, is in peril. Boccaccio has found time in the midst of his literary labors to fall in love with Fiametta, the adopted daughter of Lambertuccio, the grocer. He, as well as Lambertuccio, is unaware of the fact that the girl is the daughter of the Duke of Tuscany, who for political reasons has had her brought up in this humble fashion. Her father has destined her for a fitting marriage and he sends to Florence at this time, Pietro, Prince of Palmero, to claim as his wife, Fiametta, who has been betrothed to him in infancy. Pietro is acting in accordance with the wishes of his father and not because he desires to assume marital ties, for, as he himself confesses, he is far too fond of wine and flirting to care to take on himself the role of husband.

Upon his arrival in the city, he joins in several adventures with the students and meets Boccaccio, for whom he has had, for some time, a profound admiration. He fancies that by his adventures he may gain such experience that he, too, may write of life as Boccaccio does. But his literary ardor is somewhat cooled when, on account of a resemblance which he bears to Boccaccio, he is seized by Florentine citizens who have figured unpleasantly in the novels of "the miserable scribbler" and given a sound drubbing.

Boccaccio, who has learned that Fiametta is to marry, succeeds in stealing interviews with her in the disguises of a beggar and a simpleton, and finds that his love is returned.

Meantime Pietro's adventures go on merrily. He is introduced to Isabella, the wife of the drunken cooper, Lotteringhi, and proceeds to fall in love with her, for the students represent that she is the cooper's niece. On one occasion, when Lotteringhi returns before he is expected, the lady hides her princely lover in a barrel and when he is discovered, glibly explains his presence by saying that he had purchased the barrel and had gone in to examine it. To be brief, after much flirting and serenading, Pietro accomplishes the business for which he has set out and meets

Fiametta whose foster-father is overcome with awe to learn her true identity.

In the last act, Fiametta is found at the ducal palace in Palmero, about to be solemnly betrothed to Pietro. Boccaccio, for whom the Prince has a profound liking, comes as a guest to the festivities. He knows well that his love is reciprocated, and he has Pietro's own admission that he feels only indifference for Fiametta, so he decides to help fate to a more gallant role. He is asked to arrange a play for the evening and, in the impromptu affair he illustrates the situation with such fidelity and shows up the follies of Pietro so vividly, that the young man who looks it over previous to its performance decides not to have it played and instead surrenders the hand of Fiametta to the one who truly loves her. Fiametta is better pleased to wed a professor of the University of Florence, for such Boccaccio is now made, than to be Princess of Palmero and the happy Boccaccio promises that it shall be quite the last of his literary practical jokes.

The opera is full of genuine comedy which is generously furnished by the superstitious Lambertuccio, who sees dreadful signs and portents in every occurrence; by Checco the beggar and by Peronella, the elderly sister of Lambertuccio, who is engaged in hunting a rich husband.

The numbers include in Act I, Leonetto's song, "I will follow thee;" Boccaccio's song, "There is a jolly student;" Fiametta's song, "Love is a tender flower" and the duet of Fiametta and Boccaccio, "A poor, blind beggar." In Act II are found the song, "Always in twos and in threes;" the serenade of Boccaccio, Leonetto, and Pietro before Fiametta's window, "I'd be a star;" the cooper's song and chorus; the letter trio of Fiametta, Isabella and Peronella and Boccaccio's simpleton song. In Act III, occur "How pleasing his novels;" "I'm the father of a Princess;" the duet of Boccaccio and Fiametta, "The language of love" and the septet, "You tho'tless, blind and silly men."

NERO

"Nero," an opera in four acts with music by Anton Rubinstein and text by Jules Barbier, was produced in Hamburg in 1879.

CHARACTERS.

Nero Claudius, Imperator.
Julius Vindex, Prince of Aquitania.
Tigellinus, Prefect of the Pretorians.
Balbillus, an astrologer.
Saccus, a poet.
Sevirus, High Priest of Evander's temple.
Terpander, Citharist, Agrippina's freedman.
Poppæa Sabina, Otho's wife, Nero's mistress.
Epicharis, a freedwoman.
Chrysa, her daughter.
Agrippina, widow of the Emperor Claudius and mother of Nero.
Lupus, a Roman gamin.
Calpurnius Piso, Fænius Rufus, Sporus, Valerius Messala, } plotters.
Thraseas Pætus, Senator.
Salvius Otho, Governor of Lusitania.
Delia, Poppæa's slave.
An aged Christian.
The leader of a band of jugglers.

A public crier, a street vender, a centurion.

Shades: The Emperor Claudius, Britannicus, Seneca, Burrus, Lucanus, Petronius, Octavia and others.

Senators, patricians, Augustans, priests, lictors, players, musicians, Christians, Greeks, Gauls, Germans, Ethiopians, slaves, vestals, courtesans, dancers, female slaves.

The opera, like all other chronicles of this ill-famed person, deals in unpleasant deeds. It opens in the house of Epicharis, a courtesan, where a number of prominent Romans are assembled for a feast. Of the company is Vindex, Prince of Aquitania, a man somewhat above the moral standard of the age. As the hostess leads the way to the banquet hall, Chrysa, a lovely young girl, rushes in, falls at the feet of the tarrying Vindex, and, white and trembling, tells him of pursuit by a band of ruffians who, having killed her slave, have cast his body into the river and are now hard upon her track. She begs piteously for protection and, as he promises it, shouts are heard and a party of masked men burst into the apartment. Epicharis indignantly demands the reason of the intrusion and, to the general astonishment, the leader throws off his mask and reveals the dissipated features of the Emperor. Saccus, the poet and sycophant, who by some remark has aroused the imperial anger, now, to divert him, proposes that the victim shall be brought forth and a mock marriage celebrated. Nero welcomes this prospect of a new entertainment with delight and the miserable girl is dragged in to play the bride. Epicharis and Chrysa utter simultaneous cries of astonishment, for they are mother and daughter, the latter being ignorant of the former's mode of life and living apart from her. Vindex has been upon the alert to protect the girl, but now that he discovers her relationship to this notorious woman, he abandons her cause. The mocking maidens deck her with ornaments; place the bridal wreath upon her brow and admonish her in the duties of wifehood. Nero chooses Saccus for his groomsman and ceremoniously signs the contract. The dice are thrown by Balbillus the astrologer and a joyous life predicted for the two, the company being in convulsions of laughter over the chaste nuptials. Just before the ceremony takes place, Chrysa's mother brings her a bowl of wine and commands her to drain it and, as the procession starts, the girl suddenly reels and falls as if dead. To save her from a horrible fate, the mother has drugged the wine and Nero is cheated of his bride.

The second act opens in the Imperial Palace in the apartments of Poppæa, the favorite of Nero. She has just learned of the death of Octavia, the wife of Cæsar, and believes that now her ambition to share the throne is about to be realized. Nero's mother, Agrippina, who is in banishment, has heard of her son's last escapade and has captured Chrysa, whom she plans to present to him as a means of effecting a reconciliation. She has sent Terpander to Rome to pray Nero's pardon and while the Emperor is singing of the "loves and griefs of Iphigenia" and occasionally glancing contemptuously at some victim doomed to death, who is brought before him, Epicharis enters and pleads for the return of her daughter, who has disappeared from her house. Thus Nero learns for the first time that Chrysa is not dead. He rushes forth to find her and in the public square meets Agrippina, to whom he becomes wholly reconciled when she tells him of the gift she has in her power to bestow. In honor of the event, he invites the people to the Circensian games. In the midst of the revelry, the jealous Poppæa leads Vindex and Epicharis to Chrysa, who carry her to temporary safety. Above the tumult is heard the voice of Nero proclaiming himself not only Emperor but God.

The third act discovers Chrysa hidden in a secluded cottage of her mother's and guarded by Vindex, who declares his honorable love for her. Nero has released the imprisoned Epicharis in order to follow her as a decoy to Chrysa and while Vindex goes to seek a refuge for the women outside the city, Nero appears. He offers the girl a place beside him on the throne but she spurns him and his softness turns to fury. Poppæa follows to remind him that Rome is in flames and with sinister laughter he remembers that it was he who started the conflagration. With Chrysa and her mother dragged in his footsteps, he goes forth gleefully to watch his work. He stops to sing and play upon the wall and intersperses his song with imprecations upon the Christians. At this, Chrysa, who is a convert to the faith, publicly announces the fact and is struck down by the people. In a moment the house, upon the steps of which she lies with her penitent mother bending over her, falls and buries them in its ruins.

In the fourth act, Nero flying from the infuriated people, takes refuge in the mausoleum of Augustus, where the shades of his numerous victims pass before him in review. Terror stricken, he rushes out into the storm. Vindex, who has mustered the legions, is close upon his heels, and the Emperor realizes that the end is near. Exclaiming "Ah! what an artist here will be lost!" he points the dagger at his own breast. As he hesitates, Saccus, who accompanies him, aids him to the accomplishment of the best of his deeds, plunging the weapon into his body and the earth is rid of the greatest of its tyrants. As he falls, dying, there appears in the heavens a shining cross to proclaim the triumph of Christianity.

Rubinstein's setting of this elaborate tale of lust, vanity and bloodshed is brilliantly colored and, while uneven in values, includes some passages of great beauty. The ballet music in the second act has endured and Chrysa's song "Oh mother, oh mother, why from me wert taken?" is much admired. Other numbers that are attractive are the chorus of maidens at the mock marriage, "Deck thee with the tunic fair;" the intonation of the bridal song by Vindex, "My song to thee, guardian of marriage;" "Crowned my dreams by love," sung by Poppæa; "Oh my fate, how remorseless," the song of

Iphigenia sung by Nero; Chrysa's prayer, "Father in Heaven, Father of Mercy;" the berceuse of Epicharis, "Oh sleep my child, free from all sorrow;" Nero's song while Rome is burning, "O Ilion, O Ilion, thou by the gods upreared in pride" and the chorus of Gallic Legions, "He sang so much, so much did Cæsar."

JENNY LIND,

1820-1887.

In the words of Meyerbeer, "One of the finest pearls in the world's chaplet of song."

She was born in Stockholm, where her father was a lawyer in very moderate circumstances. She made an early appearance in opera, in which she was extremely successful, not only in her native land but in London.

In 1849 she left the stage and thereafter sang in concerts only. In 1850, toured the United States and was received so enthusiastically that the crushes at her concerts were positively dangerous. She died in 1887 universally lamented.

She was notable for her technical control of a soprano voice of great compass, power, sweetness and perfect purity. She possessed a remarkable memory being able to sing and play the accompaniments of entire operas and oratorios. Wherever she appeared, whether in the smallest cities or in the grandest theaters, she made the same effort to please and she was as much beloved because of her beautiful personality as because of her wonderful voice.

THE PIRATES OF PENZANCE

"The Pirates of Penzance," or "The Slave of Duty," a comic opera in two acts with text by W. S. Gilbert and music by Sir Arthur Sullivan, was first produced in New York Dec. 31, 1879, under the personal direction of both Mr. Sullivan and Mr. Gilbert, some of the music being finished after their arrival in this country.

CHARACTERS.

Richard, a pirate chief.
Samuel, his lieutenant.
Frederic, a pirate apprentice.
Major-General Stanley of the British Army.
Edward, a sergeant of police.
Mabel, General Stanley's youngest daughter.
Kate, Edith, Isabell, } General Stanley's daughters.
Ruth, a piratical maid-of-all-work.
Pirates, policemen.

It is discovered soon after the rising of the curtain that the festivities in progress in the pirate's camp are in honor of the termination of the apprenticeship of their loved Frederic, which makes him really one of them. What is the general consternation when the youth tearfully announces that he is among them only owing to a mistake and that now he is free to do so, he must leave them. Thereupon the remorseful Ruth, his one-time nurse, who has been allowed to accompany him, confesses that it was all her fault, that being a little hard of hearing, when his father told her to apprentice her charge to a pilot, she understood him to say "pirate." Frederic declares that although individually he loves them all with an affection unspeakable, collectively he looks upon them with a disgust which amounts to absolute detestation and that so keen is his sense of duty that once out of his indentures, he shall feel it incumbent upon him to exterminate them. All weep and deplore the fact that they can offer him no temptation to remain owing to the fact that they can't seem to make piracy pay. Frederic declares it to be owing to faulty business methods, that as they make it a point never to attack a party weaker than themselves, naturally when they attack a stronger one they get thrashed, and that it is also a bad thing that their rule never to capture an orphan has been noised about, for the last three ships they tackled have been entirely manned by orphans.

Ruth urges Frederic to take her along with him as his bride and, as she is the only woman he has seen since he was eight years old and as she assures him, upon being questioned that, compared with other women, she is quite beautiful, he consents, especially as the pirates generously refuse to deprive him of his middle-aged darling. Shortly afterward, he sees the numerous pretty daughters of Major-General Stanley, and denouncing her as a deceiver, becomes deeply involved in a love-affair with Mabel, the youngest of them. The rest of the sisters are surprised by the pirates, who each seize one and propose to conduct them at once to a doctor of divinity located near by.

The military parent appearing, expresses an objection to pirates as sons-in-law but the pirates return that, although they have a similar objection to major-generals as fathers-in-law, they will waive the point. Just as the way seems clear to happiness, the Major-General announces that he is an orphan, and the pirates gnashing their teeth at the sound of the fatal word, give up their brides.

The second act discloses the Major-General sitting in a draughty old ruin he has just purchased, with all the illustrious ancestors thrown in. He is a prey to remorse over his prevarication about being an orphan and confesses as much to Frederic who is marshaling his trembling police to march against the pirates. That young gentleman is surprised by the vindictive Ruth and the pirate chief, who inform him that they have discovered that he was born on the 29th of February, which makes him only a little over five years old. They remind him that he was bound to the pirate chief until his twenty-first birthday. They do not mean to hold him to anything but merely leave it to his sense of duty. Of course, when it is put that way, Frederic has to go with them, duty also forcing from him the confession that the father of his beloved Mabel ignobly escaped on the false plea that he was an orphan. He bids his bride-elect a fond adieu, promising to return to her when he is of age, which will be in 1940. The rest of the story is devoted to the struggles between the scared policemen and the pirates, the former conquering because they order their braver enemy to give way in the name of the queen. When all seems lost, the chief tells General Stanley that most of his band are noblemen gone wrong. This brings about a miraculous change in the general's attitude. He says:

No Englishman unmoved that statement hears,
Because with all our faults we love our House of Peers.

. . . .

I pray you pardon me, ex-pirate king,
Peers will be peers, and youth will have its fling.
Resume your rank and legislative duties,
And take my daughters, all of whom are beauties.

The principal numbers are Ruth's recountal, "When Frederic was a little lad;" the song of the pirate king, beginning, "Oh better far to live and die;" Frederic's song, "Oh! is there not one maiden breast?" Mabel's song, "Poor wandering one;" the amusing number of General Stanley, "I am a very pattern of a modern Major-General;" the "Tarantara" of the Sergeant; the pirate king's song, "For some ridiculous reason;" Mabel's ballad, "Oh! leave me not to pine" and the Sergeant's song, "When a fellow's not engaged in his employment."

BILLEE TAYLOR

"Billee Taylor," or "The Reward of Virtue," a comic opera in two acts with text by Stephens and music by Edward Solomon, was first presented in Londŏn in 1880.

CHARACTERS.

Captain, the Hon. Felix Flapper, R. N. of H. M. S. "Thunderbomb."
Sir Mincing Lane, a knight.
Billee Taylor, a sailor.
Ben Barnacle, a sailor.
Christopher Crab, a tutor.
Phœbe Fairleigh, a charity girl.
Arabella Lane, an heiress.
Eliza Dabsey, the beloved of Ben Barnacle.
Susan.
Jane Scraggs.
Charity girls.

The story is founded on the old song of "Billee Taylor," a well known English nautical ditty. The scene is laid in Southampton in 1805. The first act opens at the Inn of the Royal George which overlooks the harbor. The villagers are found rejoicing over the holiday which celebrates the approaching wedding of Billee Taylor and Phœbe. Arabella Lane, a lady of greater fortune than the pretty Phœbe, has done Billee the honor to fall in love with him and so overcomes her maidenly modesty as to tell him so, though only to have the tempting offer of her hand and fortune refused. The kind-hearted old Sir Mincing Lane arranges a feast in honor of the wedding and invites his friend, Captain Flapper, to join in the fun. This impetuous guest falls in love with Phoebe at first sight and vows to marry her himself. Still another swain who sighs over Phœbe is the tutor, Christopher Crab. A guest present, also disturbed by heart-trouble, is Ben Barnacle, who has gone to sea "all on account of Eliza," who is bestowing her smiles elsewhere. Ben is ordered by the press-gang, which is in full sway at this time to abduct Billee Taylor, and before the ceremony can unite the lad to the charming Phœbe, the deed is done.

Two years elapse before the second act, which takes place in Portsmouth harbor. A characteristic scene is shown. Ships sail gently in and out the harbor, returned sailors bask in the smiles of their sweethearts and some of them dance a hornpipe on the quay. A great many things have happened in the two years. Phœbe and all the charity girls disguised as boys have followed Billee to sea and that gentleman has proved worthy of their devotion by rising to be a lieutenant. Arabella still forces her attentions upon him and he is gradually warming in the glow of her persistent love-making. Phœbe learns of this from Captain Flapper. Sir Mincing Lane, who is organizing a company of volunteers, tries to get some of the sailors to join him and Phœbe decides to enlist but is claimed by Barnacle as a messmate and a quarrel is brought on between the soldiers and sailors. Crab incites Phœbe to fire at the unfaithful Billee and she yields but the shot goes wild and hits her adviser. She is sentenced to be shot but declares that she is a woman and, when her identity is discovered, Billee claims her as his own.

"Billee Taylor," which has had frequently to face the accusation of being an unmistakable copy of "H. M. S.

Pinafore," is by no means devoid of merit of its own and has enjoyed deservedly no small measure of popular favor.

Among the many taking numbers contained in this opera are Billee's song, "The Virtuous Gardener;" the duet, in which Arabella confesses her love to Billee; "The Two Rivers," sung by Susan and Phœbe; Sir Mincing Lane's song, "The Self-Made Knight;" Phœbe's song, "The Guileless Orphan;" Barnacle's popular offering, "All on account of Eliza;" "The Poor Wicked Man," sung by Crab; Angelina's "Billow" ballad and Captain Flapper's musical remarks on "Love, Love, Love," beginning

Do you know why the rabbits are caught in the snares,
Or the tabby-cats shot on the tiles?

THE MASCOT

"The Mascot," a comic opera in three acts with music by Edmund Audran and words by Chivat and Duru, was first produced in Paris in 1880.

CHARACTERS.

Bettina, the Mascot.
Fiametta, daughter of Lorenzo XVII.
Pippo, a shepherd.
Lorenzo XVII., Prince of Piombino.
Rocco, a farmer.
Frederic, Prince of Pisa.
Parafante, sergeant.
Matheo, innkeeper.
Peasants, lords and ladies of court, soldiers and others.

The scene of the opera is laid in Piombino, Italy, in the Fifteenth Century. The curtain rises on a farm, where the peasants are celebrating the vintage festival. Rocco, the farmer, sits morose and aloof and when asked the reason of his gloom, declares that he is pursued by ill-luck. Pippo arrives from Rocco's brother to whom he has sent for aid, bringing only a basket of eggs and a letter in which he informs him that he is sending his turkey-keeper, Bettina, who has the gift of bringing happiness and prosperity to any hearth at which she resides. But when she appears, a very rosebud of a girl, she does not receive an overwarm welcome, for the practical Rocco would have preferred more tangible benefits to a mascot.

A royal hunting party, including Prince Lorenzo and his daughter, Fiametta, Prince Frederic and the members of the court arrive for rest and refreshment. Lorenzo also fancies himself ill-starred and, learning by accident of the almost supernatural virtue said to belong to Bettina, he determines to take her to his court. To make amends to Rocco for appropriating his mascot, he promises to make him Court Chamberlain. He also creates Bettina Countess of Panada, while poor Pippo, who has fallen in love with the girl, is left disconsolate.

In the second act, a fête is to be given at the palace in honor of the approaching marriage of Fiametta and Frederic, the crown prince. Bettina, now a fine lady and supposed to be the king's favorite, is weary of splendor and wants only her shepherd lover, Pippo. A play given by a company of strolling actors is one feature of the entertainment. A leading member of the troupe turns out to be Pippo in disguise. He and Bettina plan to fly from Court but Rocco, recognizing him, causes his arrest. The bride, meantime, falls in love with handsome Pippo and discards Frederic and, to make better her chances with the shepherd, tells him that Bettina is false and is about to be married to her father. But Pippo and Bettina have an understanding and escape by leaping from a window overlooking the river.

The third act takes place in an inn in the Duchy of Pisa. Naturally, the friendship between Lorenzo and Frederic has come to an end. The soldiers are celebrating the victory of Frederic's troops over the army of his whilom son-in-law that was to be. Pippo, who is one of Frederic's captains, and Bettina, who has fought through the war in the disguise of a trooper, are here and they decide to be married without delay. While preparations are under way for the happy event, Lorenzo,

Fiametta and Rocco who, owing to military reverses have been reduced to minstrels, arrive at the inn. Fiametta goes back gladly to her old lover, Frederic, and the two rival Pippo and Bettina in happiness.

Favorite portions of this melodious and merry opera are the peasants' chorus, "Now the vintage time is over;" Pippo's ballad, "One day, the arch-fiend, drunk with pride;" Bettina's "Kiss Song;" the song of superstition sung by Lorenzo and the chorus; the coaching chorus at the end of the first act; the number for Pippo as Saltarelle, "All hail to you, my lords;" the mutual admiration duet of Pippo and Bettina; the Rataplan song of Frederic; the Orang-Outang song of Fiametta and the chorus, beginning

> The big ape, who at Piombino
> Ruled, and ruined with red tape.

THE QUEEN'S LACE HANDKERCHIEF

"The Queen's Lace Handkerchief," a comic opera in three acts, with text by Genée and Bohrmann-Riegen and music by Johann Strauss, was first produced in Vienna Oct. 2, 1880.

CHARACTERS.

The King.
The Queen.
Donna Irene, the Queen's confidante.
Cervantes, an exiled Spanish poet.
Count Villaboisy Roderiguez, Prime Minister.
Don Sancho de Avellaneda, the tutor to the King.
The Marquis de la Mancha Villareal, Minister of War.
Dancing Master.
Master of Ceremonies.
Antonio, an innkeeper.
Ministers of various departments, students, doctors, courtiers, toreadors, brigands.

The scene is laid in Portugal in the Sixteenth Century. Among the characters are a king and queen of the Mother Goose type, one of the prominent characteristics of the former being his passion for truffles and other good things to eat. A flavor of verity is secured by the introduction of the literary man, Cervantes, who has been banished from Spain and who is now a captain in the Royal Guard. He is in love with Irene, first lady in waiting to the Queen, and the two work together to further the interests of the young rulers. There is for a villain, a bad Prime Minister, who is in league with the King of Spain in trying to keep the power in his own hands. To this end, he tries to stir up discord between the King and Queen, who are really too young to be very wise, for the King has seen but nineteen years and the Queen but seventeen. The King is encouraged in various irregularities and showers attention on the charming Irene, who is too true to the Queen and her loving Cervantes to accept them. Cervantes is appointed Queen's reader and her neglected heart conceives a sentiment for him which is chiefly gratitude for his genuine friendship and sympathy. As she is an impulsive young woman, she writes on her lace handkerchief, "A queen loves you," and placing it in the manuscript of Don Quixote, hands it to him. The manuscript is seized and read with avidity. It is indeed most interesting matter, for two of the characters are drawn from life, Don Quixote being the Portuguese Minister of War, and Sancho Panza the Minister of Instruction. Cervantes is arrested for treason but the King and Irene effect his release by pretending that he is insane.

The two young monarchs now ascend the throne, announcing that the regency is at an end. The Prime Minister, in fright at the apparent failure of his plans, plays his last card. He gives the King the Queen's lace handkerchief, with the compromising words written upon it. Cervantes is arrested again and the Queen is banished to a convent. Cervantes escapes from his guards, however, and joins a party of brigands who capture the Queen. He disguises himself as the host and the Queen as the waiting-maid of an inn and, when the King comes that way hunting, they serve him, and explain everything. Under the circumstances, they will have to be forgiven for their ingenious explanation that the words on the handkerchief were only a message sent by the Queen to the King through Cervantes' friendly hand.

This romance with its sprightly music is one of the most popular of the Strauss operas. The numbers include the Queen's romanza, "It was a wondrous fair and starry night;" the King's truffle song; the duet of the Premier and the King in praise of the oysters; Cervantes' number, "Once sat a youth so fair and pensive;" the Premier's song with chorus, "When great professors;" the Queen's "Bright as a ray from heavenly heights gleaming;" Sancho's song, in the third act, "In the night his zither holding;" the Queen's "Seventeen years had just passed o'er me," and the final choruses.

OLIVETTE

"Olivette," a comic opera in three acts, with music by Edmund Audran and libretto by Chivat and Duru with an English adaptation by H. B. Farnie, was first presented in Paris in 1879.

CHARACTERS.

Captain De Merimac, of the man-o'-war "Cormorant."
Valentine, an officer of the Rousillon Guards, his nephew.
Duc des Ifs, cousin and heir presumtive to the Countess.
Coquelicot, his foster-brother and henchman.
Marvejol, local pluralist, Seneschal to the Countess and Mayor of Perpignan.
Olivette, daughter of the Seneschal Marvejol.
Bathielde, Countess of Rousillon, in love with Valentine.
Veloutine, the Seneschal's housekeeper.
Moustique, the captain's boy.
Courtiers and nobles, citizens, wedding guests, sailors and pages.

The scene of the story is laid in Perpignan on the shore of the Mediterranean in the time of Louis XIII. All the village is stirred over the approaching marriage of the Seneschal's daughter, Olivette, to the old sea-captain, De Merimac. Olivette is just out of the convent, where she has met and fallen in love with Valentine, nephew of De Merimac. The youth haunts the house of his lady love and, when the unprepossessing bridegroom arrives, the girl, who has been described to him by her parent, as an "angel of sweetness and obedience" tells him sharply to pack his valise, and depart as the marriage will not take place. The Captain is not at all dismayed, for he thinks he has it in his power to force her to a marriage with him. He has secured the eternal gratitude of the Countess of Rousillon by rescuing her chimpanzee from a watery grave and she has promised him anything he wants. He writes to her asking her to order the wished-for marriage but at this critical moment he is sent off on a three months' voyage. The Countess has fallen in love with Valentine and has come to Perpignan to be near him. She requests the marriage according to instructions and Valentine, pretending to be the elder De Merimac, quietly weds Olivette himself.

The second act opens with a ball, given by the Countess in honor of the wedding, and Valentine has a strenuous time impersonating both his uncle and himself by frequent changes of costume. The uncle arrives in person, however, and is greeted as the bridegroom. Valentine, coming in suddenly, this time as the old man, is confronted by the original and an explanation is unavoidable. The Captain declares that the bride taken in his name belongs to him, while Olivette faces the prospect of being Valentine's aunt instead of his wife.

Olivette gets rid of her elderly claimant by means of a little conspiracy but the Countess upsets her calculations by announcing her intention of marrying the loyal soldier, Valentine, who has put down the conspiracy. As a last resource, he joins the conspiracy which is to send the Countess out of the kingdom. She is imprisoned on De Merimac's ship, the Cormorant. When Olivette and Valentine, disguised as sailors, are seeking a boat to take them away, the husband is seized. Olivette manages to set the Countess free and assumes that lady's dress, passing her own on to her maid Veloutine. The fickle Duke courts the maid, thinking her the mistress and boasts of his success so loudly that both uncle and nephew disown Olivette until she is able to prove an alibi. Finally, things straighten themselves out, Valentine and Olivette are free to acknowldge their union, the Countess accepts the Duke at last and De Merimac is left to console himself

Pretty numbers are Olivette's Tyrolienne song, "The Convent Slept;" the marine madrigal, "The Yacht and the Brig," by De Merimac and the quartet; the Countess' waltz song, "O Heart, Wherefore so light?" the Duke's couplets, "Bob up serenely;" Valentine's serenade, "Darling, Good Night:" Olivette's "Sob" song, "O My Father;" Valentine's duet with De Merimac, "What! she your wife?" "Jamaica Rum;" the Romance of the Countess, "Nearest and Dearest" and the "The Torpedo and the Whale."

LES CONTES D'HOFFMANN

"Les Contes d'Hoffmann," or "The Stories of Hoffmann," a fantastic opera, in three acts and a prologue and epilogue, with text by Jules Barbier and music by Jacques Offenbach, was first performed at Offenbach's residence in Paris, May 18, 1879, and was formally produced Feb. 10, 1881.

CHARACTERS.

Olympia.	Cochenille.
Giulietta.	Pitichinaccio.
Antonia.	Franz.
Nicholas.	Coppelius.
A voice.	Dapertutto.
Hoffmann.	Dr. Miracle.
Spallanzani.	Luther.
Nathaniel.	Hermann.
Crespel.	Schlemihl.

The prologue is played in Luther's tavern in Nuremburg. It is a favorite resort of the students, who enter to make merry. While they are remarking the delay of their favorite Hoffmann, that gentleman appears with his friend, Nicholas, and calls for a place, a glass and a pipe. The students ask for a song and Hoffmann sings the ballad of Kleinzach, with its "clic clac" chorus. Some one mockingly accuses Hoffmann of being in love. He utters a vehement word of protest, whereupon they hasten to assure him that such a condition is nothing to be ashamed of and refer to sweethearts of various of their number. Hoffmann disdains them all. They then inquire if his love is such a jewel that none of theirs may compare with her.

"My love!" exclaims Hoffmann. "Say rather my three. Shall I tell you my adventures?"

"Yes, yes, we listen!" shout the students.

"The name of my first was Olympia," begins Hoffmann.

At this the stage grows dark and the curtain falls. When it rises Hoffmann's first love-story lives upon the stage. A luxurious office is shown. Dr. Spallanzani is plotting to recover through "Olympia" the five hundred ducats he lost to the bankrupt Jew, Elias. Hoffmann and Nicholas arrive and the physician goes away temporarily. Hoffmann parts the curtains of the adjoining apartment and sees Spallanzani's daughter, the lovely Olympia, asleep. He falls in love with her at sight and gives vent to many extravagant expressions. Nicholas advises him to know her better and he replies that it is easy to understand the soul one loves.

Coppelius arrives and Spallanzani, who has returned, speaks of marrying Olympia to the "young fool." For payment of his debt to Coppelius, he sends him to get his money from the Jew, Elias, whom Coppelius does not know is bankrupt. Coppelius leaves. Now Spallanzani leads in his charming daughter and introduces her to the company. Her father declares that she is ever amiable, exempt from fault and accomplished. He asks her to sing and as if to arouse her from her excessive modesty, he touches her reassuringly upon the shoulder. She consents, and again he touches her on the shoulder and she sings. It is a brilliant performance with many trills and flourishes.

Supper is served but the lady does not care for refreshment. Hoffmann ıemains to hover over her breathing his devotion. He is grieved that Olympia is so taciturn. Occasionally, it is true, she utters a monosyllable. Nicholas comes from the supper-room to tell his friend that the company are laughing at him. Coppelius returns furious, having learned that Spallanzani has duped him with a worthless note. He mutters that he will get even. The music plays for the ball. They give Olympia to the infatuated Hoffmann, placing her hand in his. She dances divinely, but goes swifter and swifter in spite of the protests of her father. She shows no exhaustion, but not so with Hoffmann, who grows dizzy and faint. Suddenly there is a sound of snapping springs and Olympia falls. taking Hoffmann with her. She is a skilfully made automaton. Coppelius has wound her up to the breaking point and thus gets even with Spallanzani for his failure to pay him for making the puppet's eyes.

The second act or story is placed in Venice at the Palace of Giulietta, a lady with many lovers. Hoffmann and Nicholas are with her. Schlemihl, a jealous lover, arrives unexpectedly and reproaches Giulietta for amusing herself during his absence. Nicholas tries to get Hoffmann away but Hoffmann boasts that he is absolutely unsusceptible. On hearing this boast, Dapertutto resolves to have Hoffmann victimized, like all his predecessors have been. He induces Giulietta to try her arts upon the newcomer. She does and wins, coaxing his likeness from him as a love-token. Schlemihl discovers them and he and Hoffmann fight a duel. Hoffmann vanquishes his opponent but when he comes to claim Giulietta she mocks him and runs away laughing with Pitichinaccio. Hoffmann calls for revenge but Nicholas persuades him to go away.

The scene of the third adventure is laid in Cremona, where Hoffmann, after long wandering, again finds Antonia, she of the beautiful voice, whom he loves. She is weak-lunged and Crespel, her father, fearing that she will share the fate of her mother, who died of consumption, makes her promise never to sing. He is angry with Hoffmann, for he knows that the youth loves his daughter's art and is reluctant to see her sacrifice it. Hoffmann draws from her the promise to marry him secretly on the morrow. Crespel's enemy, Doctor Miracle, who is also jealous of Hoffmann, arrives. Crespel is wild, calling him a grave-digger and accusing him of hoping to murder his child as he did his wife. Miracle sweetly declares that he will cure Antonia, and that she will feel no more pain, offering the contents of certain mystic flasks. He urges her to sing, telling her that a great career is better than love which will not last. Antonia persistently refuses. Finally, Miracle calls the mother's voice from the grave and it urges her to sing. Antonia obeys and falls fainting to the floor. Crespel comes in to find her dying and, seeing Hoffmann present, blames him and calls for a knife that he may bring the color to Antonia's cheeks with Hoffmann's blood.

In the epilogue the company praises Hoffmann's stories and he ends the song of Kleinzach begun in the prologue.

Personally, Offenbach considered this his best opera. He expended infinite pains upon it, and hoped that this more serious work would crown his musical achievement. He died, however, before the orchestration was completed and at his funeral part of the music was adapted to the service. "Les Contes d'Hoffmann" is the opera which was being performed at the Ring Theatre at Vienna when it was burned with enormous loss of life.

PATIENCE

"Patience," or "Bunthorne's Bride," a comic opera in two acts with music by Sir Arthur Sullivan and text by W. S. Gilbert, was produced at the Opéra Comique, London, Aug. 23, 1881.

CHARACTERS.

Reginald Bunthorne, a fleshy poet.
Archibald Grosvenor, an idyllic poet.
Colonel Calverly,
Major Murgatroy,
Lieutenant, The Duke of Dumstable, } officers of the Dragoon Guards.
Chorus of Dragoon Guards.
The Lady Angela,
The Lady Saphir,
The Lady Ella,
The Lady Jane, } rapturous maidens.
Patience, a milkmaid.
Chorus of maidens.

Like most of its fellows, this Gilbert-Sullivan opera is a satire, this time directed against the æsthetic school which flourished at the time of its composition, and which, it may be added, declined immediately thereafter. Mr. Gilbert hints not too subtly, in Bunthorne's confession, that the æsthetic culture may be a pose rather than a great new thought.

Am I alone
And unobserved? I am!
Then let me own
I'm an æsthetic sham!

It is an opera with two heroes, the æsthetic Bunthorne and the idyllic Grosvenor. The curtain rises on the twenty rapturous maidens dressed in æsthetic draperies and playing dolefully on lutes, apparently in the last stages of despair for unrequited love. Their concerted affections have alighted upon Bunthorne. Patience, a buxom unaffected milkmaid, in whose dairy the loved one recently has been discovered eating butter with a tablespoon, arrives and is much concerned at the spectacle of their woe, voicing her delight however that she never has known this disturbing thing, love. She hopes to cheer them by the announcement that the Dragoon Guards, for whom a year ago they were sobbing and sighing, are in the village. But it seems that since the etherealization of their tastes they care nothing for such earthy creatures as Dragoon Guards. When these heroes appear on the scene of their former conquests and find that a melancholy literary man has routed them, they are deeply indignant. Utterly ignoring them, the maidens fall on their knees and beg to hear Bunthorne's poem. He bids them cling passionately to one another and think of faint lilies and taking care to retain the hand of Patience in his, he recites a dreary composition on the general commonplaceness of things, entitled, "Oh Hollow, Hollow, Hollow!" When finally left alone, Bunthorne makes a declaration of love to Patience, and the milkmaid has to confess that she does not know the meaning of the tender passion, never having loved anyone save her great-aunt. She goes to Lady Angela for enlightenment, and that person gives her an æsthetic definition of which she can understand little except "that it is the one unselfish emotion in this whirlpool of grasping greed." Patience, greatly impressed, vows that she will not go to bed until she is head over heels in love with someone, and Grosvenor, the apostle of simplicity, conveniently enters. They discover that they have been playmates in childhood and fall mutually in love, but their brief bliss is spoiled by the thought of Patience that since it makes her happy, it must be selfish to love him, so they decide that they must sunder. The scene is enlivened by the arrival of Bunthorne, who, crowned with roses and hung with garlands, is followed by a procession of maidens dancing classically and playing on archaic instruments. He nobly has decided to be raffled off. Patience, who perceives that to devote herself to loving Bunthorne would be very unselfish indeed, brushes the others aside and offers to wed him herself. The poet overjoyed to escape the possibility of falling into the hands of the antique Jane, accepts without hesitation. The maidens have recourse to the Guards, but forsake them again for the more poetic Grosvenor, whom Bunthorne recognizes with jealous discomfiture may prove a rival.

The ancient Jane is discovered at the rising of the curtain of the second act sitting in a glade and promising herself ever to be faithful to Bunthorne, whom the others have deserted because he has "glanced with passing favor on a puling milkmaid." A little later her hero arrives, but her devotion does not seem to be superlatively consoling to the jealous æsthetic.

Grosvenor appears in turn, followed by the maidens of whom he is heartily tired. Finally, in desperation he announces that he can never be theirs, and begs a respite in the following words:

"Ladies, I am sorry to appear ungallant, but you have been following me about ever since Monday and this is Saturday. I should like the usual half-holiday and if you will kindly allow me to close early today, I shall take it as a personal favor."

In the next scene the Dragoons come attired as æsthetics and struggling manfully with their "angular attitudes," having reached the decision that it is the only way to gain favor with the ladies. Bunthorne and Grosvenor have an important interview, in which the former accuses the latter of monopolizing the feminine attention. Grosvenor declares that he would be only too glad of any suggestion whereby his fatal attractiveness might be lessened. Bunthorne tells him that he must cut his hair and become absolutely commonplace. He cringes under the awfulness of this decision but Bunthorne threatens him with his curse and he yields. When the maidens find that Archibald, the All Right, has discarded æstheticism, they conclude that it proves that æstheticism ought to be discarded. Patience sees that she could be perfectly unselfish in loving such a commonplace fellow, and flies to his arms. The maidens find lovers among the Dragoons and Bunthorne is left alone with his lily, for even Jane is wrested from his side by the Duke, who chooses her as a recompense for her plainness.

Among many sparkling and melodious numbers are the Colonel's song "If you want a recipe for that popular mystery;" Bunthorne's "Oh, Hollow! Hollow! Hollow!" and "If you are eager for to shine;" the duet of Patience and Grosvenor, "Prithee, pretty maiden;" the Duke's plea, "Your maiden hearts, ah, do not steel;" the lovely sextet, "I hear the soft note of the echoing voice;" Jane's song, "Silvered is the raven hair;" Grosvenor's song of the magnet and the churn; the ballad of Patience, "Love is a plaintive song;" and the duet of Bunthorne and Grosvenor, "When I go out of door."

THE MERRY WAR

"The Merry War," a comic opera in three acts with text by Zell and Genée and music by Johann Strauss was first produced in Vienna, Nov. 25, 1881.

CHARACTERS.

Countess Violetta.
Colonel Umberto.
The Duke de Limburg.
Balthazar Groot, a Dutch Tulip Dealer.
Elsa, wife of the Former.
Spiuzzi.
Franchetti.
Biffi.
Soldiers, citizens.

The scene of the operetta is laid in Genoa in the Eighteenth Century. The not too serious hostilities are brought about by the fact that a famous danseuse has made simultaneous contracts with the theatres of two petty states, Genoa and Massa Carrara. These states go to war over the matter, each insisting upon the fulfilment of its own particular contract.

A mock siege is held, the Genoese storming the fortress of Massa Carrara and each side throwing a harmless bombshell at noon every day. The Genoese, however, succeed in making three captures of some importance, the Marquis Sebastiani, an inveterate gossip; a Dutch tulip planter, named Balthazar Groot; and the lovely Countess Violetta, who is in disguise. The feminine prisoner, making good use of her beauty, coaxes a pass from Umberto, the gallant commander of the garrison. On subsequently discovering her rank, he decides to punish her for her deception by marrying her. The fact that Violetta is engaged to the Duke of Limburg and that the marriage is soon to take place, does not present itself to Umberto as a difficulty worthy of much consideration. He arranges that the ceremony shall be performed by the field chaplain, he to appear as the proxy of the Duke. In the ceremony no mention is made of the Duke and Umberto becomes the real husband, although of this the bride is ignorant.

In the second act, several new characters make their appearance. Among them is Elsa, wife of Balthazar Groot. For the benefit of Violetta, Groot has been compelled to pass himself off as the Duke of Limburg, and the jealousy of Elsa is of course aroused. Violetta finds that she abominates her pretended spouse, who can only jabber in Dutch. She also discovers that she is fond of Umberto.

In the third act, complications are nicely untied. Balthazar and Elsa find their conjugal bliss again and Umberto reveals to the delighted Violetta that she is married to him instead of to the Duke of Limburg. A dispatch is received to the effect that the dancer, the cause of the war, has run away and, as she will not keep her engagement with either theatre, peace is concluded.

Among the gay and tuneful numbers are the song of the Marchese, "The Easiest Way's the Best;" Umberto's song, "There's not a drop of blood yet spilled;" Balthazar Groot's number, "We came all the way from Holland;" the duet of Violetta and Umberto, "Hear me! hear me!" "Very Nice Conduct" sung by Balthazar; the romanza, "So near her now and yet so far;" Umberto's love song, "Now darker falls the night;" Artemesia's war song and the duet of Balthazar and Elsa, "Two months have passed."

HERODIADE

"Herodiade," an opera in four acts and seven tableaux, with words by Paul Milliet and Henri Grémont and music by Jules Massenet, was produced at the Théâtre de la Monnaie, Brussels, Dec. 19, 1881.

CHARACTERS.

John.
Herod, King of Galilee.
Phanuel, a Chaldean.
Vitellius, Roman proconsul.
The High Priest.
A voice in the temple.
Salome.
Herodias.
A young Babylonian woman.
Merchants, Hebrew soldiers, Roman soldiers, priests, Levites, temple servitors, seamen, scribes, Pharisees, Galileans, Samaritans, Sadducees, Ethiopians, Nubians, Arabs, Romans.

The action takes place in Jerusalem in the year 30, A. D. A court outside the palace of Herod with adjacent groves of cedars and oleanders is shown. In the distance, the Dead Sea lies in the embrace of the Judean hills. A caravan rests in the valley, awaiting dawn. When the light breaks in the sky, the drowsy scene changes to one of activity and merchants from many countries, followed by slaves carrying heavy burdens, come to the gate. They are true exponents of an age of discord and come nearly to blows over the question of the comparative excellence of their horses. Sage Phanuel, the Chaldean, reproaches them for their foolish quarrel. He speaks of the evil times, of the unrest of the world, of the deaf ear it turns to the immortal voice which tells of love and pardon and eternal life. He predicts that the supremacy of Rome is nearing its end.

The girl Salome appears. She has long been searching for her mother. Phanuel regards her with deep pity, for he knows what she does not, that she is the daughter of Herod's wife. Salome speaks with great feeling of the Prophet John and, even at her words, his voice is heard in the distance, hailing Jerusalem. At the same moment, the dancing-girls file out of the palace. Herod appears and eagerly scans their ranks in search of Salome, a glimpse of whom has infatuated him. Herodias, his consort, follows in agitation, to complain that in the morning a rudely clad man had risen in her path to curse her and call her Jezebel. It was John, the infamous apostle, who preaches baptism and the new faith. When Herod inquires brusquely what she would have him do, she asks for the prophet's head, trying to beguile him with recollections of the past. Herod refuses on the ground that John is too popular with the Jews. When John comes upon the scene, he curses the wicked Herodias anew. After the court has retired, Salome runs to fall at his feet and to sob out her love and adoration. He reminds her that her youth can have little in common with his dark life and the stony road he must travel, but he speaks to her of a higher love.

The second act shows the magnificent chamber of Herod. The King reclines languidly upon his couch, while slaves perform their voluptuous dances before him. He raves of Salome. A Babylonian woman gives him a philtre more vividly to call up the young girl's image. Phanuel reproaches him for occupying his thoughts with a woman, when misery and unrest are growing in the land and when all about him is revolt and bloodshed. The strength of the kingdom is threatened for many of its allies have lately gone over to Rome. Herod boasts of his hold upon the people but the wiser Phanuel reminds him that the people are inconstant. Herod refers disdainfully to the new faith and declares that he will stifle it.

The scene shifts to the public square overlooked by the temple of Solomon on Mount Moriah. Here is assembled a motley, excited crowd. They praise Herod because he has promised to lift the Roman yoke from their necks. As the King and the people plan heroic deeds, the Roman fanfare is heard and Herodias appears in a high place to cry that the oppressor is at the door. Vitellius, the Roman proconsul, with his escort, enters the gates and as he appeals to the people offering them liberty and their just desires, to Herod's chagrin, they rally about his enemy. Above everything else is heard the voices of Salome and the women of Canaan, welcoming John. They cry "Glory to him who cometh in the name of the Lord!" Herod catches sight of Salome and Herodias following his gaze knows that she has a rival.

The scene of Act III is laid at night, in the dwelling of Phanuel. The philosopher, bowed down by his sense of the peril of the wicked city, consults the stars. Hither Herodias comes secretly to ask him the course of the star of the woman who has robbed her of the love of the king. Reluctantly he tells her that their stars are strangely associated and that hers is covered with blood. She laughs, saying that it is the blood of revenge. Phanuel reveals to her his knowledge that she is a mother and points to where below them walks her daughter. With horror Herodias recognizes that her daughter and her rival are one and the same.

The scene changes to the temple, where Salome comes to pray for the safety of John. Hither Herod also repairs.

Judea is in the hands of the hated Romans. He reasons that if he saves John, the grateful Jews will help him to throw off the yoke. Then he sees Salome for the first time face to face. The terrified girl learns that she has had the misfortune to secure his favor. He swears that with his power as King he will possess her and her love. Defiantly she returns that she already loves one greater than Cæsar and the heroes. Herod declares that he will find this man and deliver them both to the executioner. Now the priests and the people invade the temple and before the Holy of Holies with its thousand lights perform the sacred dances. John is present and the priests exhort the people to destroy this man who has proclaimed a false king of the Jews. Herod is appointed to judge him. To all questions the prophet answers well. His prophecy is peace and good will, his arms are The Word, his end is Liberty. Herod whispers to him to serve his projects and he will save his life, but John answers that he has naught to do with the schemes of kings. "Death to him," shout the priests. "Crucify the false Messiah," cries Herodias. "Let us see if God will deliver him," mock the people. Salome begs to be allowed to share his fate and now Herod knows the identity of her lover.

"And I was going to save him," he mutters. "You are right," he says sagely to the priests. "He conspires against Cæsar and Rome. A Holy prophet indeed! He is the lover of Salome, the courtesan."

"Death," cries the rabble and John, unafraid, is led away by the guards.

The last act shows the vault beneath the temple, where the prisoners are kept. John is reconciled to death but he longs for the presence of Salome, until bitterly he questions whether he is the herald of the true God and the elect of the apostles or only a man like other men. Salome finds her way to him and they delight in their reunion, careless of death. They are interrupted by the priests who take John to execution while slaves drag Salome to Herod.

The scene shifts to a banqueting-hall in the palace of the proconsul. Hither Salome is brought. She prays for death with John, first to Herod, then to the Queen whom she invokes as a wife. "If only you were a mother," she moans. Herodias shudders at the word, and Salome speaks bitterly of the unnatural mother who abandoned her to make an infamous marriage. The executioner appears upon a terrace with a sword dripping with blood and Salome, with a terrible cry, precipitates herself upon Herodias crying that she has killed the prophet.

"Pity," begs Herodias, "I am your mother." At this frightful announcement Salome thrusts the dagger into her own bosom and dies.

THE BEGGAR STUDENT

"The Beggar Student," a comic opera in three acts with music by Carl Millöcker and text by Zell and Genée, was first produced in Vienna in 1882.

CHARACTERS.

The Countess Palmatica.
Laura and Bronislava, her daughters.
Symon Symonovicz, the Beggar Student.
Janitsky, a Polish Noble.
General Ollendorf, Governor of Cracow.
Lieutenant Poppenberg,
Major Holzhoff,
Lieutenant Walgenheim,
Lieutenant Schweinitz,
Captain Henrici,
Ensign Richtofen, } Saxon officers.
Bogumil,
Eva, his wife, } cousins of Palmatica.
Burgomaster.
Enterich, a jailor.
Piffke,
Puffke, } his assistants.
Sitzka, an innkeeper.
Onouphrie, a servant.
Alexis, a prisoner.

The action of the opera is laid in the city of Cracow in Poland in 1704. The Polish monarch, Stanislaus, has a little while before been overcome by Augustus the Strong, of Saxony, whose soldiers have charge of a military prison now filled with the captured Poles. General Ollendorf, the military governor, is in love with Laura, daughter of the Polish Countess, Palmatica, and has been spurned in his advances. He has intercepted a letter written by that haughty and patriotic lady, in which she declares that only a Pole and a nobleman can be her son-in-law. The General devises an appropriate revenge. He takes from prison Symon Symonovicz, a Polish vagabond student of fine presence, who is serving a term for poaching and tells him that if he will impersonate a wealthy nobleman and woo and marry the Countess Laura, he may have his liberty. To this the adventurous youth agrees and a fellow prisoner, Janitsky, who is held for political reasons is released to be the new nobleman's private secretary. The plot is as successful as can be. The golden bait is eagerly seized by the ladies who far too long for their own satisfaction have existed in genteel poverty, and the Prince and Laura are betrothed amid general rejoicing. Sister Bronislava and Janitsky are also busied meantime in falling in love.

In the second act, which takes place in the grand salon of the palace of the Countess, the two young people discover that it is a very real sentiment which enthralls them. The money supplied by the General to keep up the impression of opulence is exhausted, and Symon resolves to tell Laura at once of the deception practised upon her. He does not come to this decision without a fierce struggle with temptation, for he is certain that the disclosure will prevent the marriage which was to have taken place that very day. He has not the courage personally to enlighten her of his perfidy and so writes a letter instead, which he intrusts to her mother with instructions that it must be delivered before the ceremony is performed. The General, who suspects that his plans are about to be frustrated, tells the Countess that the letter is of a business nature and, in the hurry, it goes unread. When the ceremony is over, the General in high glee discloses the real station of the bridegroom in the presence of the assembled guests and the Beggar Student is driven from the palace.

In the third act, Symon, insulted and degraded, is meditating self-destruction, when his friend Janitsky reveals the fact that he is a Polish officer and is one of a party of patriots who are planning to capture the citadel and to reinstate King Stanislaus. The Governor-General has discovered that Janitsky knows the secret hiding-place of the Polish grand duke and so bribes him with 200,000 thalers to betray the duke to the Austrians. Janitsky asks Symon to personate the grand duke until the money for his capture can be paid for the surrender of the citadel. The plot succeeds with Symon's help. In return, he is knighted by King Stanislaus and accepted by his wife and mother-in-law.

Prominent tuneful numbers in the score are the chorus of sopranos, "Our husbands, alas, they've locked up in jail;" Ollendorf's song, "And they say that toward ladies;" the chorus at the springtide fair at Cracow; Symon's song, "'Twas thus it came to me;" Palmatica's advice, "If joy in married life you'd find;" the duet of Symon and Laura, "I'll put the case;" Ollendorf's humorous pieces,

> One day I was perambulating,
> Along the Ganges meditating,

and his topical song, "There in a chamber Polish;" "The Prince a beggar's said to be," sung by Bronislava; the song of the philosophical Symon, "I'm penniless and outlawed, too," and the happy concluding chorus,,

> The land is free,
> United we.

PARSIFAL

"Parsifal," a sacred festival drama with words and music by Richard Wagner, was produced at Bayreuth, July 26, 1882, all but the instrumentation having been completed three years previously. It is the last of the great composer's works and was first witnessed by him only seven months before his death. Partly in deference to a promise made to Wagner, the presentation of "Parsifal" took place for twenty-one years only in Bayreuth. It was for America to have the first complete performance outside of the original theatre, and Dec. 24, 1903, after many passages-at-arms between the promoters and the Bayreuth authorities representing Frau Cosima Wagner, it was produced at the Metropolitan Opera House, New York, by the company under the management of Heinrich Conried. Later Henry W. Savage prepared a splendid production and presented "Parsifal" in English in forty-seven different cities and towns of the United States.

CHARACTERS.

Amfortas.
Titurel.
Gurnemanz.
Parsifal.
Klingsor.
Kundry.
The brotherhood of the Grail Knights, esquires, youths and boys, Klingsor's flower maidens.

The Castle of Monsalvat (Salvation), which is the temple of the Holy Grail and the dwelling of the knights who guard it, is placed by Wagner, as by those who have spoken of it before him, in northern Spain. The Holy Grail is the chalice from which Christ drank at the last supper, and in which afterward Joseph of Arimathea, according to one legend, caught the blood which flowed from the Savior's pierced side when He hung upon the cross. To Titurel first was entrusted the care of the cup and spear and it was he who built the temple, instructed the knights chosen to guard it in the duty of leading blameless lives and impressed upon them the invincibility of the spear as long as he who wielded it resisted temptation and kept himself pure. He also taught them to be in readiness to fight for the right and to rescue the weak and the oppressed. When Titurel became old, he resigned the sacred captaincy to his son Amfortas and for many years this trust was faithfully kept. Far and wide went the holy knights, fighting for the good and always winning the victory, for the food which renewed their strength was of sacred origin and they recovered as if by magic from the wounds received in warfare. Many were the knights who desired to enter the ranks as keepers of the Holy Grail and to share in its marvelous benefits and adventures. Those whose lives could stand the test were admitted but many were turned away. One of the latter was Klingsor, a magician, whose life could not bear the scrutiny to which it was subjected. His repulse filled his sinful soul with thoughts of revenge and he established himself in the valley beneath Monsalvat and erected there an enchanted castle. He changed the surrounding desert to a magic garden, peopled with sirens of transcendent beauty. Many of the knights of the Grail were beguiled thither and many fell from their high estate. Finally, his wicked triumph was crowned with the fall of the very head of the order itself, for Amfortas, resolved upon ending his enemy's sway, sallied forth armed with the sacred spear and all-confident in his own impregnability. But Klingsor sent Kundry, fairest of all the hosts of temptresses, and Amfortas, forgetful, yielded to her seductions. To complete the Knight's dishonor, the spear was snatched from him by Klingsor and with it the magician inflicted a wound which would be eased by no remedy. After Amfortas had suffered long, the Grail oracle decreed that help could come only through a guileless fool made wise through fellow-suffering.

All these things have happened when the curtain rises on the quiet woodland glade near the castle of the Grail. It is daybreak and Gurnemanz, one of the aged knights, rouses two young sleeping squires. Across the peaceful fields comes the fierce, wild Kundry dressed in coarse garb and with flying hair. She offers, for the help of Amfortas, a rare balsam from Arabia. Kundry, when in the heavy sleep Klingsor's magic puts upon her, is the beautiful enchantress of the charmed garden but when free from the spell, she is a half-savage silent creature, who, seemingly oppressed by a consciousness of some great sin, seeks to find relief and redemption through performing menial services for the knights of the Grail. She laughs when she fain would weep, she does evil when she longs to accomplish good, and she fears to sleep, for then it is that she falls under Klingsor's baleful influence.

As Amfortas, coming from his bath in the sacred lake, is borne past upon his litter, Gurnemanz and the squires discuss his sad plight and hope for the coming of the blameless fool. Their conversation is interrupted by a sound and a moment later a wild swan hit by an arrow flies unsteadily across the lake and falls dead at their feet. Indignant that a deed of violence should thus desecrate the peaceful vicinity of the Grail, some of the younger knights drag forward the culprit, who is only a forest lad of innocent mien and wholly unconscious of having done anything wrong. When it dawns upon him that he has hurt and killed a harmless creature, he breaks his bow and flings away the arrows. The knights, softened by this act, question him. He discloses a strange ignorance, which extends even to his origin; but upon this subject Kundry is able to enlighten both him and them.

'Twas fatherless that his mother bore him,
For in battle slain was Gamuret;
And from a like untimely death
Her son to shelter, peacefully,
In a desert, the foolish woman reared him.
A fool too!

As the youth watches her with wide eyes she concludes thus

As I rode by I saw her dying
And fool, she bade me greet thee.

In a passion of sorrow and indignant at her laughter, he flies at her throat, but is restrained by the knights, and falls fainting on the ground. Kundry now is filled with pity, and revives him with water from the spring. Then suddenly she is overcome by drowsiness, and, struggling against it, she staggers toward the thicket and sinks down on a grassy knoll.

In the heart of Gurnemanz has been growing the hope that this boy may be the "pure fool." Led by this hope, he conducts him to the temple where the holy rites of the love-feast are to be performed. Amfortas, the one sinner in that pure brotherhood, pleads not to be asked to perform his duty of uncovering the Holy Grail, which act, since his sin, entails for him untold agony. But his father, Titurel, lying in the tomb between life and death, bids him not shirk, for only the sight of the Grail can restore the waning strength of the old monarch. Amfortas then makes passionate inquiry as to how long this torment must last and is answered by voices which bid him await the coming of the "blameless fool, wise through pity." Parsifal, at one side, watching as the shrine is uncovered, feels a pang of sorrow at Amfortas' suffering, but not being as yet "wise through pity" he does not understand and the vexed Gurnemanz thrusts him forth from the temple exclaiming "Thou art then nothing but a fool!"

The second act takes place in Klingsor's enchanted palace. The magician, gazing into his magic mirror, perceives that a struggle is at hand, that Parsifal, the pure, is coming and that Kundry must be the means of his ensnarement. He summons her and she appears in a bluish mist, as if just awakening from sleep. When she knows the use which is to be made of her, she breaks forth into a tempest of remonstrance and grief but Klingsor forces her to do his bidding and mocks her for seeking the knights, who reckon her not even "as a dog."

The scene changes to the enchanted garden abloom with tropical flowers and bathed in a strange light. Already Parsifal has gained the ramparts and stands gazing with astonishment upon the scene below. For his further bewilderment there now appear the sirens, who, as flower maidens, flit about in gauzy garments and dance and sing before him. When he draws nearer they surround him, laughing, caressing him and gently reproaching him for his indifference, which indifference they attempt to dissipate by decking themselves like veritable flowers, and by hovering in fragrant crowds about him, uttering soft cries of

> Come, gentle lover!
> Let me be thy flower.

At first he enjoys the novel sight, looking upon them as children and offering to be their playmate. But finally as they press about him quarreling for his favor; and becoming freer and bolder with their kisses, he repulses them half angrily and is about to escape, when a beautiful voice, issuing from a thicket of flowers, stops him.

"Parsifal, tarry!" It is the name his mother once called him and she who knows it shall have his attention. There comes to his dazzled view, Kundry the enchantress, beautiful as a dream and lying on a couch of roses.

"Didst thou call me, the nameless?" he inquires, wonderingly. Subtly she wins his interest by telling him of his own life and of his dead mother "Heart's sorrow," who loved him so dearly. He is overcome with distress and emotion at this memory and falls at her feet. Kundry attempts to exercise her spell in the guise of pity. She gently draws him to her, puts her arm about his neck and kisses him. With a cry he starts to his feet, his hand pressed to his side, for in this kiss he feels the wound that Amfortas received from the sacred spear when it was yielded by Klingsor. Within him has been born the wisdom which shall enable him to heal Amfortas. He speaks the name of the sufferer with pitying lips, his sympathy springing from the depths of a marvelous new comprehension. He is the fool no longer. He now is "wise through pity." He realizes in himself how Amfortas was tempted, he understands the frailty of the human heart; he is overwhelmed with compassion for the whole world of sin.

As Kundry attempts to renew her endearments, he pushes her away with loathing but a moment later the new compassion extends even to her and he promises to give her deliverance, if she will show him the way to Amfortas. She is Klingsor's agent, however, and she cannot but cry aloud in this crisis for aid. The magician appears on the steps of the castle, bearing the sacred lance, which he hurls at Parsifal but the holy weapon hangs suspended over the pure youth's head. He seizes it and makes with it the sign of the cross. The castle falls as if overthrown by an earthquake, the garden withers to a desert and the ground is scattered with faded flowers, while Kundry lies prostrate amid the ruins.

Many years pass before the beginning of the third act but evil years they have been, for misfortune has fallen upon the knights of the Holy Grail. The wound of Amfortas never has healed. The light of the Grail has not been allowed to cast its benignant glow upon the knights, for its guardian has not had the courage to incur the agony attendant upon uncovering it. The sacred food has been withheld and the aged Titurel, whom the holy light had kept alive, has perished in despair.

These years Parsifal has spent wandering through the world in search of Amfortas. Many have tried to wrest from him the sacred lance, but have failed. As the curtain rises we see again the precincts of the Grail. It is spring and early morning, the morning of Good Friday. Gurnemanz, grown very old, comes from his hermit's hut. He hears a noise in the thicket near by and pressing aside the branches discovers Kundry, lying there in a half-stupor. He arouses her and she, responding to his inquiry as to what she would have, utters but the words "Serve! Serve!" She enters the hut but coming forth again fetches water from the sacred spring. Suddenly a stranger is seen approaching clad in black armor, his visor down and in his hand a spear. He plants the spear in the earth, removes his helmet and kneels in prayer. Both Gurnemanz and Kundry recognize him as the "pure fool" now grown to man's estate. To his marveling auditors Parsifal imparts the tidings that he has brought back the sacred weapon undefiled. The old man tells him that once again on that day are the knights to assemble in the temple as they did of yore and that once more they hope to see the holy light, for Amfortas has promised to perform for the funeral rite of Titurel the long-neglected office, whatever may be the cost to himself.

The humble Kundry bathes the feet of Parsifal with water from the sacred spring and dries them with her hair. He, knowing her heart, baptizes her, and as she falls to the ground weeping in gratitude, he kisses her gently on the forehead. Habited like the guardians of the Grail and bearing the sacred spear in his hand, he proceeds to the temple, whither is borne Amfortas on his litter and whither the knights bring in solemn procession the dead body of Titurel. When the coffin is opened and the knights realize how their aged King longed for the light and died because it was withheld, they break forth into lamentations and press upon Amfortas renewing their importunities for the revelation of the Grail. In anguish their suffering leader refuses and, tearing open his garment, he bids them plunge their swords into his bleeding wound and kill him, so that they then may unveil the Grail themselves. But Parsifal enters and touching the wound with the sacred spear that made it, bids Amfortas "be whole, absolved and atoned." He also bids him to consider his suffering blessed, for through it divine pity and the might of knowledge have been given to a fool. Then Parsifal, destined henceforth to be the guardian of the Grail, shows the knights the sacred spear which he brings back to them and now places on the temple's altar. While he uncovers the chalice and kneels before it, a white dove descends from heaven and hovers above his head. Kundry, gazing at the holy sight, sinks lifeless to the ground, her redemption complete, while the voices of knights and angels mingle in praise of the Redeemer.

The idea of "Parsifal," called by one writer an "inspired dramatic Te Deum," first was suggested to Wagner by the epic poem of Wolfram von Eschenbach, while searching for material for "Tannhäuser." Evidently, the theme lay but partly dormant in his mind, for fifteen years later, while at Zurich, he drew up the first sketch of the opera. But not until another interval of twenty years had elapsed, was it finished at Bayreuth. Thus it may be regarded as the result of thirty-five years of reflection and as the embodiment of a mellow and deliberately developed philosophy. It is considered by many to be Wagner's masterpiece, while others go a step farther and call it the most marvelous and impressive achievement in the history of music.

The basis of the drama is derived from the cycle of the Holy Grail myths, made familiar by the stories of King Arthur and his knights, which have come down to us in manifold guises. These Grail romances were written at the time of the earlier crusades, when the supposed discovery of the sacred cup and spear still was fresh in the minds of the Christians. In Tennyson's "Idyls of the

King," the chalice is carried to Great Britain by Joseph of Arimathea, to whom, when cast into prison after preparing the body of Christ for burial, Christ appeared, bringing the sacrament in it.

Wagner has bestowed his own individuality upon the legend and he has changed the name of the hero to indicate this hero's character. In the Arabian, " fal " signifies foolish and " parsi " pure one. " Parsifal," freely translated, means " blameless fool." Amfortas, in all the legends, is the visible symbol of suffering whose healing depends upon the asking of a question. Gurnemanz is always present in the original Parsifal legends. Klingsor also appears though never so malignant as here, but Kundry, with her many-sided soul, is the creation of Wagner and his greatest contribution to the myth.

Musically, " Parsifal " contains the fullest and most complete exposition of all Wagner's theories concerning the music drama and its construction. While the most zealous admirers of the work declare it the Bayreuth master's greatest achievement, more careful students find it not the equal of " The Mastersingers," " Tristan and Isolde " or certain portions of " The Ring of the Nibelungs " so far as vitality, power and originality of the thematic material is concerned. It is a master work but not the highest reach of Wagner.

Portions of the score which are familiar through more or less frequent performance in concert, are the prelude built up upon three motives from the work itself; the " Good Friday Spell," which is heard in the scene of Parsifal's return and the preparation for his progress to the temple to assume the kingship of the Grail; the so-called " Transformation," which is the music played by the orchestra during the march of Gurnemanz and Parsifal to the temple, the scenery moving slowly from side to side and changing the setting gradually from the woodland and fields to rocky recesses and finally to the interior of the temple itself; and the finale of the music-drama, the tonal illustration of Parsifal's unveiling of the chalice and its glowing from delicate pink to blood-red as the dove descends and hovers above him. The "Flower Girl" music is of exceptional grace and beauty. The "Lament" of Amfortas and the scene of Kundry's attempted ensnarement of Parsifal have also been heard in concert performance. They, together with the foregoing, constitute the "big" moments in the truly remarkable score.

WILHELMINA SCHRÖDER-DEVRIENT,

1804-1860.

One of the great dramatic singers and operatic tragediennes, who in dramatic power, feeling and fascination, has never been surpassed and hardly ever equaled. She came of histrionic stock, her mother, Sophia Schroeder being a tragedienne, who was compared to the great Sarah Siddons. Her father was a baritone singer. Wilhelmina was born at Hamburg and her childhood was passed with her parents, wandering about Germany, playing and singing in the various towns.

Her greatest fame and triumph followed her appearance in Fidelio, her conception of which, was thoroughly approved of, even by the composer, the arbitrary Beethoven.

The singer was connected with the Dresden Opera for twenty years and she was on good terms with many of the famous composers, among them Wagner, in whose Rienzi, The Flying Dutchman and Tannhauser she appeared.

Although eminently successful in Italian Opera, the singer's greatest triumphs came to her in German opera and she did much to make it popular. She was thoroughly in earnest in her work and labored hard for the cause of German music. Her voice was a mellow soprano, which united softness with volume and compass. A marble bust of her is in the opera house at Berlin.

WILHELMINA SCHRÖDER-DEVRIENT,

1804-1860.

One of the great dramatic singers and operatic tragediennes, who in dramatic power, feeling and fascination, has never been surpassed and hardly ever equaled. She came of histrionic stock, her mother, Sophia Schroeder being a tragedienne, who was compared to the great Sarah Siddons. Her father was a baritone singer. Wilhelmina was born at Hamburg and her childhood was passed with her parents, wandering about Germany, playing and singing in the various towns.

Her greatest fame and triumph followed her appearance in Fidelio, her conception of which, was thoroughly approved of, even by the composer, the arbitrary Beethoven.

The singer was connected with the Dresden Opera for twenty years and she was on good terms with many of the famous composers, among them Wagner, in whose Rienzi, The Flying Dutchman and Tannhauser she appeared.

Although eminently successful in Italian Opera, the singer's greatest triumphs came to her in German opera and she did much to make it popular. She was thoroughly in earnest in her work and labored hard for the cause of German music. Her voice was a mellow soprano, which united softness with volume and compass. A marble bust of her is in the opera house at Berlin.

IOLANTHE

"Iolanthe," or "The Peer and the Peri," is a comic opera in two acts, with music by Sir Arthur Sullivan and text by W. S. Gilbert. It was produced at the Savoy Theatre, London, Nov. 25, 1882.

CHARACTERS.

Strephon.
The Earl of Mount Ararat.
The Earl of Tolloller.
Private Willis.
The train-bearer.
The Lord Chancellor.
Iolanthe.
The Fairy Queen.
Celia.
Leila.
Fleta.
Phyllis.
Chorus of peers.
Chorus of fairies.

The first act is played in Arcady. The queen of the fairies and her court appear and lament the absence of Iolanthe, who married a mortal. In fairy-land that is a sin punishable by death but the queen, in this case, had commuted the sentence to desertion of her husband and penal servitude for life. This punishment Iolanthe has chosen to undergo at the bottom of a stream so as to be near her son Strephon who is twenty-four years of age and of whom his father knows nothing. The Queen decides to recall the banished fairy and forgive her. As Iolanthe is immortal, she still looks about seventeen and it is difficult to believe that she is the mother of the full-grown Arcadian shepherd, who appears playing on a flageolet. It develops that Strephon is fairy to the waist and that his legs are mortal, a situation fraught with difficulty, It also appears that he loves Phyllis, a ward in chancery, and that the match is seriously opposed by the Lord Chancellor, who has a liking for her himself. But the young people have decided to be married in spite of his opposition.

While they are expressing their approval of each other, a procession of peers, headed by Lords Ararat and Tolloller with the Lord Chancellor as an impressive finale, comes in, each of the Lords proclaiming his own merits.

Phyllis is persuaded to present herself and her case before the bar of the House. Lord Tolloller generously announces that he would be glad to have her even if her origin is rather lowly, since he has "birth and position in plenty and grammar and spelling for two." But Phyllis prefers to share a lowly cot with Strephon. The Lord Chancellor declares such a thing can never be, as Strephon has disobeyed an order of the Court of Chancery. Iolanthe tries to dissipate her son's dejection by reminding him that the Queen of the fairies has promised him special protection. Her words are partially overheard by Lord Tolloller, who draws Phyllis' attention to the affectionate interview between her lover and a pretty girl. When Phyllis scolds him, he avers that it was only his mother, which statement gives rise to general mirth. Strephon insists that what is more she is and has been his mother ever since his birth. Phyllis will not believe such a flimsy tale and, in pique, tells the Lord that any one of them may have her.

The Queen of the fairies realizes that the time for her assistance has arrived. To the dismay of the peers, she announces that Strephon shall discard his crooks and pipes and go into Parliament, and that,

> Every bill and every measure
> That may gratify his pleasure,
> Though your fury it arouses,
> Shall be passed by both your Houses.

Private Willis opens the second act, which is played in the palace yard at Westminster. He has a musical soliloquy about Parliament and then the fairies trip in followed by the peers, from whose conversation it may be gathered that Strephon has entered Parliament and is creating havoc "running amuck of all abuses." It also appears that the fairies are beginning to become enamored of the peers. Phyllis has an affecting scene with the two peers to whom she is engaged, Lord Ararat and Lord Tolloller.

As it is a tradition in both families always to kill successful rivals, which tradition they have sworn on affidavit to respect, the situation is delicate. To settle the matter, Phyllis is resigned by them to the smitten Lord Chancellor, who seems in a fair way to take possession of her. Iolanthe, however, who knows that Strephon and Phyllis would like to make up, reveals herself as the Lord Chancellor's wife who so mysteriously disappeared and pleads his son's cause, to which he cannot refuse to listen.

The Queen discovers now that all her ladies are betrothed to peers. She reminds them of the penalty but the Lord Chancellor exerts the "subtleties of a legal mind" and suggests the insertion of a single word which will change the law to mean that any fairy shall die who doesn't marry a mortal. This is highly satisfactory to everybody. The Queen chooses Private Willis and Iolanthe is restored to the Lord Chancellor. It occurs to somebody that since the House is to be recruited from persons of intelligence, there can be no use for the members in question. So all become fairies, with wings springing from their shoulders, and exchange the House of Peers for the House of Peris.

This harmless and unmalicious burlesque on the dignity of peers and the British constitution contains the following among its numbers: Strephon's song, "Good morrow, good mother;" the duet of Phyllis and Strephon, "None shall part us from each other;" the Lord Chancellor's song, "When I went to the Bar;" Private Willis' song, "When all night long a chap remains;" the Lord Chancellor's patter song, "When you're lying awake with a dismal headache" and Iolanthe's song, "He loves! if in the bygone years."

LAKME

"Lakmé" is a romantic opera in three acts, the music written by Léo Delibes. The words, by Goudinet and Gille, are taken from the story "Le mariage de Loti." It was first presented in Paris in 1883.

CHARACTERS.

Lakmé, daughter of Nilakantha.
Nilakantha, a Brahmin priest.
Gerald, an English officer, lover of Lakmé.
Frederick, a brother officer.
Mallika, } slaves of Lakmé.
Hadji, }
Ellen, } daughters of the viceroy.
Rose, }
Mrs. Bentson, a governess.
A fortune-teller.
A Chinese merchant.
A Sepoy.
Hindoos, English officers and ladies, sailors, bayaderes, Chinamen, musicians, Brahmins.

The scene is laid in India and the choice of characters is in itself promising. Lakmé's father, the Hindoo, hates with a mighty hatred, all foreigners. Quite naturally, the damsel falls in love with the first young Englishman who presents himself. This happens to be Gerald, who, with a party of English people, comes to the sacred grounds from the viceroy's palace. Lakmé and Gerald encounter each other alone. The girl, who has been raised by a jealous father to know naught of the great world outside the bamboo enclosure, is completely fascinated by the charming stranger, while Gerald, ravished by the beauty of the girl and by the charm of her retreat with its tropical glory of lotus and rose, surrenders to what is to him an episode but to her is everything. They unfortunately are discovered by Lakmé's furious father. The Englishman escapes his rage for the moment but ultimately falls a victim to his plotting. Nilakantha and his daughter disguise themselves as penitents and he requires the girl to sing in the market-place. As he has hoped, the lover at once recognizes the voice of his dear one and discloses himself. Nilakantha approaches him stealthily, stabs him in the back and flees, thinking his enemy dead. This hope is false, however, and in some fashion, Lakmé and her slave Hadji convey the wounded man to a luxurious bungalow in a jungle where every comfort is available. Here they conceal him and patiently nurse him back to health, the girl meanwhile dreaming fair dreams and hoping desperately that she may retain his love. With the characteristic superstition of her people, she leaves Gerald for a while to seek the sacred water which can make love eternal. While she is gone, the music of his regiment summons him to duty and the charms of his own world, among them a lovely English girl, call loudly to him. Their voices become irresistible when Frederick, who discovers him, adds his entreaties. When Lakmé returns and her beloved one's very evident faithlessness mocks her hope of eternal love, she poisons herself with the flowers of the datura and goes to the arms of Brahma.

Delibes was little known save as a composer of exquisite ballet music until the appearance of this graceful work. In Lakmé, he used much of oriental color and always with rare good taste and skill. Especially appropriate is the scene in the jungle, which is filled with dreamy and sensuous charm. The opera suffers, however, from a sameness of coloring. Despite the beauty of many of its numbers it is apt to impress one as somewhat monotonous, when heard in its entirety. The duet for Lakmé and her slave, " 'Neath yon Dome," is one of the finest pages in the score; Gerald's passionate love-song, "The God of Truth," forms an effective incident of the first act; Nilakantha's song, "Lakmé, thy soft looks," has true pathos in it, while Lakmé's "Bell-song," with its wealth of vocal ornamentation, is a piece of writing which not only forms the climax in brilliancy of the opera but has won triumphs for many a concert singer. Lakmé crooning " 'Neath the Dome" is the gem of the third act.

FALKA

"Falka," a comic opera in three acts, with score by Francis Chassaigne and text by Leterrier and Vanloo, was first produced, Oct. 29, 1883, at the Comedy Theatre, London.

CHARACTERS.

Folbach, Military Governor of Montgratz.
Tancred, his nephew, usher in a village school.
Arthur, a student, son of a rich Hungarian farmer.
Lay-Brother Pelican, doorkeeper of the convent.
Konrad, captain of the Governor's pages.
Tekeli, sergeant of the patrol.
Boboky, a Tzigan scout.
Boleslas, chief of the Tzigani.
The seneschal, Folbach's steward.
Falka, niece of Folbach, at the convent school.
Edwige, sister of Boleslas.
Alexina de Kelkirsch, a young heiress.
Minna, her maid.
Janotha, landlady of the inn.
Military pages, soldiers of the watch, maids of honor, peasants, Bohemians.

The action passes in Hungary, about the middle of the Eighteenth Century. Folbach is a military governor and is promised by the emperor a patent of nobility on condition that he can show a male heir, direct or collateral, on whom the succession may be settled. He is childless but has a nephew, Tancred, and a niece, Falka, of both of whom he has disposed, upon the death of his brother, by sending the boy to be an usher in a village school and by putting the girl into a convent. He builds his hope upon Tancred, whom he never has seen and whom he has summoned from his humble post. But while the youth is on his way through the forest at night he is waylaid by gypsies and bound to a tree. Edwige, the chief's sister, offers to release him on condition that he will marry her. He promises and then ignominiously takes flight. Tancred is closely pursued by his fiancée and her brother, neither of whom has seen his face. Their meager clues are limited to the sound of his voice and to certain pet words in which he has indulged. Learning that he is a nephew of the Governor, they decide to lurk about until the meeting and thus identify him. But of this scheme Tancred learns and to baffle them he sends word to his uncle that he is ill and cannot appear.

Meantime, Falka has been making history for herself and has eloped from her convent with Arthur, the son of a rich Hungarian farmer. They come to the inn where the Governor is waiting for Tancred and are closely followed by Brother Pelican, doorkeeper of the convent. Falka eludes her pursuer by dressing in Arthur's clothes. Finding that her brother is expected at the inn, she impersonates him. Folbach is greatly pleased with his heir. Things are further complicated when Pelican finds Falka's convent dress and, suspecting that she is disguised as a boy, arrests Arthur for Falka. Edwige and Boleslas, witnessing the meeting of the Governor and Falka, believe that they have found the faithless Tancred. As the act ends the cortège sets out to the castle, where the heir presumptive is to be betrothed to Alexina de Kelkirsch, the bride assigned to Tancred by the emperor.

In Act II, Arthur is made to put on convent dress and is marched away by Pelican leaving Falka, in huzzar uniform, to win her uncle's forgiveness, which, on account of his antipathy to girls, she knows will be difficult. Tancred comes, in footman's costume, to watch over his own interests and to defeat the schemes of the young impostor not knowing that it is his sister. He dares not yet reveal himself because of the gypsies but he hopes that these persons will dispose of his rival for him, under the impression that it is he. Falka is challenged to a duel by Boleslas and averts it by a private confession to Edwige that she is a woman. Arthur is brought back from the convent in haste and has to own up to an exchange of clothes with Falka, and in disgust the Governor orders the pair out of his presence. At this desired consummation, Tancred cries "O joy! O rapture!," familiar words which reveal him to his pursuers. The Governor's state of mind is unpleasant when he learns that Tancred is betrothed to a gypsy and that he possesses such a madcap niece.

In Act III, the Governor, obliged to carry out the emperor's will, dispiritedly goes on with the marriage of Tancred and Alexina. Falka is consigned to a tower to await her restoration to the convent. Edwige and Alexina have an interview and, as a result, the gypsy presents herself as the bride. Meantime Falka escapes from her tower only to be recaptured and led before her uncle. Admiring her pluck and spirit in spite of himself, he pardons her just as a despatch from the emperor arrives, settling the succession on the female line.

The principal numbers are the patrol chorus, "While all the town is sleeping;" the air and refrain, "I'm the Captain Boleslas;" the rondo duet of Falka and Arthur, "For your indulgence we are hoping;" the "Tap tap" chorus of the maids of honor; Falka's song "You must live strictly by rule;" the pretty Bohemian chorus, "Cradled upon the heather;" the trio "Oh Joy! Oh Rapture!;" the quintet, "His aspect's not so overpow'ring;" the bridal chorus "Rampart and bastion gray;" the Hungarian rondo and dance, "Catchee, catchee;" the romanza, "At eventide;" the duet, "Slumber, O Sentinel" and the finale, "And now a long good-bye."

SIGURD

"Sigurd," an opera in four acts with music by Ernest Reyer and text by Du Locle and Blau, was produced at the Théâtre Monnaie, Brussels, Jan. 7, 1884. Its hero is the hero of the Nibelungen myths. Although written previous to the presentation of Wagner's "Ring," many of the scenes are similar to scenes in that great cycle.

CHARACTERS.

Sigurd.
Gunther, King of the Burgundians.
Hagen, a warrior, Gunther's companion in arms.
A priest of Odin.
A bard.
Envoys from Attila.
Brunhilde, a Valkyrie, banished by the gods.
Hilda, Gunther's sister.
Uta, Hilda's foster-mother.
Burgundian warriors and people, Icelandic people, priests, servants.

The action opens in Gunther's palace, where the women are making ready the standards and armor of the King and his followers, who will, on the morrow, go forth to undertake fresh conquests. The pensive Princess Hilda reveals to her foster-mother, Uta, her love for Sigurd, an heroic warrior, who a short time before aided her brother against his enemies and rescued her from captivity, although evincing no further interest in her fate. The older woman has divined her secret and has sent to Sigurd a magic message which will insure his coming. She also has prepared a philtre potent to change his indifference into love.

Soon Gunther enters to receive the ambassadors sent by the King of the Huns to sue for the hand of his sister. He informs them that because of Hilda's desire not to wed, the suit is vain. She is, nevertheless, presented with a bracelet as a gage of love, which, if sent by her to Attila, will insure his coming to aid or avenge her.

A bard sings the legend of Brunhilde banished from heaven for disobedience and condemned to lie sleeping in a palace in Iceland surrounded by fire and demons until awakened by a warrior capable of encountering them. Gunther is so fired by the tale that he declares he will start at morn to rescue her. Sigurd arrives and Gunther, discovering that his visitor is the warrior who rescued him from the Burgundians, offers him the half of his kingdom. Eternal friendship is sworn between the two men. The love-philtre is administered and Sigurd becomes at once enchanted with Hilda. He offers to accompany Gunther to Iceland on condition that upon their return he be granted any reward he may ask.

The priests who know the danger which threatens Sigurd and Gunther, reluctantly present them with the magic horn of Odin as an aid in the enterprise. They warn them that none can gain Brunhilde's fastness save one who is perfectly pure. Sigurd knows that he alone is fitted for the task. But he promises that should he win the lovely Valkyrie he will resign her to Gunther, with whom he exchanges helmets.

After a series of contests with valkyries, kobolds and phantoms he crosses the lake of fire and enters the enchanted chamber of Brunhilde. Lowering his visor, he awakens her. She offers him her love and gratitude and then falls asleep again. Her couch becomes a barque and with Sigurd's sword between them they are drawn away by norns who have assumed the form of swans.

The third act opens in Gunther's garden at Worms, where the two warriors meet and Sigurd renounces his lovely prize. At the first gleam of dawn, Brunhilde's sleep slips from her. Assured that it was Gunther who set her free, she consents to be his bride. Hilda is full of joy because she sees in Sigurd's transferral of the Valkyrie to her brother, an evidence of his love. But Uta foresees disaster. Sigurd demands, as a reward, to be wedded to Hilda and Brunhilde is asked to join their hands. As hers touches Sigurd's a peal of thunder is heard, but blind to the omen, the double marriage procession goes forth to the grove of Freya.

In the last act, the people deplore the continued melancholy of their Queen, Brunhilde, and in a soliloquy she laments the decree of Odin that she should wed Gunther instead of Sigurd. Hilda, perceiving her brother's bride tremble at the name of Sigurd, reveals in a passion of jealousy that it was Sigurd who set her free, taunting her with the fact that he gave her up and showing her the Valkyrie's belt, given as a love-token. Brunhilde accuses her of sorcery, and when Gunther comes, she denounces his baseness and throws her crown at his feet. He is about to kill himself when Hagen assures him that Sigurd is the greater culprit. The two watching, see Brunhilde join him and dispel the influence of the love-charm, and listening, they hear them swear eternal fidelity. Sigurd is ultimately slain. The Valkyrie's spirit follows him, and they are seen soaring through the clouds to the paradise of Odin.

"Sigurd," although a work of undoubted power, has borne the ungrateful fate of frequent comparison with the Wagnerian music clothing the same story.

Prominent passages in the score are the chorus of women engaged in embroidering the standards, "Brodons des étendards et préparons des armes" ("We 'broider the standards"); Uta's interpretation of Hilda's dream, "Je sais des secrets merveilleux" ("I know of secrets wonderful"); the bard's story of Brunhilde, "C'était Brunhilde, la plus belle" ("'Twas Brunhilde"); Sigurd's song at his entrance, "Prince de Rhin, au pays de mon père" ("Rhineland's King, the country of my sire"); his song in the forest, "Les bruits des chants s'éteint dans le forêt" ("'Mid Forests vast"); Brunhilde's aria of awakening, "Salut, splendeur de jour" ("Hail, thou glory of the day"); and the duet after the love-spell is broken, "Avec ces fleurs que l'eau traîne en courant" ("With every flower").

MANON

"Manon," an opera in five acts, with music by Jules Massenet and words by Meilhac and Gille after the novel of Abbé Prévost, was first presented in Paris, Jan. 19, 1884.

CHARACTERS.

The Chevalier des Grieux.
The Count des Grieux, his father.
Lescaut of the Royal Guard, Manon's cousin.
Guillot Merfontain, minister of finance, a roué.
De Brétigny, a nobleman.
An Innkeeper.
Attendant of St. Sulpice.
A sergeant of guards.
A soldier.
Rossette, Poussette, Javotte, } actresses.
Manon, the adventuress.
Gamblers, croupiers, guards, travelers, townspeople, ladies, gentlemen.

The opera opens in the courtyard of the inn at Amiens, which is filled with a somewhat motley crowd, including Lescaut of the Royal Guard, who, according to the present opera-book, is Manon's cousin and not her brother, as in the version of the Puccini opera. When Manon alights from the coach, she creates a sensation on account of her remarkable beauty. She is on her way to a convent and is as ill-fitted for such a life as one could well be, for she responds with unusual abandon to the joy of living.

The young student, Des Grieux, musing with happy anticipation upon the morrow, when he shall be in Paris again with his father, sees Manon. It is a case of love at first sight for both of them. Manon's motive is largely a worldly one, for she is of the peasantry and Des Grieux's position fires her vanity. In almost less time than it takes to tell it, the two reckless children are on their way to Paris in the coach in which the old roué Guillot, who had been making merry at the inn, had hoped to carry off the girl.

Before Des Grieux can secure the coveted consent of his father to their marriage, he and Manon are tracked to their simple but happy retreat by Lescaut and De Brétigny. The former has many reproaches and a great deal to say about "the honor of his house" but it develops that he is willing to sell Manon to a higher bidder. Des Grieux is delivered to his father's spies who abduct him. Manon is left to console herself with De Brétigny and the luxury with which his wealth makes it possible for him to surround her.

Manon is seen in the third act in the midst of the magnificent evidences of her dishonor and apparently enjoying the flattery of the swarm of admirers about her. From Des Grieux's own father, she learns that her unhappy lover is now a priest at St. Sulpice. She flies to him at once. In this scene, remarkable for its dramatic power, Manon succeeds in prevailing upon Des Grieux, who tries in vain to deceive himself into thinking that all his love is dead, to break his vows and to return to enjoy the world at her side.

In the fourth act, which takes place in a gambling-house in Paris, Lescaut, surrounded as usual by his favorites, Poussette, Javette and Rossette, is joined by Manon and Des Grieux who now are destitute. Manon urges the Chevalier to the gaming-table much against his will, hoping that thereby he will mend his fortunes. He does win but he is accused of cheating by the jealous Guillot, who causes his arrest. In this dilemma, he is saved by his father who pays his debts. But also through the influence of Guillot, Manon is sentenced to deportation. This is never accomplished, for she dies from shame and exhaustion on the road to Havre where the embarkation is to be made, but not before she has been clasped in the arms of the faithful Des Grieux who bends over her as her soul takes flight.

"Manon," which is one of the more important products of the modern French school and is probably the ablest of all of Massenet's operas, is so closely knit in music and text that the naming of portions of particular and especial excellence or interest is difficult. The system of short phrases (leit-motifs) to characterize and distinguish the various personages of the drama has been employed by the composer. The orchestra web throughout is intricate and elaborate yet of great eloquence and beauty. Portions that will impress the hearer as effective and interesting are Manon's first song, "Je suis encor tout étourdie" ("I'm still confused and dazzled quite"); the duet in the first act for Manon and Des Grieux; Des Grieux's "Dream song" in the second act; Manon's gay admonition "Obéissons quand leur voix appelle" ("Let us obey when they shall call"); the intensely impassioned music of the duet at St. Sulpice; Manon's exultation when Des Grieux wins at gaming and her lament following his arrest.

THE TRUMPETER OF SAKKINGEN

"The Trumpeter of Säkkingen," an opera in three acts and a prologue, with music by Victor E. Nessler and text based on J. Victor von Scheffel's poem, with several original songs added by the librettist, Rudolf Bunge, was produced at the Stadt Theatre, Leipzig, May 4, 1884.

CHARACTERS.

Werner Kirchoffer, a law student, afterward a trumpeter.
Conradin, army trumpeter and recruiting officer.
The Baron of Schönau.
Maria, his daughter.
The Count of Wildenstein.
His divorced wife, the Baron's sister-in-law.
Damian, the Count's son by his second marriage.
Steward of the Electress' household.
The Rector of Heidelberg University.
Students, soldiers, citizens, peasants, school children, knights, members of the May ballet and many others.

The time of the opera is during the latter part of the Thirty Years' War and just after its conclusion. The prologue is played in the courtyard of Heidelberg at night, where the soldiers and students are lustily singing one of the many panegyrics dedicated to that famous collegiate town.

Old Heidelberg victorious
In honors rich and rare,
No other town so glorious
On Rhine, or Neckar fair.
Thou town of jolly fellows,
Of wisdom ripe and wine,
Bright roll thy merry billows,
Blue eyes upon them shine.

Werner, a law student, and chief among the "jolly fellows" takes up the strain alone, followed by Conradin, an old trumpeter and a recruiting officer. A college steward interrupts the music and expostulates with the noisy students for disturbing the slumbers of the Electress. The spirit of mischief prompts them to direct their tunefulness to the lady in a serenade. Werner takes the trumpet from Conradin's hands and the soldiers and students sing in chorus with trumpet interludes. So skilfully is the latter done, that the recruiting officer, declaring that such good material should not be wasted on the desert air of a college, tries to persuade Werner to enlist but the youth declines to be caught by a bit of flattery.

The steward. who has made repeated demands for a cessation of the noise, engages the aid of the Rector Magnificus, with the result that all the students are expelled. The dashing Werner, not half sorry to be "dispossessed of debts and lawbooks," enlists in the army, with which incident the prelude closes.

In the first act, for which we are taken to Säkkingen, the peasants are celebrating the fête of Saint Fridolini. Werner appears just in time to protect the Countess and her niece from the rudeness of certain mutinous peasants. Love at first sight ensues between the handsome trumpeter and the lovely Maria. The Countess, too, is impressed with the bearing of the young man, but her warmth is cooled when she learns that he was a foundling brought up by gypsies and afterwards adopted by a college professor. This vividly recalls to her the sad fact that her own son, who would be about Werner's age, was kidnaped in childhood by a roving tribe.

While Conradin and Werner escort the ladies to the church where the fête-day ceremonies are in progress, the scene changes to the apartment of the Baron of Schönau, who, owing to a bad attack of gout, is a prisoner at home. He is diverted by a letter from Count Wildenstein, the divorced husband of his sister, the Countess, who, his second wife having recently died, hopes to effect a reconciliation with the first one, from whom he has been separated by unprincipled persons. He also suggests a union between Maria and Damian, a son by the second marriage. The Baron is delighted, for the match is desirable from the viewpoint of both family and wealth.

The Countess and Maria return to relate their adventure. The Baron regrets the death of his faithful old trumpeter, whose vigilance had afforded such protection to the lonely, badly guarded castle. The trumpet of Werner is heard in the distance. At the enthusiastic recommendation of Maria he is sent for and speedily wins the approval of the Baron, who engages his services.

In the second act, Werner gives Maria a music lesson under the blossoming chestnut-trees, or rather he forgets his business and employs the time in making love to his pupil. The happy pair are discovered by the watchful Countess, who indignantly tells her brother, whereupon that wrathful gentleman summarily dismisses Werner from the castle. Meantime, the Count of Wildenstein arrives with the foolish Damian and the parents talk of an immediate wedding. Maria will have nothing to do with her new suitor and breaks down completely when Werner departs.

The dénouement is brought about speedily in the third act. The rebellious peasants lay siege to the castle. The trembling Damian is sent out "to be a hero" and to disperse them. Soon knocking is heard at the gate and the shrieking Damian implores admittance. He whimpers that the common herd do not even know the rules of fighting;

they have crushed his helmet and torn his jacket. It remains for Werner and the soldiers to drive the peasants back. He is brought in with his arm wounded. While it is being dressed, there is discovered a mark upon it which proves that he is the lost son of the Count and Countess of Wildenstein. The Baron tells Maria that she has won and that he has no further desire to possess the cowardly Damian for a son-in-law. As the citizens raise their voices in praise of the brave young soldier, we are left to draw our own conclusions as to whether the restoration of the true heir of Wildenstein effected a reconciliation between his father and mother. From the happy tone of the final chorus, one is led to conclude that everything turned out satisfactorily.

In the prelude are heard the student and soldier choruses; among them being the love song, "A vassal e'er faithful now lies at your feet." In the first act occur the peasant dances and choruses celebrating the fête; the fuming of the Baron at his gout; Maria's song in praise of the trumpeter, "His gait is proud and stately." In the second act are the love duet of Werner and Maria, "Shinest not warmer? sunlight golden;" Young Werner's farewell song, "God shield thee, love," the most popular number in the score. The third act contains the battle song sung by the soldiers before marching against the peasants and Conradin's song with a chorus "Love and merry trumpet-blowing." All these charming numbers go to make up a light opera which placed Nessler among the most admired of the lesser composers of Germany and secured for the work itself performance and enduring popularity in every country where the German language and German sentiment are understood and appreciated.

THE MIKADO

"The Mikado" or "The Town of Titipu," a comic opera in two acts, with words by W. S. Gilbert and music by Sir Arthur Sullivan, was produced at the Savoy Theatre, London, March 14, 1885.

CHARACTERS.

The Mikado of Japan.
Nanki-Poo, his son, disguised as a wandering minstrel, and in love with Yum-Yum.
Ko-Ko, Lord High Executioner of Titipu.
Pooh-Bah, Lord High Everything Else.
Pish-Tush, a Noble Lord.
Yum-Yum, Pitti-Sing, Peep-Bo, } three sisters, wards of Ko-ko.
Katisha, an elderly lady in love with Nanki-Poo.
Chorus of school-girls, nobles, guards and coolies.

In this delightful opera there is always something delightful happening, from the instant that the curtain rises upon the courtyards of Ko-Ko's palace in Titipu disclosing a company of nobles who explain that

If you want to know who we are,
We are gentlemen of Japan:
On many a vase and jar,
On many a screen and fan,
We figure in lively paint:

Our attitude's queer and quaint—
You're wrong if you think it ain't,

to the final chorus:

For he's gone and married Yum-Yum, Yum-Yum.

Nanki-Poo, son of the Mikado, is pursued by Katisha, an elderly lady with matrimonial intentions. He flees from the court, in the guise of a minstrel, to escape punishment for his reluctance to marry his persistent admirer. Ko-Ko is a gentleman who successfully combines the office of Lord High Executioner with the profession of tailor. True to the traditions of comic opera, he wants to marry his ward, Yum-Yum, who, in turn wants to marry someone else. This someone else is no other than Nanki-Poo, the heir-apparent, who is badly in love with the maid. He comes in disguise to Titipu to find Yum-Yum and approaches Poo-Bah for information. Poo-Bah is a haughty and exclusive personage, who can trace his ancestry back to a "protoplasmal, primordial, atomic globule." He also retails state secrets at a low figure. He furnishes Nanki-Poo with the sad news that when Yum-Yum comes home from school, that very day, her wedding to Ko-Ko is to occur. A damper is put on the happy plans of Ko-Ko, however, by a message from the Mikado, informing him that His Majesty is struck by the fact that no executions have taken place in Titipu in the past year and that unless somebody is beheaded within a month, the executioner will be degraded. Nanki-Poo appears at this juncture, announcing that he is about to terminate an existence made unendurable because he can't marry the girl he adores. He and Ko-Ko then and there make a bargain that if Nanki-Poo can marry Yum-Yum and live with her a month, he will, at the end of that time, be a subject for the execution which will preserve Ko-Ko's dignity. Yum-Yum's philosophical attitude in the matter is somewhat impaired by the news that when a man is beheaded, it is customary to bury his wife alive at the same time. She objects on the grounds that it is such a "stuffy" death, whereupon Nanki-Poo threatens suicide again. Thereupon Ko-Ko arranges for a false statement of the execution. The Mikado comes unexpectedly, and when he sees the statement, instead of praising Ko-Ko, threatens him with terrible things because he has killed the heir apparent. That youth's appearance in the flesh causes Ko-Ko to be forgiven on condition that he will marry Katisha, whom his friends assure him has a "left elbow that people come miles to see," even if her face isn't what it should be. Finally, Nanki-Poo and Yum-Yum are happily married.

"The Mikado" is in some respects the most universally appreciated of any of the Gilbert-Sullivan operas. These collaborators, who usually enjoy satirizing British institutions have refrained from this tendency in "The Mikado," which, in consequence, gains in general interest. It is especially popular with the Germans and its revival in Berlin in 1907 was greeted with delight. While it has to do with characters having caricatured Japanese names and stations, it is not too heavily painted with local color. It came at a time when the passion for the Japanese was at its height and added to the craze, while at the same time benefiting from it. The text is filled with charming wit and philosophy, and the music is bright and humorous, the instrumentation being a model of its kind.

Among the many popular numbers are Ko-Ko's song, "They'd none of 'em be missed;" the trio for Yum-Yum, Peep-Bo and Pitti-Sing, "Three little maids from school are we;" Nanki-Poo's "A Wandering Minstrel I;" the trio by Ko-Ko, Pooh-Bah and Pish Tush, "My Brain it teems;" Yum-Yum's song "The Sun whose rays are all ablaze;" the quartet, "Brightly dawns our wedding-day;" the Mikado's song, "My object all sublime;" Ko-Ko's ballad, "On a tree by a river a little tomtit" and the duet of Nanki-Poo and Ko-Ko, "The flowers that bloom in the spring, tra la."

ERMINIE

"Erminie," a comic opera in two acts with libretto by Bellamy and Paulton after Charles Selby's "Robert Macaire" and music by E. Jakobowski, was first produced at the Comedy Theatre, London, Nov. 9, 1885.

CHARACTERS.

Marquis de Pontvert.
Eugene Marcel, the Marquis' secretary.
Vicomte de Brissac.
Delaunay, a young officer.
Dufois, landlord of the Lion d'Or.
Chevalier de Brabazon, the Marquis' guest.
Ravennes, } two thieves.
Cadeaux, }
Cerise Marcel, Erminie's companion.
Javotte, Erminie's maid.
Princess de Gramponeur.
Erminie de Pontvert.
Soldiers, peasantry, guests, waiters.

There are two bad men in "Erminie," thieves named Ravennes and Cadeaux. They are very clever in their knavery, and account for their deeds in the most plausible way. They say, for instance,

We're a philanthropic couple, be it known,
Light fingered, sticking to whate'er we touch.
In the int'rest of humanity alone,
Of wealth relieving those who have too much.

The sour old gent, whose worship vile is dross,
We hate to see a-wallowing in tin;
It ain't 'cos gain to us to him is loss,
We eases him 'cos avarice is sin.

Erminie, daughter of the Marquis de Pontvert, is about to be betrothed to Ernst, a young nobleman. He is on his way to the betrothal ceremony when he has the misfortune to meet this philanthropic pair, who, after depriving him of his wardrobe, tie him to a tree. They go in his stead to the Lion d'Or for the betrothal festivities, Ravennes presenting himself as no other than the fiancé and introducing Cadeaux as his friend of high degree. They explain their inappropriate apparel by a fine tale of a holdup and robbery at the hands of a highwayman. Cadeaux is half intoxicated and his remarkably bad manners and language nearly bring them to grief. However, Ravennes tells that the "Baron" is erratic and original and all suspicions are allayed. The betrothal, it must be explained, has not been anticipated with delight by the parties most concerned. Erminie is already in love with her father's secretary, Eugene, and Ernst is cherishing a secret passion for Cerise Marcel, the friend of Erminie. Ernst, in due season, escapes his bonds and arrives somewhat late and in disordered attire. Ravennes throws the guests and the soldiers, who are in pursuit of two thieves, off the scent by raising a cry of "Seize the villain," and by claiming that Ernst is the thief who attacked them earlier in the day.

Ravennes convinces Erminie of his entire unselfishness and nobility of character by pretending sympathy for her in her love for Eugene and promising her his help in securing happiness, while she aids him, all unwittingly, in his plan for a wholesale robbery of the house, which plan just fails of being successful.

The opera is brought to a satisfactory conclusion with the robbers in the hands of the law and the happy pairing off of Eugene and Erminie and Ernst and Cerise.

This tuneful and interesting work has enjoyed great and enduring popularity in the United States. It was produced in New York at the Casino, March 10, 1886, with Francis Wilson as Cadeaux and has been one of the most frequently performed of the light operas.

The music is unusually tuneful and pleasing throughout. Numbers that have proven great favorites are "Ah! When love is young;" the martial song of the Marquis, "Dull is the life of the soldier in peace;" Erminie's song, "At midnight on my pillow lying;" Eugene's song, "The Darkest Hour;" Erminie's widely-sung lullaby, "Dear Mother, in dreams I see her;" the amusing solo for "Caddy" with a whistling chorus, "What the dickey-birds say" and the vocal gavotte, "Join in Pleasure, dance a measure."

THE BLACK HUSSAR

"The Black Hussar," a comic opera in three acts, the music by Carl Millöcker, was produced at Vienna in 1886.

CHARACTERS.

Friedrich von Helbert, colonel of the Black Hussars, disguised as an army chaplain.

Hans von Waldmann, adjutant of the Black Hussars, disguised as a student.

Theophil Hackenback, Magistrate of Trautenfeld.

Piffkow, his factotum, with numerous offices.

Mefflin, a tragedian of the Meininger Company No. 14.

Francois Thorillière, a captain of the French army.

Rubke, a captain of the Prussian army.

Wutki, Hetman of the Cossacks.

Shadow,	Black Hussars disguised variously as	a pedler.
Bruck,		a scissors-grinder.
Eiken,		a beggar.
Selchow,		a ratcatcher.
Prittwitz,		a bookseller.
Putnam,		a quack doctor.

Minna, Rosetta, } Hackenback's daughters.

Barbara, an orphan, Hackenback's housekeeper.

The scene is laid in and near the town of Trautenfeld, on the border of Germany and Russia. The time is 1812.

The piece opens at the Magistrate's house, where a chorus of citizens are descanting on the disadvantages of living on the border at this time of Napoleonic activity, for they are continually involved in turmoil and the French and Cossacks pay them unwelcome attentions.

Hackenback, Magistrate of Trautenfeld, is a pompous fellow, who spends so much time congratulating himself on his might and wisdom that the weight of his office falls upon his factotum, Piffkow. The aforementioned consumes a large part of the first act enumerating his duties, which range from collecting the taxes to airing the poodles.

At this time news has been brought to camp by a chaplain with a "Dragoon's bold air" (Colonel von Helbert of the Black Hussars who is in disguise) that two hundred Germans, four hundred Frenchmen, and a large number of Cossacks will soon be quartered on the town. Helbert is trying to foment an insurrection against the Napoleonic oppression and the French are busily hunting for him. Hackenback is a sad trimmer and his aim in life is to carry himself diplomatically between the French and the Russians, so when he takes down the description of the miscreant, Helbert slyly manages to make it the magistrate's own, such complimentary terms as "spindle legs," "vermilion red nose," "aggressive mole" and "crazy old topknot" being included.

Upon being introduced to the Magistrate's daughters, Minna and Rosetta, we find that their parent has another eccentricity, that of disguising them in the most frightful fashion, so that the men will not carry them off. They are compelled to paint their faces grotesquely, "roam on crutches," erect humps on their backs, and wear dresses that are "simply wild and weird." But rebellion is brewing in the domestic camp, especially since the arrival of the good-looking chaplain, whom they shrewdly suspect to be no chaplain at all. As soon as the girls rid themselves of their atrocities, Helbert falls in love with Minna, which is fortunate, since Rosetta and his adjutant, Hans von Waldmann, are already very fond of each other.

The second act opens in the market-place with an amusing gossiping chorus by the village wives. They succeed in arousing the curiosity of the men and then laugh at them for exhibiting this supposedly feminine trait. Piffkow arrives in the guise of a hero and relates an adventure, in which it appears that he has broken into a company of actors playing "Julius Cæsar," has taken it all seriously, and has carried off the assassin, Brutus.

Hackenback, embarrassed by the arrival of both French and Russian troops, is reduced to the necessity of making use of the mongrel cry "Napolexander." In spite of his precaution, he is arrested on the evidence of the posted description and marched away to jail. Matters are simplified by the arrival of the Black Hussar regiment, which captures the French troops, just after they have captured the Russians. So all disguises are cast aside, and the remainder of the opera is devoted to love-making.

OTELLO

"Otello" or "Othello," a grand opera in four acts with text by Arrigo Boito after the drama of Shakespeare, and with music by Verdi, was first presented at La Scala, Milan, Feb. 5, 1887.

CHARACTERS.

Othello, a Moorish general.
Iago, his ancient.
Cassio, his lieutenant.
Roderigo, a Venetian gentleman.
Lodovico, an ambassador.
Montano, Othello's predecessor as governor of Cyprus.
Desdemona, Othello's wife.
Emilia, wife of Iago.
Herald, soldiers, sailors, Cypriots, children.

The scene is laid in Cyprus at the end of the Fifteenth Century. The story follows closely that of the Shakespearian tragedy. The curtain rises upon the seafront. A storm is raging and the crowd watches Othello's ship, which is battling with the waves. Among the spectators are Cassio, Iago, and Roderigo. The landing is safely accomplished and Othello comes ashore to receive an ovation for his victories in warfare against the Turks. After the storm has subsided and the Moor has withdrawn Cassio, Iago and Roderigo make a convivial gathering about the table. The villainy of Iago, which is seemingly a villainy for villainy's sake alone, becomes at once apparent. He makes Cassio drunk and incites him to a fight with Montano, who is wounded. Othello, appearing at the moment, deprives Cassio of his rank. Othello then returns to the side of his wife, the gentle Desdemona. A noble love scene follows, in which Othello declares that

> Were it to die now, 'twere to be now most happy,
> While thine arms surround me
> In tender embraces.

Iago now begins to plot and the seeds of jealousy are sown in Othello's breast. He sends Cassio to Desdemona to beg her to intercede with her husband and then with many insinuations draws Othello's attention to the incident of the visit. Desdemona, surrounded by the adoring people, comes to Othello to present the case of the sorry Cassio but her request for clemency is refused with suspicion. His agitation is so evident that in tender solicitude, she attempts to tie her handkerchief about his throbbing forehead. He casts it away petulantly. Emilia picks it up and has it snatched from her fingers by Iago, who later brings news to Othello that he has seen this bit of lace "spotted with strawberries" in Cassio's hands and whispers that he has heard Cassio murmur Desdemona's name in his sleep. Both Iago and the Moor take a solemn oath to avenge the latter's honor. Accordingly, Othello feigns a headache and asks for the lace handkerchief which the unsuspecting wife confesses she has lost. She still pleads Cassio's cause and is charged in cruel terms with being unfaithful, the injustice of which she in vain protests. Iago brings in Cassio and leads the conversation to Bianca, skilfully turning the dialogue to make Othello, whom he knows is concealed near by, believe they are speaking of Desdemona. Cassio draws forth the fatal handkerchief which Iago has left at his house and the maddened Othello believes the evidence to be final. In his rage and jealousy, he seeks council of Iago, who advises him to punish the erring wife by strangling her. Desdemona again is repulsed in the presence of the Venetian Embassy, while the feelings of Othello are so overwrought, that he falls in convulsions.

The last act takes place in Desdemona's apartment. She is filled with foreboding but at last falls asleep, only to be awakened by Othello's kisses, and to be told that she is to die. Deaf to her pathetic assertions of innocence, he stifles her. Emilia, hearing the sound of a struggle, comes in. She discloses Iago's villainy and the remorseful Moor stabs himself.

"Otello" ranks high among Verdi's works and marks a distinct and notable advance in the composer's style. The influence of Wagner's theories is plainly shown. Verdi did not imitate slavishly any of the achievements of the Bayreuth master, but rather accepted as correct the principles governing music drama which Wagner laid down and then, preserving his own musical individuality and the art attributes of his own nation, he applied those principles in the creation of "Otello." The orchestra is given a more prominent and important role to play than in any of his previous works, the set aria and the concerted number are largely done away with, while certain phrases are employed frequently in the score, somewhat in the manner of the Wagnerian leading motive. The rich flow of melody and the passion which are characteristically Verdian are finely in evidence, however, throughout the entire work, and there is no mistaking the individual or the nation that created it. Verdi was fortunate in having Boito as his librettist, for the Shakesperian text has been adapted with rare intelligence and understanding. All superfluous detail has been omitted, yet the essential strength and power of the tragedy have been preserved. Nothing new has been added save a "credo" for Iago, in which that arch-villain voices his distrust and contempt for all that is good and noble in humanity and life. This is a forceful bit of writing which forms the basis for one of the strongest moments in the opera. In addition to this credo for Iago, the score contains, as notable portions, the music accompanying the storm in which Othello arrives; the drinking song for Iago; the beautiful love duet between Othello and Desdemona at the close of the first act; the dramatic duet by Iago and the Moor; a graceful mandolinata, sung by children who bring flowers and shells to Desdemona; Othello's "Farewell to war;" Desdemona's plea for mercy after Othello's great outburst in the third act; the sextet which follows; Desdemona's exquisite "Willow Song" and the "Ave Maria," which is equally beautiful and which shows Verdi as past master in the writing of simple, pure melodies.

LE ROI D'YS

"Le Roi d'Ys," or "The King of Ys," is an opera in three acts and five tableaux, the music by Édouard Lalo set to the poem of Édouard Blau who has made use of an old Breton legend. It was first presented in Paris in 1888.

CHARACTERS.

Mylio.
Prince of Karnac.
The King.
Saint Corentin.
Margared, }
Jahel, } daughters of the King.
Rozenn, }
People, soldiers, gentlemen, pontiffs, horsemen, ladies and followers.

On the terrace of the palace of the king, we are introduced to a gay company among whom the monarch's daughters Margared and Rozenn are prominent. It is upon the fair Margared that all eyes are centered, for she is soon to be led to the altar by Prince Karnac, to whom her father has promised her in order to end a bloody war. She is pensive and distrait in the midst of the rejoicing. When she and her sister gain a moment apart, Margared admits that although she is glad to be of service to the country, she carries the image of another in her heart. As Rozenn suspects, it is that of Mylio, who is a captive in other lands. It is Mylio whom Rozenn loves, too, although of this Margared is unaware. To make the unhappiness of the Princess all the more poignant, her women remind her that the bridal hour approaches. The King, addressing the Prince as the rival "in whom he has found a son" commends him with stately compliment to the people as their future sovereign. Suddenly Mylio appears upon the scene and the impulsive Margared sacrifices her resolution to save the kingdom to her own desires rekindled by the sight of the long-absent companion of her childhood. She declares that the marriage shall never come to pass, and is deaf to the remonstrances of her father and the people. The Prince of Karnac, furious at the insult, thrown down his glove and Mylio accepts it.

In Act II, Margared, from a window of the palace, watches Prince Karnac lead his soldiers against the city, and overhears a loving interview between her sister and Mylio before he goes forth to meet the foe. He encounters Rozenn's fears with his own confidence of victory which he believes assured from the fact that while praying before Saint Corentin he heard a voice from on high promising protection. As the two are folded in each other's arms, Margared overhears Rozenn murmur the words, "my husband" and reels against a pillar with the thirst for revenge born in her heart.

In the combat, the victory goes to Mylio, and the worsted Prince takes refuge in the chapel of Saint Corentin calling upon all the powers of evil for assistance. Margared comes out from the shadows.

"Hell listens," the woman scorned says quietly. If he so desires, yesterday may be made as but a remembrance. But how can that be with an army already perished? She suggests that there is an ally more terrible than war, the ocean. She will give him the keys to the sluices which protect her father's city from the sea.

At this the sky is obscured, and in contrast to the ominous darkness, a strange glow fills the chapel. The statue of Saint Corentin rises to hurl reproaches at the betrayer, while a voice from the tomb urges repentance. Gradually the vision is effaced, leaving Margared upon her knees.

Act III opens with the marriage of Rozenn and Mylio, a scene full of charm and tenderness. Margared has disappeared from the ken of her relatives, but Karnac seeking her to fan the possibly ebbing flame of her revengefulness finds her watching the ceremony from afar. It is as he has feared, the crime appears too hideous now. But he taunts her, knowing the weakness of her jealous heart. Does she not see her hero bending to gaze into another woman's eyes? Does she not hear the sound of the bridal music? The ceremony must be now about at an end. He paints the picture which Margared's averted eyes shrink from beholding. The newly wedded pair are issuing from the chapel; their hearts are fluttering with a sweet emotion; one is thinking, "He is mine;" the other says, "How fair she is;" he bids her fancy how the evening breeze will carry to her the echo of their kisses.

Karnac succeeds. Margared goes to get for him the keys of the sluices. Coming back, she hears her father sorrowing over the loss of both his daughters, one by marriage, the other a fugitive from the palace. She hears Rozenn trying to comfort his sadness, and learns that they speak of her tenderly. It is too late for regret. The water is rising in the streets. The people fly to a hill, the King carrying the reluctant Margared with him. As they watch in temporary safety from the eminence, they see the stately palace devastated and many victims claimed by the sea. Then Margared, stricken with remorse, acknowledges herself to be the guilty one and throws herself into the flood. Saint Corentin accepts the sacrifice and the angry sea retires.

Striking passages in the brilliantly modern score are the opening chorus in which the people rejoice in the conclusion of the war, "C'est l'aurore bénie" ("'Tis the dawn of blessed peace"); in the second act, Margared's reverie, as she watches at the window; in the third, the wedding chorus of girls and young men; Mylio's bridal song, addressed to the door of Rozenn, "Vainement, O bien-aimée ("Vainly, oh! dear beloved"); the scene in which Karnac goads Margared to persist in her revenge and the prayer of the people that the waves may recede, "O Puissance infinie" ("O God of mighty power").

THE YEOMEN OF THE GUARD

"The Yeomen of the Guard," or "The Merryman and His Maid," a comic opera in two acts with music by Sir Arthur Sullivan and text by W. S. Gilbert was first produced at the Savoy Theatre, London, October 3, 1888.

CHARACTERS.

Sir Richard Cholmondeley, lieutenant of the Tower.
Colonel Fairfax, under sentence of death.
Sergeant Meryll, of the Yeomen of the Guard.
Leonard Meryll, his son.
Jack Point, a strolling jester.
Wilfred Shadbolt, head jailor and assistant tormentor.
The Headsman.
First Yeoman.
Second Yeoman.
Third Yeoman.
Fourth Yeoman.
First Citizen.
Second Citizen.
Elsie Maynard, a strolling singer.
Phœbe Meryll, Sergeant Meryll's daughter.
Dame Carruthers, housekeeper of the Tower.
Kate, her niece.
Yeomen of the Guard, gentlemen, citizens.

Through the machinations of a jealous kinsman, the gallant Colonel Fairfax has been sentenced to death for sorcery and is pining in the Tower. He has, however, two stanch friends who do not propose that he shall perish, and these are his daughter Phœbe and Sergeant Meryll, whose life he has twice saved in battle. The Sergeant's son Leonard lately has been appointed to the Guard and a plan to substitute Fairfax for Leonard in the ranks occurs to them. Fairfax is brought to the Tower and declares that he is ready to die but that he cherishes one wish before the event, this being to contract a marriage so as to frustrate his wicked kinsman's plan to succeed to the estate. An impromptu bride is sought in all haste and Elsie Maynard, a strolling singer, who happens along in company with Jack Point, a jester, consents to go through the ceremony blindfolded, like unto a certain Maritana, known, in operatic lore.

The next thing is to get the yeoman suit to Fairfax in his cell. Phœbe brings into use her love affair with Wilfred the head jailor. She steals the keys, releases Fairfax in his yeoman uniform, and returns the stolen implements before their absence has been discovered. Just as the executioners are preparing for the beheading of Fairfax, the first act closes.

In the second act, we find the warders submitting to a tongue-lashing from Dame Carruthers for allowing Fairfax to escape. Wilfred, who is desirous of shining as an amateur comedian, is told by Point that if he will hold a mock execution, i. e., fire off the arquebus and state that it has caused the taking off of Fairfax, he will possess all the essentials of a jester. Accordingly the shot is fired and the governor notified that the prisoner is dead.

The watchful Dame Carruthers, meantime, has made a discovery. She has heard Elsie talking in her sleep and learns from her somnolent remarks that Fairfax is the man she married, and that the little strolling singer is his widow. Fairfax makes love to her in the interest of Point, but as usual in such cases, to his own undoing, for he falls a victim to her winsomeness himself. All is cleared up by the production of the governor's pardon, which has been held back by the wicked kinsman. Fairfax and Elsie are entirely willing to have their marriage stand; Phœbe and Wilfred make one happy pair and the Sergeant and Dame Carruthers another.

It is interesting to know that of all the charming Gilbert-Sullivan family of operas the "Yeomen of the Guard" was the favorite child of its parents. With the public it has never reached the height of popularity occupied by either "The Mikado" or "Pinafore."

Among the most attractive solos and ensembles are Phœbe's song, "When a Maiden loves;" Dame Carruthers' "When our gallant Norman foes;" the entrance of the crowd and players, "Here's a man of jollity;" the duet of Elsie and Point, "I have a song to sing, O!" Phœbe's song, "Were I thy bride;" Point's delightfully funny offering, "Oh, a private buffoon is a light-headed loon;" Fairfax's ballad, "Free from his fetters grim;" the trio, "If he's made the best use of his time;" the song, "Rapture! Rapture! when love's votary flushed with capture" and the charming finale.

ROBIN HOOD

"Robin Hood," a comic opera in three acts with score by Reginald De Koven and text by Harry B. Smith, was produced in Chicago, June 9, 1890.

CHARACTERS.

Robert of Huntington, afterward Robin Hood.
Sheriff of Nottingham.
Sir Guy of Gisbone, his ward.
Little John, } outlaws.
Will Scarlett, } outlaws.
Allan-a-Dale, } outlaws.
Friar Tuck, } outlaws.
Lady Marian Fitzwalter, a ward of the crown, afterward Maid Marian.
Dame Durden, a widow.
Annabel, her daughter.
Villagers, milkmaids, outlaws, kings, foresters, archers, pedlers.

The scene is laid in England at the time of Richard I. The story opens on May-day at the market-place in Nottingham, where a merrymaking is in progress. The outlaws come to join in the fun and finally Robin Hood appears, dashing and handsome, and declares that he is earl and that the Sheriff shall so proclaim him. That worthy, however, has other plans. He swears that Robin Hood has been disinherited by his own father, who, shortly before the youth's birth, was secretly married to a peasant girl who died when her child was born. This child whom he has reared, he asserts is Sir Guy and the rightful heir of Huntington. It has been arranged that the fair Maid Marian shall marry Sir Guy but her eyes are all for Robin Hood. She hopes that she may postpone her wedding until King Richard comes back from the crusades and thus be able to find a way out of the engagement. Robin Hood hopes, on the monarch's return, to obtain help to prove his right to his own. Incidentally, Robin Hood and Maid Marian, to the deep disgust of Sir Guy, exchange vows of mutual affection. The outlaws are all on Robin Hood's side and invite him to join their jolly crew, promising that instead of an earl he may be their king and rule beneath the greenwood tree. Robin agrees and they place the Sheriff in stocks from which he finally is rescued by Sir Guy and his archers.

In the last act a message from the king brought by Robin Hood saves Maid Marian at the very door of the church from the marriage which has seemed inevitable, and there is a general rejoicing that

Tho' clouds were dark and drear
The sky is now so blue above.

"Robin Hood" is generally conceded to be the best musical score Reginald De Koven has written, while the libretto is easily the best of the many Harry B. Smith has given the stage. The work has enjoyed widespread and enduring popularity. Much admired are the spirited overture; the chorus, "A morris dance must you entrance;" the auctioneer song of Friar Tuck; the milkmaid's song with the chorus, "When Chanticleer Crowing;" Robin Hood's entrance to the chorus, "Come the Bowmen in Lincoln Green;" the duet of Robin Hood and Maid Marian, "Though it was within this hour we met;" the song and chorus, "I am the Sheriff of Nottingham;" the trio of the Sheriff, Sir Guy and Maid Marian, "When a peer makes love to a maiden fair;" the chorus, "Cheerily soundeth the hunter's horn," which opens Act II; Scarlett's story of "The Tailor and the Crow," sung to humming accompaniment; the song of Little John and the chorus, "Brown October Ale;" the tinker's chorus; the sextet "Oh See the Lambkins Play;" Marian's charming forest song; Robin's serenade, "A Troubadour sang to his love;" and, in Act III, the Armorer's song, "Let hammer on anvil ring;" the "Legend of the Chimes," by Allan-a-Dale and chorus; the duet of Marian and Robin Hood, "There will come a time;" the quintet, "When life seems made of pains and pangs, I sing to my too-ral-loo ral-lay" and the country dance, "Happy day! Happy day!"

CAVALLERIA RUSTICANA

"Cavalleria Rusticana," or "Rustic Chivalry," is an opera in one act with words by Targioni-Tozzetti and Menasci, after the tale of the Sicilian novelist, Verga, and with music by Pietro Mascagni. It was performed at the Teatro Constanzi, in Rome, May 20, 1890, having been written in competition for the prize offered by a music publisher for the best three one-act operas. To "Cavalleria Rusticana" was awarded the first prize. It is said to have been written in a week, and virtually in a day it lifted its young composer from obscurity to world-wide fame.

CHARACTERS.

Santuzza, a village girl, betrayed by Turiddu.
Lola, wife of Alfio and mistress of Turiddu.
Turiddu, a young soldier, returned from the wars.
Alfio, a village carter.
Lucia, mother of Turiddu, keeper of the tavern.

The scene is laid in a Sicilian village, the curtain rising on a public square, one side of which is occupied by a church decked for Easter. the other by Mother Lucia's inn. Turiddu, her son, has but recently returned from military service. Before enlisting he was engaged to Lola but he finds her not "faithful and true," she having married Alfio, the well-to-do carter. Turiddu tries to be philosophic and speedily woos and wins, but alas, not honorably, the pretty peasant girl,

Santuzza, who loves him as ardently as he has loved the fickle Lola. The thought that Turiddu can console himself so easily and can mend the heart she has fancied fatally shattered, does not please Lola. Her jealousy is aroused and she exerts all her coquetry to regain his attentions. The task is not difficult, for Turiddu already is beginning to tire of the too-loving Santuzza.

Before the curtain rises, we hear the song of Turiddu in praise of Lola, supposedly sung as a morning greeting before her house. Santuzza goes to Lucia's door to ask the whereabouts of Turiddu. The mother brusquely tells her she does not know and bids her be off. However, in reply to Santuzza's tearful pleading she informs her that her son has gone to the neighboring village, Francoforte, for wine. Santuzza is doubtful, for she has had a glimpse of him the night before. Lucia, who begins to feel pity for the girl, asks her to come in but she sobs out that she is an outcast, having been excommunicated for her sin. Now Lola's husband, Alfio, runs gaily upon the scene boasting of his happiness and good fortune in which Lola is an important factor. Much to Lucia's astonishment, he too refers to having seen Turiddu lingering near his house that morning. The people are celebrating Easter and the music of the mass issues from the church, its sacred strains being echoed by the people in the square. When silence comes again, the desperate Santuzza tells Lucia her sad story and of Turiddu's infatuation for Lola. Shamed and depressed, Lucia goes into the church to pray. Just then Turiddu arrives and is greatly annoyed to encounter Santuzza. With a supercilious air he inquires why she is not at church on Easter. Quietly she asks him where he has been staying and he lies, saying at Francoforte. She returns that she knows this to be false, that he has been at Lola's. He accuses her of spying upon him, cursing her jealousy and expressing his distaste and disdain for her. While this is going on, Lola comes flaunting by. She mocks Santuzza, asking her whether she is going to mass. Santuzza answers that only those who are without sin can go there. Lola does not take this to herself but virtuously refers to her own freedom to go where she pleases. Santuzza by her importunity prevents Turiddu from going into the church with Lola, which makes him all the more furious. When Santuzza pleads with him to be just to her, he forgets himself and throws her down in rage. Then he hastens into the church after the woman who has infatuated him.

"Your Easter shall be bitter; that I swear," cries Santuzza wildly.

Alfio now returns to attend service and Santuzza in a frenzy of grief, reveals to him the perfidy of his wife and her lover. Swearing to obtain vengeance, Alfio rushes away, followed by the unhappy girl. At last the services are at an end and the crowd issues from the church. Turiddu and Lola steal a word before they separate at the doors. Many of the people flock to the tavern for wine at Turiddu's invitation. Finally Alfio comes. He refuses to accept of Turiddu's hospitality which means that he knows his injury at the other's hands. At this ominous sign and the fury displayed by the two men, the women run away frightened. Turiddu throws away the wine Alfio has just refused and asks him what else he has to say. Alfio answers grimly that all has been said. At this Turiddu bites Alfio's ear, which is the Sicilian form of challenge. However, before going to meet his adversary behind the garden, the repentant Turiddu embraces his mother and commends Santuzza to her care in case he is killed, confessing that he should have made her his wife. He leaves and Santuzza and Lucia cling to each other in terrible suspense. The women rush in crying that Alfio has slain Turiddu.

Mascagni, who at the time of the composition of "Cavalleria Rusticana," was only twenty-seven years of age, had the distinction of founding with his work a new school of opera, the "verissimo" school, with flesh and blood characters whose deeds follow the logic of passionate human nature. He benefited by the reaction from the excessive craze for Wagner and his legendary operas, the people receiving the new realism with delight. The opera is extremely brief but it runs the gamut of the passions, is sincere and fresh, dramatic and original, while its local coloring is true and vivid. Few operas have met with such instant and lavish favor.

Preëminent in popularity among the numbers is the famous intermezzo for the orchestra which has place between the duet for Alfio and Santuzza and the exit from the church service. Other conspicuous numbers are Turiddu's song, heard behind the curtain during the prelude, "O Lola c'hai di latti la cammisa" ("O Lola, fair as flow'rs in beauty smiling"); Alfio's whip song with chorus, "Il cavallo scalpita;" the Easter chorus in the church and square "Regina Cœli" ("Queen of Heaven"), Santuzza's romanza, "Voi lo sapete" ("Now shall you know"); the impassioned duets for Santuzza and Turiddu and for Santuzza and Alfio; Turiddu's drinking-song, "Viva il vino" ("Hail the ruby wine") and his farewell to his mother.

LE REVE

"Le Rève" or "The Dream," a lyric drama in four acts and eight tableaux, with music by A. Bruneau and poem by Louis Gallet, after the romance of Émile Zola, was produced in Paris in 1891.

CHARACTERS.

Angelique.
Hubertine.
The Bishop, Jean **d'Autecœur.**
Felicien.
Hubert.
An invisible choir.

The curtain rises on a simple French interior, an embroidery shop, from whose windows are seen a blossoming garden and the Cathedral of St. Agnes. Angelique sits with her needlework abandoned in her lap, absorbed in the Golden Legend. In fact, so much has she mused upon the characters of this loved book, that they have assumed for her actual being. She numbers among her friends Saint Marceline, who was burned; Saint Solange, who was scourged and Saint George, who bravely slew the fearful dragon.

While her foster-parents, Hubert and Hubertine, watch her revery with loving indulgence, the humble cottage has the honor of a visit from the Bishop. He seems interested in the delicate, deft-fingered girl. They tell him how, years before, they found her half-dead in the snow and adopted her. As he examines the ecclesiastical embroidery which she is making at his order and finds it excellent, he relates the story of an ancestor who healed the plague-stricken people with the touch of his lips and the words, " Si Dieu veut, je veux." These words have been since that time the motto of this family. As Angelique listens she hears her invisible choir and the Bishop observes her ecstasy with amazement. When he has gone, they speak tenderly of the reverend man and Hubertine tells how once he was married, how his adored young wife died, and that there is a son who is in disfavor because he will not be a priest. "He is as beautiful as an angel and as rich as a king," she adds.

Angelique naively relates her own day-dream, which is that she shall marry a king and spend her life in good deeds. When the shocked Hubertine bids her silence her pride and remember that kings are not always available, she declares that she has had a vision of him. Even then her face lights up, for through the window she catches a glimpse of the beautiful youth of her dreams.

In the second scene, we are taken to the field, where all day long the people have been washing linen in the stream. Angelique who is scattering lavender in the snowy folds, gaily sends her foster-parents home and remains behind on pretext of finishing some task, but really in the hope that, in the lily-scented quiet, the voices may come to her. As the rays of the setting sun strike the window of the chapel, they disclose the figure of a man whom for a moment she fancies may be Saint George in person. He disclaims the distinction, assuring her that his name is Felicien and that he is only a worker in stained glass. She returns the compliment giving the simple facts about herself. Her name is Angelique. She is an embroiderer; the shop and the garden of her parents are yonder. " But why do you look at me so? " she falters. " It is because

I love you," he answers. And that is the whole story of the courtship.

Her parents are not inclined to accept him as unquestioningly as Angelique. They want some explanation of a workman who wears diamonds and whose hands are so white. He has promised that they shall know all on the morrow, the fête of Corpus Christi. And on the morrow, when they watch the procession, they see Felicien in the suite of the Bishop. The resemblance tells the story. "The son of Monseigneur!" Angelique cries gladly but her foster-parents gaze at her with profound sorrow.

In the next scene, the Bishop is resolved not to give his consent to his son's marriage, as he hopes to save him from the human ties in which he himself has found little but sorrow. The humble, heartfelt pleading of Hubert and Hubertine for their darling do not in the least move his iron will. No more do the entreaties of Felicien, nor those of poor drooping Angelique who comes to kiss his hands and fall at his feet in supplication, and who swoons at the sound of his relentless "never."

Felicien seeks Angelique, although he has been told that her love is cured, and finds her asleep in the little cottage but so white and frail that his heart is torn with compassion. She consents to fly with him but the symphony of the invisible friends detains her, bidding her submit to the harshness of fate and to remember that renunciation is good. In the enthusiasm of sacrifice, she refuses to listen to her lover. He goes to his father to tell him that Angelique is dying and to pray him to heal the broken-hearted girl as his ancestor did the plague-stricken. Still the father is obdurate. But kneeling at his prie-dieu he hears the heavenly symphony which so often has sounded in Angelique's ears, and, crying that his dead wife has spoken, he takes the holy oil and sets forth for Hubert's cottage. Angelique's spirit seems almost to have departed but murmuring the words of his ancestor "Thy will be done," he kisses the girl's forehead. As the chants of the priests sound about her, she revives and declares that she will live to see her dream accomplished.

On the morrow, Angelique and Felicien go to the cathedral to be married, but on the theshold the frail creature faints, almost as if with too much joy and dies on her lover's breast.

Bruneau has been called the standard-bearer of the young French School and his treatment of Zola's romance in his opera "Le Rève" was sufficiently original to cause a stir, and to bring him prominently before the music world. He uses representative themes and displays a marked gift for characterization.

The Bishop's recountal in the first act, "Pendant une peste cruelle" ("During a plague most cruel"); his monologue in the fourth tableau of Act II, "Seigneur, J'ai dit: Jamais!" ("O God, I swore the vow") and Angelique's appeal to the Bishop are especially noteworthy pages in the score.

L'AMICO FRITZ

"L'Amico Fritz" or "Friend Fritz" is a lyric comedy in three acts, the music by Pietro Mascagni, the book by P. Suardon after the novel of Erckmann-Chatrian of the same name. It was first presented at the Teatro Constanzi in Rome, Oct. 31, 1891.

CHARACTERS.

Fritz Kobus, a rich bachelor.
Rabbi David.
Federico, a friend of Fritz.
Hanenzo, a friend of Fritz.
Suzel, the head farmer's daughter.
Beppe, a gypsy.
Caterina, a housekeeper.
Chorus behind the scenes.

The most interesting character in the opera is David, the Rabbi, the consummate match-maker, whose good humor and knowledge of human nature permeated every situation.

Fritz Kobus is a rich bachelor who has reached the age of forty without becoming a convert to matrimony. In fact, he is openly averse to it and declares himself "A friend to all, a husband, never." The Rabbi knows his excellent qualities and believes that marriage would bring him happiness. So he sets very cleverly about it to find him a suitable wife. Fritz's birthday is celebrated by his friends with a feast. Among those who come to do him honor is Suzel, the daughter of one of his farmers, who brings him violets and presents her father's respects. In spite of all his boasted indifference to women, the girl's beauty and simplicity appeal to him and he speedily makes the visit to her father's farm which she has requested. They pick cherries together and the pretty incident comes near to completing the capture of the bachelor. The Rabbi sees them and is satisfied that his plans are prospering. To make sure of the state of the maiden's affection, he bids her tell him the old love-story of Isaac and Rebecca and her deep confusion convinces him that she is truly in love with Fritz. Believing that a little jealousy is necessary to bring the wary bachelor to capitulation, he casually informs him that he has found Suzel a husband. Fritz is very indignant at the thought of trying to marry off "such a baby" and, in rage, vows it shall not be done. He is miserable indeed when David tells him later that everything is arranged. When Suzel appears, looking sad and pale, he inquires ironically whether she has come to invite him to the wedding, whereupon she bursts into tears. He suspects for the first time that she is not indifferent to him and, in the prettiest and simplest of love-scenes, they are betrothed. Fritz's wager of his vineyard, Clairfontaine, made at the birthday feast apropos of the marriage question is lost and the delighted winner, Rabbi David, hands it over to Suzel for a dowry.

This opera, which the public awaited with eagerness, did not meet the expectations aroused by "Cavalleria Rusticana." Although it has many merits of its own, it is generally agreed that the subjct is too gentle for the dramatic and sensational style of Mascagni.

Among the more notable numbers in the score are Suzel's presentation of the violets; Beppe's song in the first act; the charming "cherry" duet, which is the best number; Suzel's story of Isaac and Rebecca and the final duet of Fritz and Suzel, "Io t'amo, t'amo, o dolce mio tesor" ("I love thee").

I PAGLIACCI

"I Pagliacci" or "The Players," a tragic opera in two acts and a prologue, with words and music by Ruggiero Leoncavallo, was first performed at the Teatro dal Verme, Milan, May 21, 1892.

CHARACTERS.

Canio (in the play, Punchinello), master of a troupe of strolling players.
Nedda (in the play, Columbine), wife of Canio.
Tonio (in the play, Taddeo), the clown.
Beppe (in the play, Harlequin), one of the troupe.
Silvio, a villager.
Villagers.

In the prologue, sung in front of the curtain, a hint of coming gloom is given and Tonio, who sings, suggests that back of the motley and tinsel are human hearts beating with passion.

"I Pagliacci" is a play within a play. The scene of the story is laid in Calabria and the plot concerns itself with the members of a traveling troupe of players. They arrive in the Italian village and are warmly welcomed by the curious inhabitants. It soon develops that all is not harmony in the little company. The beautiful Nedda is far too attractive to be really creative of happiness, and not only does she possess a husband, Canio, whom she does not love, but two lovers as well. Tonio is madly in love with her but she is enamored of Silvio, a villager, and scornfully rejects the somewhat loutish advances of the clown. She summarily dismisses him, cutting him across the face with a riding whip when he tries to embrace her and thereby securing his active enmity.

Shortly thereafter, his opportunity comes. Overhearing her planning with Silvio to elope, he rushes away to inform Canio who is drinking at the tavern. Canio comes post-haste but Silvio escapes over the wall. The husband has not been able to recognize him and Nedda cannot be terrified into disclosing his identity. Canio is about to stab his unfaithful wife when Beppe, the clown, interferes, warning him that it is high time to prepare for the play. In no heart for play-acting, Canio postpones his vengeance and, lamenting, makes ready to appear as Punchinello.

The second act opens on the same scene. It is evening and the rustic audience has assembled before the little theatre. Nedda, while collecting the admission fees, has managed a word with Silvio. When the curtain on the rude stage is drawn aside, it soon becomes apparent that the play is to be a replica of the state of affairs existing in the troupe. Nedda, as Columbine, is alone on the stage listening to the tender songs of Harlequin, her lover in the play. Tonio, as Taddeo, the fool, enters to serve them with food, and, just as he has done a few hours before in real life, he now makes love to her and she repulses him haughtily. To complete the resemblance between the mimic and the real play, the fool brings back the wronged husband who finds Columbine and her lover dining merrily together and plotting to poison Punchinello. But the anger which Punchinello shows soon becomes too terrible in quality to be merely acting and even the audience which is being well entertained begins to realize this. When Punchinello rushes upon Columbine and in maddened tones again demands the name of her lover, they feel that it is a real tragedy which is developing under their eyes. Nedda sees her necessity and calls upon Silvio in the audience to save her. He leaps upon the stage but is too late. Canio has thrust his erring wife through with a dagger and with its dripping blade he turns and stabs Silvio, too. Then Canio turns to the audience, in whose eyes he is vindicated. "Go," he says hoarsely, "the comedy is ended."

This fiery melodrama, distinctly Italian, dramatic and forceful in method is generally compared to "Cavalleria Rusticana" which it follows closely. The music is consistent, making an effective, illustrative and enhancing accompaniment to the exciting incidents of the plot. There is much of the modern Italian short-phrased melody in the score. The intense nature of the story, together with the strongly impassioned, unquestionably sincere and, in many respects, beautiful character of the music lend the work qualities which promise to secure for it long enduring favor in the public's esteem and to make it one of the best products thus far received from the young Italian school.

Especially admirable are: The "prologue" sung by Tonio before the curtain, a number which virtually takes the place of an overture; the chorus imitative of bells, "Dong, ding, dong;" Nedda's cavatina, "O, che volo d'augelli" ("Ah, ye birds without number"); the duet for Nedda and Silvio, "E allor perchè" ("Wherefore I pray thee"); Canio's "Lament" which closes the first act, "Recitar! mentre preso dal delivio" ("To go on! When my head's whirling"); the "Intermezzo" between the two acts; Harlequin's serenade sung behind the scenes of the mimic theatre, "O Columbine, il tenero" ("Columbine, your Harlequin") and the music accompanying the play.

FALSTAFF

"Falstaff," an opera in three acts, with music by Giuseppe Verdi and text arranged after Shakespeare by Arrigo Boito, had its first performance at La Scala, Milan, March 12, 1893.

CHARACTERS.

Sir John Falstaff.
Master Ford.
Master Fenton.
Dr. Caius.
Bardolph, } followers of Falstaff.
Pistol, }
Mrs. Alice Ford.
Mrs. Quickly.
Mrs. Page.
Nannetta, her daughter.
Host of the Garter Tavern.
Robin, page to Falstaff.
A page to Master Ford.
Town and country people, Ford's servants.
Scene, Windsor Forest in the reign of Henry IV.

The libretto is based mainly upon the "Merry Wives of Windsor," which Shakespeare is said to have written in compliance with the wish of Queen Elizabeth to see the "Fat Knight" in love. Boito's arrangement is supplemented with several passages from "Henry IV."

In the first act, Falstaff and his henchmen, Bardolph and Pistol, are discovered eating and drinking mightily at the Garter Tavern. They exchange compliments with Dr. Caius, who accuses them of emptying his purse while he slept. He and Pistol engage in a verbal battle in which such choice epithets as "sprout of the mandragora" and "yardstick" are hurled as missiles, while the fat knight looks on with magnificent condescension and occasionally lets drop some maxim from a very practical philosophy.

Falstaff, it develops, has fallen in love with the Mesdames Ford and Page, the Merry Wives. He bids Bardolph and Pistol carry to them each a billet-doux. They refuse to meddle in the matter, their "honor" forbidding. The mention of this superfluous little word gives occasion for the famous monologue from "Henry IV." depicting the impotency of honor.

In the second scene of Act I, we are introduced to the joke-loving Merry Wives to whom a page has delivered the fat knight's "inflammatory" epistles. Under a promise of secrecy, they tell each other of "such an adventure" and find that the poetical effusions with which they have been favored are alike and from the same gallant. They plot to take a merry revenge upon their amorous "wine-cask."

The treacherous, time-serving Bardolph and Pistol warn Ford of the designs of the obese Don Juan, virtuously referring to the fact that they have refused to carry his messages. While the injured husband is preparing a frustration, Nannetta (sweet Anne Page) and her adorer, Fenton, make love delightfully. The curtain falls as the Merry Wives conclude the arrangements for the practical joke and, with shaking sides, quote from their love-letters,

> Your lovely eyes shall shine on me,
> Like stars from the immensity.

The curtain of the second act rises to discover Falstaff drinking sack at the Garter Tavern. Thither comes Mrs. Quickly to tell him that the ladies are flattered and would meet him.

"You bewitch them all," sighs the gossip.

" 'Tis not witchery," explains the modest Sir John, "but a certain personal fascination."

The jealous Ford visits Falstaff, under the name of Brook, and by means of a demijohn of Cyprus wine, craftily draws from him a boastful admission of his conquest of Mrs. Alice, even disclosing the hour of the visit he is about to pay her.

Falstaff excuses himself as the happy moment approaches and leaves Ford engaged in concealing his wrath. Mrs. Quickly precedes him to inform the Merry Wives that he has "fallen into the trap like a stone." Nannetta alone of all the company is not in convulsions of laughter, and, upon being questioned, confides to her mother that the course of true love is not running smoothly with her for her father wants her to marry fussy old Dr. Caius. She confesses a preference for being stoned alive and her mother promises to help her out of the dilemma.

When all have concealed themselves around a corner, waiting to enjoy the culmination of the joke, Falstaff enters and proves himself master of the honeyed phraseology of love. He is interrupted in his puffy protestations by the warning that Ford is coming "hard on his track, . . . filled with tremendous rage and cursing all the daughters of Eve."

The women hastily conceal him in the buck-basket and nearly smother him with soiled linen. Ford, with Bardolph and Pistol and all the neighbors, rage about the house and Nannetta and Fenton take advantage of the hubbub to continue their love-making behind a screen, from which suddenly is heard the sound of a rapturous kiss. All advance cautiously, remembering that "a man of that size cannot be routed with a breath." The screen is upset and Nannetta is disclosed blushing in Fenton's arms. Now orders are given to chuck the family washing into the Thames and in spite of the protests of the contents of the buck-basket, this is done.

In the third act, Falstaff is seen at his old haunt, the Garter Tavern, musing on the rascally world and calling for mulled sack to soothe his ruffled feelings. While in this mood, he is approached by Mrs. Quickly with an elaborate explanation that the buck-basket episode was no fault of the lovely Alice and that she fain would see him again. A little flattery does the work and Falstaff agrees to a midnight meeting at Herne's Oak, he to be in the disguise of the Black Huntsman. It is a weird company which awaits his arrival in Windsor Forest. Fenton is Oberon, Nannetta the queen of the fairies and there are troops of hobgoblins, sprites and elves. Falstaff is no laggard in love but is on hand at the stroke of midnight dressed as Herne the Huntsman. The supernatural bevy lies low while he greets his mistress but, at a signal from Bardolph, they fall upon him and pinch him, claw him and roll him about until he cries for mercy. Finally the breathless old sinner recognizes Bardolph by his red nose and begins to suspect that he has "been made an ass of."

Page thinks to celebrate the fat knight's discomfiture by the marriage of his daughter to Caius who is to be disguised as a monk; but it is Fenton behind the cowl and the true lovers are united instead. Page is inclined to be forgiving and everybody goes off to supper, still shaking with laughter over the night's adventure.

"Falstaff" is in every respect a remarkable work. It was composed when Verdi was eighty years of age but shows no signs of falling off in power. On the contrary, musical authorities esteem it to be his masterpiece, albeit the general public has been slow in its acceptance of the great work. It is filled with the spirit of youth and of joy. It ripples with laughter and true musical humor from beginning to end, although not without occasional moments of exquisite tenderness. Boito's libretto borders on perfection, one critic declaring it "probably the best written and planned book ever presented to a composer." He has translated Shakespeare with love and respect and has preserved admirably the spirit and the English flavor. When "Falstaff" was first presented at La Scala Theatre, it was acclaimed one of the greatest works ever heard within those famous walls.

As to notable passages in the opera, which has, by the way, no overture nor prelude there may be mentioned an effective chattering quartet in E major for the women's voices, unaccompanied, the reading of Falstaff's love-letters; the "Honor" soliloquy; the ensemble music of the second act, the buck-basket episode; the fat knight's famous scherzetto, "When I was page to the Duke of Norfolk's grace;" the love duet of Nannetta and Fenton; Nannetta's song in the scene of the haunted forest and the wonderful vocal fugue which brings the work to a close.

MANON LESCAUT

"Manon Lescaut" is a lyric drama in four acts with music by Giacomo Puccini, the libretto being the work of the composer and a committee of friends, with an English version by Mowbray Marras after the familiar work of the same name by Abbé Prévost. It was first presented in Turin in 1893.

CHARACTERS.

Manon Lescaut.
Lescaut, her brother, a sergeant of the king's guards.
The Chevalier Des Grieux.
Geronte de Ravoir, Treasurer-General.
Edmondo, a student.
The Innkeeper.
A singer.
The Dancing-Master.
A lamplighter.
Sergeant of the Royal Archers.
A captain in the navy.
The Hair-Dresser.
Singers, old beaus and abbés, girls, citizens, villagers, students, people, courtezans, archers, sailors.

The opera opens at Amiens, in the later half of the Eighteenth Century, in the square where the post-chaises depart for Paris. Here frolic the gayest of throngs, students being a conspicuous element. Among the students are Edmondo and Des Grieux, the latter a youth of good family, who, when chaffed by his companions, declares gaily that he knows nothing of the dismal farce called love. While all the young fellows take time from their drinking and card-playing to flirt with the girls who stroll by upon the avenue, a diligence draws up at the inn from which alights a young girl, Manon Lescaut, accompanied by her brother and Geronte, an elderly state official. During the time the luggage is being disposed of, the girl sits down before the inn and is approached by Des Grieux, who is enchanted with her grace and beauty. With much simplicity she tells him her name. She also tells him that on the morrow she is to be consigned forever to a convent. To her admirer's expression of horror that one so well fitted for the joyousness of the world should endure such a gloomy fate, she makes answer that there is no escape from the dictates of the paternal will. Geronte, too, is fascinated by the lovely Manon and her brother shows some inclination to dispose of her to the highest bidder. While Lescaut, who is a professional gambler with, in addition, many other unsavory qualities, is engaging the students in disastrous play, Geronte, who has planned to elope with Manon, gives orders to the landlord to have a carriage waiting for a man and a maiden who will ride to Paris like the wind. Edmondo overhears these directions and having observed his friend's sudden infatuation, tells him of the girl's peril. Des Grieux speedily resolves to take Geronte's place in the carriage. When Manon appears, she offers but a half-hearted resistance to her abduction at the hands of the charming youth, and in a trice the two madcaps are on their way to Paris followed by the maledictions of the baffled roué.

The two young lovers pass an idyllic period together in Paris but their funds give out, and when Lescaut tracks them to their abode, Manon with whom the desire for luxury is a veritable passion, falls a victim to the worldly allurements held out by the rich old libertine Geronte and runs away with him.

At the opening of the second act, we find her installed in Geronte's house. She sits in a splendid salon, surrounded by servants, hair-dressers, singers and dancing-masters. Lescaut is much pleased with this arrangement, for he is not above accepting the ill-earned bounty of his sister. Just as her coiffure is finished, he comes in. He compliments her and tells her that she should thank him for rescuing her from "the modest little cottage very rich in kisses but short in money." But Manon presents many strangely constrasting phases of character and much as the luxury delights her, she finds herself unable to forget Des Grieux and his refined and poetical devotion, which forgives for her sake his exile from home and the withdrawal of his allowance. She is not very much interested in learning the minuet and when Des Grieux, dejected, appears at her apartment, having long sought trace of her, she throws her arms about him in rapture and overwhelms him with endearments. Thus they are surprised by Geronte, who angrily reproaches her for her ingratitude and faithlessness. In reply she laughs at him and bids him look in the mirror and prove to himself his inability to inspire love. Geronte, roused to fury, causes her arrest and has her sentenced to be deported as a "fille de joie."

Manon accepts her lot with the fortitude which characterizes her. She makes one attempt to escape from the harbor at Havre but is recaptured. Before this, Des Grieux has visited her to kiss her hands through the bars. The roll is called, she passes to the ship with the other women of her unhappy class, weeping and cowering under the stares and rude comments of the crowd. The agony of Des Grieux, who is a witness of her humiliation, touches the captain, who allows him to come on board and, as the original tale has it, he becomes a cabin-boy in order to be near her.

The last act finds Manon and her lover in America, wandering on the plains near the territory of New Orleans. They are lost in a strange country, weary and thirsty, and the delicate form of Manon is racked with fever. Bravely she tries to keep on and to lend encouragement to her heavy-hearted companion but at last is overcome with exhaustion and falls in a swoon. The distracted young man revives her and leaves her for a few moments in the hope of finding some woodland hut which may afford them refuge. At sunset he returns unsuccessful, to find her delirious. Finally, as her weakness increases, the terrible realization that the chill of death is upon his beloved Manon is forced upon him. With her last breath Manon finds joy in protesting the depths of her love, murmuring at the last,

> Time will obliterate my faults
> But my love will never die.

The work which captivated Italy and which has made its way successfully into other countries is an example of the new school of realism. Many of its scenes are treated with great power, notably the embarkation at Havre. There have been several operatic versions of Abbé Prévost's celebrated but unpleasant romance, among them one by Auber, one by Massenet and one by Kleenmichel, but this is generally conceded to be the best. It was Puccini's first success.

Notable passages are the song of heart-free Des Grieux, "Tra voi, belle, brunee bionde" ("With you fair ones, brunette or blonde"); the chorus which welcomes the arrival of the diligence; Des Grieux's greeting to Manon, "Oh, come gravi le vostre parole" ("Ah, how earnest are thy speech and manner"); the charming duet of Manon and her brother; the music of the minuet; Manon's song, "L'ora, O Tirsa, è vaga e bella" ("The hour, O Tersa, is fav'ring and fair"); the rapturous duet when the lovers meet in Geronte's salon; the lovely intermezzo before Act III; the roll-call of the sergeant on the dock at Havre; Des Grieux's plea to the commandant to take him on board and Des Grieux's song to Manon in the wilderness, "Non mi rispondi, amore" ("Wilt thou not answer? beloved").

I MEDICI

"I Medici," an historical opera in four acts, with words and music by Ruggiero Leoncavallo, was produced at La Scala in Milan, in November, 1893.

CHARACTERS

Lorenzo de' Medici.
Giuliano de' Medici.
Giambattista da Montesecco, a Papal captain.
Francesco Pazzi.
Bernardo Bandini.
Salviati, the Archbishop.
Il Poliziano.
Simonetta Cattanei.
Fioretta de' Gori.
The Mother of Simonetta.
Citizens, populace, public singers, conspirators.

The action passes at Florence, in the latter part of the Fifteenth Century. When the curtain of the first act rises, a wooded hill near the city is seen, with glimpses of a river in the background. It is noon. Lorenzo de' Medici and his younger brother Giuliano, enter and Lorenzo admits that he long has felt that the enmity of the Pope is directed against their family. His suspicions are not without ground, for at that very moment Montesecco and his fellow conspirators are plotting near by. Voices are heard and all disperse, some joining the hunt. When all are gone Simonetta strolls in. She is followed by her friend, Fioretta. Simonetta is oppressed by sadness, although she has no tangible reason for it. Fioretta leaves her and she is suddenly confronted by Montesecco. Taken with her beauty, he tries to seize her but she evades him, her scorn only increasing his admiration. He is distracted by the tumult arising from the pursuit of a deer by hunters and dogs. The terrified animal eludes its pursuers, much to Simonetta's delight. Giuliano returns and Simonetta falls in love with him at first sight. As they converse Montesecco spies upon them from the bushes. Giuliano tells the girl only his first name and makes an appointment with her for the morrow. Fioretta comes unexpectedly to rejoin Simonetta and she, too, falls in love with the attractive patrician youth.

In the second act, the scene shifts to the Square of Santa Trinita. The night is falling. Here are gathered the Archbishop, Francesco Pazzi, Montesecco and the other conspirators. There is much talk of the "cause," which is to assassinate the dangerously ambitious Medici. They are interrupted in their plotting by the arrival of the crowd. Among them is Lorenzo de' Medici and his musicians. His singing is so excellent that the people are delighted, and when his identity becomes known, the cry of the Medici is echoed from many approving throats. Simonetta and her mother appear and against the advice of her parent, the girl dances and sings. At last she sinks to the ground unconscious. Giuliano is in deep distress, while Fioretta watches him half jealously. Simonetta is borne away and Giuliano, left with Fioretta, asks to be kept informed of Simonetta's condition. Giuliano, noticing his companion's sadness, questions her about it. Finally she confesses that she loves him and, kissing him, hurries away.

Act III reveals through the darkness the interiors of the adjacent houses of Simonetta and Fioretta, and, in the foggy distance, Montesecco's house and an old bridge over the Arno. Fioretta climbs the stairs leading from Simonetta's house to her own. The memory of Simonetta's kisses brings deep compunction to her, for she knows that her friend little guesses her intimacy with Giuliano. The conspirators gather and see Giuliano cross the bridge and hurry to the house of Fioretta. They spy upon him and find that he is on business of love. Giuliano asks anxiously about Simonetta and Fioretta tells him that the girl speaks continually of him.

Simonetta, meantime, overhears the plot of the conspirators to kill the Medici on the morrow. She is discovered by Montesecco and admits that she knows all. When asked what she will do, she declares stanchly that she will warn the victims. The crafty Montesecco leads her to Fioretta's window, where she sees her friend in Giuliano's embrace. Montesecco has miscalculated, however, for instead of desiring revenge, she rushes in to tell her story. She has merely gasped " Tomorrow, the Medici " when she falls dead.

The interior of the church of Santa Reparata is seen in the fourth act. Mass is being said and the church is filled with people. Montesecco and his allies circulate among them, inciting them against the Medici. Fioretta, upon her knees, fervently implores pardon for her sins. Lorenzo enters with Il Poliziano, followed by four gentlemen. Murmurs of disapproval are heard and it is evident that the conspirators have worked to some avail. Finally Giuliano joins his brother and the conspirators find that the time is ripe for action. They creep upon Giuliano and stab him but Lorenzo and his followers defend themselves. There is general confusion and cries of " Death to the tyrants " are heard. Lorenzo, gaining a point of vantage, tries to show the people that they are wrong. He finally succeeds in getting their attention, and they begin to distrust the conspirators. Fioretta leans over the wounded Giuliano, weeping. With his last breath, he confesses to his brother that she should have been his wife and consigns her to his care. Now the people cry that Giuliano's death shall be avenged and the church resounds with the Medici cry, " Palle! Palle! "

HÄNSEL AND GRETEL

"Hänsel and Gretel" is a fairy opera in three acts, the music being by Engelbert Humperdinck and the libretto by his sister, Frau Adelheid Wette. It is the nursery legend of "The Babes in the Wood," told in German fashion. The work was first produced in Munich, Dec. 30, 1893.

CHARACTERS.

Peter, a broom-maker.
Gertrude, his wife.
Hänsel, } their children.
Gretel, }
The Witch, who eats children.
Sandman, the sleep fairy.
Dewman, the dawn fairy.
The enchanted children.
The fourteen angels.

There are three scenes, the first of which is laid in the wretched little cottage of Peter, the broom-maker. He and his wife, Gertrude, have gone to town to sell their wares and have left Hänsel and his sister Gretel in possession of the house. For a while they are very good children, the boy working at a broom and the girl knitting stockings. But soon they realize that they are hungry. Except for the jug of milk with which the mother is to make a porridge when she comes home, the house is in the sad condition of Mother Hubbard's cupboard. They do not quite dare to drink the milk and they do not care to work, so they begin to dance. This is such great fun that they keep it up until they grow dizzy and fall laughing upon the floor. But the mother comes in just then and, angry at finding them idle, boxes the boy's ears and accidentally knocks over the milk, not only spilling it but breaking the pitcher as well. This is such a catastrophe that the poor woman bursts into tears and curtly tells the children to go and hunt strawberries in the wood and not to come home until the basket is full. They have been gone but a little while when the father comes back and it is apparent at once that he has had fine luck, for he is singing a song and the basket on his arm is full of good things to eat. He has indeed sold all his brooms and there will be something beside dry bread for a while. When his wife tells him that the children have been sent away to the forest of Ilsenstein, he is horrified, for he knows that it is there that the witches ride and that they live on children. In terror, they both rush out to find Hänsel and Gretel.

In the second act, we find the two children in the forest. It is sunset and the basket is brimful of fruit. The boy crowns his sister with a rose-wreath, while she gives him a strawberry as a reward. It tastes good and he eats another. Then she tries one, and behold! in a few moments the basket is empty. They would even brave the wrath at home but it is dark and they cannot find the way and the forest is full of terrifying sounds and peering faces. Thoroughly frightened, they lie down in each other's arms, trying to say their evening prayers. They find comfort in the familiar words,

When at night I go to sleep
Fourteen angels watch do keep:
Two my head protecting,
Two my feet directing,
Two upon my left in sight,
Two there are who warmly cover,
Two above me always hover,
Two to whom the word is given,
To guide my steps to heaven.

Then the Sandman comes in a mist, sprinkling sand in their eyes, and they sink to sleep. The mist becomes a staircase, and the angels descend and stand guard about the children.

In the third act, they are awakened by the little Dewman, and, wandering into the woods, they find the Witch's house with its fence of gingerbread figures about it. They are hungry, so invited by a gentle voice within, they nibble at the cakes that are on the house and, of course, the Witch comes out and seizes them. She puts Hänsel in a cage to fatten on almonds and raisins and is about to thrust the plump Gretel into the oven, when the clever brother, who has freed himself, picks up the enchantment wand and slipping up behind the Witch, pushes her head first into the oven.

A great many fine things happen in the finale. The oven cracks open, revealing the Witch, turned to gingerbread The gingerbread children become flesh and blood again simply by the touching of the fingers of Hänsel and Gretel and Peter and Gertrude find their children safe and sound.

This charming setting of a simple nursery tale was originally intended to be only an unpretentious work for home presentation. The composer's sister wished a little singspiel for the use of her children and thus began the writing of the text. Humperdinck was asked to supply the music. He composed the work, using as his thematic material a number of the well-known German folk-songs. As he worked, his enthusiasm and interest grew and soon the determination was reached to make the work an opera. The influence of Wagner was strong on the composer and, while the musical setting he has supplied is perhaps disproportionately elaborate and complex for so simple a story as is this nursery tale, the beauty of the music itself and the irresistible appeal of the book have made the opera a recognized masterpiece throughout the world.

Among the numbers which linger in one's memory are the orchestral number, "The Witch's Ride;" the beautiful prayer of the children in the forest scene; the Sandman's lullaby; the music accompanying the appearance of the angels; the waltz of Hänsel and Gretel before the house of the Witch and the final "Hymn of Thanksgiving,"

> When past hearing is our grief,
> God, the Lord, will send relief.

LA NAVARRAISE

"La Navarraise," termed by its composer "a lyric episode in one act," with text by Jules Claretie and H. Cain, and music by Jules Émile Frederic Massenet, was produced in London in 1894.

CHARACTERS.

Garrido, a general of the Royalist troops.
Remigio, a farmer.
Araquil, his son, sergeant in the Biscayan regiment.
Ramon, a lieutenant in the same regiment.
Bustamente, a sergeant in the same regiment.
Anita, a girl of Navarre, betrothed to Araquil.
Officers, soldiers, villagers, military chaplain and surgeon.

The opera opens in a public square in a village near Bilboa. It is an evening in springtime, soldiers begrimed with powder straggle past and a group of women pray in silence before a Madonna. The booming of cannon and the rattle of musketry fill the air and bring the terrified women to their feet. It develops that Garrido, general of the Royalist troops, has tried vainly to retake a Basque village from the Carlist leader, Zuccaraga. One of his officers, Ramon, is timidly approached by Anita, a girl of Navarre, who inquires breathlessly for news of her soldier sweetheart, Araquil. But he can tell her nothing. As she is praying to the leaden medallion of the Virgin, which hangs about her neck a battalion appears and Anita scans the ranks eagerly. It passes and Araquil is not of it. Finally he comes, having been delayed by military duty, and Anita casts herself into his arms and covers his face with kisses. Oblivious to everything but each other they are interrupted in their endearments by the approach of Remigio, Araquil's father, who is delighted at the safe return of his son of whom he is very proud. But he has no gentle words for this girl of Navarre, for he is ambitious for his son and looks higher for a wife for him. Whoever weds Araquil must have a dowry equal to his own property. Anita loves too well to be angry, she only asks how much that dowry must be and is hopeless when he answers carelessly, "Two thousand douros." He might as well ask her to bring him the moon. Araquil entreats his father to be lenient but to no avail.

Garrido comes to raise Araquil to a lieutenancy and his father, prouder of him than ever, hurries him away from Anita. Night comes on and the girl still lingers in the square, dejected. Araquil's father was right. She is only a stranger, an outcast, a beggar. What is there left for her but to go on alone and broken-hearted? Finally she overhears Garrido talking with Ramon. Zuccaraga has been having fresh victories, all the general's friends have fallen before him. He would give a fortune to any one who would take Zuccaraga. A fortune! Pale and with staring eyes, she goes to Garrido and tells him that she will do the deed. Astonished, he aske her name but she answers that she has no name, that she is only a girl from Navarre, and runs away into the darkness. "Mere empty threatening," mutters the officer.

Araquil comes back, seeking his sweetheart. Yes, the soldiers have seen her. She was bound for Zuccaraga's camp. They are full of insinuations. The Carlist leader loves pretty women, it seems. Araquil is wild and, as the day breaks, he rushes away to find out for himself. Shots are heard, for the Carlists have risen. Anita comes back to the Royalists, deathly pale, her arm wounded. She tells Garrido that she has fufilled her part of the bargain and demands the money. Remorsefully he pays it, binding her to secrecy.

While Anita is gloating over the gold which will bring her such joy, Araquil, who has traced her to the Carlist camp and who believes in her guilt, is brought, wounded. He accuses her of unfaithfulness but she cares only that he is hurt. When he sees the gold, he tells her that she has sold herself. Just then the bells ring out for Zuccaraga's death. The people say that he was killed last night by an assassin. The eyes of Araquil are fixed upon Anita's hands and she fancies that he can see the blood upon them and hides them in terror. Then he understands and, pointing to the money, cries in an awful tone, "The price of blood," and falls back dead. Remigio drives her away from his son's body and she is about to curse the Madonna, who has forsaken her, when she hears the bells in the distance and fancies it is her wedding-day. Then she kisses the little leaden medallion and laughs joyfully, for La Navarraise is mad.

Upon the histrionic ability of the one cast in the role of Anita depends chiefly the success of this warlike drama, with its persistent din of battle, for it is more of an acting than a singing part.

Among the important passages in its vivid score may be mentioned the duet of Anita and Araquil upon their meeting, "Ton souvenir m'a protégé" ("I thought of thee, my darling only") and Araquil's song, when he comes back to look for Anita in the square, "Que deviens-tu donc mon aimée?" ("Why comest thou not?"). Also effective are the strangely beautiful nocturne which accompanies the sleep of the soldiers who are stretched upon their blankets in the road; Anita's song over the gold and her raving when she goes mad, and the song sung by the soldiers and Sergeant Bustamente to the music of his guitar, when just before "lights out," they gather around the soup-pot. The English translation of this sinister piece is effective:

Bustamente. I've three houses in Madrid!
Chorus. Oh, you poor old soldier!
Bust. The gaol, and the place where the dead are hid!
Chorus. And the hospital, too, for the soldier!
Bust. But I've my sweetheart Isabelle!
Chorus. He has his sweetheart, you can tell!
So, as for sorrow — let it fly!
Sing away, boys, let the dead men lie!
Bust. The soldier's love is but a flower,
Chorus. Oh, you poor old soldier!
Bust. The bugle sounds the parting hour,
Chorus. "Good bye" says the poor old soldier.
Bust. But I've another sweetheart yet!
Chorus. He has another, don't forget!
So as for sorrow, let it fly!
Sing away, boys, let the dead men lie!

MADAME MARCELLA SEMBRICH,

As Mimi, in La Boheme.

Famous Polish prima donna, who was born in 1859 and who was an accomplished violinist and pianist before her voice developed. Was sent to Leipsic Conservatory to study under Wilhelm Stengel, and later became his wife. Made her debut in 1877 as a singer in I Puritani. Visited the United States first in 1883. Her greatest successes have been made in Mozart's operas, and she has sung with great success in Barber of Seville, Martha, La Traviata and La Sonnambula. Mimi in La Boheme and the leading role in The Daughter of the Regiment, are two of her greatest roles.

She is now and has been for several years a member of the Metropolitan Opera Company, and has given many recitals throughout the country.

LA BOHEME

"La Boheme" or "Bohemia," an opera in four acts with book by Giacosa and Illica and music by Giacomo Puccini, was first presented at the Teatro Reggio, Turin, Feb. 1, 1896. The plot is based on Murger's novel, Bohemian Life.

CHARACTERS.

Rudolph, a poet.
Marcel, a painter.
Colline, a philosopher.
Schaunard, a musician.
Benoit, an importunate landlord.
Alcindoro, a state councilor and follower of Musetta.
Parpignol.
Musetta, a grisette.
Mimi, a maker of embroidery.
Students, work-girls, citizens, shopkeepers, street-vendors, soldiers, restaurant waiters, boys, girls, etc.

Time, about 1830.

The action begins in an attic-studio in the Latin Quarter in Paris, where are discovered Rudolph and Marcel, the latter painting on what he announces is to be his masterpiece, "The Passage of the Red Sea." It is cold and there is no fuel and Marcel is about to sacrifice one of the rickety chairs, when Rudolph insists upon using instead his drama manuscript.

As a cheerful blaze is kindled, Colline joins them, grumbling because he has been unable to pawn his books. Their joy is great when Schaunard comes, bringing a supply of food and fuel. and a feast is soon in progress. Benoit, the landlord, interrupts it with demands for rent money but they give him wine and lead him to confess that he is a sad old rogue, until under the pretense of fearing contamination, they forcibly eject him. Finally they all leave with the exception of Rudolph who begins to write, but stops at the knock of Mimi, a girl of beautiful but delicate appearance, who comes to his door to ask for a light. She faints at the threshold but is restored with wine. As she is leaving, she loses her key, and both candles are accidentally extinguished. While groping about for the key, their hands meet in the dark, and they acknowledge their sudden and mutual love. They go out together, the enamored Rudolph and the frail poetical girl, who lives alone in an attic and by her embroidery earns a meager living.

The second act takes place near the Café Momus, where the lights are gay and the picturesque and motley crowd of the Latin Quarter flit about; where the air is full of the cheerful cries of the street-vendors, acclaiming their wares, hot coffee, chestnuts and sweetmeats; while above all is heard the strident inquiry, "Who'll buy some pretty toys from Parpignol?" This spot is regularly frequented by the four inseparable companions, who are nicknamed "The Four Musketeers." Rudolph buys Mimi a bonnet and introduces her to his comrades, whom he finds at supper. At this instant, Musetta, a famous grisette, whose "surname is Temptation," a being petulant and unprincipled but fascinating, appears with Alcindoro, a foolish old state councilor, who is dancing attendance upon her. Marcel has formerly been her gallant, but has been discarded. He struggles to appear indifferent, but his agitation is plainly evident. Musetta boldly tries to draw his attention and finally pretending that her shoe pinches, orders old Alcindoro off to buy her a new pair. In his absence a most ardent reconciliation is effected. The comrades find they have not the wherewithal for the meal and Musetta saves the situation by adding their bill to hers and leaving them both for Alcindoro, after which subtle strategy Marcel and Colline carry her off shoeless through the crowd.

Rudolph and Mimi have been living together for several months when Act III begins; but, alas, not happily, for the very intensity of their love brings them pain. Rudolph is continually jealous and for purely fanciful reasons. The lovers realize the advisability of saying farewell forever. Mimi has come to the tavern where Musetta and Marcel are staying and have been joined by Rudolph, with this purpose in mind. It is February and snow covers the ground. Over the tavern hangs, as its sign-board, Marcel's familiar canvas, "The Passage of the Red Sea." Marcel finds the girl gazing wistfully into the gaily lighted hostelry. She is in the clutches of consumption and coughing interrupts her words. The sympathetic Marcel upholds her in her intention and when Rudolph appears they say a pathetic farewell and go their separate ways.

The fourth act occurs in the attic-studio of the first act. Here Rudolph and Marcel, again separated from Musetta, pretend to work but are really absorbed in thoughts of the past. Colline and Schaunard enter with four rolls and a herring and they try to make merry over this poor fare. While thus engaged, Musetta rushes in to tell them that Mimi is on the stairs below, too weak to ascend. They bring her in and, while they get her in bed, Musetta relates how she found Mimi dying and begging to be taken to Rudolph. Mimi revives, commends to Marcel Musetta, whose real love for him she has fathomed and feigns sleepiness in order to be left alone with her lover. They embrace affectionately, she assures him of her unaltering love and he brings out for her to try on the little rose-covered bonnet he had bought for her when first they fell in love. While they are laughing over the memory, Mimi is seized with a spasm of suffocation and falls back dead, and the curtain slowly falls on the sorrow of the stricken Rudolph and his friends.

Among the striking numbers in the score are, in the first act, the duet of Rudolph and Marcel, expressive of their trials and the duet of Mimi and Rudolph; in the second act, Musetta's waltz song and in Act IV, Marcel's final scene with the dying Mimi.

SHAMUS O'BRIEN

"Shamus O'Brien," a romantic comic opera in two acts with music by Dr. Charles Villiers Stanford and text by George H. Jessop, founded on the poem by Jos. Sheridan Le Fanu, was first produced in London in 1896.

CHARACTERS.

Shamus O'Brien, "on his keeping," outlawed.
Father O'Flynn, the parish priest of Ballyhamis.
Captain Trevor, of the British army.
Mike Murphy, a peasant farmer.
Sergeant Cox, of Captain Trevor's company.
Nora O'Brien, wife of Shamus.
Kitty O'Toole, sister to Nora.
Little Paudeen, the heir of the O'Briens.
Soldiers, peasants, villagers, etc.

The scene is laid in Ireland, after the suppression of the rebellion of 1798. Shamus O'Brien, a young Irish patriot, chafing against the heavy hand of England, has committed some act of insubordination and Captain Trevor and his men are on his track. It soon becomes apparent that Shamus is a hero worth having, for even before he appears, the various characters celebrate the merits of their "darlint," and we learn that

If Romulus and Ramus
Had lived along o' Shamus
They'd be like two puppy jackals wid a lion.

Such a conquering hero has succeeded, of course, in winning the girl of his choice and some time before the story begins, Shamus has married the charming Nora O'Toole, much to the distaste of the farmer, Mike Murphy, who has wanted her for himself. Murphy has vowed vengeance on his more fortunate rival and he is not the one to pass by such an opportunity to secure it as that of betraying Shamus into the hands of his pursuers. The prospect of receiving the blood-money and of recourting the widow Nora does away with any scruples he might have possessed. While on military duty, Captain Trevor falls in love with Nora's pretty sister Kitty. The courting of rustic swains has left this lass unmoved, although she plaintively assures us that she has a heart "if they could only get to it." She is still coy but there is some indication that the captain is on the road at any rate which leads to Kitty's heart.

Shamus comes and there is a scene in which he, the warm-hearted Father O'Flynn, Nora and Kitty figure. It is full of stanch Irish patriotism and traditional Irish hopefulness and we see for ourselves that Shamus is all that his associates think him. He is ready for any fate and, to quote his own words,

> I've sharpened the sword for the sake Ould Erin,
> I've carried a pike when she called on her sons;
> I ran the risk then, and I will not be fearin'
> The enemy's gallows no more than his guns.

Shamus, as is usually the case, is followed by a crowd of villagers. Captain Trevor comes in upon them, making inquiries for the fugitive, who keenly appreciating the joke, gaily offers to act as guide in the search through the bogs and succeeds in completely blinding his pursuers. Poor Nora cannot share in the care-freeness which her husband exhibits and Father O'Flynn questions her as to her downcast looks. She admits that for two nights she has heard the Banshee cry and that she fears the third cry, which will mean death for her Shamus. The gloom which her recountal has occasioned is banished by the arrival of the old Piper ready for a dance. Father O'Flynn tells them that he has

> Looked upon sorrow of several types,
> But seldom seen one wouldn't yield to the pipes.

and the crowd troops away to profit by the reverend counsel.

When night is falling, the traitorous Mike leads the Captain to the cottage of O'Brien and Shamus is seized. As he is led away, the Irishmen shout defiance to the oppressors.

Act II finds Captain Trevor lamenting the fact that, forced to obey the imperial decree in respect to Shamus O'Brien, he will lose the love of the latter's pretty sister-in-law, Kitty. While plunged in gloomy meditation, he is approached by Mike who finding Glengall too warm for him, wants his blood-money in order that he may depart. Mike finds that the Captain has no gratitude to bestow upon him for making his duty all too plain.

Nora comes to plead for Shamus and is supported by the people, who argue that the rebellion is over and that clemency is in order. But with real regret, Captain Trevor reads the court's decision that at dawn Shamus shall be hanged near Ballyhamis.

In the third act, we find our characters waiting to take their last look at Shamus, who, like a true Irishman, tries to be debonair even at the hour of death. Father O'Flynn is there to furnish what comfort he may and there is a note of cowed desperation evident in the words of the people, who have learned the bitter lesson that struggling against the stronger power is futile. Free now to speak the truth with no fear of the consequences, Shamus makes his last oration to the British soldiers:

> You call me a rebel, and still I defy you!
> You're slaves and you're cowards, again and again.
> If yourselves had a foe in your own land to try you,
> Perhaps the experience might make of you men.

Then Nora bravely lifts up the baby Paudeen for him to kiss and Shamus O'Brien goes to his death.

"Shamus O'Brien" is Dr. Stanford's most convincing work. He has drawn upon the native music of his own country for his inspiration and the opera exhibits a warm sympathy for downtrodden Ireland. The text is happy with its seasoning of delectable brogue and the music has the matchless Irish swing which makes "The Wearin' o' the green" and kindred melodies so fetching. Among the spirited numbers are Kitty's query, "Where is the Man that is coming to marry me?" Nora's song of the Banshee; Mike's number, "When I used to be young" and Captain Trevor's songs, "My Heart is Thrall," "I love old Ireland" and "Glengall."

MADAME LILLIAN NORDICA,

As Brunhilde in Wagner's Valkyrie.

American prima donna who was born at Farmington, Me., in 1859, and who has become the greatest Brunhilde of the day and famous in all the great Wagnerian music-dramas such as Lohengrin, The Valkyrie and Tristan and Isolde. After a course of study in Boston and a season as vocalist with Gilmore's band, she made her operatic debut at Brescia in 1879 in La Traviata. Studied the role of Elsa under Mme. Cosima Wagner, creating the part at the Bayreuth festival.

Mme. Nordica has a repertoire of forty operas. She recently announced that she would establish on the banks of the Hudson an institution modeled after Bayreuth, where American music students could receive the best training without journeying to Germany.

FEDORA

" Fedora," a lyric drama in three acts with text by V. Sardou, and music by Umberto Giordano, was first produced in Milan in 1898.

CHARACTERS.

Princess Fedora Romazov.
Countess Olga Sukarev.
Count Loris Ipanov.
De Siriex, a diplomat.
Dimitri, a groom.
Desiré, an attendant.
Baron Rouvel.
Cyrill, a cook.
Borov, a doctor.
Grech, a police officer.
Lorek, a surgeon.
Boleslav Lazinski.
Dr. Müller.
Marka, a waiter.
Basil, a domestic.
Ivan, a detective.

The action of the beginning of the opera takes place in St. Petersburg at the house of Count Vladimir Andrejevich, captain of the guard. The servants are making merry in the parlors. They are well aware of their master's dissolute habits and do not look for his return before the dawn, especially as this is his last night of freedom, his wedding to the handsome young widow, the Princess Fedora Romazov, being set for the morrow. The retainers laugh as they suggest the ease with which he will dissipate her millions and enumerate his extravagant and questionable tastes.

They are surprised by a call from the Princess herself, who comes to seek her fiancé on some important matter. Dimitri, the groom, departs hurriedly in the hope of finding the count at his club, and Fedora, meantime, fondly examines the apartment and delights in it because of its association with her lover. It is apparent that she knows nothing of his dissolute life. She seizes his photograph from a bracket and kisses it, eulogizing the nobility of the original and voicing her belief that a new life will begin for her on the morrow.

But as she waits absorbed in happy dreams, the count is brought in mortally wounded. The house speedily fills with officers, doctors and priests. Vladimir dies and Fedora is wild with grief. Suspicion fastens on Count Loris Ipanov and search is at once begun for him. Fedora swears solemnly by the cross to avenge his death.

The scene of the second act is laid in Paris. The Princess Fedora is holding a brilliant reception. Among the gentlemen who surround her is Loris, whom she has tracked to the city and infatuated. She feels that she has him at her mercy but, to her chagrin, finds that she does not hate him as she should. She begins to hope that her suspicions are wrong and that he is innocent. In his presence, Fedora announces that she returns to Russia on the next day. The prospect of losing her drives him to an impassioned declaration of love. He admits that he cannot bring her honor for he is proscribed for implication in the murder of Vladimir. It is a terrible moment for Fedora. Her vow of revenge bids her pursue her advantage and draw from him a confession; her heart fears to know the truth. He asks her if she loves him, and when she gives a breathless affirmative, he says "Yes, I killed him." Promising on the next day to bring proof that he was justified, he leaves.

Before his return the net has been spread for him. A letter has gone to the Russian Government; guards stationed in the garden are to whistle when all is ready and Fedora shall dismiss him and send him down; the Russian ship on the Seine will be his prison.

He comes. He tells her that Vladimir, his professed friend, had seduced his wife who afterwards died. He shows her letters which not only prove the truth of this, but Vladimir's utter perfidy to Fedora on the very eve of their wedding. The guards whistle below. Fedora gasps at the sound of the signal. It is late. Loris says he must go. She urges him to stay. He reminds her of the world and its bitter tongue. She says she does not care and turns the key in the door.

In the third act, Loris and Fedora are enjoying the delights of her villa in the Bernese Alps. Their happiness is almost childlike in its simplicity. They swing, they gather flowers. Loris leaves Fedora a moment to go for his mail. While he is gone she learns that her incriminating letter has resulted in the arrest and execution of his brother, and the death of his mother, whose heart has broken under the cumulation of tragedy. When Loris comes back he opens a despatch announcing his pardon. The thought of return to mother, brother, friends and country, and the realization that now it is in his power to honor Fedora, fills him with joy. Then he opens the letter which preceded the despatch and learns of the irreparable loss that has been his, and that it has been brought about by an unknown woman in Paris. He begs Fedora to help him bring to justice the fiend who has betrayed him. Faltering she pleads the cause of this erring woman, who might have loved Vladimir. Finally he sees it all: she is the woman! He flings her down and is about to kill her but even in her despair she thinks to save him. She has, foreseeing some dénouement like this, poured the poison from a cross she wears into a cup of tea. She drains it at a gulp and receives before she dies the pardon of the broken-hearted Loris.

VERONIQUE

"Veronique, the Flower Girl," a comic opera in three acts, with music by André Messager and book by Van Loo and Duval, was first produced in Paris in 1898.

CHARACTERS.

Florestan de Valiancourt.
Monsieur Loustot, a bailiff.
Seraphin, a groom.
Octave, } Florestan's friends.
Felicien, }
Monsieur Coquenard.
Ermerance, Countess de Champ Azur.
Agatha, Madame Coquenard.
Aunt Benoit.
Denise, her niece.
Hélène de Solanges.
An orderly of the national reserve, waiters, florists, and others.

The action of the opera takes place in 1840 in Paris, the merry pleasure-loving Paris of the reign of Louis Philippe. The scene shifts from one picturesque spot to another; Coquenard's flower-shop being shown, the woods in the park at Romainville and the reception-room in the Tuileries. Monsieur Coquenard is a whimsical old flower-shop proprietor, who, in spite of his eminently peaceful pursuit, greatly covets military honor. His flirtations with the girls in the shop, the aforesaid military ambition and the difficulty he has with his sword, when he finally possesses one, form the principal comedy elements.

The story chiefly concerns itself with the prank of Hélène de Solanges, a maid of honor at the Bourbon Court. She is to be a party to a *mariage de convenance* and much dislikes the idea of a union without love. The affianced, by the way, have never met. Hélène and her aunt visit the florist and from a gallery the girl beholds Florestan, her betrothed, for the first time. He is flirting desperately with the handsome Madame Coquenard and the whole shopful of fascinating flower girls. He is sufficiently pleasing to Hélène to rouse her jealousy and later her deep resentment, when he describes the dismay with which he awaits his approaching marriage.

The sly Hélène herself assumes the guise of a flower girl and as the bewitching Veronique, wins the exclusive attention of the fickle Florestan to the chagrin of Madame Coquenard, whose susceptible husband also shows symptoms of undue interest in his charming employée. Florestan bewails more bitterly than ever his approaching martyrdom, Hélène now enjoying these expressions to the utmost.

They meet again at a rustic wedding, where Coquenard engages in a lively affair with Hélène's aunt, who is also in disguise, while Florestan makes an impassioned declaration to the humble flower girl who has so spoiled his peace of mind. As the hour is approaching for her formal reception of her fiancé, she hastily escapes from Florestan's attention by donning the veil of the bride. A little later, when in great state she meets the sad young nobleman in the reception-room of the Tuileries and he discovers that the charming Veronique and Hélène are one and the same, his delight and embarrassment may easily be imagined.

The success which awaited this opera shows that the world finds itself just as much in sympathy with the maiden who wants to be loved for herself as it did in the days of the "Rose of Castile." A more graceful, refined and wholly amusing creation than "Veronique" could not be desired. The repartee is delightfully witty and the music is dainty and tuneful. The captivating "Swing Song," sung by Veronique and Florestan in the second act usually soon appears on the pianos of those who have heard it; the song and chorus, "The bloom of an apple tree;" the quartet "Between us all is over;" and Coquenard's humorous song "Ask me not" also are deservedly popular.

DER BÄRENHÄUTER

"Der Bärenhäuter," or "The Bearskin Weaver," an opera in three acts, with text and music by Siegfried Wagner, was produced at the Hof Theatre in Munich, Jan. 22, 1899.

CHARACTERS.

Hans Kraft, a young soldier.
Melchior Frölich, the burgomaster.
Lena, Gunda, Louise, } his daughters.
Parson Wippenbeck.
Nicholas Spitz, the innkeeper.
Anna, a waitress.
Carl Muffel, Kasper Wilde, a sergeant. } from Plassenburg, the fortress.
The Stranger.
The Devil.
Peasants, soldiers of Muffel's company.
Nymphs, children, a troop of little devils.

The action takes place at the close of the Thirty Years' War and the scene is laid in the country about Bayreuth. A summer landscape near a village is first shown. A joyous crowd of peasants are hurrying to town to welcome the soldiers returning from the war. They all are warmly received and welcomed by their friends. Finally, Hans Kraft comes, looking anxiously for his mother. After many vain inquiries, an old peasant informs him that his mother died about three years before, that little property had been left and that the old home is now in the hands of strangers. Hans endeavors to obtain lodging from some of the peasants but is refused in no very kindly manner. As all run merrily on to feast at the inn, Hans sinks to the ground and gives way to grief over the death of his mother and to indignation over his treatment by the villagers.

Just then there appears, laughing heartily over Hans' discomfiture, a person whom the young soldier easily recognizes as the Devil. His Satanic Majesty reminds Hans that the war is over and that he has no money and offers him rich treasure if he will serve for a year in Hell. His duties will be to keep the kettle boiling in which souls are tortured for punishment for their sins and to see that no one escapes. Hans, not caring much what happens, accepts the offer, and, having shut his eyes for a moment, reopens them in Hell.

The Devil, reminding the newcomer of his duties, leaves him alone after ordering him to get to work. First, Hans wafts a message to his mother, assuring her that his stay in Hell is only temporary. Voices now are heard from the kettle and among them Hans recognizes his colonel's scolding tones. When he climbs up a ladder at the side of the kettle and looks in, the colonel flatters him, hoping that he will let him out. Hans reminds him that he ill-treated him on earth and, climbing down, gleefully builds up the fire. A stranger, who is no other than Saint Peter, approaches to plead for the souls but Hans will not listen. Saint Peter proposes a game with dice, he staking gold and Hans the souls in the kettle. Hans loses and the Saint announces to the souls that they are free, at which a chorus above sings "Hallelujah."

Fearful wind and thunder are heard and the Devil rushes in. He stamps and howls and curses Hans and, calling up a troop of lesser devils, commands them to cover the miscreant with soot and dirt from the oven. In time his nails and beard will grow long and he will look like the Devil himself. Satan gives him a sack which always will contain gold for his needs, throws a bearskin over his shoulders, which he is to wear without washing for three years, and, opening the kettle, reminds him that he shall suffer in it if he does not find a wife within that time. Whereupon Hans is put to sleep.

Act II opens at night in the tavern. The parson, the burgomaster and many peasants are there, playing cards and drinking. Hans knocks at the door but when Anna, the waitress, opens it, she at once slams it shut crying that the Devil is outside. After some delay the window is shoved up and Hans is told to show his feet, and when it is found they are those of a man, he is admitted. The landlord and the burgomaster quarrel about an unpaid bill and Hans gives the burgomaster sixty florins. The burgomaster tells Hans about his three daughters. Hans immediately asks for one and is promised that he may see them on the morrow and take his choice.

Filled with hope, Hans goes to bed, forgetting the sack lying on the table. When all is quiet, the landlord in his nightcap steals in and plunges his hand into the sack. He finds there not gold but a strange, sticky mass. With great difficulty he withdraws his hand, when bats, scorpions, and the like come forth from the sack. Hans, roused by the man's shrieks, runs in and taking the sack, which the landlord admits he was trying to steal, goes to bed again.

It is morning when the next scene is shown. People are going past to church, and among them are the burgomaster and his three daughters. To Lena is given the first opportunity to see Hans. She calls Gunda and they ridicule him, pointing at his black face, long nails and dirty ears and calling him a devil. Soon Louise arrives, and seeing a tear on Hans' face, she is moved to pity and is very gentle with him. He shows her the half ring the Devil gave him and tells her that if she will wear it for three years and if the gold does not fade, the curse which is upon him will depart. She places it upon a ribbon she wears about her neck and hides it beneath her bodice.

Loud voices are heard and the landlord and the peasants rush in. The landlord has told them about the bag and they accuse Hans of being in league with the Devil. Hans asks about the sixty florins and the landlord declares that he gave them back because they were the Devil's gold. At this, Hans seizes him and takes the gold from his pocket. He throws it upon the ground and where it falls a hell flame shoots up. The peasants attack Hans but Louise remonstrates, declaring that he is a good man.

The third act shows first a wild pine forest where, upon a stone in a pool of water, the Devil sits with an hour-glass in his hand. The three years are at an end and Hans has won. Hans is sleeping on a grassy knoll and the little devils are busy about him. They cut his hair and beard, trim his nails, and wash the soot and dirt from his face. When he wakes up, Hans reminds the Devil of the three wishes which, as loser, he must grant. Hans' first wish is to be what he was; the second, to have the bag free from gold and ghosts; the third, that the Devil will leave him alone in the future. All these are granted and he bids the Devil farewell, going to his bride. As he is hastening along he is accosted by the stranger, who urges him to warn the sleeping fortress that Wallenstein's army is about to attack it.

The scene shifts to the burgomaster's garden, which looks out on the Plassenburg. Excited peasants cry that an army is coming to storm the fort and that all the soldiers are sleeping. The worst of it is that no one dares to go to waken them. In the midst of their trepidation, the sergeant rushes in and tells them that the danger has been averted by Hans Kraft, whom they formerly knew as a soldier. The colonel details soldiers to bring Hans to the glory which awaits him. While Louise, left alone, is thinking of him whose ring she wears and longing for his return, a soldier enters, slightly wounded, and she binds his wrist. He asks for a drink of water and drops his part of the ring into the glass.

To be brief, everything ends happily; the people learning that their idol, Hans, is no other than the black man who wore the bearskin and that through the love of Louise the curse has been removed.

The music of "The Bearskin Weaver" is naturally after the style of Richard Wagner and many of the orchestral effects as well as the motifs themselves are more than merely reminiscent. The opera has known but a short life in Germany and has not made its way into other lands, facts which tend to prove that the interest it aroused when it first appeared was due more to curiosity concerning the abilities of Siegfried Wagner, the son of Richard Wagner, than to any enduring values in the work itself.

FLORODORA

Florodora is a musical comedy in two acts, with music by Leslie Stuart, dialogue by Owen Hall and lyrics by Ernest Boyd Jones and Paul Reubens.

It was first presented in London in 1899.

CHARACTERS.

Cyrus W. Gilfain, holder of the Island of Florodora.
Capt. Arthur Donegal, Lady Holyrood's brother.
Frank Abercoed, Mr. Gilfain's manager.
Leandro, the overseer.
Anthony Tweedlepunch, a detective, disguised as a phrenologist.
Dolores, the rightful heir to the island.
Valleda, Lady Holyrood's maid.
Estelle Lamont, a stenographer.
Angela, the daughter of Gilfain.
Lady Holyrood.
Farmers, flower-girls and others.

The scene is laid partly on the semi-tropical island of Florodora "set in the Eastern sea" and partly in Wales. The time is the present. As usual with musical comedies, there is a small plot which does not interfere seriously with the music. There is a species of villain, Cyrus Gilfain, who has stolen the island of Florodora from its rightful owner. Gilfain is the manufacturer of a perfume, which he has named after the island, and Dolores, the daughter of the real owner, works in the factory. To make his claim to his possession indisputable, Gilfain determines to marry his charming employée but her affections have been previously engaged by the chief clerk, Abercoed. Gilfain has a daughter Angela and she and Captain Donegal are in love with each other. After one of Gilfain's visits to England, he returns with an addition to his party in the person of Lady Holyrood, a London society woman, who has matrimonial designs upon him. Another addition to the population of Florodora is Tweedlepunch, a detective, disguised as a palmist and phrenologist, whose mission is to find the daughter of the real owner. He gives much valuable advice as to the choosing of life partners according to phrenological specifications. Gilfain, who has discovered that his chief clerk is really Lord Abercoed, bribes Tweedlepunch to decide that the young peer and Angela must wed and that he and Dolores are fitting mates. Lady Holyrood offers him more money and the phrenologist changes his mind and announces that she and Gilfain are destined for each other. Abercoed gets out of the distasteful affair by going back to England, promising, however, to return for Dolores.

The second act is laid in Wales. The prosperous Gilfain has acquired the Abercoed Castle and refuses to admit the son of the former owner, who has been so unpleasant about falling in with his matrimonial plans. Abercoed gets in, however, in company with Dolores and Tweedlepunch and with the aid of a story of a castle ghost forces from Gilfain the confession of his dishonest dealing. So everything ends beautifully. Dolores comes into her own, Abercoed gets back the ancestral castle and marries her; Angela and her captain are married and Lady Holyrood falls to the lot of Gilfain.

Seldom have songs persisted in being sung and whistled and parodied so long and so vigorously as have those of "Florodora." The vogue enjoyed by the tuneful production was greater than that of any similar work in recent years. True, when the musical comedy was brought from London to New York, the humor with which it was invested was found to be so essentially English that it fell flat on American ears. But this was patched up and a more sprightly dialogue resulted. It is safe to say, however, that with the elimination of one number, "Tell me, Pretty Maiden," sung by the double sextet of English girls and clerks, its popularity would have been many times diminished. With the charm of its words and rhythm increased by very clever stage business, this number proved so taking that audiences insisted upon hearing it over and over again. The double sextet is not, however, the only popular number. In the long list of them there are the chorus, "The credit due to me;" "When I leave town," sung by Lady Holyrood; Abercoed's "In the shade of the sheltering palm;" Lady Holyrood's topical song, "Tact;" Angela's number, "The fellow who might;" Donegal's "I want to be a Military Man" and the song and dance by Leandro and Valleda, "We get up at 8 a. m."

LA TOSCA

"La Tosca," an opera in three acts, with score by Giacomo Puccini and text by Illica and Giacosa after Sardou's drama, was produced at the Constanzi Theatre, Rome, in January, 1900.

CHARACTERS.

Floria Tosca, a celebrated songstress.
Mario Cavaradossi, a painter.
Baron Scarpia, chief of the police.
Cesare Angelotti.
A sacristan.
Spoletta, a police agent.
Sciarrone, a gendarme.
A jailor.
A shepherd-boy.
Executive, scribe, judge, cardinal, officer, sergeant, soldiers, police-agents, ladies, nobles, citizens, artisans.

Scene, Rome, June, 1800.

Cesare Angelotti, a political prisoner, escapes in the garb of incarceration and takes refuge in the chapel of the church of Sant' Andrea alla Valle, where his sister has concealed for him woman's apparel in which he may disguise himself. The artist, Mario Cavaradossi, is at work in the church and the refugee, recognizing him as an old friend, makes himself known, delighted at the thought of finding succor. While they are conferring, Floria Tosca, the painter's mistress, calls from without and Angelotti is hastily concealed but not before Mario has managed to get into the hands of the famished man his luncheon basket, filled with food and wine.

Floria proves to be what her lover has called her, the most jealous of women. Her ears have caught the sound of a whisper in the church. Her fancy has supplied the swish of skirts. When she tells Mario that she will meet him at the stage door that night after her song and paints in anticipation the beauty of the moonlit Italian night, he responds to her rhapsodies absently, for his thoughts are with his friend in his peril. She is hurt and petulant when he dismisses her on the pretext that he must be at his work, and when, as she is leaving, she perceives that the magdalen on the easel is in reality a portrait of a beautiful, blue-eyed woman (Angelotti's sister, who comes frequently to the chapel to pray), she is consumed with unhappiness, until Mario succeeds in convincing her that her own dark eyes are the most lustrous in the world.

As soon as she has gone, Mario lets Angelotti out of the chapel and the condemned man is about to venture forth when the cannon of the fortress is heard, the signal that his escape is discovered. Mario nobly resolves to go with his friend and fight for him if need be. As the doors of the church close behind them, a crowd of people arrive, rejoicing that reverses have overtaken Napoleon. Scarpia and his policemen trace Angelotti to the church, where they find evidence of his recent presence. As they search for clews, Floria comes back with a message for Mario, and Scarpia, who wants her for himself, seizes the opportunity to rouse her jealousy, pointing out a fan dropped by the prisoner's sister and insinuating that Mario has been inspired by more than a glimpse of a stranger's face to paint the picture on the easel. His poison works well. Floria leaves weeping, followed by Scarpia's spies.

In the second act, Scarpia is seen at supper in his apartments in the Farnese Palace. He learns from Spoletta that both Floria and Mario have been followed to their villa but no trace of Angelotti can be found. Floria is singing at an entertainment given by Queen Caroline in the palace below but Mario has been seized by Scarpia's agents and brought to the house, from thence being conducted to the Chamber of Inquisition. Though subjected to frightful torture, the painter steadfastly refuses to disclose his friend's whereabouts. Floria comes but she is just as steadfast under Scarpia's pleas and threats, until she realizes what agony her lover is undergoing and is promised that her confession will release him from it. Then she informs Scarpia that Angelotti is hidden in a well in the garden. Mario is at once brought in unconscious and Floria tries to soothe his bruised head with tears and kisses. He rouses to hear Scarpia's orders to search the well, and, knowing that Tosca has betrayed his friend, he curses her. News comes that Napoleon has just conquered the Royalists, and Mario, fearlessly rejoicing in the event, is carried away to be shot.

Floria would follow, but Scarpia restrains her, telling her that he holds Mario's life in pawn for her. She spurns him, but he shows her the scaffold where her lover shall die in an hour, and she agrees to yield to his lustful desires. He writes the passport which the next day shall enable her and Mario to leave the city, and he promises her that Mario shall now have only a mock execution. When he comes toward her to claim his reward, she seizes a knife and stabs him to the heart, crying "It is thus that Tosca kisses."

After this tumult and tragedy, the curtain of the third act rises upon a quiet scene. It is the Castello St. Angelo, where Mario is held prisoner. The Vatican and St. Peter's are visible in the background, the clear sky is thickly studded with stars, church bells sound from afar, a shepherd sings a love song in the distance. While Mario, who has forgiven Floria, is lamenting that he must leave a world which holds this matchless woman, she appears with the safe-conduct she has taken from Scarpia's dead hands. She tells him everything, that she has killed Scarpia, of his insults and of the execution which is to be a farce. Gaily she coaches him to simulate death for a moment, he answering, "Do not fear love; I shall fall at the right moment and quite naturally," and caresses the gentle hands which Fate has driven to such bitter deeds.

The jailor leads him out, Floria giving him many last instructions. "You must not laugh," she whispers. The sergeant offers to bandage his eyes but smiling he declines. When the soldiers fire, Floria stops her ears and nods as a signal that he must fall. How cleverly he acts! As soon as she dares, she runs to tell him to get up but staggers back shrieking. He is dead. Spoletta and his men rush in to find her talking to her murdered lover. "It was Tosca who killed Scarpia," they cry, "she shall pay with her life." She thrusts them aside, springs to the parapet of the terrace and, calling upon Mario to meet her in heaven, throws herself into the depths below.

"La Tosca," like all Puccini's operas, is written in the modern style, without clearly defined aria or ensemble. Among the most nearly individualized passages in the score are Mario's aria, comparing the blue-eyed beauty of the portrait and Floria's dusky charm, "Recondita armonia" ("Strange harmony of contrast"); Tosca's song, "Non la sospiri la nostra casetta" ("Dost thou not long"); Scarpia's malicious soliloquy, "Va, Tosca! nel tuo cuor" ("Go, Tosca! There is place in your heart"); Tosca's touching appeal to heaven when in the grasp of Scarpia, "Vissi d'arte e d'amor" ("Love and Music, these have I lived for"); the shepherd's song; Mario's recollection of Floria, "E lucevan le stelle" ("When the stars were brightly shining") and their duet when Floria tells him of her bloody deed, "O dolci mani mansuete e pure" ("O gentle hands").

LOUISE

"Louise," an opera or, as its composer terms it a musical romance, in four acts and five tableaux, was first produced in Paris in 1900. Both music and text are from the pen of Gustav Charpentier.

CHARACTERS.

Julien, an artist.
The Father.
Louise.
The Mother.

MEN:—

The night-walker.
The old Bohemian.
A song writer.
Philosophers, a painter, a sculptor, a ballad writer, a young poet, a student, a ragpicker, a jack of all trades, policemen, an apprentice, a street urchin, guardians of the peace, an old Bohemian, vendors of potatoes, chickweed, green peas, brooms, barrels, old clothes.

WOMEN:—

Irma,
Marguerite,
Camille,
Blanche,
Gertrude,
Suzanne,
Elise,
Madelaine,
} sewing-girls.

Dressmakers, apprentices and forewomen.
A ragpicker, a street-sweeper, a milkwoman, various street vendors.

The heroine, Louise, is the daughter of a workingman and spends her daylight hours in the shop of a dressmaker. Her parents are simple folk with strict ideas of honor. They keep her as a recluse and refuse her hand to Julien, a penniless young artist of alleged bad character, whom she adores. When the opera opens there is disclosed a room in a tenement where the little family resides. The girl is at the window talking to Julien, who stands outside. They speak of their love and recall incidents of their forcedly surreptitious courtship and Julien urges Louise to elope with him since they cannot get her parents' consent to the marriage. The mother, overhearing them, bluntly terminates the interview, mockingly repeats some of their tender words, and overwhelms Louise with reproaches.

After a little while, the father comes home. While Louise sets the table, he reads a letter from Julien asking him for her again. He feels her suspense and when he has finished, he holds out his arms to her. The little family sit down to supper. The father talks of the day's toil. He is tired, for he is no longer young and the days are long.

"And to think that there are some who pass their lives making merry," says the mother, bitterly, thinking of Julien. "I believe that all the world should work," concludes this maternal socialist.

"Equality is a fine word but it is impossible," returns the father, "and if one has the right to choose, let him choose the least arduous labor."

"Ah! quite true," says the mother, ironically, "all the world wants to be an artist."

But the father has a more cheerful philosophy. Each has his lot in the beautiful life and possession of wealth is not happiness. Happiness is the fireside where one finds a place and, near to those one loves, forgets the evil turns of life. Have they not love and health? He kisses the daughter and seizing the protesting mother, waltzes heavily about the room with her.

When the subject of the letter and Julien's request come up again, the father tenderly tries to reason with Louise. He reminds her that she has had no experience; that love is blind. At her age everything is rosy and beautiful and one chooses a husband as one chooses a doll. He tries to tell her that she soon will get over the pain. It is their love for her that makes them so hard. He asks her to read the newspaper aloud to him, hoping thus to divert her thoughts but she breaks down, her voice choked with sobs.

The scene of the second act is laid on the hill of Montmartre. It is five o'clock of an April morning and the workers are beginning their day's toil. All the sounds of waking Paris are heard. "At this very moment, if you can believe it there are women sleeping in silk," sighs a wretched woman whose trade is ragpicking. A debonair night-walker accosts some girls with flattering words and, throwing off his cloak, appears garbed as Spring. He jauntily explains that he represents the pleasures of Paris. As he runs off, he knocks over an old ragpicker, who tells with weeping how his daughter was tempted away by this same night-walker. An old street-sweeper stops to paint the glories of other days which, through the grayness of the present, look like Paradise.

At last Julien enters with his gay Bohemian friends and speaks of carrying off Louise. He ponders half fearfully on the step he is about to take and wonders what persuasion he can use with her. The manifold street cries of Paris are heard; the girls pass chattering on their way to work with occasional glances at the handsome artist. At last Louise comes guarded by her mother. Julien waits until the latter leaves and flies to the girl's side to entreat her to go with him. She refuses half-heartedly, painting her parents' misery, and leaves him plunged in deep depression.

The second scene of the act shows the interior of the dressmaker's shop, with Louise among the sewing-girls. Because she sits pensive and distrait, her associates allude to it, and someone says that her parents are very hard with her — that her mother strikes her, that her father treats her as a child; another accuses her of being in love and the rest take the cue and tease her. The sound of someone singing to the guitar is heard and the girls flock to the window. It is Julien and his voice is fraught with emotion. After a while Louise rises to leave, saying that she is ill. The girls watch from the window and a moment later see her go away with Julien.

The lovers go to live in a little house on Montmartre and there the third act finds them. Louise is very happy, although the thought of the sorrow she has left behind her disturbs a little her content. She cannot help remembering that her mother sometimes struck her and that her father treated her like a child. Julien laughs and calls them Mother Routine and Father Prejudice. When she doubts the righteousness of her course, he tells her that everyone has the right to freedom and to love. When the lights begin to twinkle in the city which is spread like a panorama before them, the two burst into jubilant song celebrating their liberty and affection. While they are singing, a crowd of Bohemian friends arrive and crown Louise as the Muse of Montmartre. In the midst of the gaiety the mother appears to tell her that her father is ill and humbly asks her to return for a little while, in order that his grief may not kill him. The thought of the old man whose affection for her she knows so well moves her deeply. The old ragpicker passes by babbling of his lost daughter and Louise, promising her lover that she will return, goes away.

The fourth act is played in the little home in Paris. The parents hope desperately that Louise will be willing to forsake what they consider her dishonor and take up the old life. Her father, still feeble from illness, tries to present to her the parents' side of the case. He shows her how their love has followed her all the way, from the baby just born, guiding the young steps, greeting the first smile. Fatigue and hardship have been nothing when they have been for her. The child grows; she becomes a pretty girl; gallants flock about her. She is charming. The old parents are proud of their daughter for she is a model of honor and goodness. A stranger passes one day. He lures her away from them and drives the past from her heart. As the father speaks his indignation grows and he curses the robber, Love, who has estranged their daughter. The mother calls Louise to the kitchen on the pretense of needing her aid and pleads with her to take pity on her father, who listens eagerly from the other room. It is evident that Louise cannot promise and the mother mocks bitterly at this free love and, seeing the discussion is fruitless, tells Louise that it is bedtime and bids her say good-night to her father. When she goes up to him he seizes her violently in his arms, covering her face with kisses. Louise disengages herself coldly, and when he speaks her name turns away her eyes.

But is she not his child, he pleads. Did he not once rock her in his arms? Although she struggles gently to get away, he takes her upon his lap and croons to her as to a baby and begs her to remember the happy bygone days. "Such a good little baby," he says, and she forces a smile. He speaks of happiness but she reminds him that she must lead her own life and that happiness cannot come in the prison they would make for her. Would they have her abandon all her hopes and break her vows?

Through the window steals the gay invitation of Paris going to play. "The dear music of the great town," whispers Louise in delight. She runs to the window and watches the lights bloom out. It brings with added force to her the rapture of returning to Julien, her Prince Charming. She will be no longer the little daughter with the timid, fearful heart but the wife with the heart of flame. She runs to the door but her father bars her passage.

But when she speaks again of her lover, his anguish displays itself in a paroxysm of anger. He throws open the door and in a terrible voice bids her go. She passes out into the night. He looks after her, and his anger fades. "Louise" he calls madly, but she has gone too far to hear. Her mother gazes sadly from the window into the darkness. Then the father stumbles again to the door and shakes his fist at the Paris which has stolen his child.

"Louise" made the sensation of the year in which it was produced. It received extended criticism, and much was found in it besides the surface indication. Charpentier was fortunate in producing it just at the right time, for a few years previously it would not have been understood. It is full of human interest. Charpentier's own words sum it up. "The essential point of the drama is the coming together, the clashing in the heart of Louise, of two sentiments, love which binds her to her father, the fear of leaving suffering behind her, and on the other hand, the irresistible longing for liberty, pleasure, and happiness, love, the cry of her being which demands to live the life she wishes."

The opera is an odd mixture of realism and idealism and possesses decided revolutionary tendencies. Into the orchestration all the street noises of Paris are cleverly worked. Besides the leading characters, all the every-day people of Paris, clad in the garb of the present, walk through the story. Some one has said that the opera has to do with only three characters, Louise, Julien, and the City. But the father and mother are also drawn with consummate skill.

ZAZA

"Zaza," a lyric comedy in four acts, founded on a play by Pierre Berton with words and music by Ruggiero Leoncavallo, was produced in Milan in 1900.

CHARACTERS.

Zaza.
Anaide, her mother.
Floriana, a concert singer.
Natalie, Zaza's maid.
Signora Dufresne.
Milio Dufresne.
Cascart, a concert singer.
Bussy, a journalist.
Malardot, the proprietor of the concert café.
Lartigon, a monologue artist.
Duclou, the stage manager.
Michelin, a journalist.
Marco, the valet of Signor Dufresne.
Courtois.
Toto, Signor Dufresne's little daughter.
Singers, dancers, supernumeraries, clowns, firemen, property-men, machinists, scene-shifter and others.

When the curtain rises there is disclosed part of a concert café. At one side is the dressing-room of Zaza, the singer, and at the other a section of a stage setting, before which may be discerned some of the audience seated at round tables upon which are glasses and trays.

Nearly all of the characters are introduced in this act. Zaza's rival, Floriana, sings a gay aria and is applauded; two clowns do an act; Malardot, the proprietor, bargains with Lartigon, the monologist, for something lively and scolds the waiters for not leaving the foam on the beer, so that four glasses might pass muster for five; Cascart, a singer, who looks upon Zaza as his special property, visits her in her dressing-room to tell her of his new engagement at Marseilles and to propose taking her along. Zaza's drunken mother, Anaide, who always is begging for money to indulge her weakness, comes in on the usual errand and accomplishes it. Zaza also has a chat with Bussy, the journalist, her "discoverer." They speak of Milio Dufresne, his friend, and it is plain that Zaza is interested. Taunted by Bussy, she declares that she will have Dufresne at her feet. Bussy tells her she flatters herself too much. Floriana and Zaza, of whom all the women are jealous, have a lively tilt, Dufresne looking on from the background.

Afterwards Zaza lures Dufresne to her dressing-room and exerts all her well-tried charms. At first he is cold and very much on his guard but finally she conquers and he abandons himself to the affair.

The second act is played in the reception-room of Zaza's house. Here, as usual, is Dufresne. This time he tells her that he must leave her to go to America for some months. She abandons herself to childish grief over the matter, displaying the force of her warm and heedless love. She pleads so piteously that he finally consents to postpone his journey. He tells her, however, that he must at once go to Paris on business. He departs and Zaza watches his retreating form from the window, wafting kisses to him and fairly weeping for joy when he turns around for a last smile.

Her mother comes but Zaza is in no mood for gossip and runs away. When she comes back all laughter and happiness in the thought of Dufresne, Cascart is there.

He speaks of the Marseilles engagement but Zaza is indifferent. Then he tries to reason with her about her present love-affair, warning her that no happiness can come from the attachment. He refers to their own past love and she gently tells him that Dufresne's love is finer than that of the rest of them. But he suggests that possibly Dufresne has other ties and tells of seeing him with a woman in Paris. All the jealousy of which a nature like Zaza's is capable is aroused. Her mother joins Cascart in his advice to give him up. Zaza, however, announces her intention to follow him.

Act III shows an elegant apartment in Dufresne's Paris house. He arranges the papers on his desk and goes away with Signora Dufresne. Zaza enters with her maid. Dufresne's valet, who has been enjoying his master's best cigars, fancies she is a caller who has been expected and retires. The succeeding events dispel Zaza's hope that Cascart might have been wrong. She finds a letter addressed to Signora Dufresne on the desk. A child enters in search of a piece of music and being cajoled by Zaza prattles of her father and mother. Then the wife herself arrives and gazes astonished at the intruder. Zaza, merely saying that she has made a mistake in the door, goes away.

The scene of the fourth act is again at Zaza's house. Malardot chides her about the uncertainty she has lately displayed in fulfilling her engagements and with the indifference of despair she promises to sing. The loyal Cascart, who has learned the story of the Paris visit, again pleads with Zaza to give up her lover. She laughs at the suggestion and Cascart reminds her sternly that it is now a question of duty. He leaves and Dufresne is announced. He greets Zaza in the old affectionate way. Then she allows him to understand that she knows he is married but freely expresses her forgiveness for his deception and talks touchingly of her love and her belief that they were destined for each other. He responds very warmly but some casual expression arouses her suspicion that he is by no means indifferent to his wife. Thereupon she declares that she has told Signora Dufresne everything. In a rage, he throws her to the floor and reviles her for making him forget a pure woman's love for her own unworthy self. Zaza, crying that he has cured her, sends him away, having first, however, assured him that Signora Dufresne knows nothing. When he has gone, she runs to the window and tries to call him back but he does not turn and she falls by the window, weeping bitterly.

MANRU

"Manru," an opera in three acts with music by Ignace Jan Paderewski and text by Alfred Nossig, after the Polish novel by Kraszewski, was first produced at the Royal Opera House in Dresden, May 29, 1901, and was heard for the first time in New York, Feb. 14, 1902.

CHARACTERS.

Manru, a gypsy.
Ulana, a Galician girl.
Hedwig, her mother.
Asa, the belle of the gypsies.
Urok, a dwarf.
Oros, the chief of the gypsy band.
Jagu, a gypsy fiddler.

Manru is a Hungarian gypsy in whose breast lie dormant all the longings of his race. He encounters Ulana, a charming peasant girl, falls in love with her and succeeds in conquering the domestic, home-loving heart. With the peasant folk, however, the gypsies are in ill-repute and the girl is cast off by her mother, Hedwig, and by her former associates because of her unconventional marriage.

To a lonely hut in the wood the gypsy husband takes her and they are happy in their isolation until the yearning for the old, carefree, wandering life seizes Manru. He struggles hard against it, for the sense of duty is not absent from his character, but the wild hunger for the freedom of the mountains is but little softened by the human love dying in his heart. Urok, a dwarfed, unprepossessing fellow, who is in love with Ulana, is their only companion. To him she confesses her fear that the Wanderlust has seized her husband. She realizes dully that if she could shake off her love of home and go wandering with him, she might hope to retain his love. At this juncture, her mother offers to take her back again if she will renounce Manru. This she refuses to do but she begs Urok, who knows all the herbs of field and forest, to brew her a potion which shall revive her husband's love. Urok consents but hints that the effects of the draught may not be permanent.

In the second act, Manru is seen at work at his little forge, while within the cabin Ulana sings a lullaby over the cradle of her baby. Urok, who sees that the domesticity of the scene is maddening to Manru, taunts both of them. The regret for the old life, for the old gay companionship almost overwhelms Manru when he hears the sound of gypsy music echoing in the hills and when his former fellow, Jagu, the fiddler, arrives. He urges Manru to return to his people, tempting him with the chieftainship of the band and the love of Asa, his former sweetheart, whose charms he recalls to him. His arguments nearly prevail and he is about to follow Jagu to the hills when Ulana's voice restrains him and he goes back to the anvil. Now Urok appears with the promised love-potion which Ulana gives to her husband. In a few moments he is transformed into an ardent lover. The rapturous duet ensuing is one of the gems of the opera.

As Urok has suggested, the potion is but temporary in its effect. The third act finds Manru again in the grasp of a mad desire for freedom. His inner unrest is reflected in the scene. It is a wild rocky ravine near a lake; flying clouds ride across the moon and the wind wails in the hills. Manru, at last undone by the battle in his soul, falls prostrate, his face to the earth. After a while familiar music falls upon his ears, the weird measures of a Romany march which announces the coming of his people. They descend from the hills and Asa, the seductive, is with them. She recognizes Manru and welcomes him, entreating him to return and promising her own love in reward, while Oros, leader of the band, watches them with ill-concealed jealousy. It is Jagu, the fiddler, who gives success to Asa's enticements. He plays a wild strain on his gypsy strings which sets Manru on fire and he consents. In a rage, Oros throws down his staff of office and the gypsies acclaim Manru their leader in his place.

When all have gone, poor Ulana accompanied by Urok, comes seeking Manru. In despair, for she knows that she has been deserted, she finally throws herself into the lake. It is the dwarf who acts as the retributive force. When Manru appears with his arm around Asa, Urok steals up behind the unfaithful husband and pushes him over the cliff.

Paderewski has levied inspirational tribute upon the folk-songs and the dances of his own people as well as upon the strange music of the nomadic tribes of Hungary where the scene of the story is laid, and has made effective artistic use of this virile material. He has chosen a story well suited for musical expression. The music is essentially modern in that it is continually painting the inner life of the characters. Especially powerful is the portrayal of the conflict that rages in Manru's soul. Passages which show unusual power are the peasant ballet in the first act with the recurring phrase, "When the Moon is full the Gypsy runs wild;" Ulana's tender lullaby over her child in the second act and the impassioned love duet which concludes it; the elaborate orchestral prelude to the third act; Manru's dream; the strange Romany music and Asa's song of temptation.

"Manru" was performed in Cracow, Semberg, Zurich and Cologne after its original production in Dresden. Alexander von Bandrowski sang the principal role many times and was engaged to sing at the Metropolitan Opera House, New York, in 1902. The remainder of the cast included Mme. Sembrich, Mme. Homer, Fritzi Scheff, Mühlmann, Blass and Bispham.

In spite of its brilliant introduction, "Manru" seems to have had its day. Its stanchest admirers acknowledge that the story is rather badly told. Many of the criticisms arise from the fact that the public does not seem to understand that it is a story of an emotional, passionate people, whose very mode of life is conducive to lawlessness and inconstancy. National airs and warlike music have been known to inspire patriots and to lead them forth to face dangers even when their cause has not been just—then why should we marvel that the wild free music of the Gipsy fiddler, recalling all the joy and freedom of Manru's old life, should prove too strong for a nature like his?

More portent than the words is the music, which tells of the conflict between Christian and Pagan, between law and lawlessness. It depicts a soul struggle, and in the prelude to the last act the orchestra delineates this warring of passions by a seeming discussion between Polish and Gipsy voices, and as the curtain rises we find this war symbolized in the panorama of sky, where clouds and moon are struggling for mastery.

Mr. Krehbiel, in his "Chapters of Opera," says: "More than the story, more than the picturesque costumes and stage furniture, there is a fascination about the music which grew with each hearing. 'Manru' is an opera not to be disposed of with a hurried ultimatum on either book or music. From several points of view it not only invites, it clamors for discussion. The book is awkwardly constructed, and its language is at times amazingly silly; yet the fundamental idea is kept before the mind persistently and alluringly by devices of the composer."

PELLEAS ET MELISANDE

"Pelleas and Melisande," a lyric drama in five acts with music by Claude Debussy and text after the play of Maurice Maeterlinck, was first presented in Paris.

CHARACTERS.

Arkel, king of Germany.
Genevieve, mother of Pelleas and of Golaud.
Pelleas, } grandchildren of Arkel.
Golaud, }
Melisande.
Little Yniold, a son of Golaud by a former marriage.
A physician.
Servants, poor people.

In a forest, Golaud, recovering from wounds received while hunting, finds the young girl Melisande, sobbing by the edge of a shadowy pool. She repulses him when he approaches her and evades his questions. When, however, he asks her what is gleaming in the depths of the water she tells him it is a crown which has fallen from her head. He offers to restore it to her but she insists that in that case she will take its place. Golaud has no more idea of his whereabouts than Melisande has of hers, but after much difficulty he convinces her of the danger of remaining in the forest unprotected and the two lost ones depart together, as the curtain of the first scene falls.

Six months are supposed to have elapsed before the second scene. The action passes in a room in the castle. Genevieve reads to the king a letter from Golaud to his brother Pelleas, containing the information that he has married the unknown girl, Melisande. He urges his brother to intercede for him with his grandfather, who had hoped to marry him to the Princess Ursula to terminate a feud. In case a welcome is forthcoming, Pelleas is to place a lamp in the tower overlooking the sea. Arkel is inclined to be lenient to the formerly exemplary Golaud, who since the death of his first wife, has lived only for his little son Yniold.

Genevieve comes to greet Melisande, who exclaims at the gloom of the garden. Pelleas joins them, too. He speaks of the tempest which is brewing over the sea. Melisande sees a light gleaming through the mists. It is the beacon of Arkel. They talk dreamily of the spectral ships, of the falling of the night. Pelleas offers his hand to help her down the rocks. She laughs, for hers are full of flowers. He steadies her arm. "Perhaps I shall go away tomorrow," he says as if to himself. "O, why are you going away," says Melisande regretfully, as the curtain of the first act goes down.

In the second act, Pelleas leads Melisande to a fountain in the park, a fountain deep as the sea, a once miraculous fountain whose waters could cure the blind. Melisande leans over it, her wonderful, long hair trailing upon its surface and plays with the wedding-ring which Golaud has given her. Just as the clock strikes noon it slips from her fingers into the depths. In the next scene we find that at that instant Golaud's horse has taken unaccountable fright in the forest and has thrown him violently to the ground. Melisande attends him, and her tears bring him to inquire their cause. She confesses that she is wretchedly unhappy and he takes her hand to comfort her, the little hand he could crush like flowers. "Hold! where is the ring?" he exclaims.

He questions her in agitation. He would rather have lost everything he owned than the ring. He bids her call Pelleas and she goes forth sobbing to search with him in the inky grotto, where they find three white-haired old beggars, sleeping side by side. The search proves futile and they promise themselves to resume it another day.

The third act finds Melisande standing at her window in the tower singing and combing her unbound hair. Pelleas comes by. He tells her of the beauty of the night. The stars are innumerable. He never has seen so many. "Do not stay hidden in the shadow, Melisande," he pleads. He begs her to lean out that he may see the glory of her hair. Will she not put her little hand upon his lips in farewell? Tomorrow he goes away. She will not give her hand to him unless he promises not to go.

Ah, then he will wait. She leans out and her loosened hair falls about him in a shower. He grasps the silken strands in his hands and twines them about his arms and his throat, threatening to hold her thus a prisoner all night long. She urges him to run away for some one will come. Some one does come. It is Golaud. "What children you are," he laughs, nervously. "Melisande, do not lean out of the window in that fashion. You are going to fall."

That Golaud's jealousy has been growing is proved in a dramatic scene between him and the little Yniold. The father, half ashamed, questions the child as to his uncle and stepmother. "Pelleas is always with her, is he not?" "Yes," the child answers, always when his father is not there. The lamps are lighted in Melisande's apartment. Golaud lifts the child to peer through the windows his own eyes cannot reach. The child bursts into tears at the unconscious cruelty of his grasp. Never mind, he shall have presents on the morrow.

Ah! his uncle Pelleas is there with his mother. They do not speak; they do not move; their eyes frighten him. He must get down or he will cry.

In the fourth act, the wan Pelleas is ordered away on a voyage. Golaud comes in with blood upon his forehead and, when Melisande attempts to wipe it off, he repulses her. He demands his sword and, turning fiercely upon his grandfather, bids him say what he finds in Melisande's eyes. "Only a great innocence," responds the patriarch. At this, Golaud turns in a passion of ironic fury and, seizing his wife by the hair, drags her to her knees.

Melisande who has made a hazardous flight from her lord, meets Pelleas in the forest. In the midst of their rapture they hear the sound of the castle gates closing for the night. Golaud tracks them and strikes with his sword the defenseless Pelleas, who falls over the edge of the fountain, while Melisande flees through the darkness.

In Act IV Melisande is dying in the castle. Golaud, still mad with jealousy, implores her to tell him whether her love for Pelleas was guiltless. She answers "yes" and he raves that he would have further assurance.

They bring in her baby, but she is too weak to lift her arms to take her. As her spirit takes its flight, the servants fall on their knees, the sobs of Golaud break the silence, and Arkel, wise and calm, bids them leave the little dead mother with her child.

The Debussy setting is in the most modern music-drama manner, with nothing of set solos or ensembles which can be singled out as special features of the musical score. The French composer is a master in the handling of orchestral color and he has made his music merely a tonal commentary and illustration of the Maeterlinck drama.

THE SULTAN OF SULU

"The Sultan of Sulu," a musical satire with lyrics and dialogue by George Ade and music by Alfred G. Wathall was produced at the Studebaker Theatre, Chicago, March 11, 1902.

CHARACTERS.

Ki-Ram, the Sultan of Sulu.
Col. Jefferson Budd, of the Volunteers.
Lieut. William Hardy, of the Regulars.
Hadji Tantong, the Sultan's private secretary.
Datto Mandi, of Parang.
Wakeful M. Jones, agent and salesman.
Dingbat, captain of the guards.
Rastos, Didymos, } Nubian slaves.
Henrietta Budd, the Colonel's daughter.
Miss Pamela Frances Jackson, judge advocate.
Chiquita, wife number one.
Galula, the faithful one.
Ki-Ram's other wives.
The four Boston schoolma'ams.
United States soldiers, marines, imperial guards, American girls, slaves, natives and attendants.

Sulu, or Jolo, is the largest of the southerly islands in the Philippine group. The Sultan, whose real name is Hadji Mohammed Jamulul Ki-Ram, has hitherto found his rule undisputed save by certain chiefs with whom he has kept up a running warfare, one feature of which has been the abduction of women. The natives of Sulu are Mohammedans, polygamists and slaveholders. In 1899, after the Spanish-American war, the American troops land in Sulu and after some parleying, come to a peaceable agreement with the Malay ruler, who retains his title of Sultan and becomes governor at a fixed salary. "The Sultan of Sulu" shows what might have happened.

When the curtain rises the natives are celebrating in song the majesty of the Sultan and his brother, the Sun, with the Sultan somewhat in the lead. Six of Ki-Ram's wives appear for the morning round-up and Hadji, the private secretary, calls the roll. He also informs them that their uncle, the Datto Mandi of Parang, is encamped near the city, having come for the purpose of recapturing them. They express their entire willingness to be recaptured and remind him that it was only because they were offered their choice between an ignominious death and Ki-Ram that they hesitated and chose Ki-Ram.

The next important event is the arrival of Lieut. William Hardy of the United States Regulars, with a company of soldiers. He announces their mission, which is as follows:

> We want to assimilate, if we can
> Our brother who is brown;
> We love our dusky fellow man
> And we hate to hunt him down.
> So, when we perforate his frame,
> We want him to be good,
> We shoot at him to make him tame,
> If he but understood.

While the Sultan is closeted in his palace, sending out word that he will die before he surrenders, there arrives Colonel Budd, a military hero, his eye fixed on Congress, with his daughter Henrietta Budd, Wakeful M. Jones, Pamela Frances Jackson and the four schoolma'ams. Learning that the Sultan is within making his will, Mr.

Jones unheeding Chiquita's warning that death is the punishment for entering the majestic presence unheralded, rushes into the palace to talk life insurance.

"Poor man," sighs Chiquita. "Don't worry about Mr. Jones," returns Hardy, reassuringly. "He's from Chicago."

Ki-Ram comes out in funereal black, the picture of woe. He expects to die and enumerates the reasons of regret for leaving the smiling isle of Sulu. Budd interrupts his farewell speech to tell him that they have only come to take possession of the island and to teach the benighted people the advantage of free government. "We hold that all government derives its just power from the consent of the governed," he continues. "Now, the question is, do you consent to this benevolent plan?"

"Are all the guns loaded?" inquires Ki-Ram, looking carefully around.

"They are."

"I consent," says Ki-Ram.

His attention being called to the luscious quartet of schoolma'ams, he is visibly impressed with the new scheme of education. The next step is to change him from a sultan to a governor, that noblest work of the campaign committee. While Ki-Ram and Budd are left together talking politics, the former feels a draught and looking around finds his worst suspicions confirmed. Galula, the charter member of the bevy of wives, is fanning him. Reminded by him that absence makes the heart grow fonder, she sadly departs. Ki-Ram, under the influence of several cocktails (Colonel Budd has given him the glad information that the cocktail, as well as the constitution, follows the flag) suppresses his jubilant desire to climb a tree and instead proposes to Miss Pamela Frances Jackson, who, when she learns that she is merely wanted to complete a set of wives, threatens in her capacity as judge advocate to make him give up all of them. He consoles himself with the idea that he will thus get rid of Galula, while the wives are delighted with the prospect of being grass-widows, as they are getting on famously with the soldiers.

Ki-Ram is interrupted in his proposal of marriage to the four schoolma'ams by the preparations for the inaugural. One of the preliminaries is the presentation of a silk hat as the insignia of office. All the characters previously introduced enter, the Sultan assumes the hat and the band plays "The Star Spangled Banner."

Act II opens on the hanging gardens of the palace. The natives are singing a lullaby to Ki-Ram, who is oversleeping himself in the apartment below. While they are singing, Ki-Ram appears in his pajamas. His head is wrapped in a large towel. He carries in one hand a water-pitcher, and in the other his silk hat. The expression on his face is one of extreme misery. He dips the towel in the ice-water and holds it against his throbbing brow. Discovering numerous specimens of the insect family disporting themselves about him, he does battle with them and then breaks forth into a doleful song whose burden is "R-E-M-O-R-S-E." It appears that Ki-Ram has communed with the cocktail on the preceding night and has absorbed twenty-three of these concoctions. His dejection is not lessened by Judge Jackson's information that seven of his wives have been granted divorces and that he may keep only one. He is trying to decide which one to keep when Henrietta Budd appears in a stunning outfit, with her arms full of roses, and he resolves not to keep any of them. When he makes violent love to her, she warns him as a titled foreigner, that although she is an American girl she is not an heiress. "Henrietta," returns Ki-Ram, "you wrong me. I am Sulu, not English."

Pamela pursues Ki-Ram like Nemesis and informs him that he must keep one wife and that one must be the first one, who is Galula. He is further overwhelmed by the news that according to the law he will have to pay each wife alimony equivalent to one-half his income. Hadji suggests as a way out of this financial difficulty that Datto Mandi recapture the wives. Overjoyed at the suggestion, Ki-Ram immediately appoints the unwilling Hadji bearer of the message to Mandi that, while the Imperial Guards are over at the north wall repulsing an imaginary attack, he can come in by the south gate and get his nieces. Soon after Hadji's departure rifle-shots are heard and he is brought in between two marines "badly mussed up," the traitorous message having been found upon his person. Ki-Ram pleads ignorance as to who sent it but Pamela's legal mind has its suspicions. Reminding him that he hasn't paid his alimony on time, she has him handcuffed to Hadji and put under guard. The two, having opportunity to cogitate, hatch up a scheme to marry off the wives. Budd and Chiquita fall easily into the net and gradually the rest of the harem pair off with members of the Imperial Guard. They are looking for someone to perform the ceremony when the unpleasant Pamela again spoils things by the decision that a divorcée cannot remarry within the year. Meantime, a fierce and bearded warrior, none other than the Datto Mandi of Parang, approaches stealthily and is about to despatch Ki-Ram with his long sword, when that worthy is saved by Jones, who has just insured his life for 50,000 pesos.

There is a sound of brass band music and the Sulu Democratic and Republican marching clubs arrive with their candidates, the dusky waiters Didymos and Rastos. The disgusted Ki-Ram is about to go voluntarily to jail for the rest of his natural life, when a despatch-boat arrives with orders announcing among other things the Supreme Court's decision that the constitution follows the flag only on Mondays, Wednesdays and Fridays, in which case Ki-Ram is no longer convict number 47. He is the Sultan and his first act of regained authority is to send Pamela Frances Jackson back to Boston.

"The Sultan of Sulu" derives its importance not so much from its music as from the fact that in subject-matter it is probably the most national of all the comic operas written by an American. National weaknesses and idiosyncrasies are drawn with the peculiar dry humor best understood and enjoyed by a citizen of the republic.

Among the most successful songs in the opera are "Since I First Met You," "R-e-m-o-r-s-e," "Hike" (soldiers' song), "Rosabella Clancey," "Delia" and "Oh! What a Bump."

LE JONGLEUR DE NOTRE-DAME

"Le Jongleur de Notre-Dame," or "The Juggler of Notre-Dame," an opera in three acts with score by Jules Massenet and as text the poem of Maurice Léna, was first produced in 1902 at the theatre of Monte Carlo.

CHARACTERS.

Jean, the juggler.
Boniface, the cook of the abbey.
The priest.
A poet monk.
A painter monk.
A musician monk.
A sculptor monk.
Two angels.
The Virgin, an apparition.
Monks, voices of invisible angels, cavaliers, villagers, peasants, merchants, clerks, a crier monk, a comical fellow, a drunkard.

On a May-day in the Fourteenth Century, the people are frolicking in the square overlooked by the abbey, above whose door is placed a statue of the Virgin. With their songs mingle the cries of the merchants extolling such articles as leeks, cream cheeses, and white cabbages. Soon into the general tumult steal the notes of a hurdy-gurdy. The peasants, glad of a new diversion, give attention, and Jean arrives, grinding out a tune and bowing right and left. "Give place for the king of jugglers!" he says, quite grandly. He is very thin and wan and shabby and titters are heard from the crowd. "The king is not very splendid, truly a king of pitiful mien," comments one. "His Majesty, King Famine," announces another and the titters become roars.

Jean begins a grand harangue about the wonders of his performance but the crowd interrupts him to dance about the pathetic figure. As soon as he can evade them, he passes the wooden bowl. Only one piece of money rattles into it. A look of radiant gratitude comes into his face but a second glance drives it away, for the coin is bad.

Still hopeful, he begins his performance. "I can draw eggs from a hat," he suggests. "That old trick," sniffs the contemptuous audience. "I know the hoop dance," and he makes a few heavy turns. "Such lightsome grace," they remark, ironically, and dance about him again. "Shall I sing then?" he pleads, hoping against hope to light upon some way to please them. "Will the gentlemen have a love song?" The cries of the vendors drown his voice. "A battle song?" "No! no!" He mentions several by name. All are old stories and they will have none of them. He timidly enumerates all his repertory. At last in his desperation and against the inclinations of his truly pious soul, he proposes a sacrilegious drinking song and, behold! it is what they want. First he turns to the Virgin to implore her pardon, explaining his hunger and necessity, and then playing a prelude on the hurdy-gurdy, he regretfully begins his song, the people joining boisterously in the chorus.

Suddenly the abbey doors open and the priest appears upon the steps to hurl reproaches and maledictions at the irreverent crowd. All run away but Jean, who falls upon his knees and begs piteously to be forgiven. The priest has no leniency. Only hell is for such as he. Jean, crushed, falls on his face and finally drags himself before the Virgin to plead with her. The holy man, softened at last by his agony of soul, admits that there is one way to secure forgiveness for his transgression and that is to become a monk.

All his life Jean has had but one mistress, Liberty. It is hard to give her up but the priest argues unanswerably, and to crown it all, Friar Boniface, the cook, comes in carrying paniers full of flowers and food and bottles. Savory odors issue from the refectory and he hears the chanted grace. "Come," invites the priest, "to the table." "To the table!" repeats hungry Jean in ecstasy, and with a humble genuflection, he goes in, carrying his juggler's box.

In the second act, we find Jean a monk but humble, contrite and regretful. What homage can he do the Virgin? He cannot even sing, or pray to her in Latin. Feeling keenly his unworthiness, he remains silent and apart and the others chide him, all save Boniface, the cook. Humbly he acknowledges his fault. Well he knows that not one day since gentle Mary led him to this shelter has he earned his bread. Stupid, ignorant, he does nothing but eat and drink.

"A juggler, what a trade!" mocks the sculptor monk, Jean may be his pupil. There is nothing so great as sculpture. "Ah," says the painter monk, "You forget the brush. Painting is the great art." "No," cries the poet monk, coming up, "the place of honor goes to poetry," "But music ascends straight to heaven," insists a fourth voice. It is the musician monk. The discussion is heated indeed when the priest arrives to still the troubled waters with Latin admonitions.

Jean sits with his head in his hands. "Only I offer nothing to Mary," he sighs pathetically. But comforting Boniface is near. "Do not envy them, Jean," he counsels. "They are proud and Paradise is not for such as they. When I prepare a good repast, do I not do a work as meritorious? I am a sculptor of nougats; a painter in the color of my creams; a capon cooked to perfection is worth a thousand poems; a ravishing symphony is a table where order reigns. But, you see, to please the Virgin I remain quite modest, quite simple." "But, alas, I am too simple. She loves Latin and I know it not." "But she listens to French too," says the reassuring Boniface. He reminds Jean that Jesus greeted with the same smile the magi with their gold and myrrh and frankincense and the poor shepherd who had nothing to bring but an air played upon a reed pipe.

The last words linger in Jean's ears: "The poor shepherd — his reed pipe." What light illumines his soul! The shepherd, the juggler are worth as much to Mary as the king!

In the last act is seen the painter monk's new representation of the Virgin placed over the altar. The monks enter the chapel. Jean is before them, though he does not see them. He is on his knees in humble prayer. His hurdy-gurdy and his juggler's wallet are beside him. "He is mad," whisper the monks watching, "let us warn the priest." They see Jean salute the Virgin. "Give place," he cries in the accustomed words, "It is Jean, king of the jugglers! You prefer, perhaps, a love romance?" he inquires naively. He begins on several, but his memory fails him. "And now do you wish some juggling, some sorcery? Shall devils and griffins be evoked?" He stops ashamed. "It is force of habit. Between us, I do exaggerate," he falters, "the harangue is never absolutely true, you know." He juggles, he dances. The priest comes and would fall upon him but Boniface restrains him. At last, dizzy and exhausted, Jean falls prostrate in profound adoration. The indignant monks are about to precipitate themselves upon him when Boniface points to the Virgin. A light glows in her eyes. A divine smile touches her lips. From the canvas her hands extend over him in a maternal gesture. About them sound the voices of invisible angels.

"A miracle! A miracle!" cry the brotherhood. "Here am I," cries Jean, rapturously, and he falls dying into the arms of the priest. And voices of monks and of angels mingle as his soul takes its flight.

FEUERSNOT

"Feuersnot" or "The Fire Famine," a song poem in one act with text by Ernest von Wolzogen, suggested by a tale in "The Collected Legends of the Netherlands," and with music by Richard Strauss, was produced in Weimar Oct. 28, 1902.

CHARACTERS.

Schwieker von Gundelfingen, custodian of the castle.
Ortoff Sentlinger, the burgomaster.
Diemut, his daughter.
Elsbeth, }
Wigelis, } her companions.
Margret, }
Kunrad der Ebner.
Jörg Pöschel, the innkeeper.
Hamerlein.
Kofel, the smith.
Kunz Gilgenstock, a baker and brewer.
Ortlieb Tulbeck, a cooper.
Ursula, his wife.
Ruger Aspeck, a potter.
Walpurga, his wife.
Citizens, women, children, servants of the duke.

Until recently, there existed an ancient house in Audenarde, upon whose gable was inscribed the legend of the extinguished fires and the depiction of its last scene. The old witch story is the basis of the text of the opera.

The curtain rises to disclose a quaint spot in Munich in the Twelfth Century. To the right is the house of the Burgomaster and midway in the pretentious structure is a basket on pulleys, fastened to the top of the gable. There are numerous other houses, among them an inn. Two little side streets lead off in different directions. It is just before sundown, at the time of the winter solstice. A busy scene is shown; young couples pass by arm in arm and older citizens stand in the doors or look out of the windows. All are dressed in queer medieval costumes.

Down one of the side streets comes a procession of children and of pipers and drummers, pushing hand-carts on which are sticks of fire-wood that they have gathered for the big bonfire to be built outside the town in celebration of the day when the sun turns in the heavens. They stop before the Burgomaster's house and cry, "Give us wood for the solstice fires." As a final argument they suggest that the Burgomaster's daughter will not get a husband unless her father gives generously. Soon the big basket comes down filled with wood, which the children snatch eagerly. The stately Burgomaster himself appears and makes a speech and his handsome daughter, Diemut, comes out with three companions, all carrying pitchers of wine and baskets filled with sweetmeats. A feminine voice declares that Diemut looks like an angel and predicts that she will be a bride within the year. Then the children go on to the corner house near the inn and Jörg Pöschel, the innkeeper, tells of a strange guest who comes there for his meals, a quiet fellow who holds himself aloof in the old house "like an owl in a dark nest." Old Ortlieb tells of the former inhabitants of this house. They were descendants of a Moorish giant, whom Duke Henry the Lion brought with him when years before he entered the town. God gave the giant a certain time in which to become a Christian. Nobody knows how he died but, at any rate, all his descendants were wicked sorcerers, the last of whom were driven from the town many years ago.

MADAME FRITZI SCHEFF.

She is one the most popular light opera singers now before the public, is a Viennese by birth, the daughter of Mme. Hortense Scheff Yager, prima donna at the Imperial Opera House, Vienna, and of Dr. Yager, a prominent Vienna physician. From her mother she received her early musical training. Made her debut in Frankfort as Juliet. Sang in all the cities of Europe in grand opera and came to the United States in 1900, appearing in Fidelio, La Boheme, and I Pagliacci. Is in private life the wife of Baron von Bardeleben, an officer in the German Hussars. She was nicknamed by Paderewski, "the little deviling of grand opera."

Kofel, the smith, declares that what is told about the giant's descendants are only old women's tales and that they were really good men. This leads to a heated discussion. The children batter upon the doors of the former house of the sorcerer and Kunrad, disturbed at the noise, comes out. He is young and handsome and distinguished in bearing. He asks them what they want and they explain, adding that if he is a bachelor and does not give them wood no woman will look at him. He tells them to take the wooden shutters off the windows, and tear everything from the house that is combustible and take it away. He even throws in his old scripts, for he fears he has been losing all the tangible joys of life through poring over them.

While this has been going on, Kunrad has had eyes only for Diemut and the maiden has not failed to return his glances. Then, growing emboldened, he kisses her, much to the entertainment of the crowd. The Burgomaster chides him, and Diemut is indignant to the point of tears. She runs into the house, promising that he shall be sorry. Some one in the crowd says that tears mean love.

The children and the older folk go to make the bonfire outside the town. Only Kunrad lingers. Diemut comes to the window to comb her hair and Kunrad inquires what he has done to deserve such treatment. She relents, apparently, and invites him to come up in the basket. Overjoyed, he gets in and Diemut now has her revenge, for she draws it only half way up and leaves him hanging there. Then she mocks him and suggests his jumping out or climbing up on her hair. She calls her companions and they summon the others, and soon all the town is there to hoot and jeer at him. Then Kunrad invokes his master, the sorcerer, and asks for aid; and all the lights and fires upon the hearths are extinguished. The old people and the children are disconsolate but the lovers do not so much dislike the situation.

The castle custodian threatens to imprison Kunrad in the tower as soon as he can get him. Even severer threats are made. Kunrad reminds them that they brought it upon themselves and that it is for them to find the solution. Then he manages to climb upon the roof from which he delivers them an oration. He chides them for their narrow prejudices. The man whom they had driven away had not been evil but they could not see it. He had wished only to bring fame and blessing to the town. He had tried to introduce wagons with four wheels, instead of carts, and many other like improvements but they would have none of his doctrine of progressiveness. People who wished to advance with the world moved away. As for himself, he had come to finish his master's work. They distrusted him, and the woman he loved spurned him. But a woman's heart is the source of all warmth and light, he declares, and only through Diemut and her yielding herself to him can they regain their fires.

The people cry to Diemut in her house that it is her duty to get back the fires for them. Suddenly Kunrad disappears into her room. Soon a light shines from the windows and many others in the town answer it. Then Kunrad and Diemut, in each other's arms, look out from the casement and the opera ends with a pæan of joy and love.

In his operas Richard Strauss has reduced the vocal part to even greater subserviency to the dramatic action itself than did Wagner. His works are written with the voice of the singer going a way seemingly wholly independent of anything in the instrumental score. Talking is approached as nearly as is possible, and of formal melodies there is little, while set numbers are wholly wanting. The orchestra has the important part and "Feuersnot" could be given satisfactorily and with virtually as great effectiveness with the dialogue spoken as it can with it sung. Interesting moments in the score are the opening chorus for the children, in which they beg for wood for the solstice fire; the music for Diemut, when first she appears among the children; the legend sung by Tulbeck, "Als Herzog Heinrich mit dem Löwen kam" ("When great Duke Henry with the lions came"); the declamatory scene for Kunrad, in which he responds to the children's demands for wood for the solstice illumination; his lengthy song-speech, "Dass ich den Zauber lerne" ("That I should magic learn"); the Burgomaster's solo; Kunrad's "Fuersnot! Minnegobot!" ("Need of fire! Need of love!"); Diemut's song, "Mitsommernacht! Wonnige Wacht!" ("Midsummer Night! Time of Delight!") which is one of the most melodious numbers in the score; Kunrad's "Hilf mir, Meister!" ("Help me, Master!") and the long descriptive scene which follows, which is musically directed at Munich and its treatment of both Wagner and Strauss himself. In it appear motifs from the works of Wagner and from Strauss' own opera "Guntram" which are heard in both voice and orchestra when Kunrad speaks of the spirits that once dwelt in the house but which were driven forth through lack of appreciation. Another striking number is the elaborate symphonic orchestral poem, which pictures the yielding of Diemut to Kunrad and the return of light to the town, a number which has found its way into the concert repertory and has been generally admired.

ADRIENNE LECOUVREUR

"Adrienne Lecouvreur," an opera in four acts with music by Francois Cilèa and text by A. Colautti after the work of Scribe and Legouvé was produced in Milan in 1903.

CHARACTERS.

Maurice, Comte de Saxe.
The Prince de Bouillon.
The Abbé de Chazeuil.
Michonnet, prompter of the Comédie Francaise.
Quinault, Poisson, Majordomo, — sociétaires.
Adrienne Lecouvreur, of the Comédie Francaise.
The Princesse de Bouillon.
Mlle. Jouvenot, Mlle. Dangeville, — sociétaires.
The Duchesse d'Aumont.
The Marquise.
The Baroness.
A maid.
Ladies, gentlemen, valets, lackeys.
Ballet consisting of Paris, Mercury, Juno, Pallas, Venus, Amazons, and Cupids.

In the greenroom of the Comédie Francaise, Michonnet, the prompter, is having a sad time of it. Mlle. Jouvenot wants her powder; Poisson is mad for rouge; Mlle. Dangeville is dying for her fan; Quinault has instant need of his coat; a peremptory voice demands a handkerchief; another calls for a sword.

Michonnet reflects that he sometimes pays a good price for his ambition to be an actual sociétaire or a member of the Comédie Francaise, and for his desire to be ever near Adrienne. While he is thus reflecting, the Prince de Bouillon, accompanied by his sycophant, the Abbé de Chazeuil, come to pay their compliments to Adrienne, who soon appears. Dressed as Roxana, she is studying her role. A magnificent necklace, presented to her by the Queen, hangs about her neck. She rehearses a passage and the little audience breaks into applause.

It is easy to see why Adrienne's great gifts are making her the idol of Paris. With an impulse of gratitude, she goes over to Michonnet and declares that whatever success she may have had she owes to him, her faithful and disinterested friend and teacher. Pleased and happy, he is encouraged to endeavor to tell her, a little later when they are alone, what for years he has been trying to say, that he worships her. His uncle, the pharmacist, has just left him 10,000 pounds and he is at a loss what to do with it. Sometimes he has "a mad idea of marrying."

"Fine," exclaims Adrienne. Sometimes, she confesses, shyly, the same idea has occurred to her. She loves? "Yes." Why not tell this true friend, the state of whose feelings, alas, she does not guess. The object of her affection is merely a young officer in the service of the Comte de Saxe, son of the King of Poland and heir to the estates of Courland. He is fighting to regain his own and once saved her from insult at the risk of his own life. Only today he has returned from war, and will be at the theatre. And Michonnet goes away, his love too true to turn to resentment when it finds itself not reciprocated.

The lovers steal an interview before the play. Adrienne is full of questions as to Maurice's advancement. Has he won the favor of the Count? The Count is very difficult to please. Then how she would like to meet him and intercede! But the Count is a dangerous man, warns Maurice. Yes, admits Adrienne, all women love him. Maurice pretends to be jealous, and then to be consoled by her promise to meet him after the play.

Meantime, the Prince, who is trying to break off an entanglement with Duclos, the actress, intercepts a letter, which he believes she has written and which bids Maurice come that night to the villa the Prince built for her. The Prince plans to surprise them and by playing the role of a betrayed lover, to terminate the affair. He therefore invites the entire company of the Comédie to supper there. Adrienne has played as never before but her triumph is robbed of its sweetness by a message from Maurice, canceling their engagement. She has little heart for the Prince's supper-party but consents to go upon learning that the Comte de Saxe is to be present.

It is not Duclos, but the Princesse de Bouillon, whose agent she is, who has made the rendezvous at the villa. Maurice, it may be explained, is the Comte de Saxe himself. She is completely in love with him and to complicate matters, she holds the success of his political enterprises in her hands. He is delighted to learn that through her intercession the Cardinal has consented to his raising an army. From some half tangible change in his manner, she ventures, scarcely believing it herself, that he loves another woman, and sees in his face that her suspicions are correct. She haughtily demands the name of her rival and he refuses to disclose it. Just then the supper guests arrive, and the Prince orders the trap to be closed. The Princess, aghast at the sound of her husband's voice, hides in an adjacent apartment. Maurice is presented to the astonished Adrienne in his true person. He manages to whisper to her that he is true, and asks her to guard the apartment containing the other woman. Adrienne yields to an impulse of generosity and offers to unlock the garden gate for her. On the way the jealous Princess discovers that this is the woman to whom she has lost her lover. They strive to learn each other's identity but the darkness is too dense.

In Act III, the Princess, with no clue but the memory of Adrienne's wonderful voice, enlists the aid of the Abbé and goes upon her hunt. She gives a reception. Adrienne is among the guests and when she speaks, the Princess knows that her quest is ended. Adrienne from the incident of a lost bracelet also learns that she confronts her rival.

The women exchange pleasantries, referring to the night of the rendezvous. Adrienne is asked to recite and she addresses to the Princess a passage from "Phèdre" which fits her all too well.

The fourth act passes at the house of Adrienne, whose doubts of Maurice have made her ill. The faithful Michonnet comes to comfort her. He presents to her, as a birthday present, the necklace the Queen had bestowed upon her and which Adrienne had sold to pay the debts of Maurice. Michonnet has redeemed it with his little fortune. Adrienne's fellow actors flock in to pay their compliments. A belated parcel is brought to her. It appears to be from Maurice and contains a faded bouquet of hers. Its strange perfume makes her faint; its insult tears her heart. But Maurice follows soon after to offer his hand, as well as his throne, if fortune restores it to him. She tries to realize her joy but is strangely dazed. It is her happiness? No! It is his flowers? He sent no flowers!

She reels and falls, gradually losing consciousness of her surroundings. The room is full of phantasms. Just before she dies she has a moment of transcendent joy in which she realizes that Maurice loves her. But the Princess has worsted her rival. The bouquet had been poisoned.

HELENE

"Hélène" or "Helen of Troy," a lyric poem in one act with words and music by Camille Saint-Saëns, was first produced in Monte Carlo in 1904.

CHARACTERS.

Helen.
Venus.
Pallas.
Paris.
Spartans, nymphs and cupids, Trojans.

The work is founded on the immortal story of Helen of Troy. The incidents subsequent upon her abduction by Paris are set forth in a series of seven scenes.

The first scene, which is remarkably brief, shows the exterior of the palace of King Menelaus, illuminated for a fête. From within is heard the chorus chanting the praises of King Menelaus and of Queen Helen.

In Scene II, Helen is seen exhausted and distrait. standing at the top of a cliff by the sea. It is daybreak. The Queen is trying to escape from the net which Paris has spread about her. She finds her greatest difficulty in the fact that she loves him and does not wish to be free. At last, she declares she will be worthy of her race and true to her ties and is about to cast herself into the sea when Venus appears above the waves and prevents her self-destruction. It is to the Goddess' purpose that her victorious rival in the affection of Paris shall live, sin, and bear the consequences. In desperation Helen denies her love for Paris, but Venus reads her heart and says, "The story of your loves shall the Muse of History engrave on some undying monument." Warning Helen that she will soon lead the son of Priam to her retreat, she disappears with her nymphs.

Paris comes as Venus has said, and pays eloquent and impassioned suit, assuring Helen that stern Sparta is no home for such as she but that the land of the Trojans, with its radiant hills and valleys is a fitter setting for her transcendent loveliness. She protests that it is only Menelaus that she loves, but gradually is brought to confess that she, the daughter of Zeus, has lied, and that her heart belongs to him. Having thus yielded, she calls upon the gods to save her from herself. Pallas comes in thunderbolts and shows her what the consequences of her surrender to Paris will be. The Goddess places in the sky a vision and bids the lovers look upon Troy in flames and Priam done to death. The amorous Paris swears that even should the sun burst its bonds and burn up the universe he still would be true to his love. Helen casts aside her last scruple, gladly relinquishing home, husband, and children for a "love that is stronger than death or the gods." They embark in a ship sailing for Troy and are borne away.

SALOME

Salome, a grand opera in one act, its text by Oscar Wilde, its music by Richard Strauss, received its premier production at the Royal Opera, Dresden, Dec. 9, 1905. It was prohibited in England owing to the fact that Biblical characters are introduced. In America, it was first produced Jan. 17, 1907, at the Metropolitan Opera House in New York, where its further presentation was immediately forbidden, only one performance being given.

CHARACTERS.

Salome, the daughter of Herod's wife.
Narraboth, a Syrian, captain of the guard.
Iokanaan, John the Baptist, a prophet of the Lord.
Herod Antipas, Tetrarch of Judea.
Tigellinus, a young Roman.
Naaman, the executioner, a huge negro.
The Cappadocian.
Herodias, Herod's wife.
Page of Herodias.
Pages, Jews, Nazarenes, slaves of Salome.

The story is suggested by the Biblical account of the decapitation of John the Baptist at the caprice of the daughter of Herodias.

The curtain rises on a terrace of the palace of Herod, tetrarch of Judea. Here are Narraboth, the Syrian, and a number of soldiers and pages; in the background is seen a cistern surrounded by a wall in which Iokanaan, or John the Baptist, is held prisoner. The moon, which proves the subject of an ensuing multitude of amazing similes, gleams in the sapphire of the Oriental sky. Narraboth is speaking of the beauty of Salome with whom he is in love. Just then Salome herself comes in from the feast, rejoicing to be free from the caresses of her licentious stepfather, Herod. As she reflects upon the glory of the night, the voice of Iokanaan issues forth solemnly, uttering the words "The Lord hath come: the Son of Man is at hand!" Salome starts, listens and demands that he who has spoken be brought forth for her to see. Waving aside the slave of Herod, who bids her return to the royal company, she uses her arts upon the doting Narraboth so effectually that he disobeys Herod's orders and brings the prophet from the cistern. No sooner does she see him, splendid in manly beauty and stately in bearing, than her barbaric nature yields to his attraction, and she bursts forth in a passionate expression of her longing for him. He repulses her, speaking the name of the Lord, calling her daughter of Babylon and of Sodom and telling her that she is no better than her sinful mother. But unabashed, she renews her ravings over his physical beauty, and begs for a touch of his mouth. Again he repulses her and again and again she repeats, "Suffer me to kiss thy mouth, Iokanaan."

Mourning over the degeneracy of the time, he returns to his cistern but not before the unhappy Narraboth, who has witnessed the scene, slays himself, and falls between them. It is he whose father was a king, whom Herod drove from his kingdom; whose mother was a queen, whom Herodias made her slave.

Herod, the Queen and their retinue come in from the banquet-hall. They speak of Iokanaan and his prophecies and of the Nazarene who changed water into wine at a marriage in Galilee and who healed two lepers before the gate of Capernaum simply by touching them. Herod's eyes are only for Salome. He begs her to dance that he may better observe her charms. She refuses; he implores; he offers her anything that she may ask "even unto the half of his kingdom." Then she dances the dance of the seven veils and the king asks what she will have in reward. Even the degenerate Herod is shocked when she asks for the head of John the Baptist on a silver platter. He urges her to suggest something else, anything else; untold wealth, emeralds, pearls, turquoises and amber, white peacocks with gilded beaks; at last even the veil of the sanctuary, but she is obdurate. Finally he yields to her terrible will and orders the executioner to the cistern, while Salome, shaking with emotion, leans over listening for the death-struggle. Finally when the huge arm appears, she takes the bleeding head from the shield, and madly kisses its lips. Even the stars flee from the sky and the face of the moon is hidden behind clouds. As Herod, in fright and horror, hastens to depart, he hears the voice of Salome chanting "I have kissed thy mouth, Iokanaan."

"Kill that woman," cries Herod and the soldiers crush beneath their shields Salome, daughter of Herodias, Princess of Judea.

Salome had been widely heralded as unclean and revolutionary. It has proved the greatest operatic sensation since Wagner. The story is laid in the days of the decadent Roman Empire, which gives an opportunity and, perhaps, presents a necessity for a flagrant display of sensualism and earthiness. It was received with greater suspicion because the text came from the pen of Oscar Wilde, a text replete with the most unique and glowing poetical figures. Strauss in his score has caught the spirit of the text with the hand of genius. In orchestration, he is a veritable revolutionist, putting aside all previously made rules, and introducing startling effects which no one before him has been daring enough, or possibly creatively big enough to employ. The work is overpowering in the vividness of its musical description. Every sound has been pinioned in the score from the screaming of white peacocks to the dripping of blood. The whole work is dramatic to a degree and it would be difficult to find another moment in opera of tenser suspense than that in which Salome waits at the cistern for the head of John.

The diversity of opinion as expressed in the countless magazine and newspaper discussions of the opera is both amazing and amusing.

MADAM BUTTERFLY

"Madam Butterfly," a Japanese lyric tragedy, is founded on the book of John Luther Long, and the drama by David Belasco with Italian libretto by L. Illica and G. Giacosa. Its music is by Giacomo Puccini. It was first produced at the Scala Theatre in Milan in 1904 and received an adverse verdict. The following year it was revived in slightly changed form and with changed fortunes. Its first American presentation occurred in October, 1906, in Washington, D. C.

CHARACTERS.

Madam Butterfly, Cho-Cho-San.
Suzuki, Cho-Cho-San's servant.
Kate Pinkerton.
Lieut. B. E. Pinkerton, of the United States Navy.
Sharpless, United States Consul at Nagasaki.
Goro, a marriage broker.
Prince Yamadori.
The Bonze, Cho-Cho-San's uncle.
Trouble, Cho-Cho-San's child.

Lieutenant Pinkerton of the United States Navy, who is temporarily stationed at Nagasaki, is about to contract a Japanese marriage, assisted by Goro, a marriage broker, with Cho-Cho-San, known as the Butterfly. He has leased a cottage on the hills above Nagasaki and overlooking the harbor. The opera opens as he and Goro are inspecting the dwelling and its surroundings. His friend, Sharpless, United States Consul at Nagasaki, comes upon the scene and to him Pinkerton explains his plans. Sharpless makes an earnest effort to dissuade the Lieutenant from his rash idea, arguing that while a Japanese marriage might be only a joke to him, it could prove all too serious to the little bride. Butterfly, appearing with her mother and relatives, charms Sharpless by her attractive manner and evidently lovable nature. He learns from his conversation with her that, as he feared, she looks upon the marriage quite seriously. In order to prepare herself for it, she even has secretly renounced her faith, thus severing all ties with the past.

Despite the good counsel of Sharpless, Pinkerton persists in signing the contract in the presence of the relatives and friends of Butterfly. While the drinking and rejoicing that follow this event are in progress, Bonze, the Buddhist priest, the uncle of Cho-Cho-San appears, cursing and denouncing her for having given up her religion. Pinkerton ends it by ordering everyone off the premises. There follows an exquisite love-scene in which Pinkerton succeeds in winning Butterfly back to smiles and happiness.

Three years elapse. Pinkerton long ago has been called away from Nagasaki, and Suzuki, Butterfly's faithful servant, announces to her mistress that the money left for their maintenance is almost gone, and voices her fears that the Lieutenant will never come back. For this lack of faith she is severely reprimanded. Sharpless appears with a letter in his hands which Butterfly at once surmises to be from Pinkerton speaking of his return. In this surmise she is correct but Sharpless has not the courage to tell her that while Pinkerton is returning, he is returning with an American wife. The marriage broker again has been active, and has urged upon Madam Butterfly the advisability of marriage with Prince Yamadori, a wealthy nobleman. In this effort he is seconded by Sharpless, both of them explaining that under the Japanese law, Pinkerton's continued absence is sufficient grounds for divorce. After persistent refusal, Madam Butterfly sends Suzuki from the room, and the maid returns bearing Pinkerton's fair-haired child. Then Madam Butterfly turning to Sharpless says unanswerably, "Look, can such as this well be forgotten?" The Consul leaves without having delivered his news. Now across the harbor floats the boom of the gun. Rushing to the window, Madam Butterfly sees that it is the salute of the American man-of-war. She and Suzuki deck the cottage with flowers and seat themselves at the windows with the child, to await Pinkerton's coming. The maid and child fall asleep, leaving Butterfly watching alone for her lover.

The third act opens to find the new day dawning, and Butterfly still at her post. The light awakens Suzuki and she persuades Butterfly to take the child and rest. While she is gone Pinkerton comes with his American wife but he hastens away, unable to face the situation. When Butterfly comes again fluttering with happiness, the presence of the other woman seems to bring the truth to her. It is then that the little Nipponese heart breaks. Quite simply and without resentment, she tells the American wife that if her husband will return in half an hour he may have the child, and that "All will be well." When they have gone, Madam Butterfly drives Suzuki from the room, and binding the eyes of Trouble, the child, with a scarf, she places in his hands a doll and an American flag. Taking her father's sword she goes behind the screen in the rear of the room. There is a short pause, the sword clatters on the floor, she totters out and falls dead at the baby's side.

It is said that Puccini considers "Madam Butterfly" his best work. In fact, he admitted this when watching from the wings its first American performance in the language of the original libretto. "I confess" said he, "that I am very fond of my Madam Butterfly. The subject appealed to me from the first. It gives fuller expression to my temperament and to my sentiment, than any other of my works, not even excepting 'La Bohème.' "

In this idea he is supported by the critics, a thing which does not always follow. It is generally conceded to be the greatest of his works. It is a convincing exponent of Italian operatic renaissance, and justifies Puccini's admirers in their asseveration that the mantle of Verdi has fallen on his shoulders. The score is in the essentially modern manner with no distinct arias, solos or ensembles. The orchestra plays the prominent role in illustrating and describing the dramatic situations and the emotions felt by the various persons on the stage. Much of the vocal part is written in the "conversational" style of recitative but there are certain important scenes which are of great melodic beauty. Of such are the impassioned love duet for Pinkerton and Butterfly, with which the first act closes; Butterfly's description to Suzuki of how some day Pinkerton will return; her declaration to Sharpless that she will care for little Trouble and the admirable orchestral interlude which portrays musically Butterfly's long watch throughout the night before Pinkerton comes to her.

ARIANA ET BARBE-BLEUE

"Ariana et Barbe-Bleue" or "Ariana and Blue Beard," an opera in three acts, the text arranged by Maurice Maeterlinck with music by Paul Dukas was produced in Paris at the Opéra Comique in March, 1907.

CHARACTERS.

Ariana.
The nurse.
Selysette, Mélisande, Ygraine, Bellangère, Alladine (pantomime role), — the five wives.
Blue Beard.
An old peasant.
Second peasant.
Third peasant.
The crowd.

The first act shows how Ariana, the sixth wife, opened the forbidden door. A sumptuous apartment in Blue Beard's castle is disclosed. It is in the form of a semicircle. At the rear there is a great door and on each side of this are three smaller doors of ebony with locks and ornamentations of silver. Above the six smaller doors are six tall windows, which are open. It is evening and the chandeliers are lighted. Through the windows come the cries of an excited and indignant crowd below. From their disjointed utterances, it may be gathered that a beautiful, smiling young woman has just been conveyed in a coach to Blue Beard's castle. They say that she should be warned before the fatal doors close upon her forever. There have been five before her. That is too many! Some say that she knows all and that she is coming into the trap with her eyes open. But she is too lovely to die, so lovely that twenty lovers have followed her from her city and are weeping in the streets.

As the crowd discourses, the windows close quite of themselves and Ariana, the sixth wife, and her nurse enter the apartment. The nurse is full of fears about this new husband of whom such terrible things are rumored. Ariana assures her that she does not believe the wives are dead. At any rate she is going to know the secret. Her husband has given her the keys which open the bridal treasure. The six silver keys are to use, the golden key is forbidden. But that is the only one which counts with Ariana and she throws the others disdainfully upon the marble floor. The nurse hastily gathers them up and with the permission of her mistress unlocks one of the doors. It swings upon its hinges and a perfect shower of amethyst jewelry rains upon her. There are collars, aigrettes, bracelets, rings, buckles, girdles, diadems. Distracted, she plunges her arms deep into the purple treasure and fills her mantle to overflowing.

"They are beautiful," agrees Ariana. "Open the second door."

Breathless the nurse turns the key; the doors swing apart; and a dazzling eruption of sapphires falls about them. The third door is opened to release a milky rivulet of pearls; the fourth to emit a deluge of emeralds; from the fifth comes a tragic cascade of rubies, like a bloody warning; from the opened sixth flows a marvelous, bewildering cataract of diamonds. Only for a moment does the young wife gaze at the splendor. Now for the seventh forbidden door with the hinges and locks of gold! Disregarding the protests of the nurse she turns the key and throws open the door. Nothing but a dark opening is seen but from it issues, weirdly, the song of the five daughters of Orlamonde who have wandered through three hundred halls searching for the light. They see the great ocean through the window and fear to die; they knock upon the closed door but do not dare to open it.

Blue Beard comes quietly into the room and regards Ariana. "You, too," he observes, dryly. "I especially," says Ariana. "How long have they been there?" she asks.

"Some many days, some many months, the last a year. It was a very little thing that I asked."

"You asked more than you gave," returns Ariana.

"But you lose the happiness I wished for you," says Blue Beard looking sadly at his wife. "Only give up knowing and I shall yet pardon you."

But Ariana has no such idea. Blue Beard seizes her by the arm and involuntarily she utters a cry. The listening crowd below hear it; a stone crashes through the window. In a moment, the angry people rush into the house but Ariana advances calmly toward them.

"What would you?" she inquires. "He has done me no ill." And they go away shamefaced.

In Act II we see Ariana and her nurse descending the last steps of a subterranean stairway and plunging into almost complete obscurity. Five forms are crouched in a grotto, so motionless that she fears them dead. At the sound of her voice, they tremble. She runs to them to cover their faces with kisses, to caress them and to utter little cries of joy that their lips are fresh and their arms warm and living. She fancies they still are beautiful, but when the nurse brings the light they appear a desolate group, pale and emaciated, their hair disheveled, their clothing in rags. She hovers about them then with tender expressions of pity. They gaze at her beauty and inquire sadly whether she too has disobeyed.

"I have obeyed, but other laws than his," returns Ariana sententiously.

She asks them more of the experiences of their entombment. They tell her of their occupations, which are to pray, to sing, to weep and always to watch. Then Ariana scolds them gently for their passivity. Do they not know that outside is the springtide, the sunlight, the dew on the leaves, the smiling sea?

As she speaks, a jet of water falling from the roof of the vault extinguishes the lamp. Only for a moment is she disconcerted. Then she sees a faint light at the end of the vault and promises to lead them to it. With their aid, she climbs the high rocks which interpose. Groping along the wall she comes to a section bolted and barred. She would try her strength upon it but the others cry out in warning.

"My poor sisters," reproaches Ariana. "Why do you wish me to deliver you if you so adore your darkness?"

At last her struggles are successful and the prison is opened to the dazzling light of noon. Blinded, the five wives hide their unaccustomed eyes. When they can bear it, they look out and exclaim in delight at the trees, the green country, the distant village. Breathless they watch the figure of a peasant and count the strokes of the clock. Ariana tells them not to gaze at the light until they grow apprehensive but to profit by their temporary frenzy to get out of their tomb.

"Here is a stairway," she calls. "I do not know where it leads, but it is light. Come everybody." Half reluctantly they lift themselves up by the rocks and then disappear outside, dancing and singing in the light.

In Act III, we are taken again to Blue Beard's enchanted castle, where before the mirrors the five wives are decking themselves with jewels and flowers. Ariana runs from one to the other to assist in making them fine. They whisper questions about Blue Beard.

"You are going to be free and you must be beautiful," remarks Ariana. She counsels each to make the most of her special gift. She unbinds Mélisande's lovely hair; she loops back Ygraine's sleeves to show her charming arms. They have made nothing of themselves. It is not strange he did not love them for he had only their shadows.

The nurse rushes into the room, haggard and frightened, with the news that Blue Beard is coming under guard and that all the villagers have assembled to capture him. The wives hastily mount the stairway and gaze from the high windows. With hungry eyes they watch the ogre issue from his coach. They nearly faint with terror when the peasants attack him and rout him and the guards. When he falls wounded and the peasants bind him they cry out entreaties not to kill him. The mob invades the castle, and lays at the feet of the stately Ariana the bound and helpless Blue Beard.

"Here he is, madam," they say, proudly. "He shall do you no more harm." They proffer further aid but Ariana tells them it is not needed, and so they disperse. On their knees, the five wives gaze at their fallen lord. Ariana gently examines Blue Beard's wounds and the wives rise and vie with each other to do him service. Alladine, the wife who cannot speak their language, furtively kisses him.

When he has been cared for, Ariana cuts the cords which bind him and prepares to go. Blue Beard feeling himself free, raises himself and looks attentively at each of the five wives. Then, perceiving Ariana, he turns toward her. She gives him her hand in farewell and he tries to retain it but she releases herself gently and goes toward the door with her nurse. She asks them all in turn to go with her. The moon and the stars shine all along the road; the sea and the forest call; the dawn peers over the azure vault and shows the world inundated with hope. Are they coming?

But even Alladine, who sobs for a moment in her arms, cannot say yes.

"Adieu; be happy," says pitying Ariana through her tears, as she goes away. The women look intently at Blue Beard, who raises his head as the curtain goes down.

Herein we see the invasion of the opera by the problem. Woman's craving for emancipation and her reluctance to accept it when it comes to her are impressively set forth in this Maeterlinck fable. The music by Dukas, one of the younger of the French composers, is in the most advanced modern manner and has attracted to its author widespread attention, and won for him both enthusiastic approval and unqualified censure. The radicals hail him as a genius; the conservatives regard him as an extremist of almost dangerous type.

SKETCHES OF OPERAS

ABENCERAGES, Les — French opera in three acts, music by Cherubini, words by Jouy, first produced in Paris, 1813.

Abenteuer Händels, Ein (A Handel Adventure) — An operetta in one act, music by Carl Reinecke, text by W. Grove, first produced at Schwerin in 1874. This operetta is also called "Die Macht des Liedes," The Power of Song. Kathleen's parents insist upon her marrying a man whom she does not love, so she runs away from home. Händel's music awakens in the parents' hearts a longing for their child and they no longer oppose Kathleen's choice.

Abraham — German biblical opera, music by Seyfried, words by Castelli, produced in 1817.

Abreise, Die (The Departure) — Musical comedy in one act. Music by D'Albert, words by A. von Steigentesch and Ferdinand Grafen Sporck, first performed at Frankfurt A/M, 1898. Time, present; scene, the garden room of a German castle. Owing to a misunderstanding between a young couple the husband decides to leave home. In a touching song the wife laments his departure; he leaves her, returns and they become reconciled.

Abroad and at Home — English comic opera, music by William Shield, first produced in London, 1796

Abu Hassan — A one-act comic opera, music by Weber, words by Hiemer, produced at Dresden, in 1811, under the composer's own direction. The story is founded on a tale from the Arabian Thousand and One Nights.

Achebàr — Musical tragedy, words by Cardinal Alessandro Bichi, music by his secretary, the Abbé Mailly, produced at the episcopal palace of Carpentras, 1646.

Achille in Sciro, (Achilles in Scyrus) — Italian opera, music by Jomelli, words by Metastasio, produced in Vienna in 1745. Achilles was disguised as a woman at the court of Lycomedes, he was discovered by Ulysses and pursuaded to join the Greeks in the war against Troy.

Acis and Galatea — Pastoral opera, masque or serenata, music by Handel, words by Gay, with subsequent additions by Pope, Hughes and Dryden, first performed at Cannons in 1720 or 1721. Mozart rescored it for Van Swieten in 1788.

Acteon — French comic opera in one act, music by Auber, words by Scribe, first produced in Paris, 1836.

Adam und Eva — Opera by Johann Theile. First performed at Hamburg, Germany, in 1678. Text by von Richter is based upon the Bible story. This opera is significant because it is the first real German opera ever publicly performed in the German language. It was soon followed by others of its kind and the city of Hamburg thus became the birthplace of German opera.

Adieu, Hadrian — French grand opera, music by Méhul, words by Hoffmann, produced in Paris, June 4,

1799, but written in 1795. The theme is the Emperor Hadrian's campaign in Syria.

Adler's Horst, Des (The Eagle's Eyrie) — An opera in three acts, music by Franz Glässer, words by Van Holtei, first produced in Berlin in 1830. An eagle steals a child whose parents have been separated. In the end it is rescued and the parents united.

Admeto — Opera by Handel. First produced in London in 1727.

Adolphe et Clara; ou, Les Deux Prisonniers, (Adolph and Clara; or, The Two Prisoners) — French comic opera in one act, music by Dalayrac, words by Marsollier, first produced in Paris, 1799.

Adolph von Nassau (Adolph of Nassau) — Grand opera in four acts. Music by Marschner, text by von Heribert Rau, first produced at Hanover, Germany, in 1843. The story follows closely the history of Kaiser Adolph of Nassau, including the intrigue of archbishop Gerhard of Mainz, and the romance of Adolph and Imogena. This opera is one of the best of modern German romantic operas.

Adone (Adonis) — Italian pastoral opera, music by Monteverde, produced in Venice, 1639. Adonis was the youth for the possession of whom Venus and Proserpina quarreled.

Adonis — French opera, music by Cambert, produced in Paris, 1662. The story is from mythology. Adonis was a youth, loved by Venus, he was killed while hunting and from his blood the goddess caused the anemone to spring.

Adriano in Siria — Italian opera in three acts, music by Cherubini, first presented at Livourne, 1782.

Æneas — This well known hero of the Trojan War was often used as theme for operas in the Seventeenth and Eighteenth Centuries. The earliest opera on this subject is by Montverde, "Le Nozze d'Enea con Lavinia," and appeared at Venice, 1641. Others are by Franck, Hamburg, 1680; Uttini, Stockholm, 1756; Caporti, Naples, 1805.

Agnes — German grand opera by F. Motel, produced at Weimar in 1880. Agnes, the Angel of Augsburg, was the wife of Prince Albrecht III. of Bavaria. Because of her birth she was not recognized by the Duke of Bavaria, and she finally found a tragic death in the Danube in 1435. In 1834 at Dresden appeared Karl Krebs' opera on this same subject.

Agnes Sorel — Opera in three acts, music by Adalbert Gyrowetz, text by Sonnleither from the French, produced at Vienna, 1806. Joan of Arc's rescue of France forms the historical setting of the opera, and Agnes Sorel, mistress of Charles VII. of France, is the heroine.

Agnes von Hohenstauffen — German grand opera in three acts, music by Spontini, words by Raupach, the first act produced in Berlin, May 28, 1827, the entire opera June 12, 1829. The theme is the reconciliation of the Emperor Henry VI. of Germany with Henry the Lion by means of the marrige of their two children at Mainz in 1194.

Agrippina — Italian grand opera, music by Handel, produced in Venice, 1709. Agrippina was the mother of Nero and was murdered by him, when she tried to displace him with Britannicus.

Aladdin — English opera, music by William Shield, first produced in London in 1788.

Albion and Albanius — English opera. Music by L. Grabut, words by Dryden, the English poet. First performed in London in 1685. The music was of very little importance, the satire of the words is all that gained the opera any notice.

Alceste, ou le Triomphe d'Alcide (Alcestis, or the Triumph of Alcides) — French opera in five acts, music by Lully, words by Quinault, produced in Paris, Jan. 19, 1674. The story is from mythology. Alceste was the wife of King Admetus of Pheræ.

Alcestis — German opera, music by Gluck, words by Calzabigi, produced in Vienna, Dec. 26, 1767. It was produced in Paris in 1776, at which time the composer made some changes in the score, and the second version is now the more familiar one of the two.

Alchymist, Der (The Alchemist) — German opera by Spohr. First produced in 1830. Though really a very fine opera it met with only fair success and did not last long.

Alcibiade Solitaire — French opera in two acts, music by Louis Alexandre Piccinni, words by Cuvelier and Barouillet, first produced in Paris, 1824.

Alcidor — German opera, music by Spontini, words in French by Theauleon, translated into German by Herklots, produced in Berlin, May 23, 1825. The libretto was adapted from one of Rochon de Chabannes, which had been used by Dezede for his opera "Alcindor."

Alcina — Grand opera, music by Händel, produced in London, 1735. Alcina was a legendary enchantress of mediæval song and poetry.

Aleko — Russian opera, in one act, music by Rachmaninov, produced in Moscow in 1893.

Alesandro — Italian opera by Händel, produced at London in 1726 and five years later it reappeared under the title Poro. Subject is Alexander the Great, King of Macedonia, and his meeting with Porus, King of India.

Alessandro nell' Indie (Alexander in India) — Italian opera, music by Leonardo da Vinci, the painter and sculptor, words by Metastasio, produced in Rome, 1729. The subject of the libretto is the meeting of Alexander the Great and King Porus in India. It was the most successful of da Vinci's operas.

Alessandro Stradella — Romantic opera in three acts, music by Flotow, words after the French by W. Friedrich, written in 1844, and first produced in Hamburg.

Alexandre aux Indes (Alexander in India) — Opera by Mereaux, text by Morel after Racine's "Alexandre," produced at Paris in 1783. This libretto was a great favorite with Parisians.

Alfonso — Italian opera, music by Lampugnani, produced in London, 1744. Alphonse, King of Arragon and Navarre, was victorious against the Moors in the early part of the Twelfth Century.

Alfonso and Estrella — German romantic opera in one act, music by Schubert, produced in Weimar, 1854, though it was written in 1822. It was revised by Fuchs in Vienna, 1880.

Alfred, a Masque — Music by Arne, words by Thompson and Mallet, produced in 1740. It celebrated the succession of the House of Hanover to the English throne. The Masque will always be remembered as containing the song, "Rule Brittannia."

Ali Baba — French opera by Cherubini with text by Scribe and Mélesville, produced at Paris in 1833. Ali Baba is the well known hero of the story of The Forty Thieves who gains entrance to the cave by the magic phrase "open sesame."

Aline, Reine de Golconde (Aline, Queen of Golgonda) — French heroic ballet, music by Monsigny, words by Sedaine, produced in Paris, 1766. An outline for the libretto was first made by the Count of Boufflers.

Almahide — Italian opera, music attributed to Buononcini. This opera, produced in London, 1710, was the first performed there entirely in Italian.

Almira — German opera, music by Händel, produced in Hamburg, 1705 Revised by Fuchs in 1878 and given for the opening performance of the new Hamburg opera house.

Alona — German opera, music by Wilhelm Hill, libretto by O. Prechtler, first produced at Frankfurt, Germany, in 1882. Alona is the daughter of King Gudrum of Jutland. She falls in love with a young Dane, who comes to her father's court as a fugitive.

Alpenkönig und Menschanfeind (The Alpine King and the Misanthrope) — German opera in three acts. Music by Leo Blech, words by Richard Batka. First produced at Dresden, Germany, in 1903. Text is based upon the pretty folk song of the same name. Rappelkopf, the Misanthrope, hates all mankind and thoroughly enraged forsakes his family and flees to the mountains. But the Alpine King, a mountain spirit, shows him his error and he returns to his family. One of the sweetest songs is "Fair are the roses and the jessamine," sung to a polka air. The music of this opera displays the exceptional talent of the young composer. Musical effects both bold and charming, and a fearless use of tuneful melodies, mark Leo Blech as one of our best modern composers.

Alphons d'Arragone — French opera; music by Bochsa, text by Sourigiere, appeared at Paris in 1814. Alphonse I., King of Arragon and Navarre, was successful against the Moors in the early part of the Eleventh Century.

Alphonse et Leonore, ou l'Heureux Proces (Alphonse and Leonore, or the happy suit) — French comedy in one act with music by Gresnick, and text by C. L. D'Iray; produced at Paris in 1797.

Alte Mare, Die (The Old Story) — German opera in four acts. Music by Ladislaus Telenski, text by Braudrowski, first produced at Lemberg in 1907. Text is based upon Kraszewski's historical novel with the same title. The history of Poland in the Ninth Century forms the background for the Slavic myths and legends woven into an opera. The opera was very cordially received and the seventy-year-old Polish composer had reason to feel pleased.

Amadis — French opera in five acts, music by Lully, words by Quinault, produced in Paris, January 18, 1684. The hero of the opera is the Amadis of Gaul, who figured so prominently in mediæval romance.

Amalie — Czechic opera in four acts. Music by Zajc, libretto taken from Schiller's Rauber (Robbers). Produced at Agram, 1873.

Amanti Comici, Gli (The Comic Lovers) — Italian opera, music by Cimarosa, produced in Naples in 1778.

Amants de Verone, Les (The Lovers of Verona) — An opera by Marquis Richard d'Ivry, first produced in Paris, Oct. 12, 1878, and at Covent Garden, London, May 24, 1879. Shakespeare's "Romeo and Juliet" has been closely followed.

Amazones, Les (The Amazons) — Opera by Méhul, text by Jouy, produced at Paris, 1811. These fabled warrior women of antiquity are favorite subjects for operas and appear under many different titles. Méhul's opera, also called "La fondation de Thebes," tells of the founding of Thebes by the Amazons.

Amfiparnasso — A musical farce by Orazio Vecchi, produced at Modena, Italy, in 1594. This is one of the earliest forms of opera. It consisted of a series of madrigals for five persons. There was no overture and no instrumental accompaniment of any kind. When one character held the stage the other four sang behind the scenes, thus forming a forerunner for the later orchestra. These songs, which were solos, duets, or choruses (for not more than five), were full of melody and technical skill.

Amelia — See Masked Ball by Verdi.

Amica — Musical drama in two acts. Music by Mascagni, words by Bérel, translated into the German by Otto Neitzel. First produced in Cologne in 1907. Master Camoine decides that his niece Amica shall marry Giorgio who is sickly and deformed. She, however, loves Rinaldo, Giorgio's brother. Rinaldo does not know that Giorgio and Amica are betrothed and consents to elope with her. Giorgio follows the fugitives and the brothers are horrified when they face each other. Rinaldo can not forgive Amica for betraying his brother's love and flees across a raging torrent to escape to the mountains. Amica follows him but misses her footing and falls into the torrent. Rinaldo witnesses this and returns to his brother.

Amici di Siracusa, Gli (The Friends of Syracuse) — Italian opera, music by Mercadante, produced in Rome in 1824. The subject is taken from Schiller's poem "Bürgschaft."

Amor vuol Sofferenza (Love Will Suffer) — Italian comic opera, music by Leonardo Lee, produced 1739. The opera was also called Cive (That is to say) from one of the characters, who explained everything with this word. It was extremely popular.

Amours de Momus, Les (The Loves of Momus) — French opera-ballet in three acts and prologue, music by Desmarets, words by Duche, first produced in Paris, 1695.

Amphitryon, the Father of Hercules —Opera in three acts. Music by Grétry, text by Sedaine, produced at Paris, 1788. This opera was not a success, and with others of its kind proves that Gretry's field was in operas of a lighter vein.

Anacreon chez Polycrate — French opera in three acts, music by Grétry, words by J. H. Guy, first produced in Paris, 1797. This was Gretry's last opera and was very successful.

Anacreon; ou L'Amour Fugitif (Anacreon; or Love Fleeing) — French opera in two acts, music by Cherubini, words by Mendouze, first produced in Paris, 1803.

Andrea Crini — A very dramatic Bohemian opera; music by Tonecek; text by Bohnslav Benes, first produced at Prague in 1900. Andrea Crini, the son of Doge Crini of

Venice is discovered at the head of a plot to depose his father. He is brought before a tribunal for trial. The tribunal stands half in favor of his acquittal, and the father finds, to his horror, that he must decide his son's fate. Sacrificing parental affections, he sentences him to be executed. On the day of the execution the old father gives his people freedom, but when he hears the bells tolling his son's fate, he collapses.

Andrea Crini No. 2 — This opera has enjoyed a very marked success.

Andreasfest, Das (The Festival of St. Andrew) — German opera. Music by K. Grammann, libretto by R. Fels, produced at Dresden in 1882. A charming little love story at Innsbruck in which Emperor Maximilian figures.

André Chenier — Musical drama in four acts. Music by Umberto Giordano, words by L. Illica, first produced in Milan in 1896. Time, French revolution; scene, Paris. Story: André Chenier, a French poet, is condemned to die upon the guillotine. When his sweetheart, Madeline, learns this, she seeks his cell at night. Bribing the jailor she joins her lover and fearlessly the next morning she rides away with him in the death cart.

Andromaque — French lyric tragedy in three acts, music by Grétry, words by Pitra, first produced in Paris, 1780. The work is founded upon Racine's famous tragedy.

Andromeda — Italian opera, music by Manelli, words by Ferrari, produced in Venice, 1637. It is said to have been the first opera sung in a public theater.

Andromeda — Early French opera. Music by Girolamo Giacobbi. First produced at Bologne in 1610. It was so well received that it was reproduced in 1628.

Angelique et Medor — One act French comic opera by Ambroise Thomas, words by Sauvage, produced in the Opera Comique in Paris, May 10, 1843. It is no longer sung.

Angelo — Russian opera, music by César Cui, produced in St. Petersburg, 1876. The libretto is Bourenine's translation of Victor Hugo's drama by the same name. The opera is usually regarded as the composer's best, but it has never had any popular success. It is, however, sung to-day in Russia.

Angelus, The — An opera composed by Dr. E. W. Naylor, organist and lecturer in music at Emmanual College, Cambridge, with libretto by Mr. Wilfrid Thornely of Trinity Hall, Cambridge. It was first produced at Covent Garden, Jan 27, 1909, having received the £500 prize offered by Messrs. Ricordi for an original opera by a British born composer. The plot is based upon a discovery of the elixir of life.

Angiolina — Italian comic opera in three acts. Music by Antonio Salieri, text by Franceschi, produced at Prague, 1800.

Angla — Dramatic opera in one act. Music by Ferdinand Hummel, words by Axel Delmar. First performed at Berlin, 1893. Angla tries to persuade her lover, Duke Widerkind, to become a Christian. He hesitates, fearing the wrath of the gods. Later Charlemagne appears with a host of Christian women, saying that in a dream he had seen a pure woman cut down the heathen oak sacred to Wodan and now one of these women is to try this with his sword. But none has the courage. Then Angla begs for his sword, calls upon the Holy Trinity, and fells the oak. In its place appears a bright cross. When Widerkind sees this, he embraces Christianity. This is the best known of Hummel's operas.

Anna Bolena — Italian opera, music by Donizetti, words by Romani, produced in Milan, 1822. The heroine is Anne Boleyn, wife of Henry VIII., who met her death on the scaffold in 1536.

Ännchen von Tharau — Lyric opera in three acts. Music by Heinrich Hoffmann, words by Roderich Fels, first produced in Hamburg, Germany, in 1878. The poet Dach is in love with the beautiful girl Anna, the daughter of the parson in Tharau. Soon after their engagement, an old playmate of Anna's returns to the town and she realizes then that she does not love Dach and the poet generously gives her up. The little song "Ännchen von Tharau ist's die mir gefallt" ('tis the Anna of Tharau whom I love) has survived the opera, and is still very popular especially among Germans. Historically this little poem was dedicated by the poet Simon Dach (1605-1695) to the marriage of his friend Portatius and Anna Neander.

Annette et Lubin — French opera, music by Blaise, words by Favart, first produced in Paris, 1762, and again in 1800 with new music by Martini. It was very popular at the time. The plot is founded upon Marmontel's tale by the same name.

Antigone — German opera by Johann Adolph Hasse. First produced at Brunswick, Germany, in 1723. This was the first of this composer's operas, it met with success at the time, but was long since forgotten.

Antigono — Italian opera, music by Gluck, words by Métastase, first produced in Rome, 1756.

Antiochus and Stratonice — German opera by Graupner, produced at Hamburg in 1708. Antiochus I., also called Soter, fell in love with his stepmother, Stratonice. His father allowed him to marry her and made him King of all of his lands beyond the Euphrates.

Apajune (The Waterman) — Opera in three acts by Millöcker. Libretto by F. Zell and R. Genée. Place, the estate of Totroceni on the Dumbowitza River. Time, 1864. First produced at Vienna in 1880.

Apelle et Campaaspe — French opera in one act, music by Eler, words by Demonstier, first produced in Paris, 1798.

Aphrodite, Greek Goddess of Love — Opera; music by Camille Erlanger, words by Louis de Gramont. Produced at Paris in 1907 and at the Manhattan Opera House, 1908. Plot is based upon Pierre Louy's novel "Aphrodite." As produced by Mary Garden it was hailed by Parisians as one of the finest productions ever made at the Opera Comique in Paris. Mary Garden sings the leading role of Chryais, and in New York M. L. Boyle appeared as Demetrios.

Apollo et Hyacinthus — Opera with music by Mozart, produced at the University of Salzburg in 1767. The text was in Latin, and was a comedy based upon the story of these mythological characters.

Apollon et Coronis — French opera in one act, music by J. B. and Joseph Rey, words by Fuzelier, first produced in Paris, 1781.

Apothecary, The — Comic opera by Josef Haydn, written in 1768, and revived and rearranged by Dr. Hirschfield, and reproduced at Dresden in 1895 under the direction of Ernst Schuch. The story is amusing and tells us how a young man enters the service of an apothecary that he may be near the latter's ward whom he loves. The young lover with no taste for drugs is very timid and gains the hand of the girl only after many amusing incidents.

Arabi Nelle Gallie, Li (The Arabians in Gaul) — Italian opera in four acts, music by Pacini, produced in Milan, 1827. The plot is taken from Arlincourt's romance "Le Renégat."

Archers, The; or, Mountaineers of Switzerland — Opera in three acts, music by Benjamin Carr, words by William Dunlap, said to have been first produced in New York, April 18, 1796. The plot is founded upon the story of William Tell. This is incorrectly claimed to be the first American opera.

Ariane (Ariadne) — French grand opera in five acts. Music by Massenet, text by Catulle Mendes, first produced at Paris in 1907. Ariadne, daughter of Minos, falls in love with Perseus when he comes to Crete to kill the Minotaur and flies with him to Naxos. Here Perseus deserts her for her sister Phadra. The latter is killed by an accident, but at Ariadne's request Proserpine returns her to earth again. Phadra, however, deceives her sister a second time, then the despairing Ariadne, lured by the song of the Sirens, slips into the sea. The excellent poetic libretto furnished a new field for Massenet and the French opera goers greeted the opera with hearty applause.

Arianna or Ariana — Italian opera, music by Monteverdi, words by Rincuccini, produced in Mantua, 1607. It is one of the first operas written. The story is that of Ariadne and Theseus.

Ariodante — English opera by Handel, produced in London, 1734. The subject is taken from Ariosto's "Orlando Furioso."

Ariovisto — Italian opera, music by Mancini, produced in Naples, 1702 The hero of the opera is Ariovist, the German prince, whom Julius Cæsar conquered at Bescancon, 59 A. D.

Aristeo — Opera, music by Gluck, produced at Parma, 1769.

Aristippe — French opera in two acts. Music by R. Kreutzer, text by

Leclerc and Girand, produced at Paris, 1808. The music of this opera was popular and was sung by some of the most distinguished French singers.

Arme Heinrich, Der (Poor Heinrich) — Music-drama in two acts, music by Hans Pfister, words by Grau, first produced at Mainz, 1895. The willingness of the poor Agnes to sacrifice her life in order that her master Heinrich may recover his health, and his final recovery just as the sacrifice is about to be made are the essential features of the plot.

Arm Elslein (Poor Little Elsie) — German opera, music by Cyrill Kistler, first produced at Schwerin, 1902. Kistler has written some very interesting music for this little play and the opera has been very successful.

Arme Jonathan, Der (Poor Jonathan) — Opera in three acts by Millöcker. Libretto by Hugo Wittmann and Julius Bauer. Place, Boston, Monaco and New York. Time, Nineteenth Century. First produced at Vienna in 1890.

Armida — A heroic grand opera in five acts. Music by Gluck, text by Quinault, produced at Paris in 1777. In 1099 when Godfrey of Bouillon's crusaders reached Damascus, they came to the beautiful gardens of Queen Armida, an enchantress. All the warriors lost their hearts to her except Rinaldo, Godfrey's greatest hero. He scorned her. Enraged at this, the Queen vowed to win him. He was just about to yield to her charms when his sense of duty recalled him to the army. Unable to hold him, Armida cursed him and turned her beautiful garden into a desert. This opera, produced when Glück was sixty-three, is one of his greatest. Its music is so sublime that it will remain.

Armida, No. 2 — A classic for centuries. Gluck himself said that he should like to close his career with this opera.

Armin — German opera by Heinrich Hofmann, words by Felix Dahn, a German author, produced in Dresden, 1777. Armin, Arminius or Hermann, freed the Germans from Roman domination in the battle of the Teutoburgerwald in 9 A. D.

Arminio — English opera. Music by Handel. Performed at London in 1736.

Armorer, The (Der Waffenschmied) — A comic opera in three acts, words and music by A. G. Lortzing. Though this opera does not equal the composer's "Czar and Carpenter," it is nevertheless popular because of the freshness of both melodies and plot. The Count of Liebenan is in love with Mary, the daughter of the blacksmith Stadinger of Worms. In order to win her love the count woos her in his own rank, and also in the disguise of a journeyman blacksmith named Conrad. When the count tells Mary of his love, she rejects him and confesses with blushes that she loves the journeyman Conrad. Her father too rejects the count's advances, because of his social rank and likewise disdains the suit of Conrad since he proves to be such a poor blacksmith. Amid much comedy of misunderstanding the lovers finally come to an understanding.

Armourer of Mantes, The — English opera in three acts, music by Balfe, words by Bridgman, first produced in London, 1863.

Arsinoe — Italian opera, music by Francheschi, first presented in Italy in 1677. Translated and reset to music by Clayton in England and first performed in Drury Lane Theatre in 1705, with the title Arsinoe, Queen of Cyprus. Of importance since it is among the earliest Italian operas with English words. Arsinoe was the daughter of Ptolemy I. of Egypt.

Artamene — Opera by Gluck, first presented at Cremona in 1743. This opera is very Italian in its style of composition and does not show Glück's individuality as his later compositions do.

Artaserse (Artaxerxes) — Italian opera, music by Gluck, words by Matastasio, produced in Milan, 1741. Artaxerxes was king of Persia in the Fifth Century, B. C.

Artemisia — Italian opera, music by Cimarosa, produced in Venice, 1801. The composer's death prevented his finishing the opera, but it was completed by Wagner. Artemisia was the ruler of Helikarnass, she was with Xerxes on his famous march and fought at Salamis.

Artistes par Occasion, Les (Artists on Occasion) — French comic opera in one act. Music by Catel, text by Alexander Duval, produced at Paris, 1807. This opera contains the much loved concert trio for two tenors and one bass, beginning "Come, sir, let us play comedy."

Artisti alla Fiera, Gli (The Artists at the Fair) — Italian comic opera, music by Rossi, words by Ghislanzoni, produced in Turin in 1868.

Artist's Model, An — A comedy with music in two acts, music by Sidney Jones, book by Owen Hall, lyrics by Harry Greenbank, first produced at Daly's Theater, London, Feb. 2, 1895.

Arvire and Evelina — French opera, music by Sacchini, words by Gaillard, produced in Paris, 1788. The libretto is adapted from Mason's "Caractacus." The opera was left unfinished by Sacchini and Rey completed it after the composer's death.

Ascanio — French grand opera, music by Saint-Saëns, words by Gallet, produced in Paris, March 21, 1890. The text is adapted from Paul Meurice's drama "Benvenuto Cellini." Ascanio is a simple apprentice in the studio of the great sculptor.

Ascanio in Alba — Italian opera or theatrical serenade, music by Mozart, words by Parini, produced in Milan, 1771, upon the marriage of the Grand Duke Frederick of Austria to the Princess Marie of Modena. Ascanius was the son of Æneas, the founder of Alba Longa.

Aspasie — French opera in three acts, music by Grétry, words by Morel, first produced in Paris in 1789.

Aspasie et Pericles — French opera in one act, music by Daussoigne, words by Viennet, first produced in Paris, 1820.

Asraele — Italian opera in four acts, music by Alberto Franchetti, produced in Brescia, 1888. It is the composer's first opera.

Assarpai — Opera in three acts, music by Ferdinand Hummel, words by Dora Duncker, after a ballad by Wildenbruch. Assarpai is the daughter of the last king of the Incas, and the time is 1533.

Assassini, Gli (The Assassins) — Italian opera, music by Trento, produced in Venice in 1819.

Astarte — Italian opera, music by Albinoni, words by Zeno, the first lyric poet of Italy before Métastase. First performed at Venice, 1708. Astarte in mythology is the noon-goddess, chief goddess of the ancient Syro-Phenician nations.

Astianasse (Astyanax) — Italian opera, music by Leonardo da Vinci, the painter and sculptor, produced in Venice, 1725. Astyanax was the son of Hector and Andromache.

Astorga — Tragic opera in three acts. Music by Albert, libretto by E. Pasque. Produced at Stuttgart, 1866, with great success. Story is taken from the unhappy life of Astorga, the singer and composer, who lived at Parma two centuries ago.

Astyanax — Italian opera, music by Bononcini, produced in London, 1725 Astyanax was the son of Hector and Andromache.

Astyanax — French opera, music by Rudolphe Kreutzer, words by Dejaure, produced in Paris, 1801. Astyanax was the son of Hector and Andromache. After the capture of Troy, he was thrown from the walls by the Greeks, because it had been prophesied that he would rebuild the city.

Atala — Opera in two acts. Music by Mlle. Juliette Folville, libretto by M. P. Collin, first produced at Lille in 1892. This opera was not only composed but was also conducted by Miss Folville, a young Belgian lady then only twenty-two years old. It was very cordially received.

Atalanta — Italian opera. Music by Chelleri, words by the poet Zeno. First produced at Ferrare in 1713. Many other musicians used this same text. Atalanta was an Arcadian princess who promised to marry the lover who could out-run her.

Athalie — Tragedy by Racine with choruses by Abt. Vogler, produced at Stockholm in 1791.

Attila — Italian opera, music by Verdi, first produced in Venice, 1846. This is one of the least successful of Verdi's operas.

Attilio Regolo — Italian opera in three acts, music by Scarlatti, text by Métastase, produced at Rome, 1719.

Attilio Regolo (Prince Attilio) — Italian opera, music by Hasse, words by Metastasio, produced in Dresden and Berlin, 1750. It was written for Vienna in 1740, but owing to the death of the Emperor was not sung there.

Atys — French opera in five acts, music by Lully, words by Quinault, produced in Saint Germain, before Louis XIV., Jan. 10, 1676. The story is from mythology, Atys being the favorite of Cybele.

Aubergistes de Qualite, Les (The Innkeepers of Quality) — French comic opera in three acts, music by C. S. Catel, words by Jouy, produced in Paris, 1812.

Aucassin and Nicolette — French comic opera in three acts, music by Grétry, words by Sedaine, produced in Versailles in 1779. The text is founded upon a story dating from the Thirteenth Century. The opera is sung today.

Aucassin and Nicolette — Danish opera, music by August Enna, produced in Copenhagen, 1896.

Augenarzt, Der (The Optician) — German comic opera, music by Gyrowetz, words by Emanuel Veith, produced in Vienna in 1817. The opera is still sometimes given in Germany.

Aureliano in Palmira — Italian opera, music by Rossini, first produced at Milan, 1813. Though not in itself successful, it contains selections which Rossini afterward used in "Elisabetta and the Barbiere."

Aurelia, Prinsessin von Bulgarien (Princess of Bulgaria) — German grand opera in three acts, music by Konrad Kreutzer, words by Gollmick, produced in Cassel, 1851. The libretto is founded upon a drama by Frau von Weissenthurn "Der Wald bei Hermannstadt."

Aveux Indiscrets, Les (The Indiscreet Confessions) — A French comic opera in one act. Music by de Monsigny, words by Ribadieri. First produced in Saint Germaine at the Market Theatre in 1759. This opera was the beginning of Monsigny's dramatic career.

B

Babes in Toyland — Musical extravaganza, music by Victor Herbert, words by Glen MacDonough, first produced in Chicago, in 1903.

Babette — Opera in three acts by Herbert. Libretto by Harry B. Smith. Place, Belgium and France. Time, the Eighteenth Century. First produced at Washington, D. C., in 1903.

Bacchus — French opera, music by Jules Massenet, words by Catulle Mendès, first produced in Paris, 1909.

Bacio, Il (The Kiss) — Italian opera, music by Guiseppe Giordani, produced in London, 1774. It had such success that it was given continuously for eight successive years.

Bajazzi (The Merry Andrews) — Opera in two acts. Music and words by Leoncavallo. First produced at Berlin, Germany, 1892. Time, present; scene, the little village of Montalto in Italy. A small troupe of village comedians, while performing mix their earnest with their play, and the pretended jealousy in the play becomes real and the husband kills his rival, with the telling words: "The comedy is ended." This opera became successful immediately and has enjoyed an excellent run under the leadership of the composer himself in Berlin.

Baldur's Tod (The Death of Balder) — German musical drama in three acts, music by Cyrill Kistler, text by Dr. von Sohlern, first produced at Düsseldorf in 1905. Balder is the Teuton god of sunlight and love. Everybody loves him, even the giants. Loki alone envied him and plotted to kill him. Balder once dreamed that he was going to die, this alarmed the gods and they went to all animals and plants and made them take an oath not to harm Balder. They did so willingly, but a little mistletoe had been overlooked. When Loki heard this, he flew to the mistletoe, jerked it from the oak, and pronounced incantations over it till it grew to the size of a spear. One day soon after, the gods were amusing themselves by hurling missiles at Balder to test his invulnerability. Höder, the blind brother of Balder, stood by weaponless. Seeing this, Loki urged him to try his skill and offered him the spear. All unconscious of the mistletoe's ignorance of the oath, Höder hurls the spear with all his might. It pierced Balder through the heart and he fell dead to the ground. The composer who was present at the first performance was overwhelmed with congratulations. The opera is excellent.

Ballet Comique de la Royne, Le — A French comedy ballet. Music of the dances, choruses and dialogues by Beaulieu and Salmon, arranged by Baltazar de Beaujoyeaulx. First performed in 1581 at the Chateau de Moutiers in the presence of Henry III. of France, at the marriage of the Duke of Joyeuse. This famous ballet, whose magnificent setting cost three and a half million francs, is the forerunner of the French opera. The entire work is still extant, and its music has undoubtedly furnished inspiration to French composers of the following century, among them Lulli especially.

Barbarina, Die (Barbarina di Campanini) — German opera in three acts; music and text by Otto Neitzel, first produced at Wiesbaden in 1905. An episode in the life of the famous dancer, Barbarina di Campanini, a favorite of Frederick the Great of Germany, forms the foundation for the text. Pretty Barbarina is loved by the Prussian nobleman Cocceji, but her guardian wants to marry her himself and a duel results. In spite of her lover's protests, Barbarina goes to the King to beg for mercy since duelling is prohibited, but the King laughs at her. Vexed, she breaks her contract as dancer and flees to Venice. The King orders Cocceji to bring back the fugitive by force or by cunning. Barbarina returns, but not by command of the King but because she loves Cocceji, and the prettiest thing in the whole opera is her dance before the King in the royal palace as he forgives her for her escapade.

Barbiere di Sevilla, Il (The Barber of Seville) — Italian opera, music by Paisiello, produced in St. Petersburg, 1776. Paisiello was the first to use Beaumarchais' drama as the basis for an opera. The libretto of this work served as the foundation for Rossini's better known opera of the same name.

Barcarole, La (A Venetian Boat Song) — French comic opera, music by Auber, text by Scribe, produced at Paris in 1845. The Marquis of Felino is eager to gain the attentions of the Doge's wife, so he procures a barcarolle, changes the text slightly and has it put into her sewing basket. Unfortunately the Doge finds it and complications which threaten serious injury to the innocent composer arise, but the story ends happily for all concerned. The opera is also known as "Love and Music."

Bardes, ou Ossian, Les — French grand opera in three acts, music by Lesueur, words by Dercy and Deschamps, produced in Paris, 1804, but written in 1801. The scene of action is Caeldonia, Ossian is the hero and Rosalma the heroine. The opera is no longer sung.

Barfüssle (Little Barefoot) — German opera in two acts with a prologue. Music by Henberger, text by Viktor Leon. The text is based on Auerbach's popular novel by the same title. Barfüssle is an orphan who is adopted into a good family, serves later as a servant and then marries a wealthy farmer's son. This opera has been accorded a great deal of popularity.

Baroness, The — Comic opera, music and words by Cotsford Dick, first produced at the Royalty Theater, London, Oct. 5, 1892.

Baron Golosh — A musical comedy in two acts, adapted from "L'Oncle Celesrin," by Ordonneau and Audrau, with additional numbers by Meyer Lutz, first produced at the Trafalgar Theater, London, April 25, 1895.

Basilius — German opera by Reinhard Keiser. Presented at Hamburg, Germany, about 1693. This opera is first of a long series of German operas written by this bright and lively composer and it was hailed with enthusiasm by the German theatre-goers.

Basoche, La — Opera in three acts by André Messager. Libretto by Albert Carré. English adaptation by Mrs. Madelaine Lucette Ryley. Place, Paris, France. Time, Sixteenth Century. First produced in Paris in 1890.

Bastien and Bastienne — German opera, music by Mozart, words by Weiskom, slightly revised by Schachtner, produced in Vienna, 1768, in a private theatre. The libretto is founded upon Rousseau's "Devin du Village." The story consists of the quarrels of a rustic couple, who are finally reconciled by a traveling conjurer.

Battle of Hexham, The — English opera, music by Dr. Samuel Arnold, words by George Coleman, first produced in London, 1789.

Bayaderes, Les (The Bayaderes) — French opera in three acts, music by C. S. Catel, words by Jouy, produced in Paris, 1810. A Bayadere is an East Indian dancing girl. Goethe's poem, "Der Gott und die Bajadere," is on the same theme. The god descends to earth, finds only a Bayadere faithful to him unto death, when she is carried by him up to heaven.

Bayard a La Ferté (Bayard at La Ferté) — French comic opera, music by Plantade, text by Gentil and Desauguers, produced at Paris in 1811. An attempt is made to bring Bayard into disfavor with the King. But the attempt is futile and Bayard proves himself to be the knight without fear or blame.

Bearnaise, La — Comic opera in three acts, music by André Messager, words by Leterrier and Vanloo, first produced at the Bouffes-Parisiens in December, 1885. An English version by Alfred Murray was given at the Prince of Wales' Theater, London, Oct. 4, 1886. This opera brought Messager his first great success. It is still occasionally produced.

Beatrice and Benedict — French opera in two acts, music and words by Berlioz, produced in Baden-Baden in 1862. The composer adapted his text from Shakespeare's "Much Ado About Nothing." The opera was written for the impresario of the Kursaal in Baden-Baden.

Beatrice di Tenda — Italian opera, music by Bellini, words by Romani, produced in Venice, 1833, and revived three years later in London. Philip, Duke of Milan, made suspicious of the faithfulness of his wife, Beatrice, has her and her supposed lover executed.

Beautiful Galatea, The — Comic opera in two acts; music by Suppé; text by Zell and Genée. First produced in Vienna in 1865. Scene is laid in Greece and the opera is based upon the mythological story of Pygmalion and Galatea. The opera is light, the music melodious and the whole is very cleverly set.

Beauty Spot, The — Opera by Reginald De Koven. Libretto by Joseph W. Herbert. Place, France. Time, the present. First produced at New York in 1909.

Beauty Stone, The — Romantic musical drama, music by Sir Arthur Sullivan, words by A. W. Pinero and Comyns Carr, first produced in London, 1898.

Beichte, Die (The Confession)— German opera in one act. Music by Ferdinand Hummel, words by Axel Delmar. First performed in Berlin, 1900. Time, a century ago; scene, a cliff in Portugal. The confession and sorrow of a hermit, twenty years after he had betrayed the confidence of his best friend who had entrusted his wife to his care while he was forced to go on a long journey.

Beiden Neffen, Die (The Two Nephews, or The Uncle from Boston) — An operetta by Felix Mendelssohn, produced at Berlin in 1824. This was produced in honor of the composer's fifteenth birthday at which occasion he graduated from the tutelage of his master Zelter.

Beiden Schützen, Die (The Two Grenadiers) — German comic opera in three acts, music and words by Lortzing, produced in Leipzig, 1837, under the title, "Die Beiden Tarnister." (The Two Knapsacks.) Lortzing adapted his text from a French vaudeville, "Les Deux Grenadiers."

Belisaire (Belisarius) — French opera in three acts, music by Philidor, words by Dartiguy, produced in Paris, 1796. The libretto is founded upon Marmontel's novel. Berton is said to have composed the second act. Belisarius was a Byzantine general under Justinian I. who fell from favor with the Emperor and died in 565 B. C. Legend relates that he was blinded and wandered about as a beggar with his daughter Irene. The opera was not produced till a year after Philidor's death.

Belisario — Opera in three acts, music by Donizetti, words by Cammarano, first produced at Venice, 1836. It is founded upon the drama by Schenk, and relates the tragic incidents preceding the death of Belisario who lived in the Sixth Century,

B. C., and was commander of the forces of Emperor Justinian.

Bella Donna, or The Little Beauty and the Great Beast — Comic opera, music by Alfred Cellier, words by Alfred Thompson, first produced at Manchester, 1878.

Belle Arsene, La (The Beautiful Arsene) — French fairy opera, music by Monsigny, words by Favart, produced in Paris, Aug. 14, 1773. The libretto is founded upon Voltaire's "La Begueule," (The Prude).

Belle of Mayfair, The — Comic opera, music by Leslie Stuart, words by Charles H. E. Brookfield and Cosmo Hamilton, first produced in England, later in New York, 1907.

Bellerofonte (Bellerophon) — Italian opera, music by Mysliwecsek, produced in Naples, 1765. The theme is a mythological one.

Belmont und Constanze, Die Entführung aus dem Serail (The Rescue from the Harem) — Comic opera in three acts by Mozart, words by Bretzner, revised by Stephanie for Mozart, produced in Vienna, July 12, 1782. The national "Sangerfest," established by the Emperor Joseph II. in 1778, first became a significant institution through the production of this opera.

Benoiuski — French opera in three acts, music by Boieldieu, words by Alexander Duval, first produced in Paris, 1800. The plot is founded upon a drama by Kotzebue, and relates the adventures of the famous Hungarian general, Beniousk. In 1824 it was revived with some changes.

Berenice—Italian opera, music by Porpora, produced in Rome, 1710. Berenice was the daughter of King Magas of Cyrene.

Berenice — English opera by Handel. Represented at Covent Garden Theatre in London in 1738. Probably founded on one of the Italian operas founded on many of the Italian operas of the same title.

Bergère Châtelaine, La (The Lady of the Manor as a Shepherdess) — French comic opera in three acts, music by Auber, text by Planard, produced at Paris in 1820. La Bergère Châtelaine was Auber's first operatic success; it attracted Scribe's notice and from this time on these two men collaborated with excellent results for nearly forty years.

Bergers, Les (The Shepherds) — A French operetta, music by Offenbach, text by Gille and H. Crémieux, produced at Paris in 1865. The operetta consists of three parts: "L'Idylle," which describes the shepherd life in ancient times; "Le Trumeau," which describes shepherd life in the Seventeenth Century; "La Bergerie Réaliste," a description of shepherd life as it really is.

Berggeist, Der (The Mountain-spirit) — A romantic opera by Spohr. First produced at Cassel, Germany, in 1825. Though this opera is not generally as well known as Spohr's Faust, it is in some respects finer. As the title suggests it gives room for the same mysterious magic music that marks the Brocken scene in Faust. The overture to the Berggeist is especially noteworthy.

Bergknappen, Die (The Miners) — German operetta, music by Hellwig, text by Korner, produced at Berlin in 1820.

Betby — Italian opera, music and words by Donizetti, produced in Naples, 1836. The libretto is based on Adam's "Châlet" an adaptation of Goethe's "Jouy and Bätely."

Betrug durch Aberglauben, Der (Deceived by Superstition) — German operetta by Dittersdorf, produced in Vienna, Oct. 3, 1786.

Bettler von Samarkand, Der (The Beggar of Samarcand) — German comic opera, music by Ignaz Brüll, produced in Vienna, 1864. Samarcand is a city of Turkestan.

Bettlerin von Pont des Arts, Die (The Beggar Girl of the Bridge of Arts) — German lyrical opera, music by Karl von Kaskel, words by Ludwig, produced in Cologne, 1900. Hauff's story formed the basis for the libretto. The scene is laid in Germany and Paris in the year 1828.

Betty — French ballet, music by Ambroise Thomas, produced in Paris, 1846.

Bianca — German comic opera in three acts, music by Ignaz Brüll, words by Schirmer, produced in Dresden, 1879, and revised in 1880. The opera had very little success.

Bianca e Fernando — Italian opera, music by Bellini, first produced in Naples, 1826. This was one of Bellini's first operas, and while not very well known in Europe, became quite popular in Naples and laid the foundation for the young composer's future fame.

Biarritz — A musical farce in two acts, music by F. Osmond Carr, words by Jerome K. Jerome and Adrian Ross, produced at the Prince of Wales Theatre, London, April 11, 1896. Biarritz is the name of the place in which, at the Hotel du Palais, the scene of the farce is laid.

Bijou Perdu, Le (The Lost Jewelry) — French comic opera, music by Adam, text by DeForges and Scribe, produced at Paris in 1853. The lost treasure is a watch which makes a strange tour through different people's pockets. The opera was not a success.

Bion — French opera in one act, music by Mehul, text by Hoffmann, produced at Paris in 1801. A love story of ancient times in which Bion loves Nisa, but, when he sees that she loves some one else, he helps her and her lover to marry.

Black Crook, The — A spectacular fairy opera in three acts, music by Frederick Clay and J. Jacobi, first produced in London, in 1872. Re-written by Harry Paulton and produced at the Alhambra Theatre, London, Dec. 3, 1881. It is founded upon "La Biche au Bois."

Blaise et Babet — A French comic opera in two acts; music by Dezéde, text by Monvel, produced at Paris in 1783. This opera is a continuation of Dezede's "Les Trois Fermiers" (The Three Farmers). It is considered his best work, was very successful, and held the stage for two years.

Blaise le Savetier (Blasius the Cobbler) — French comic opera in one act, music by Philidor, words by Sedaine, produced in Paris, 1759. It was the composer's first opera and a brilliant success.

Blanche de Nevers — English opera in three acts, music by Balfe, words by J. Brougham, first produced in London, 1863. The plot is taken from the French drama by Bossu.

Bluebeard — English opera, music by Michael Kelly; text by his valued friend, George Coleman. First produced at Drury Lane in 1798. It was with this opera that Kelly established his name as a composer. Overflowing houses greeted the opera night after night and it kept its popularity for over twenty-five years. Coleman based his text upon a French version of "Bluebeard."

Blue-Eyed Susan — Comic opera, music by F. Ismond Carr, words by G. R. Sims and Henry Pettitt, first produced at the Prince of Wales Theatre, Feb. 7, 1892. It was at first severely criticised, but after being revised, met with great popularity.

Boabdil — Opera in three acts, music by Moszkowski, libretto by Carl Wittkowsky, first produced at Berlin in 1892. Boabdil was the last Moorish king of Granada. An episode in the last war of the Moors against Spain forms the basis for the story. This opera achieved a splendid success.

Bondman, The — English opera, music by Balfe, words by Bunn, first produced in London, 1846.

Bondura — English opera, music by Purcell, first produced in 1695. The text is an adaptation of Beaumont and Fletcher's play by the same name.

Bon Fils, Le (The Good Son) — French comic opera, music by Philidor, words by Devaux, produced in Paris, 1773. No longer on the stage.

Bonhomme Jadis (A Good Fellow of Old) — French comic opera in one act by Jaques-Dalcrose, produced at Paris in 1907, and at the same time in Berlin with the German title "Onkel Dazumal" (Uncle of the Past). A good natured old soldier still quite capable of falling in love is the charming character in this wholesome little opera.

Bonsoir Monsieur Pantalon (Good Evening Mr. Pantalon) — French comedy in one act. Music by A. Grisar, text by Morvan and Lockroy, produced at Paris, 1851. Plot takes place at Venice and is full of amusing situations. The son of Mr. Pantalon has himself carried to his mistress in a basket; on the way the basket is tumbled into the Grand Canal.

Bonsoir, Voison (Good Evening, Neighbor) — French operetta, music by Poise, produced in Paris, 1853.

Boris Godunoff — A Russian opera by Modest Mussorgski, first produced at St. Petersburg in 1874. The hero is the chief counsellor of Fedor I., Czar of Russia. At the death of the Czar in 1594, he usurps the Russian crown after having murdered the next in line, Fedor's nine-year-old brother. This opera is the most characteristic of the new Russian school. It is a great favorite in its own country but had never been produced outside of Russia until 1908, when it appeared in Paris. It was sung in Russian, but so greatly did it please the Paris public that a French production has been promised.

Bouffe et le Tailleur, Le (The Clown and the Tailor) — French comic opera in one act. Music by Gaveaux, text by Villiers and Gouffe, produced at Paris, 1804. Although over a century old, this opera is occasionally played, and for over half a century was a great favorite in France.

Bouquet de L'Infante, Le (The Prince's Bouquet) — Comic opera in three acts. Music by Adrien Boieldieu, text by Leuven and Planard, produced at Paris, 1847. Don Fabio, a Portugese gentleman, is exiled by his King, and plans revenge. His plot is discovered and he is condemned to die, but the King's pardon is made known by the appearance of the Infante's bouquet, the royal symbol of pardon.

Bouquetiére, La (The Flower-Girl) — French opera in one act, music by Adolphe Adam, words by Hippolyte Lucas, first produced in Paris, 1847. This is a pretty romance of a flower-girl who marries a vicomte.

Bourgeois de Reims, Le (The Citizen of Reims) — French comic opera in one act, music by Fétis, words by St. Georges and Ménissier, first produced in Paris, 1825.

Bourgeois Gentilhomme, Le — A comedy with ballet, music by Lully, text by Molière, produced in Paris and Chambora in 1670. In 1852 this opera was revised for the Moliere celebration; and in 1876 it was again revised by Wecherlin.

Boyarina Vera Sheloga — Musical dramatic prologue to the "Maid of Pskov, music by Rimsky-Korsakov, produced in Moscow, 1899.

Brasseur de Preston, Le (The Brewer of Preston) — French comic opera in three acts. Music by Adam, text by Leuven and Brunswick, produced at Paris, 1838. An amusing story of mistaken identity. The brewer and his twin brother look so much alike that when the sergeant comes after the brother, whose furlough has expired, he forces the brewer to go in his stead.

Brandenburger in Böhmen, Die (The Branderburgers in Bohemia) — Czechish opera, music by Smetana, produced in Prague, 1863.

Braut der Gnomen, Die (The Gnome Bride) — A Swedish opera by Ivor Halström, produced at Stockholm, 1875. A Czechic opera by Skraup appeared at Prague in 1836.

Brautmarkt zu Hira, Der (The Bride-Market at Hira) — Romantic comic opera in one act. Music by Bugomil Zeplar, words by Oscar Justinius. First produced at Berlin, Germany, 1892. Time, 580, B. C.; scene, the city of Hira or Alexandria in Babylonia. Story deals with the ancient custom of selling marriageable girls to the highest bidder.

Bravo, Le — Grand opera in four acts, music by Gustav Salvayre, words by Emile Blavet, first produced in Paris, 1877.

Bride-Elect, The — Words and music by John Philip Sousa. Place, Capri. Time, Nineteenth Century. First produced at New Haven, Conn., in 1897.

Bride of Messina, The — Opera in three acts, music by J. H. Bonawitz, words by Hermann Müller, first produced in Philadelphia, 1874. The libretto is founded upon Schiller's tragedy "Braut von Messina."

Grigants, Les (The Brigands) — Comic opera in three acts, music by Offenbach, words by Henri Meilhac and Ludwig Halévy, first produced at the Theatre des Varietes, Paris, Dec. 10, 1869. English version adapted by W. S. Gilbert and first produced at the Avenue Theatre, London, Sept. 16, 1889. H. S. Leigh had previously adapted the same opera into English under the title "Fal-sac-ap-pa" which appeared at the Globe Theatre, London, April 22, 1871.

Briganti, I (The Robbers) — Italian opera, music by Mercadante, words by Crescini, produced in Milan, 1841. The libretto is adapted from Schiller's drama, "Die Räuber."

Briseis — Unfinished French opera, music by Alexis Emmanuel Chabrier, produced at the Grand Opera in Paris, May 8, 1899. But one act had been completed at the time of the composer's death.

Britannico — Opera by Graun. Text after Racine's tragedy, "Britannico," produced at Berlin, 1752.

Bruder Lustig (The Jolly Brother) — German opera, music and text by Siegfried Wagner, first produced at Hamburg in 1905. Text is based on one of Grimm's fairy tales. Critics claim that this opera indicates a downward step in Wagner's compositions. It is even less good than "Der Kobold." Neither music nor text offers any striking originality.

Buddha, Der (The Budda) — German grand opera in three acts. Music and text by Max Vogrich. First production at Weimar in 1904. Story is of a time about 400 B. C., and is in part legend, and part historical. By chance Gantana, a young prince, learns that there is misery in the world. Eager to enlighten his soul he gives up his wife and all the princely luxury and wanders forth as a beggar. He returns as Buddha, the prophet, after fifteen years, but nothing will induce him to stay. He and his followers go forth again; unknown to him, his loving wife follows him, but they are not united until years later when he is dying. Prophetically he proclaims a new Buddha, the god of love. The music of this opera has much originality. The Leit-motif is not as noticeable as in Wagner music; Vogrich reminds us more of Meyerbeer and Goldmark. Der Buddha was received with great enthusiasm.

Buove d'Antona, Il (The Chains of Antona) — Italian comic opera, music by Traetta, words by Goldoni, produced in Florence, 1756.

Burgha — German opera in one act. Music by F. A. Kohler, libretto by Professor Lvovsky, produced at Barmen, Germany, in 1907. The story is drawn from the late Boor struggle for independence. A Boor general, his daughter Burgha, and her lover are caught in their attempt to carry off some ammunition from the English camp. Seeing no chance for an honorable escape, Burgha hurls a torch into the ammunition wagon; by the explosion all are mortally wounded.

C

Cabinet, The — English opera, music by Moorhead, assisted by John Davy and John Braham, first produced in London, 1802. The success of this opera, which was great at that time, was probably due to Braham's singing.

Cabrera, La — Opera. Music by Gabriel Dupont, text by Henri Cain, first produced at Milan in 1904. Story takes place in a Spanish village. Pedrito loves the fifteen-year-old shepherdess Julia, but is forced to leave Spain in order to serve in the war against America. He returns in three years to find that Julia has been untrue to him and he spurns her. Broken hearted she leaves the village. In six months she comes back sick and starving and when he sees her thus, his old love is rekindled, but it is too late, she dies in his arms forgiven. This opera won the great Sonzogno prize in 1904 and it has been a tremendous success, making many friends wherever heard.

Cadi Dupe, Le (The Duped Judge) — Comic opera in one act. Music by Monsigny, words by Lemonnier. Presented at the theatre of Saint-Laurent in 1761. The comedy of this opera made it a great success at the time. Story taken from the Arabian Nights.

Caduta de Decemviri, La (The Fall of the Decemvirs) — Italian opera, music by Scarlatti, produced in Naples, 1697. None of its score is now in existence.

Caduta de Giganti, La (The Fall of the Giants) — Italian opera, music by Gluck, produced in London, 1746. The opera was written in honor of the Duke of Cumberland, who had just returned victorious from his encounter with the Scotch under Charles Edward, the young Pretender. Cumberland was the Jupiter who had put down the giants.

Cagliostro — French comic opera in three acts. Music by Adolphe Adam, text by Saint Georges and Scribe, produced at Paris, 1844. Cagliostro, a famous magician and adventurer of the Eighteenth Century, is hero of the plot; place, a salon in Versailles. Strauss' operetta, "Cagliostro," appeared in Vienna, 1875.

Caid, Le — French light opera, music by Ambroise Thomas, words by Sauvage, produced in Paris, 1849. The Caid is a stupid police official in Algiers. The opera is sometimes regarded as the precursor of opera bouffe, later so successfully taken up by Offenbach and his imitators. It was Thomas' first permanent success and is still sung in France.

Cain — German tragic opera, music by Eugen d'Albert, words by Bulthaupt, produced in Berlin, 1900. The story is the biblical one.

Cajo Fabrizio — Italian opera, music by Caldara, libretto by A. Zeno, produced at Vienna in 1729.

Cajo Mario (Cains Marius) — Italian opera, music by Cimarosa, produced in Rome, 1780. Marius, the hero of the opera, is the old Roman general and statesman.

Calife de Bagdad, Le (The Calif of Bagdad) — French comic opera in one act. Music by Boieldieu, text by Saint Just, produced at Paris in 1800. With this opera began Boieldieu's fame; it was very popular at its time and is occasionally heard to-day.

Calypoe — Italian opera, music by Peter von Winter, produced in London, 1803. The story is mythological and deals with Ulysses' wanderings.

Calypso and Telemachus — English opera, music by Gaillard, words by John Hughes, produced in London, 1712. The libretto is on a mythological subject. It was one of the very earliest attempts to write opera in English. It had very slight success, being sung but five times.

Camargo, La — An operetta in three acts, music by Lecocq, words by Leterrier and Vanloo, first produced in Paris, 1878. The story centers in Camargo, a famous opera dancer of the Eighteenth Century.

Camilla — Italian opera, music by M. A. Bononcini, text by Silvio Stampiglio, produced at Vienna in 1692. Camilla is a huntress and warrior maiden who, according to Virgil's story, aids one of Æneas' opponents but is herself killed. In 1706 this opera appeared in London with an English text and met with success.

Campanello, Il — Operetta in one act, music and words by Donizetti, first produced in Naples, 1836. The libretto is adapted from a French vaudeville called "La Sonnette de Nuit."

Candance — Italian opera by Lampugnani, produced at Venice in 1740. Candance is the Egyptian queen who defended her realm against Roman aggression.

Canterbury Pilgrims, The — English opera in three acts, music by Charles Villiers Stanford, words by G. A. Beckett, produced in London, April 28, 1884. The opera has been called an English Meister Singer. Goeffrey, the host of Tabard Inn, Cicely his daughter, and her lover Hubert are the main characters.

Canterina, La (The Singer) — An opera by Haydn written in 1767. Gasparina, a singer, accepts the attentions of two lovers and they lavish costly gifts upon her.

Capitaine Fracasse, Le — An opera in three acts, music by Emilé Pessard, words by Catulle Mendes, first produced in Paris, 1878. It is an adaptation from Gautier's novel by the same name.

Capitaine Henriot, Le (Captain Henry) — French comic opera; music by Gevaert, text by Valz, produced at Paris in 1864. The story is laid in France during the Siege of Paris by Henry IV., first Bourbon King of France, and is a comedy of love and misunderstandings with Henry himself as hero. The incompleted libretto was finished by Victorien Sardou.

Capitan, El — Comic opera in three acts; music by John Philip Sousa, text by Klein. First produced at Boston in 1896. The music of this opera is very catchy and has enjoyed great popularity. The scene is laid in Peru; time, the Eighteenth Century. Cazarro, the viceroy of Peru, has been deposed by the King of Spain, and a Spaniard named Medigna has been appointed in his place. Cazarro starts a revolution and sends to Spain for a noted soldier, El Capitan. El Capitan and Medigna, disguised as a sailor, sail from Spain on board the same boat. On the way over El Capitan is killed. Medigna learns who the slain soldier is, and when he lands, finding that his faction is hopelessly weak, he joins the revolutionists proclaiming himself El Capitan. His secretary impersonates the Viceroy. Later when the Spanish troops arrive, Medigna discloses his identity, the rebellion is put down and the story ends happily.

Caprice de Femme, Un (A Woman's Caprice) — Italian comic opera in one act. Music by Paër, text by Lesguillon, produced at Paris, 1834.

Captain Therese — Comic opera in three acts, music by R. Planquette, words by Alexander Bisson and F. C. Burnand, first produced at the Prince of Wales' Theater, London, Aug. 25, 1890.

Captif, Le (The Captive) — French opera, music by Edward Lassen, produced in Brussels, 1865, and later on sung in Germany.

Captive in the Caucasus, The — Russian opera, music by César Cui, produced in St. Petersburg, 1859. A poem of Poushkin's formed the basis for the libretto. In 1881-2 a middle act was added by the composer.

Capuleti ed i Montecchi, I (The Capulets and Montagues) — Italian opera in three acts, music by Bellini, words by Romani, produced in Venice, 1830. The story is the well known tale of Romeo and Juliet.

Caque du Convent, Le (Convent Gossip) — Comic French opera in one act. Music by Henri Potier, text by Planard and Leuven, produced at Paris in 1846.

Caravan du Caire, La (The Caravan from Cairo) — French opera in three acts, music by Grétry, words by Morel de Chedeville, first produced at Fontainbleau, 1873. It was very popular at the time, and contains the well known air "Victoire est a nous."

Carillonneur de Bruges, Le (The Bell-ringer of Brussels) — French opera in three acts. Music by Albert Grisar, text by Saint-Georges, produced at Paris, 1852. At the time of the revolt of the Netherlands against Spain, the honest bell-ringer becomes deaf, but recovers his hearing at the moment when he sees the flag of Brabant fly from the tower of his liberated city.

Carina — Comic opera, music by Julia Woolf, words by E. L. Blanchard and Cunningham Bridgman, first produced at the Opera Comique, London, Sept. 27, 1888. The story is suggested by Damaniant's drama, "Guerre Ouvert ou Ruse contre Ruse," given in Paris in 1786. This is a love story with the scene laid in Barcelona.

Carline — French comic opera in three acts, music by Ambroise Thomas, words by Leuven and Brunswick, produced in Paris, 1840.

Carlo Broschi — Opera in three acts by Auber. Libretto by Scribe. Place, the vicinity of Madrid and Aranjuez, Spain. Time, Eighteenth Century. First produced at Paris in 1843.

Carnaval de Venise, La (The Carnival of Venice) — French comic opera in three acts, music by Ambroise Thomas, words by Sauvage, produced in Paris, 1857.

Carro di Fedelta d'Amore (Car of Love's Loyalty) — Italian opera, music by Suagliati, words by his pupil Pietro della Valle, produced in Rome, 1606. It was performed on a car drawn through the streets at Carnival time and was one of the first Italian operas.

Cartouche — German comic opera in one act by Heinrich Hofmann, words by Fellechner, produced in Berlin, 1868. Cartouche is the well known Parisian sharper.

Cascina, La (The Dairy) — Italian opera by Scolari, produced at Venice in 1756.

Casilda — Opera, music by Ernst II., Duke of Saxe Cobourg Gotha, first produced in Brussels, 1855. A later production in England was unsuccessful.

Casque et les Colonbes, La (The Helmet and the Doves) — French opera by Grétry, text by Harleville and Guillard, produced at Paris in 1801. This opera was written to celebrate the truce with England, the doves nesting in the helmet of Mars being the significant symbol.

Castle of Andalusia, The—English comic opera, music by Dr. Samuel Arnold, words by O'Keefe, first produced in London, 1782.

Castles in the Air — Comic opera in three acts by Kerker. Libretto by C. A. Byrne. Place, West Indies. Time, Nineteenth Century. First produced at New York in 1890.

Castor and Pollux — French opera in five acts, music by Rameau, words by Bernard, produced in Paris, 1737. Since then the music has been twice revised. Castor and Pollux are mythological characters. The opera is Rameau's masterpiece.

Catarina Cornaro — German opera by Franz Lachner, produced at Munich, 1841. Time, the latter part of the Fifteenth Century when Cyprus falls before the Venetians. Catarina, also called "Queen of Cyprus," is heroine of the plot.

Catherine Grey — English opera music by Balfe, first produced in London, 1837.

Catone in Utica — Italian opera, music by Vinci, words by Metastasio, first produced in Rome, 1728. In 1732 the same libretto, with music by Leonardo Lev, was presented in Venice.

Cavaliere Errante, Il (The Knight Errant) — Italian opera in two acts, music by Traetta, first produced in Naples, 1777, and in Paris, 1779.

Cavalieri di Malta, I (The Knights of Malta) — Italian opera, music by Nani, words by Golisciani, produced in Malta, 1880.

Caverne, La (The Cave) — French opera in three acts, music by Lesueur, words by Dercy, produced in Paris, 1793. The theme is taken from Gil Blas. The opera was a brilliant success, but is no longer sung.

Cecchina La, sia La Buona Figliuola (Cecchina, or the Good Daughter) — Italian opera, music by Piccinni, words by Goldoni, first produced in Rome, 1760. Cecchina is a foundling who has two lovers, a gardener and a marquis. Her mother puts Cecchina into a convent from which she is rescued by the gardener, but the marquis carries her off. In the end Cecchina's father proves to be a colonel and she marries the marquis. This is said to be the most popular comic opera ever produced. It was played for years all over Europe.

Celestine — Comic French opera in three acts. Music by Bruni, text by Magnitot, produced at Paris, 1787. Music is excellent.

Cendrillon (Cinderella) — French comic opera in three acts, music by Nicolo Isouard, words by Etienne, produced in Paris, 1810.

Cenerentola, La (Cinderella) — Italian opera, music by Rossini, words by Ferretti, produced in Rome during the Carnival time of 1817.

Cent Vierges, Les (The Hundred Virgins) — Opera in three acts, music by Lecocq, words by Chivot, Duru, and Clairville, first produced in Brussels, 1872. It was performed in London, in French, at the St. James Theatre, June 21, 1873.

Cephale et Procris — Grand opera in three acts, music by Grétry, words by Marmontel, first produced at Versailles, 1773. This was one of Gretry's least successful operas.

Chaises à Porteurs, Les (The Sedan Chairs) — French comic opera in one act; music by V. Masse, text by Clairvill and Dumanoir, produced at Paris in 1858. A jealous husband and wife procure separate Sedan chairs in order to spy upon one another. They get mixed up with two cavaliers who have also hired chairs for a similar purpose, and the occupants of the four chairs furnish some very amusing incidents.

Chalet — French comic opera in one act, music by C A. Adam, words by Scribe and Melesville, produced in Paris, 1834. The libretto is adapted from Goethe's "Jery and Bately." The opera is still occasionally sung.

Chambre a Coucher, La, ou Une Demi-Heure de Richelieu (The Bed Room, or A Half Hour of Richelieu) — A comic French opera in one act. Music by Guenée, text by Scribe, produced at Paris, 1813.

Chambre Gothique, La (The Gothic Chamber) — French comic opera in one act, music by Massé, words by Carmonche, produced in Paris, 1849.

Chanson de Fortunio, La (Fortunio's Song) — Operetta in one act. Music by Offenbach, text by Cremieux and Servieres, produced at Paris, 1861. Offenbach's first offering for the stage.

Chant de la Cloche (The Song of the Bell) — French dramatic legend, music by Vincent d'Indy, produced in Paris, 1884. It gained a prize offered by that city for musical compositions.

Chanteuse Voilée, La (The Veiled Singer) — French comic opera in one act; music by V. Massé, text by Leuven and Scribe, produced at Paris in 1850. A pretty romance in the life of Valesquez, the Spanish artist. The veiled singer is his servant who sings at night in order to help her master out of debt. When Velesquez discovers her and her motive he marries her.

Chapeau au Roi, Le (The King's Hat) — French comic opera in one act; music by Caspers, text by Fournier, produced at Paris in 1856. Louis XI., that queer King of France, helps two bourgeois lovers to marry.

Chaperons Blancs, Les (The White Hoods) — French comic opera in three acts, music by Auber, words by Scribe, first produced in Paris, 1836.

Chapitre Second, Le (The Second Chapter) — French comic opera in one act, music by Solie, words by Dupaty, produced in Paris, 1799.

Char, Le (The Chariot) — French comic opera in one act, music by E. Pessard, text by Alphonse Daudet and P. Arène. While Alexander the Great is studying mathematics under Aristotle he falls in love with a washerwoman. The latter is to be dismissed but she manages so well that Aristotle himself falls in love with her. She induces him to prove his love by harnessing himself to a chariot into which she mounts. Surprised at the weight of his load, the mathematician looks behind him and discovers that Alexander is also an occupant of the cart.

Charlatan, The — Opera by Sousa. Libretto by Charles Klein. Place, Russia. Time, the Nineteenth Century. First produced at Montreal, Canada, in 1898.

Charles II.— English opera in two acts, music by Sir George Alexander Macfarren, words by Desmond Ryan, produced in London, 1849. Charles II. was King of England, 1660-1685.

Charles VI.— French grand opera in five acts, music by Halévy, words by Casimir and Germaine Delavigue, first produced in Paris, 1843. The story departs from historic facts. Odette, the daughter of an old guard, plays a similar role to that of Joan of Arc, supporting and inspiring the weak king.

Chat Botté, La (Puss in Boots) — French comic opera; music by Foignet, text by Cuvelier, produced at Paris in 1802.

Chateau de La Barbe Bleue, Le (Blue Beard's Castle) — French comic opera in three acts, music by A. Limnander, words by St. Georges, produced in Paris, 1851.

Chat Perdu, Le (The Lost Cat) — Comic French opera in two acts by de Laborde, produced at Paris, 1769.

Chatterton — Italian opera, music by Leoncavallo, produced in Rome, 1896. The librettto is an adaptation from Alfred de Vigny's play. The theme is the closing events of the wonderful English boy's career.

Chemineau, Le (The Vagabond) — Opera by Leroux. Libretto founded upon the drama in verse by Jean Richepin. Place, a locality between Burgundy and Ile-de-France. Time, the Nineteenth Century. First produced at Paris in 1907.

Chercheuse d'Esprit, La (The Blue Stocking) — French comic opera, music by Audran, produced in Marseilles, 1864. It is a new setting for an old opera of Favart's, produced in Paris, 1741. Audran's version was revived in Paris, 1882.

Cherubin — A French musical comedy in three acts; music by Massenet, libretto by Francis de Croisset and Henri Cain, first produced at Monte Carlo in 1905. The story is laid in Seville at the close of the Eighteenth Century. Cherubin is celebrating in honor of his being promoted to an officership. All the nobility attend, and the young gallant pays court to all the ladies. He flirts audaciously with the countess, the baroness and little Nina, but in reality loves only Eusoleillad, a famous dancer, but she won't have him. The King has cast his eyes upon her and she forsakes Cherubin. The latter is in despair till his attention is called to Nina who accepts him with open arms. This opera is a happy conception, eye and ear enjoy the melody, romance and the Spanish dances. It has scored an immense success.

Cheval de Bronze, Le (The Bronze Horse) — Comic opera in three acts, music by Auber, words by Scribe, first produced at the Opera Comique, Paris, March 23, 1835, revived with additions at L'Academie de Musique, Sept. 21, 1857. Various English versions of the opera have been given, the latest being that of Howard Paul which appeared at the Alhambra Theatre, London, July 4, 1881. The plot is founded upon a Chinese legend.

Chiara di Rosemberg — Italian opera, music by Luigi Ricci, words by Gaetano, produced in Milan, 1831. The libretto is based upon Genlis' novel "Le Siege de Rochelle," (The Siege of Rochelle). The opera was very successful.

Chieftain, The — An opera in two acts, music by Sir Arthur Sullivan, words by F. C. Burnand, produced at the Savoy Theatre, London, Dec. 12, 1894. It was elaborated from an earlier work of Burnand's given twenty-seven years before.

Chien du Jardinier, Le (The Gardener's Dog) — A comic French opera in one act. Music by A. Grisar, text by Cormon and Lockroy; produced at Paris, 1855. An amusing little love story in which the gardener's dog plays a very important part.

Children in the Wood, The — English opera in two acts, music by Dr. Samuel Arnold, words by Thomas Morton, produced in London, 1793. Later it became quite popular in America.

Children of the Plains, The — Opera in four acts by Rubinstein. Libretto adapted from Beck's "Yanko" by Mosenthal. Place, the plains of the Ukraine. Time, middle of the Nineteenth Century. First produced at Vienna in 1861.

Chilperic — Opera in three acts, music and words by Hervé, first produced Oct. 24, 1868. It was then a failure, but later became very popular, and has had many revivals. June 3, 1872, it was performed at the Globe Theatre, London, in French. An English version by H. Hersee and H. B. Farnie was given at the Lyceum, London, Jan. 22, 1870, at the opening of the Empire Theatre, London, April 17, 1884, and in 1903 at the Coronet Theatre, Notting Hill.

Chinese Honeymoon, The — Musical comedy, by George Dance and Howard Talbot, first produced in London, and in New York in 1902.

Chi Sofre Speri — Italian musical comedy, music by Mazzocchi and Marazzoli, produced in Florence under the patronage of the Cardinal Barberini in 1639. This is given by some authorities as the origin of opera buffa; it was without doubt one of the first comic operas.

Christoforo Colombo — Italian opera in four acts, music by Alberto Franchetti, produced in Genoa, October, 1892. Its success is mainly due to some wonderful scenic effects, descriptive of the voyage of Columbus to America.

Christus — Sacred Russian opera, music by Rubinstein, produced in Berlin, 1888. With this composition and Moses, a similar one, the composer may almost be said to have produced a new form of music. It has had but a partial success.

Cid, Le — Opera in three acts, music and words by Peter Cornelius, first produced at Weimar, in 1865. The scene is Burgos, Spain, in the year 1064. The incidents described are the triumph of the Cid, Ruy Diaz, Spain's national hero, over the Moors and his happy union with his love, Chimine, although he had been compelled to kill her father in order to defend his own honor. This opera is the best work of Cornelius and shows the Wagnerian influence.

Cigale, et le Fourmi, La (The Grasshopper and the Ant) — Comic opera in three acts, music by Audran, words by Chivot and Duru, first produced at the Gaite, Paris, October 30, 1886. English version by F. C. Burnand and Ivan Caryll, produced for the first time in England at the Lyric Theatre, London, Oct. 9, 1890.

Cimarosa — Comic French opera in two acts. Music by Nicolo Isouard, words by Bouilly, produced at Paris, 1808.

Cinna — Opera by Graun, text by Villati, produced at Berlin, 1748.

Cinq-Mars — French opera in four acts by Gounod, words by Poisson and Gallet, produced in Paris, 1877. The libretto is freely adapted from a novel by de Vigny. The scene is the French court in the time of Louis XIII.

Circassian Bride, The — English opera, music by Sir Henry Bishop, first produced in London, 1809. This was Bishop's first opera.

Circassienne, La (The Circassian) — French comic opera; music by Auber, text by Scribe, produced at Paris in 1861. Some Russian officers in garrison produce the opera "Adolphe et Clara." The general thinks he recognizes in "Clara," one of the young officers disguised, a former sweetheart.

Circe ed Ulisse (Circe and Ulysses) — Italian opera, music by Astarita, produced in Naples, 1777. The story is from mythology.

Circus Girl, The — Musical play in two acts, music by Ivan Caryll and

Lionel Monkton, book by James T. Tanner and W. Palings, lyrics by Harry Greenbank and Adrian Ross, first produced at the Gaiety Theatre, London, Dec. 5, 1896.

Ciro in Babilonia — Italian opera, music by Rossini, produced in Ferrara, 1812. This was composed when Rossini was but twenty-one and though not in itself successful, it contains a few good selections afterward used in other operas. As "Cyrus in Babylon" it was performed in London, 1823.

Ciro Riconosciuto — Italian opera in three acts, music by Albinoni, words by Métastase, produced at Rome in 1710.

Clari, The Maid of Milan — Dramatic opera by John Howard Payne, first produced in New York, 1823. The famous song, "Home, Sweet Home" was contained in this opera.

Claude Duval; or, Love and Larceny — A romantic and comic opera in three acts, by H. P. Stephens and Eduard Solomon, first produced at the Olympic Theatre, London, Aug. 24, 1881.

Claudine — Comic French opera in one act, music by Bruni, text by Deschamps, produced at Paris, 1794. Story after Florian's novel "Claudine," the little messenger.

Claudine von Villabella — German lyric opera. Text by Goethe, and set to music by a great number of German composers, among them J. Andre (Berlin, 1780); Gottfried Weber, (Stuttgart, 1783); Franz Knappe, (Dusseldorf, 1882). Franz Schubert also wrote an opera for it but it was never put on the stage.

Claudius Cäsar — German opera, music by Keiser, words by Hinsch, produced in Hamburg, 1703. Claudius was the husband of Agrippina and was poisoned by her, that she might make Nero emperor.

Cle d'Or, La — Opera, music by Gautier, first produced in Paris, 1877. The plot is taken from Octave Feuillet's novel by the same name.

Clemenza di Tito, La (The Mercy of Titus) — Italian opera, music by Gluck, words by Métastase, produced in Naples, 1751. Vitellia, daughter of the deposed emperor Vitellius, plots to overthrow Titus, but he escapes, pardons all implicated and marries Vitellia.

Clemenza di Tito, La (The Mercy of Titus) — Italian opera, music by Mozart, produced in Prague, Sept. 6, 1791, upon the coronation of Leopold II. The libretto was adapted from a much earlier one by Métastase. This opera was one of Mozart's last, and its cold reception by the public did much to embitter his last years.

Cleofide — An Italian opera. Music by Buini, produced at Venice, 1721. Cleofide is identical with Alexander the Great.

Cleopatra — German opera, music by Mattheson, words by Feustking, produced in Hamburg, Oct. 20, 1704. At this first performance occurred the famous duel between Händel and Mattheson, which was fought out on the stage before a crowd of spectators.

Clochette, La (The Little Bell) — French comic opera in one act. Music by Duni, text by Anseaume, produced at Paris, 1766.

Colomba — English opera in four acts, music by Sir Alexander Mackenzie, words by Hüffner, produced in London, 1882. The libretto is founded upon Mérimée's tale by the same name. The scene is Corsica and the story deals with a feud between the two families of Rebbia and Barracini.

Colombe, La (The Dove) — French comic opera, music by Gounod, words by Barbier and Carré, produced in Paris, in 1866. The libretto is an adaptation of one of Lafontaine's fables.

Colon, El (Columbus) — Spanish opera, music by Carnicer, produced in Barcelona in 1818.

Colonie, La (The Colony) — Comic opera in two acts. Music by Sacchini, text by Framery, produced at Paris, 1775. The situations are very ludicrous and the music charming.

Colonnello, Il (The Colonel) — Italian opera, music by L. and F. Ricci, words by Ferreti, produced in Naples, 1835.

Colporteur, Le; ou, L'Enfant du Bûcheron (The Peddler; or, the Wood Woodcutter's Child) — French comic opera in three acts, music by G. Onslow, words by Planard, produced in Paris, 1827. The story is taken from an old Russian chronicle. As "The Emissary" it was later produced in England.

Comte de Carmagnole, Le (The Count of Carmagnole) — French opera, music by Ambroise Thomas, words by Scribe, produced in Paris, 1841. It was not a success and is no longer sung.

Comte Ory, Le — French lyric opera in two acts, music by Rossini, words by Scribe and Delestre-Poirson, first produced in Paris in 1828. The libretto was adapted from a vaudeville by the same authors founded upon an old legend. Rossini adapted to these words some of the music from his "Viaggio à Reims."

Concert a la Cour, Le; ou, La Debutante (The Concert at Court; or, The Debutante) — Comic French opera in one act, music by Auber, text by Melesville and Scribe, produced at Paris, 1824.

Concert Interrompu, Le (The Interrupted Concert) — French comic opera in one act. Music by Berton, words by Favieres and Marsollier, produced at Paris, 1802.

Condor — Italian opera, music by Antonio Gomez, produced in Milan, 1891.

Confidences, Les (The Secrets) — French comic opera in two acts. Music by Niccolò Isouard, words by Hoffmann, produced at Paris, 1803. Text is lively, and the music added to Isouard's reputation.

Connétable de Clisson, Le — French opera in three acts, music by Porta, words by Aignan, produced in Paris, 1804.

Conradin v. Schwaben (Conrad of Swabia) — German opera in three acts, music by Conradin Kreutzer, produced in Stuttgart, 1812. Conrad was the best of the Hohenstauffens and was executed in Naples in the year 1268, at the command of Charles of Anjou.

Constanza e Fortezza (Constancy and Courage) — Italian opera; music by Johann Joseph Fux in collaboration with François Conti. First produced at Prague in 1723 at the coronation of Charles VI. as King of Bohemia. Extra musicians from Prague and from Italy were hired for this grand occasion, and Fux received great praise for his work. His compositions are now wholly unknown.

Consuelo — Opera by Alfonso Rendano, libretto by Francesco Cimmino, first produced in Milan in 1901. Text is adapted from a once popular novel by George Sand. Consuelo (Consolation) is a young singer who saves an unfortunate soul by the wonderful power of her music. This opera soon after appeared in Germany and though the plot is slender, the music has given a great deal of pleasure.

Conte d'Avril (Story of Avril) — French musical comedy, text by Auguste Dorchain, music by Charles M. Widow, produced at Paris in 1885. This first appeared as a play, music was added later. Music is excellent.

Contessa d'Amalfi, La (The Countess of Amalfi) — Italian opera, music by Petrella, produced in Turin, 1864.

Contrabandista (The Smuggler) — Operetta in two acts by Sir Arthur Sullivan with text by Burnand, produced at London in 1867. It was completely overshadowed by "Cox and Box" which appeared in the same year. In 1894 "Contrabandista" was revived as "The Chieftain."

Convito, Il (The Banquet) — Italian opera by Cimarosa, produced at Venice, 1782.

Coppélia, ou La Fille Aux Yeux d'Email (Coppelia, or The Girl with the Glass Eyes) — A French ballet by Clement Delibes, first produced at Paris in 1870. This ballet is based upon the pretty comedy "Coppélia." It is Delibes' greatest success and has kept the boards ever since its first performances.

Cora — Swedish opera, music by J. G. Naumann, produced in Stockholm, 1780. The libretto is adapted from Marmontel's "Incas." Cora, the heroine of the opera, was a Priestess of the Sun in Peru. The work is Naumann's best.

Cordelia — Russian opera, music by Soloviev, produced in St Petersburg, 1885. The libretto is adapted from Shakespeare's tragedy, King Lear. The opera has been widely given in Russia and was sung in 1890 in Prague. It is Soloviev's best work.

Coriolano (Coriolanus) — Italian opera, music by Ariosti, produced in London, 1723. Coriolanus was the Roman patrician and general who lived in the Fifth Century, B. C.

Corisandre — French opera comedy in three acts, music by Langle, words by Le Bailly and Livières, first produced in Paris, 1791. The plot is taken from Voltaire's "Pucille."

Cornelius Schutt — Opera in three acts, music by Swareglia, words by Illica, first produced at Prague, 1893. The time is 1630, in Antwerp. The opera rehearses the unfortunate loves of Cornelius Schutt, a painter.

Corona, La — Opera in one act, music by Glück, words by Métastase, produced at Vienna, 1765.

Corrado d'Altamura (Conrad of Hohenstauffen) — Italian opera, music by F. Ricci, produced in Milan, 1841. This Conrad was the last of the Hohenstauffens, executed at the command of Charles of Anjou, in 1268, at Naples.

Corregidor, Der (A Spanish Magistrate) — German opera in four acts, music by Hugo Wolf, text by Rosa Mayreder-Obermayer, first produced at Mannheim, 1896. Text is from a Spanish novel by Alarcon called "The Trideut." A miller and his beautiful wife live very happily together when the corregidor tries to separate them. The situations are funny and light, and though the music is at times a little heavy for the text, it is a splendid opera and must appear on every stage of any operatic pretensions.

Corsaro, Il (The Corsaire) — Italian opera by Verdi, produced at Trieste in 1848.

Cosaque, La — Comic opera in three acts, music by Hervé, words by Henri Meilhac and Albert Millaud, first produced February 1, 1884. An English version by Sydney Grundy was put on at the Gaiety Theatre, Hastings, April 7, 1884, and at the Royalty Theatre, London, April 12, 1884.

Cosi fan Tutte (As All Do It) (So Machen's Alle) — An Italian comic opera in two acts; music by Mozart, and text by L. da Ponte, Vienna, 1790. The music does not equal the best of Mozart's compositions probably because the foolishness of the libretto failed to inspire the composer. In spite of this the opera was very popular and many attempts were made in Germany, England and France to change the libretto. The plot is founded upon a foolish wager between an old cynic philosopher and two young Neapolitan officers to prove the constancy of their respective sweethearts. The test is to last one day and if the cynic wins, the wager is to cost the young noblemen a feast. After a touching farewell, the young officers leave their fiancées and soon return disguised as Albanians and make violent love each to the other's sweetheart. At first the girls resist all their pleadings and charms, but toward the close of the day the ardent foreigners win and the girls accept their protestations of love. But when the girls discover who these supposed lovers are their repentance wins them forgiveness from their real lovers, and when they in turn are told of the wager the scene ends merrily in a big feast. The music is often very delightful and sparkling.

Cosimo — French opera in two acts, music by Eugène Prévost, words by Saint-Hilaire and Paul Duport, produced in Paris, 1835. The plot is founded upon an Italian story of a prince who changes clothes with a workman named Cosimo.

Coupé du Roi de Thulé, La (The Goblet of the King of Thulé) — French fairy opera in three acts and four tableaux, music by Eugene Diaz, words by L. Gallet and Edouard Blau, first produced in Paris, 1873.

Cour de Célimène, La (The Courting of Célimène) — French comic opera, music by Ambroise Thomas, words by Rosier, produced in Paris, 1855. Célimène is a coquette, whose hand is sought by two French officers. The opera is no longer on the stage.

Courte Échelle, La (The Short Ladder) — French comic opera; music by E. Membrée, libretto by De la Rounet, produced at Paris in 1879. To make a ladder for some one means to let some one step on your shoulder. In the opera a young chevalier really does reach his sweetheart's window by stepping on the shoulders of his rival. The libretto is excellent.

Cox and Box — English operetta in one act and seven tableaux, music by Arthur Sullivan, words by Bernand, produced in London, 1867. The libretto is adapted from Morton's farce "Box and Cox." This is the germ from which sprang all of Sullivan's later operas.

Creole, La — Comic opera in three acts, music by Offenbach, words by Milland, first produced in Paris, 1875. In 1877 it was compressed into one act by Reece with lyrics by Farnie and presented at the Folly Theatre, London.

Cricket on the Hearth, The (Das Heimchen am Herd) — An opera in three acts, music by Carl Goldmark, words by A. M. Willners, first produced in Berlin, June 27, 1896, has been performed with marked success in numerous German theatres. The story is founded on Dicken's tale by the same name.

Crociato in Egitto, Il (The Crusader in Egypt) — Heroic opera, music by Meyerbeer, words by Rossi, first produced in Venice, 1825. This opera, in which the German and Italian styles are combined, brought the composer his first great recognition, and was soon presented in London and Paris.

Crœsus — German opera, music by Reinhard Keiser, words by Bostel, produced in Hamburg, 1711. Crœsus, the mythological King of Lydia, is the hero of the opera.

Cross and the Crescent, The — Opera, music by Colin McAlpin, words arranged by the composer from Davidson's translaton of "Pour la Couronne," a tragedy by Coppée, first produced in London, 1903. This opera won the Manner's prize of £250.

Crown Diamonds, The (Les Diamonts de la Couronne) — Comic opera in three acts by Auber, words by Scribe and St. George, first produced in Paris in 1841, and in English, May 2, 1844, at the Princess Theatre, London. The scene of the opera is laid in Portugal in 1777. The Queen, masquerading as the Countess Villa Fln and as Caterina, a brigand maid, pawns the crown diamonds after causing false duplicates to be made of them. After various exciting adventures she marries Enrico whom she first met as a captive among the brigands. It is considered one of the best of Auber's operas and scored its greatest success at Drury Lane in 1854.

Cruche Cassée, La (The Broken Pitcher) — French comic opera, music by Léon Vasseur, words by Moinaux and Noriac, produced in Paris, 1875.

Crusaders, The — English opera, music by Sir Julius Benedict, produced in London, 1846. The German and French versions are called "The Old Man of the Mountain." The opera is one of Benedict's best and has been given with great success.

Cupid's Revenge — English opera, music by James Hook, produced in London, 1772.

Curioso Indiscretto, Il (An Indiscreet Curiosity) — Italian opera in three acts, music by Pasquale Anfossi, produced at Milan, 1778.

Cymbia; or, The Magic Thimble — Comic opera in three acts, music by Florian Pascal, words by Harry Paulton, produced at the Strand Theatre, London, March 26, 1883.

Cymon — English opera, music by Michael Arne, produced in London, 1767.

Cyrus und Kassandra (Cyrus and Cassandra) — Opera by J. D. Hensel. Produced at Vienna, 1800. Cyrus, the founder of the Persian dynasty, in the Sixth Century before Christ, forms subject of operas by many European composers. The earliest under the Italian title "Ciro," by Cavalli and Mattioli, appeared in Venice, 1665.

Cythère Assiegée (The Siege of Cythere) — A ballet opera in three acts. Music by Gluck, text by Favert, produced at Paris, 1775. This opera had appeared a year before as a ballet with songs by Fagan. It can not be said that Glück's music added much to the piece.

D

Dafne — Italian opera, music by Peri, Caccini and Corsi, words by Rinuccini, produced privately in Corsi's house, 1597. The heroine is the Daphne of mythology, whom Zeus changed into a laurel tree, that she might escape the pursuit of Apollo. It is one of the first real operas.

Dalibor — Czechish opera in three acts, music by Smetana, words by Wenzig, produced in Prague, 1867. The scene is laid in Prague in the Fifteenth Century.

Dame de Monsoreau, La (The Lady of Monsoreau) — French opera, music by Salvayre, produced in Paris, January 30, 1888. The libretto is founded upon Dumas' drama.

Dame de Pique, La — French comic opera in three acts, music by Halévy, words by Scribe, produced in Paris, December 28, 1850. The libretto is founded upon Poushkin's novel by the same name, but the tragic ending is changed. The young lieutenant is successful at the gaming table, he wins from his rival, Colonel Zizianoff, and marries Poloska, the girl they both love.

Dame du Lac, La (The Lady of the Lake) — Opera in four acts. Music by Rossini, text by A'Epagny, Rousseau and Horace Raisson, produced at Paris, 1825.

Dame Invisible, Le (The Invisible Lady; also called "L'Amant à l'Epreuve," The Lover on Trial) — French comic opera, music by Berton, written in 1783, but not produced till December, 1787, in Paris. It was Berton's first opera and a great success.

Damnation of Faust, The — Opera in four parts by Hector Berlioz. Libretto founded upon Goethe's "Faust," and adapted by Berlioz, Gérard and Gadonnière. Place, Hungary and Northern Germany. Time, Seventeenth Century. First produced in Paris in 1846.

Damon and Phillida (Damon and Phillis) —English comic opera. Music by Dibdin, produced at London, 1767.

Danaïdes, Les — French opera, music by Antonio Salieri, words by Rollet and Tschudy, produced in Paris, 1784. The Danaïdes were the fifty daughters of King Danaus, who murdered their husbands and were punished in the lower world by having continually to dip up water in perforated vessels. Salieri was a pupil of Gluck's and the opera was produced the first twelve times under the latter's name.

Dante, Le — French opera in four acts, music by Benjamin Godard, produced in Paris, 1890.

Daphne — German opera, music by Heinrich Schutz, words by Opitz, produced in Torgan, 1627. Opitz merely translated the libretto by the same title, which Rinuccini had written for "Peri." It is the oldest and was for fifty years the only German opera. All of it, score as well as book, is no longer extant.

Daphnis et Alcimadure — Opera in three acts and prologue, words and music by Mondonville, produced in Paris, 1754. The opera is written in the patois of Languedoc, of which the composer was a native.

Dardanus — Tragic opera in five acts. Music by Rameau, words by La Bruere. First represented at Paris in 1739. Dardanus was the mythological founder of the Trojans.

Das War Ich (That Was I) — Simple comic opera, a village idyl, in one act. Music by Blech, words by Hutt V. Batka. First produced at Dresden in 1902, at Berlin in 1907. Best songs are: "In My Sweetheart's Garden"; "Am I Crazy?"; "Where Love and Love Unite," the closing quartette.

Daughter of St. Mark, The — English opera, music by Balfe, first produced in London, 1845.

Déa — A French comic opera; music by J. Cohen, text by Carré and Cormon, produced at Paris in 1870. The opera tells of the quest of a young Peruvian for his sister Déa. Finally he finds a girl whom he believes to be his sister, but she is not, they fall in love, and marry.

Defender, The — Comic opera, music by Charles Dence, words by Allen Lowe, produced in New York, 1902.

Deidamia — Italian opera, music by Handel, first produced at London in 1739. Deidamia was the wife of Achilles.

Delila — Opera in three acts. Music by Camille Saint-Saëns, words by Ferdinand Lemaire. German translation by Richard Pohl. First performed at Dresden in 1900. Libretto is based upon the Bible story; scene is laid in Gaza in Palestine, 1150 years before Christ. The opera was written thirty years ago but at first met with no success. Liszt had it produced at Weimar in 1877 but it failed. In 1890 it was performed at Rouen, and in 1892 at Paris, and since then it has been a great favorite at Paris.

Delire, ou Les Suites d'Une Erreur, Le (The Delirium, or The Sequels of a Blunder) — Comic opera in one act, music by Berton, text by Saint-Cyr, produced at Paris in 1799. Opera is almost too dramatic to be called a comic opera, the music is one of Berton's best efforts.

Demente, La (The Mad Woman) — Italian opera, music by Marchetti, produced in Turin in 1857.

Demetrio (Demetrius) — Italian opera, music by Perez, words by Métastase, produced in Turin, 1752. Demetrius was King of Syria, 161-150, B. C.

Demofoonte (Demophoon) — Italian opera, music by Jomelli, words by Métastase, produced in Stuttgart, 1770. Demophoon was son of Theseus and King of Athens.

Demoiselle d'Honneur, La (The Bridesmaid) — Comic opera in three acts. Music by Theophile Semet, text by Kauffmann and Mestepes, produced at Paris, 1857. Action is melodramatic and the music is largely dependent upon the orchestra.

Demon de la Nuit, Le (The Demon of the Night) — French opera in two acts, music by J. Rosenhain, words by Bayard and Etienne Arago, produced in Paris, 1851.

Demophon — Lyric tragedy in three acts, music by Cherubini, words by Marmontel, first produced in Paris, 1788. The libretto is founded upon Métastase's "Demofoonte." This opera marks Cherubini's transition from a light, trivial attitude to the grand style of his later works.

Denys le Tyran, Maître d'École à Corinthe (Denys the Tyrant, Schoolmaster at Corinth) — French opera in one act, music by Grétry, words by Sylvain Marechal, produced in Paris, 1794. This is one of the composer's poorest efforts.

Deseret — Romantic comedy opera, music by Dudley Buck, produced in New York, 1880. The theme is a Mormon one. The opera's lack of success was largely due to the inadequacy of the company which presented it.

Deserteur, Le (The Deserter) — French opera, music by Monsigny, words by Sedaine, produced in Paris, 1769. The story is one of a soldier, who deserts in a fit of jealous rage, is captured and sentenced to be shot, when his sweetheart begs and secures his pardon of the king.

Deux Averes, Les (The Two Misers) — French comic opera, music by Grétry, words by Falbaire, produced in Paris, 1770. It has been revised several times since, notably by Isouard and Agnelli.

Deux Billets, Les (The Two Letters) — A French comic opera in one act; music by C. Poisot, libretto by Florian, produced at Paris in 1858. A young lover loses two letters, one from his sweetheart and another containing a lottery ticket and he loses thereby both his treasures.

Deux Familles, Les (The Two Families) — Comic opera, music by Labarre, words by Planard, first produced at Paris, 1831. The text is taken from the story of the "Cid." The music is excellent, and contains numerous pretty airs for which Labarre was famous. The bass solo "Non, de Ma Just Colere" has become a classic, it is one of the best French songs.

Deux Gentilshommes, Les (The Two Gentlemen) — Comic opera in one act, music by M. J. Cadaux, text by Planard, produced at Paris, 1844.

Deux Maris, Les (The Two Husbands) — French comic opera in one act. Music by Isouard, text by Etienne, produced at Paris, 1816.

Deux Nuits, Les (The Two Nights) — French comic opera in three acts, music by Boieldieu, words by Scribe and Bouilly, produced in Paris, 1829. This, the composer's last opera, was not a success owing to the dullness of the libretto. An English adaptation is called "The Night Before the Wedding."

Deux Reines, Les (The Two Queens) — French comic opera in one act. Music by H. Monpou, text by Arnould and Soulie, produced at Paris, 1835. A comedy full of amusing incidents in which the Queens of Denmark and Sweden travel incognito and in disguise. Music and libretto are both excellent.

Deux Salem, Les — French fairy opera in one act, music by Daussoigne, words by Paulin de Lespinasse, produced in Paris, 1824.

Deux Sergents, Les (The Two Sergeants) — Comic opera by N. Louis, produced at Orleans, 1850.

Deux Sœurs Jumelles, Les (The Twin Sisters) — French comic opera in one act, music by Fétis, words by Planard, produced in Paris, 1823.

Deux Suisses, Les (The Two Swiss) — French song play, music by Gaveaux, words by Demonstier, produced in Paris, 1792.

Deux Voleurs, Les (The Two Thieves) — French comic opera in one act; music by Girard, text by Brunswick and de Leuven, produced at Paris in 1841. The two thieves, Jean Beauvais and a marquis, decide to rob Adeline on her wedding night. One decides to steal her diamonds, the other to rob her of her honor. After all the wedding guests have gone the new husband is called away from home through a forged message, but when Adeline discovers the robbers she cleverly holds them till her husband returns. She manages to make each thief believe that he is protecting her against the other. The text is full of clever incidents.

Devil's Bridge, The—English opera, music by John Braham, produced in London, 1816. Much of the popularity of this opera was due to the singing of the composer, who took one of the principal roles.

Devil's in It, The — English opera, music by Balfe, first produced in London, 1852.

Devin du Village, Le (The Village Soothsayer) — A comic French opera by Rousseau. First performed at the Academie de Musique in 1753. So popular did it become that it kept the stage for more than sixty years and travelled all over France. This little opera really became epoch making since it inaugurated a reaction against the stiff, pompous tragedies and turned the tide in favor of simple, natural musical expression. Itself an imitation of the Italian comic opera, it was soon copied by German and English composers. The plot is simple; Colette, who fears that she has lost the love of her sweetheart Coem, consults a soothsayer. He advises her to pretend that she no longer loves Coem and by being indifferent to win him back; she does this and succeeds in regaining her lover.

Diable à l'École, Le (The Devil at School) — Comic French opera in one act. Music by Boulanger, text by Scribe, produced at Paris in 1842. The Devil pays a visit to Italy hoping to seduce some soul to Hades. A young Italian plays cards with the Devil, stakes his whole fortune and loses. The Devil returns him his money on condition that he will give him his soul. The young man readily agrees. When his sister hears this, she offers to go in his place and puts herself under the protection of her patron saint. Unable to cope with the saint, the Devil is foiled, and must return alone to Hell. Scribe made a bright libretto of a somewhat worn subject, and Boulanger's music added color to the text.

Diable à Quatre, Le (The Devil's to Pay) — A French comic opera in four acts. Music by Philidor, text by Sedaine, produced at Paris, 1756. Other composers have used the same subject.

Diable à Seville, Le (The Devil at Seville) — Comic opera in one act. Music by Gomis, text by Hurtado and Cave, produced at Paris, 1831.

Diadeste — English opera, music by Balfe, first produced in London, 1838. Diadeste is Arabian for "A Game of Chance."

Diana and Endymion — French opera, music by Piccini, words by Leron, produced in Paris, 1784. The story is from Greek mythology.

Diana von Solange — Grand opera in five acts. Music by Ernst Duke of Saxony-Coburg-Gotha, words by O. Prechtler. First produced at Coburg in 1858, and at Leipsic, 1872, in the presence of the composer. Time of the story is 1586, and scene is laid in Portugal.

Diarmid — English grand opera in four acts, music by Hamish McCunn, words by the Duke of Argyll, produced in London, 1897.

Diavole a Quattro, Il (The Devil to Pay) — Italian opera, music by Luigi Ricci, produced in Trieste, 1859. It was Ricci's last opera.

Dichter und Welt (The Poet and the World) — Musical drama in three acts with prologue and epilogue. Music by Waldemar von Baussnern, words by Julius Petri. First performed at Weimer in 1897. Time of story about 1350; scene Swabia and the Alps. "Sacred Rest" for the bass; "The Water's Roar," for the soprano, are among the solos.

Dick — Comic opera in two acts, music by Edward Jakobouski, words by Alfred Murray, produced at Globe Theatre, London, April 17, 1884. This amusing version of the career of Richard Whittington, thrice mayor of London, was most popular in its day.

Dickshädel, Die (The Obstinate Daughter) — Bohemian comic opera in one act, music by Antonin Dvořák, words by Stolba, produced in Prague, 1882, but written in 1874. The theme is such a national one, that the opera has not been given with success outside of Bohemia.

Dido and Æneas — English opera in three acts, music by Purcell, words by Nahum Tate, poet laureate of England at the time, produced in a young ladies' school in Leicester Fields near London, 1695. Virgil's version of the story of Dido and Æneas is followed fairly closely. The opera is said to be the first ever written in England.

Didone Abbandonata (Dido Abandoned) — Italian opera, music by Galuppi, words by Métastase, produced in Naples, 1724. It is the old story of Dido and Æneas.

Dieu et la Bayadére, Le (The God and the Danseuse) — French opera-ballet in two acts, music by Auber, words by Scribe, produced in Paris, 1830. Text is adapted from Goethe's ballade, and the opera is a great favorite in France. It is one of Auber's best productions.

Dieux de la Foire, Les (The Gods of Market-Day)—French comic opera, music by Jean Claude Gillier, produced in Paris, 1724. It is important as one of the earliest French comic operas.

Dilettante d'Avigon, Le (The Dilettante of Avigon) — A comic opera in one act; music by F. Halévy and text by Hoffmann and Leon Halévy, produced at Paris in 1829. The text satirizes Italian music.

Dinorah (Le Pardon de Ploermel) — A fanciful opera in three acts; music by Meyerbeer, words by Barbiere and Carré. First produced in Paris, in 1859. The story is founded upon a Brittany idyl, and the music is full of the witchery of elf folk, the raging of the storm winds, and the song of birds. On a holiday set aside by the villagers of Ploermel for a pilgrimage to the shrine of the Virgin, Holl, the goatherd, and his affianced, Dinorah, set out to receive the holy benediction. On their way to the shrine a violent thunderstorm wrecks Dinorah's home. Believing he can find the key to treasure to console Dinorah for her loss, Holl sets out to look for it. He is gone a year, during which Dinorah believing he has forsaken her becomes demented and wanders about the woods with her goat seeking him. At the end of a year he returns and Dinorah becomes herself again.

Disgrazie d'Amore, Le (The Accidents of Love) — Italian opera by Cesti, words by Sbarra, produced in Vienna in 1667.

Disperazione di Filene, La (Philene's Distress) — This little sketch done in recitative by Cavalieri and produced at private entertainments in Florence in 1590 is important in opera history because it is one of the earliest forms of opera.

Distruzzione di Gerusalemme, La (The Destruction of Jerusalem) — Sacred opera; music by Zingarelli, text by Sografi, produced at Rome, 1810. This subject forms the text for many operas.

Djamileh — French comic opera in one act, music by Bizet, words by Gallet, produced in Paris in 1872. It is an Oriental story, the scene is laid in Cairo, Djamileh is a slave girl, devotedly attached to her master, Harun.

Docteur Magnus, Le—French opera in one act, music by Ernest Boulanger, words by Cormon and Carré, produced in Paris, in 1864.

Docteur Ox, Le — Comic opera in three acts, music by Offenbach, words by Gille and Mortier, first produced in Paris, 1877. The plot is taken from one of Jules Verne's scientific stories.

Docteur Tamtam, Le (Doctor Tam Tam) — French operetta in one act by F. E. Barbier, produced at Paris, 1859.

Doctor of Alcantara, The — Comic operetta in two acts, music by Eichberg, words by Benjamin E. Wolfe, first produced in Boston, Mass., April 7, 1862, at the Museum. Dr. Paracelsus, of Alcantara, Spain, has a daughter, Isabella, whose mother, Lucrezia, has selected a suitor for her, but she loves an unknown serenader. After many amusing incidents the selected suitor proves to be the unknown serenader and with this happy denoument the clever operetta is concluded.

Doktar und Apotheker, Der (The Doctor and the Apothecary) — German operetta by Dittersdorf, words

Doktar und Apotheker, Der by Stephanie, produced in Vienna, July 11, 1786. The humor is rather broad but it is sound, and the operetta is still sung to-day.

Dolly Dollars, Miss—Musical comedy in two acts, music by Victor Herbert, words by Harry B. Smith, produced in New York, 1905.

Dolly Varden—Comic opera, music by Julian Edwards, words by Stanislaus Stange, produced in New York at the Herald Square Theater, 1902. The story is founded upon Wycherley's "Country Girl."

Dolores, La—Lyrical drama in three acts, words and music by Toimas Breton, produced in Madrid in 1895.

Domino Noir, Le (The Black Domino)—Comic opera in three acts, music by Auber, words by Scribe, first presented in Paris in 1837. The scene of the plot is laid in Madrid in the past century. The heroine, Angela, has entered a convent and is destined to become its Lady-Abbess, although she has not yet taken the vows. Seized with a desire for merry making, she dons a black domino and attends a mask ball. Here she meets a young nobleman, Horatio di Massarina, and mutual love is the result. Other disguises and meetings follow. Angela is about to become Abbess when Massarena goes to her to be relieved from a marriage with Ursula, an inmate of her convent who is destined for his bride. He recognizes his love of the black domino and, through the intervention of the Queen, is at length permitted to marry her.

Don Bucefalo—Italian comic opera, music by Cagnoni, produced in Milan, 1847.

Don Carlos—Opera in four acts, music by Verdi, words by Mery and Camilla du Locle, written for the Paris Exposition of 1867. The story tells of the love of Don Carlos for his step-mother, Elizabeth of Valois, Queen of Spain, and ends in a tragedy. This is one of Verdi's earliest operas and shows the faults of inexperience.

Don César de Bazan (Don Cæsar of Bazan)—French comic opera in three acts. Music by Massenet, libretto by Chantepie, Dumenoir, and Demmery, produced at Paris in 1872. This was preceded by a play written by these same gentlemen. The hero is one of the characters in Hugo's "Ruy Blas."

Don Chisotte (Don Quixote)—Italian comic opera, music by Ristori, produced in Dresden, 1727. It was one of the best of the operas founded upon Cervantes' romance.

Donna del Lago, La (The Lady of the Lake)—Italian opera in two acts, music by Rossini, words by Tottola, produced first in Naples, 1819, in London, 1823, Paris, 1824. The libretto is founded upon Scott's famous poem.

Donna Diana—German comic opera by Heinrich Hofmann, words by Wittkowsky, produced in Berlin, Nov. 13, 1886. Adapted from a comedy by Moreto.

Donna Diana—German comic opera by Reznicek, words by Moreto, produced in Prague in 1894. The story is a Spanish one at the time of the independence of Catalonia.

Don Quijote (Don Quixote)—Musical tragi-comedy in three acts. Music by Anton Beer-Wollbrunn, words by G. Fuchs. Founded on the well known Spanish romance. First produced at Munich, 1908, with Mr. Fritz Feinhals (high baritone) as the hero.

Don Quixote—Musical tragi-comedy in three acts, music and words by Wilhelm Kienzl, first produced in Berlin, 1898.

Don Sebastien, Roi de Portugal (Don Sebastian, King of Portugal)—French opera in five acts, music by Donizetti, words by Scribe, produced in Paris, 1843. This is one of the least successful of Donizetti's operas owing to the impossible situations of the plot.

Doralice—Italian opera, music by Mercadante, produced in Vienna, 1824.

Dorfbarbier, Der (The Village Barber)—Comic opera in one act. Music by Johann Schenk, words by Josef Weidmann. First performed in Vienna in 1796. Barber Lux is not only a clever hair-dresser but a village quack as well. He wants to marry his ward Susie but she and her lover outwit him. The comedy is still played in Germany.

Dorf im Gebirge, Das (The Village in the Mountains)—Musical comedy in two acts by Weigl with text by

Kotzebue. Produced in Vienna in 1798.

Dorflunys, Der (The Village Fair) — A musical comedy by G. Benda, first produced in 1776 and a great favorite.

Dorflunys, Der (The Village Scamp) — German opera in three acts, music by Jenö Hubay (Eugene Huber), text by Dr. Anton Verady after the folk-drama of the same title by E. Toth, produced at Berlin. A Hungarian village love affair in which several of the young folks are mixed up.

Dorfmusikanten, Die (The Village Musicians) — Opera by the Bohemian composer Karl Weis, text by R. Haas, first produced at Prague in 1905. Libretto is based on a slavic folk-story by Kajetan Tyl. It is the story of an old musician who goes out into the world to earn money enough to marry off his daughter. The elves help him and he nearly has a princess forced upon him for a wife, but after all his good fortune, he finds there's true happiness only in his simple home. The story is a quaint mixture of human and fairy folk and is decidedly Slavic in character. Its material is such that it will probably achieve its greatest success as a children's or Christmas performance.

Dori, La — Italian opera by Cesti, produced in Venice, 1663. The invention of the Da Capo was by Cesti and appeared for the first time in this opera.

Doriclea — Italian opera, music by Cavalli, produced in Rome, 1645. This composition marks the introduction of the comic element into opera.

Dorinda — Italian opera, music by Pescetti, and Galuppi, produced in Venice, 1729.

Doris — Comedy opera in three acts, music by Alfred Cellier, words by B. C. Stephenson, first produced at the Lyric Theater, London, April 20, 1889. This opera was almost a failure at first, but later it became very popular and has been revived several times.

Dormeur Eveille, Le (The Sleeper Awakened) — Comic opera in four acts, music by Piccinni, words by Marmontel, produced in Paris, in 1784. The plot is taken from the Arabian "Thousand and One Nights."

Though one of Piccini's lesser works, it is among the most popular of his productions and has been reproduced many times under different names.

Dornröschen (Sleeping Beauty) — German children's opera in four acts; music by Weweler, text by Eschenbach, first produced at Braunschweig in 1905. Libretto follows the fairy tale very closely and neither the composer nor the librettist has been able to rise to the occasion. The charm of this beautiful little story was lacking in the musical production.

Dorothy — A three-act English comic opera by Alfred Cellier, with text by Stephenson. It was produced at the Gaiety Theater in London, Sept. 25, 1886. Dorothy and her Cousin Lydia masquerade as peasant girls and fall in love with two young men to whom they give rings. Then in their own proper persons, but unrecognized by the two lovers, they manage to get their rings, accuse the two men of infidelity, and much fun and confusion results. The scene is laid in Kent, England, a hundred years ago. Dorothy was the most popular comic opera of its day and was performed nine hundred and thirty-one times consecutively in London.

Dot de Suzette, La (Suzett's Dowry) — French comic opera; music by Boieldieu, text by Fievée, produced at Paris, 1795. With this opera Boieldieu made his debut in dramatic music with a decided success.

Double Echelle, La (The Double Ladder) — Comic opera in one act. Music by Ambroise Thomas, text by Planard, first produced at Paris, 1837. This little opera is the first hit in the brilliant success of the composer.

Dov è Amore e Pietà (Where is Love and Pity) — Italian opera, music by Pasquini, produced in Rome, 1679.

Dragons de Villars, Les (Known in German as the Little Bell of the Hermit) — Comic opera in three acts. Music by L. A. Maillart, text by Cormon and Lockroy, produced at Paris in 1856. Time of the story is about 1704. Scene is laid in a little mountain village near the frontier. This is the only opera by Maillart that has survived and its wit, gaiety, and charming simplicity make it still a favorite in France and Germany.

Dragon of Wantley, The — Burlesque opera. Music by J. F. Lampe, text by the English poet Henry Watley. Produced at London about 1832. The aim of both composers and librettist was to "display in English the beauties of nonsense so prevalent in Italian operas." So well did the burlesque succeed that the opera gained an immense success.

Drame en 1779, Un — Operetta by Hervé. An English adaptation by Farnie, called "Up the River," was presented in London, 1877.

Drapier, Le (The Clothier) — French opera in three acts, music by Halévy, words by Scribe, produced in Paris, 1840.

Drei Pintos, Die (The Three Pintos) — Uncompleted comic opera by Weber, finished by Mahler and produced in 1821. The libretto is on a Spanish subject.

Drot og Marsk (King and Marshal) — Danish Grand opera, music by Heise, words by Richardt, produced at Copenhagen, 1878. The plot is founded upon incidents in the life of the wicked King Ehrich Christoffersen who was murdered in the year 1286, after dishonoring the wife of his marshal.

Dubrowski — Russian opera in four acts, music by Napravnik, libretto based on Puschkin's poem by the same title. Produced for the first time at St. Petersburg in 1895. The score is very musical and well adapted to the dramatic text. The opera has met with great success.

Duc d'Albe, Le (The Duke of Alba) — Early and unperformed Italian opera by Donizetti, one song, "Spirto Gentil," to which a later opera "La Favorite" owes most of its popularity was taken from the "Duc d'Albe."

Duc d'Olonne, Le (The Duke of Olonne) — Comic opera in three acts. Music by Auber, text by Saintine and Scribe, produced at Paris 1842. A Spanish entanglement in which political episodes are used as an excuse for some most improbable intrigues. The music is one of the best of Auber's compositions.

Dudelsackpfeifer Svanda, Der (The Bagpiper Svanda) — A Bohemian opera in three acts with a ballet. Music by Karl Bendl, libretto by Jaroslav Urchlisky, first produced at Prague in 1907. The old legend that the piper Svanda played upon his pipe every midnight for the evil spirits who danced on the gallows, forms the basis for the plot. The opera was produced at the tenth anniversary of the composer's death and it met with an enthusiastic reception.

Due Contesse, I (The Two Countesses) — Italian opera in two acts, music by Paisiello, first produced in Rome, 1777.

Due Foscari, I (The Two Foscari) — Italian opera in three acts, music by Verdi, words by Piave, produced in Florence, 1845. A doge of Venice in the Fifteenth Century, compelled to condemn his own son to death, is the leading figure in this tragic opera, which is not considered one of Verdi's best.

Due Gemelli, I (The Twins) — Italian comic opera, music by Guglielmi, produced in Rome, 1787.

Due Illustri Rivali, I (The Two Illustrious Rivals) — Italian opera, music by Mercadante, words by Rossi, produced in Venice, 1839.

Duenna — English opera. Music by Linley, words by R. B. Sheridan who married Linley's daughter. First produced at Convent Garden in 1775. Its success was immediate, though not lasting.

Dürer in Venedig (Durer in Venice) — Comic opera in two acts. Music by Baussnern, text by Adolph Bartels. First performed at Weimar in 1900. Text is based upon Adolph Stern's story by the same title. Time of story, 1506; scene is laid in Venice.

Dwe Vdovy (Two Widows) — Czechish opera in three acts, music by Smetana, words by Zungel, produced in Prague, 1874. The libretto is adapted from Malefille.

E

Earl and the Girl, The — Musical comedy in two acts, music by Ivan Caryll, book by Seymour Hicks, lyrics by Percy Greenbank, produced in New York, in 1905.

Echo et Narcisse (Echo and Narcissus) — Three-act French opera by Gluck, words by Baron Tschudi, produced in Paris, September 24, 1779. The story is from mythology.

Eddystone — Opera in three acts. Music and text by Adolph Wallnoefer. First produced at Prague in 1889. Text is based on Jensen's legendary novel by same title. Time of story, 1703; scene, The Eddystone, near the English coast.

Edgar — Italian opera by Puccini, words by Fontana, produced at La Scala, April 21, 1889. The text is founded upon La Coupé et les Lèvres, a melodrama by Alfred de Musset, full of extravagant adventures.

Eduardo e Christina (Edward and Christine) — Italian opera. Music by Rossini, text by Schmidt, first produced at Venice in 1819. Princess Christine of Sweden is expected to marry Prince James of Scotland. But she has already been secretly married to a Swedish officer, Edward. Both are thrown into prison; after a while Edward is liberated and when Russian ships fire upon Stockholm he saves the King's life. The gracious sovereign then forgives the lovers.

Edwin and Angelina, or The Banditti — Opera in three acts, music by Victor Pelissier, words by Elihu Hubbard Smith, produced in New York, December 19, 1796. One of the first American operas. Plot is based upon Goldsmith's "Edwin and Angelina."

Egmont — French opera, music by Salvayre, produced in Paris, 1883. The libretto is based upon the play by Goethe bearing the same name.

Eherne Pferd, Das (The Bronze Horse) — Fairy opera. Music by Daniel François Esprit Auber, text by Eugen Scribe. First produced in Paris, 1835. The scene is laid in China, and the opera has been rearranged by Humperdinck. Since the recent political events in China, the the opera has gained renewed interest on the German stage.

Eine Nacht in Venedig (A Night in Venice) — German operetta in three acts; music by Johann Strauss, text by Genée and Zell, produced at Berlin in 1883.

Ein Feldlager in Schlesien (A Camp in Silesia) — Opera in three acts, music by Meyerbeer, words by Rellstab, first produced in Berlin, 1843. Vielka and her lover, Konrad, save the life of Frederick the Great and later are rewarded when he for their sakes pardons Leopold, the foster-brother of Konrad.

Ekkehard, the Monk — Opera in five acts. Music by Johann Josef Abert, text based upon Viktor von Scheffel's novel by the same title. First performed in Berlin, 1878. Time of the story is the Tenth Century; scene is laid in castle and monastery in Switzerland. Coloring of the text is most exquisite.

Elaine — An English opera in four acts. Music by Herman Bemberg, text by Paul Ferrier, produced at New York in 1894. Elaine is a beautiful maiden who loves Lancelot, one of the Knights of King Arthur's Round Table. The music of the opera is pleasing, but it is not great. Madame Melba and the de Reszkes appeared in it; the composer has dedicated the opera to them.

Electra — Tragic opera, music by Richard Strauss, text is adapted from the drama by Hugo von Hoffmannsthal, first produced at Dresden in 1909 and soon after in New York. Electra's father, Agamemnon, has been foully slain by her mother, Clytemnestra, and her paramour. This fires Electra's soul with a thirst for revenge, she loses all her womanliness, and becomes a living demon as she plots to have them killed. She makes her brother, Orestes, become their mother's murderer, and when the deed is done she dances frantically till she falls breathless to the ground. Strauss has made even a stranger opera than was Von Hoffmannstahl's drama. It has provoked blame and praise, but even though the theme may be abhorrent, the music is that of a genius, a master who has been truly inspired.

Elements, Les (The Elements) — French ballet opera, music by Destouches with two numbers by Lalande, words by Roy, produced in Versailles, 1721, and in Paris, 1725. It is Destouche's best work. At the first production Louise XV. of France danced in the ballet.

Elena and Malvina — Italian opera, music by Carnicer, words by Felice Romani, produced in Madrid, 1828.

Eleonora — Italian light opera by Paër, produced in 1804 in Dresden. The idea of writing "Fidelio" came to Beethoven after hearing a performance of Eleonora.

Elisa and Claudio — Italian comic opera, music by Mercadante, words by Romanelli, produced in Milan, 1822.

Elisa, ou, Le Voyage au Mont Bernard (Elisa, or, The Voyage to Mount Bernard) — French opera in two acts, music by Cherubini, words by Saint-Cyr, first produced in Paris, 1794.

Eliza — English opera, music by Thomas Arne, produced in 1843. The Spanish Armada is the subject of the piece, and Queen Elizabeth the leading character.

Emerald Isle, The; or, The Caves of Carrig Cleena — Comic opera, music completed by Edward German from fragments left by Sir Arthur Sullivan, words by Captain Basil Hood, first produced in London, 1901. The action takes place in Ireland one hundred years ago and deals with an incipient rebellion.

Emma d'Antiochia — An Italian opera in three acts; music by Mercadante, libretto by Romani, produced at Venice in 1834. When Conrad of Montferrat returns from a successful siege he brings with him Emma of Antiochia as a hostage and he expects to make her his wife, but she secretly loves his nephew, and when she and Conrad's nephew are surprised at a secret meeting, the nephew is banished. Emma ends her unhappy life by taking poison.

Emma; ou, La Promesse Imprudente (Emma; or, The Imprudent Promise) — French comic opera in three acts, music by Auber, words by Planard, produced at Feydeau, 1821.

Emma und Eginhard — German opera with music by G. P. Telemannand, text by Wend. Produced at Hamburg, 1728. Subject is the love story of Emma, daughter of Charlemagne.

Emmeline, die Schweizerfamilie (Emmeline, the Swiss Family) — German comic opera in three acts. Music by Josef Weigl, text by Castelli, produced at Vienna, 1809. Subject is a popular theme in Germany and France. Weigl's musical setting is especially happy and is a general favorite.

Emmerich Fortunat — Opera by Reznicek, the Czechish composer, produced in Prague, 1889.

Enchanted Castle, The — English opera, music by William Shield, produced in London, 1786.

Enchanteresse — An opera by Flotow, first produced in Paris, April 9, 1878. On July 9, 1878, it was produced in London under the title, "Alma, l'Incantatrice." This is a revised version of Flotow's "Indra," and is founded upon the romantic adventures of the Portugese poet, Camoëns.

Enchantress, The — English opera, music by Balfe, produced in London, in 1844.

English Fleet, The — An English opera by Braham, produced at London in 1825.

Enrico Clifford (Henry Clifford) — Spanish opera, music by Isaac Albeniz, produced in Barcelona, 1894.

Enrico Conte di Borgogna — Italian opera by Donizetti, produced in Venice, 1818. It was Donizetti's first opera.

Enrico (Henry) — Italian opera, music by Galuppi, produced in Venice in 1743.

Enrico Quarto al Passo Della Marna (Henry IV. at the Pass of Marna) — Italian opera, music by Balfe, first produced at Milan, 1833.

Erbe von Morley, Der (The Heir of Morley) — A German opera in three acts; music and text by F. von Holstein, produced at Leipzig in 1872. The last heir of the house of Morley, Charles, a marine officer disappears. Some time later a naval officer comes to the castle to announce the death of Charles, but the officer resembles Charles so closely that the family accept him for the heir. In due time Charles returns and claims his rights.

Ercole Amante (Hercules in Love) — Italian opera, music by Cavalli, produced in Paris, 1662.

Erismena — Italian opera, music by Cavalli, produced in Venice, 1655.

Erminia Sul Giordano — Italian opera, music by Michael Angelo Rossini, produced privately in Rome, 1625. The libretto is founded upon an incident in Tasso's "Jerusalem Delivered." It was one of the earliest of Italian operas.

Ernelinde — French tragic opera, music by Philidor, words by Poinsinet, produced in Paris, 1767. The libretto is founded upon an Italian one "Ricimero," used by Pergolesi and Jomelli. Ernelinde was a princess of Norway. The opera is regarded as Philidor's finest work. It was reproduced in 1769 as "Sandomir."

Ero e Leander (Hero and Leander) — Italian opera, music by Luigi Mancinelli, first performed in concert form at the Norwich Festival, 1896, first produced on the stage at Madrid, 1897, at Covent Garden, London, 1898.

Erostrate — French opera in two acts by Reyer, words by Mery and Pacini, produced in Baden, 1862.

Erschaffena, Gefallene, und Aufgerichtete Mensch, Der (The Created, Fallen, and Risen Man) — German opera by Johann Theile produced in Hamburg, 1678. It was one of the first operas to be performed in Germany.

Erwin und Elmire — German operetta, music by Schweitzer, words by Goethe, the German poet, produced in Stuttgart about 1780.

Esclarmonde — French lyric drama in four acts by Massenet, produced in Paris, May 15, 1889. An old French romance forms the basis of the libretto.

Esmeralda — Russian light opera, music by Dargomijsky, finished in 1839, but not produced till 1847 in Moscow. The libretto is a translation of a French one founded upon "Notre Dame de Paris," by Victor Hugo.

Esmeralda — English opera by Goring Thomas, words by Marsials and Randegger, produced in London, 1883. Victor Hugo's "Notre Dame" served as foundation for the libretto.

Es War Einmal (Once Upon a Time) — A fairy opera. Music by Zemlinsky. Original text is that by the Danish poet, Holger Drachmann, and it follows pretty closely Anderson's fairy tale from which it was taken. As a play this joyous little thing is loved by the people of Denmark and appeared as such more than twelve years before Zemlinsky's opera. The opera has given great pleasure in Germany. It appeared in Berlin in 1900.

Étienne Marcel — French grand opera by Saint-Saëns, words by Gallet, produced in Lyons, 1879. The story is historical, the scene being laid in Paris in 1358 at the time of the uprising of the Parisians under Marcel.

Eulen Spiegel — German comic opera by Cyrill Kistler, produced in Wurzburg, 1889. Kotzebue's comedy by the same name forms the basis for the libretto. The opera has been without much success.

Eumene — Italian opera, music by Jomelli, produced in Naples, 1746. The theme is the same as that of Sophocles' tragedy, "Antigone."

Euphrosine et Coradin; ou, le Tyran Corrige (Euphrosine and Coradin; or, The Tyrant Reformed) — French comic opera in three acts, music by Méhul, words by Hoffman, produced in Paris, 1790. This was the first of Méhul's operas to be produced, and it at once established the composer's fame. The duet, "Gardez-vous de la Jalousie," was especially popular.

Europe Galante (Gay Europe) — A French ballet opera in four acts. Music by Campra, text by La Motte, produced at Paris, 1697.

Eurydice — Italian opera by Peri, Giulio Caccini, words by Rinuccini, produced in Florence at the court upon the marriage of Marie de Medici to Henry IV. of France, October 6, 1600. The libretto is the story of Orpheus and Eurydice. It is said to be the first real opera ever written.

Evangelimann, Der (The Evangelist) — Musical drama in two acts, music and words by Wilhelm Kienzl, produced in Berlin, 1894. The libretto was adapted from a work of Meiszner's. The success of the opera was phenomenal in Austria as well as in Germany.

Evelina — Italian opera by Coccia, produced at Milan, 1815.

Evenements Imprevus, Les (Unexpected Events) — French opera in three acts, music by Grétry, words by Hele, produced at Versailles, 1779.

Ewige Feuer, Das (The Eternal Fire) — German opera in one act by Richard Wetz, first produced at Düsseldorf in 1907 with moderate success. It is a story of ancient times in which Gana's lover dares to defy the gods and her father, the high priest. He takes her away from the altar where she is about to be made priestess of the eternal fire, and carries her away. He proclaims to the terror stricken friends that the gods do not exist, but that in his heart there is a stronger god, the god of love.

Ezio (Ætius) — Opera belonging to

the Eighteenth Century. The libretto by Métastase was so popular that at least twenty operas were written for it by European composers. Among them Porpora, Venice, 1728; Handel, London, 1733; Jomelli, Bologne, 1741; Glück, Vienna, 1763; Celli, Florence, 1830. Text is based upon historical events in Rome in 451-455. Ætius, the Italian general, successful against Attila, returns to Rome where he is received with great honor. The emperor, Valantinian III., becomes suspicious of him and condemns him to death, but is himself killed.

Ezio (Ætius) — Italian opera, music by Jomelli, words by Métastase, produced in Bologna, 1741.

F

Fabier, Die — German grand opera in five acts; music by A. Langert, text by G. von Meyern, produced at Coburg in 1867. The story is taken from Freytag's historical drama. Fabia, the daughter of a patrician, marries a plebian. The scene is laid in Rome in the Fourth Century before Christ.

Fahrende Schüler, Der (The Traveling Scholar) — A German comic opera in one act; music and libretto by Edgar Ital, now being produced on the German stage. An amusing comedy of the Sixteenth Century by Cervantes forms the basis for the story. The traveling scholar by his quick wit prevents a young wife and her lover from being discovered by her outraged old husband.

Fair Co-ed, The — Musical comedy in three acts, music by Gustav Luders, words by George Ade, first produced in Detroit, in 1908. It has had a great deal of success.

Fair Rosamund — English opera in four acts, music by John Barnett, produced in London, 1837. Rosamund was the beloved of Henry II. of England, and was called the Rose of Woodstock.

Fairy Queen, The — English opera by Purcell, appeared in London, 1692. Shakespeare's "Midsummer Night's Dream" furnishes the text for the libretto.

Falkner's Braut, Des (The Falconer's Bride) — German opera, music by Marschner, produced in Leipzig, in 1832. It was dedicated to King William IV. of England.

Fanal, Le (The Light-house) — French opera in two acts, music by Adolphe Adam, words by St. Georges, produced in Paris, 1849.

Fanatico per gli Antichi Romani, Il (The Fanatic for the Ancient Romans) — Italian comic opera, music by Cimarosa, produced in Naples in 1777. The opera was produced later as "Il Fanatico Burlato," (The Fanatic Ridiculed) and "Il Fanatico in Berlina" (The Fanatic in the Pillory). It is said to have been the first instance in which concerted numbers were inserted in the midst of the action.

Fanchon, the Zither Girl — German comic opera, in three acts. Music by T. H. Himmel with text by Kotzebue, produced at Berlin, 1804. Enjoyed a great popularity at its time.

Fantasio — French comic opera in three acts. Music by Offenbach with text taken from Musset's comedy, "Fantasio." Produced at Paris in 1872. The music lacked character and was not a success.

Faramondo — Opera by Handel, first produced at London, 1737. Hero is a legendary King of the Franks, Faramund, who lived in the Fourth Century.

Faramondo — Italian opera, music by Polarolo, produced in Venice in

1699. It was one of the first operas to contain arias in "da capo" form, and accompanied recitatives.

Farfadent, Le (The Goblin) — French comic opera in one act; music by Adam, text by Planard, produced at Paris in 1852. A sailor who is believed to be dead, returns to his home one stormy night, and his terrorized family believe him to be a goblin.

Farinelli — English opera, music by John Barnett, produced in London in 1839. It is generally regarded as the composer's best work.

Farnese (Pharnaces) — Italian opera, music by Sarti, produced in Venice, 1776. The hero of the opera is Pharnaces II., son of the great Mithridates, King of Pontus.

Fassbinder, Der (The Cooper) — German operetta by Schenk, produced at Vienna in 1790. The subject is adapted in part from a novel by Boccacio.

Faublas — German opera in three acts. Music by R. Würst, text by E. Wichert, produced at Berlin in 1873. Text is adapted from the French by Louvert. Young Baron Faublas is in love with Sophie de Pontis and visits her clandestinely at the convent where she is being educated. Faublas' father discovers the lovers but will not permit them to marry believing Sophie not to be his son's equal by birth. The lovers elope and it is then discovered that Sophie is the daughter of a baron from whom she had been stolen thirteen years before.

Faule Hans, Der (Idle Jack) — Opera in one act. Music by Alexander Ritter, text by Felix Dahn. First produced at Munich, 1885. Story is a fairy tale very poetically told. The orchestral composition of the opera deserves especial mention for its excellent coloring. In 1892 the opera was revived in Dresden and very cordially received.

Fausse Adventurière, La (The Pretended Adventuress) — A French operetta; music by Laruette, text by Marcouville and Anseaume, produced at Paris in 1757. An old man is inconsolable because his son has married a poor girl. The girl disguises herself and tells the old man sad experiences which she is supposed to have suffered. The old man loses his heart to her, and wants to marry her. Then the girl tells him who she is and the story ends happily. This operetta was exceptionally popular.

Fausse Magie, La (Mock Magic) — Comic opera in two acts. Music by Grétry, text by Marmontel, first produced at Paris, 1775. It was reduced to one act and has appeared on the French stage many times in the past century.

Faust — German opera by L. Spohr, text by J. C. Bernard, (a nom de plume) written for Vienna in 1813 but produced in Frankfurt in 1818. The libretto is not founded upon Goethe's drama, but more upon the folk-legend.

Fauvette — Comic opera in three acts by André Messager, produced in Paris at the Folies Dramatiques, November 17, 1885. An English version by Alfred Rae, lyrics by L. Foutaine was given in London, at the Royalty Theatre, November 16, 1891.

Faux Lord, Le (The False Lord) — French comedy in two acts. Music by Piccini, words by his son, first produced at Paris, 1783, and received with great favor.

Favorito, Il (The Favorite) —Italian opera, music by Pedrotti, produced in Turin in 1870. It was one of the composer's last operas, and the fashion for his music having somewhat abated, it never achieved much success.

Fée Aux Roses, La (The Rose Fairy) — French comic opera in three acts, music by Halévy, words by Scribe and Saint-Georges, produced in Paris in 1849. The story is a Persian fairy-tale. A spell has been cast over a beautiful slave, Nerilha, who is destined to become hideous, as soon as she falls in love.

Feen, Die (The Elves) — Wagner's first opera, music and words by him, written in 1851, but not produced until 1888 in Munich, five years after the composer's death. It is interesting, as showing the germ from which some of his later characteristics developed.

Fée Urgele, La (Urgele, the Fairy) — A French musical comedy by Duni, text by Favert, produced at Paris in 1765. The fairy Urgele is in love with Sir Robert and she disguises herself as a peasant girl and offers him some flowers. He steals a kiss. For this she has him sentenced to death. An old woman comes to his rescue but as a reward he is forced to marry her. Great is his joy when he finds that the old hag is Urgele who did it all to test his courage. This opera was very popular.

Félicie — French comic opera, music by Catrufo, words by Dypaty, produced in Paris in 1815.

Félix et Léonore (Felix and Leonore) — French comic opera in one act. Music by Benoist, text by Saint-Marcelin, produced at Paris, 1821.

Félix, ou l'Enfant Trouve (Felix, or The Foundling) — French opera, music by Monsigny, words by Ledaine, produced in Paris in 1777. It was the composer's last work

Felsenmühle zu Etatieres, Die (The Mill by the Cliff at Etatieres) — German opera. Music by Reissiger, text by Von Miltitz, produced at Dresden, 1833.

Femmes Vengies (The Avenged Women) — Comic opera in one act. Music by Philidor, text by Sedaine after "Remois," by La Fontaine. Produced at Paris, 1775. In 1811 Blangini wrote new music for the text.

Fencing Master, The — English comic opera in three acts, music by Reginald De Koven, words by Harry B. Smith, produced in New York in 1892. The scene is Milan and Venice in the first quarter of the Fifteenth Century. Francesca, the daughter of a fencing master, who has been brought up as a boy, is in love with Fortunio, the rightful heir to the throne of Milan. After some delay the two are united and the Duke is restored to his throne.

Feramors — Opera in three acts, music by Rubinstein, words by Rodenberg, adapted from Moore's "Lalla Rookh," first produced at Dresden in 1863.

Fernand Cortez; ou, La Conquête du Mexique (The Conquest of Mexico) — French opera by Spontini, words by Jouy and Esmenard, produced in Paris in 1809, revised in 1817 and in 1821. Libretto is founded upon a drama by Piron.

Fernando — German opera in one act, written by Franz Schubert at Vienna in 1815, but never put upon the stage. One by Carlo Arrigoni appeared in London, 1734.

Fervaal — French opera in three acts and prologue, music and words by Vincent d'Indy, produced in Brussels, March 12, 1897. It is d'Indy's most important opera.

Festa d'Imenei, La (The Marriage Festival) — A ballet opera, text by Mauro, music by Rieck and Ariosti. First produced at the wedding anniversary of Prince Frederick of Hesse-Cassel and the daughter of the Elector of Brandenburg, in 1700.

Feste Galante, La (The Gay Festivals) — Italian opera. Music by Graun, text by Villati, produced at Berlin, 1747.

Fête du Village Voisin, La (The Festival in the Neighboring Village) — A lively little French comedy in three acts. Music by Boieldieu, text by Sewrin, produced at Paris, 1816. Tiring of her lovely castle, a young widow disguises as a peasant and visits a fair in the next village. A friend, also in disguise, seeks her there and a love affair results.

Fêtes de l'Amour et de Bacchus (Festivals of Love and Bacchus) — French pastoral opera in three acts and a prologue, music by Lully, words by Molière, Benserade, Quinault, and others, produced in Paris, 1672. With Bacchus and other Olympian characters, are seen men and women of Lully's own time. The idea did not originate with the composer, but was customary before his time.

Fêtes de l'Été, Les (Summer Festivals) — Ballet opera in three acts with a prologue. Music by Monteclair, words by the Abbé Pellegin (under the pseudonym Mlle. Barbier). First produced at Paris, 1716, and very popular there for over thirty years. In this opera Monteclair introduced the contrabass into the French orchestra.

Fêtes d'Hébé, Les (The Festivals of Hebe) — French ballet-opera, music by Rameau, words by Gaultier and Mondorge, produced in Paris, 1739.

Fetonte (Phaeton) — This picturesque son of Apollo was a favorite theme for operas in the Seventeenth and Eighteenth Centuries. In Rome, 1630, appeared the Italian opera "Fetonte," by Hieron. Lully's "Phaeton," with text by Quinault, appeared at Versailles in 1663. Jomelli's "Fetonte" was produced at Stuttgart in 1767.

Fiancée, La — French comic opera in three acts, music by Auber, words by Scribe, produced in Paris, 1829. The libretto is adapted from Masson and Brucker's "Contes del' Atelier."

Fiancée de Corinth, La (The Bride of Corinth) — French opera in one act, music by Duprato, words by Du Locle, produced in Paris, 1867. The libretto is very freely adapted from Goethe's poem, "Die Braut von Corinth."

Fiancée du Diable, La (The Devil's Fiancée) — A French comic opera in three acts; music by Massè, text by Romand and Scribe, produced at Paris in 1854. The superstitious villagers accuse the daughter of a poor peasant of being the devil's bride.

Fidele Bauer, Der (The Faithful Peasant)—A German operetta in two acts with a prelude. Music by Leo Fall, libretto by Viktor Leon, first produced at Mannheim in 1907. Stefan, the son of the jolly farmer, is the hero. Brought up in poverty, the young man studies diligently, rises to a professorship and marries the daughter of a rich Berlin lawyer. Ashamed of his birth, Stefan now tries to sever all connections with his relatives but they swoop down upon his household. At first the situation is very embarrassing but it all ends happily for all concerned. "Der Fidele Bauer" is a decidedly successful production.

Fidele Berger, Le (The Faithful Shepherd) — French comic opera in three acts. Music by A. Adam, text by Saint-Georges and Scribe, produced at Paris, 1838.

Fiends von Salamanka, Die (The Fiends from Salamanca) — German comic opera in two acts. Music by Franz Schubert, text by Meyerhofer. Schubert composed this opera in 1815 but it was not produced upon the stage.

Fierabras — Romantic opera by Franz Schubert, words by Kupelwiesel, written in 1823 but first produced in Vienna in 1861.

Figlia dell Aria (The Daughter of the Air) — Italian opera, music by Garcia, produced at New York, 1826.

Figlinol Prodigo, Il (The Prodigal Son) — Italian melodramatic opera in four acts, music by Ponchielli, words by Zanardini, produced at Milan in 1880.

Filibustier, Le — French opera, music by César Cui, produced in Paris in 1894, but written in 1889. The libretto is adapted from a French drama by Jean Richepin. It is no longer sung.

Filosofo di Campagna, Il (The Philosopher of the Campagna) — Italian comic opera, music by Galuppi, words by Goldoni, produced in Venice, 1754. It was the most popular of all of the composer's comic operas. It was produced in England under the title, "The Guardian Trick'd."

Fils du Mandarin, Le (The Mandarin's Son) — Russian comic opera, in one act, music by César Cui, produced in 1859.

Fils du Prince, Le (The Son of the Prince) — French comic opera in two acts. Music by Alphonse de Feltre, text by Scribe, produced at Paris, 1834.

Finta Giardiniera, La (The Disguised Gardner Maiden) — Italian comic opera in three acts by Mozart, words by Calzabigi, revised by Coltellini, produced in Münich, January 13, 1775. The opera was written for the Carnival of 1775 at the order of Count Ferdinand of Leil.

Finta Parigina, La (The Parisian Trick) — Italian comic opera, music by Cimarosa, produced in Naples, 1773.

Finta Pazza, La (The Mad Deceit) — Italian opera, music by Sacrati, words by d'Almeida, produced in Venice, 1641. It was given in Paris in 1645 before the court, and is said to have been the first opera ever performed there.

Finta Semplice, La (The Simple Deceit) — Italian comic opera, music by Mozart, words by Coltellini, produced in Salzburg, 1769. It was written in 1768 for the Emperor Joseph II. of Austria, but was not produced before him because of intrigues at court. It was Mozart's first Italian opera, and he was but twelve years old at the time.

Finte Gemelle, Le (The Twins Disguised) — Italian comic opera, music by Piccini, produced in Naples, 1775.

Fior d'Alpe (Flower of the Alps) — Italian opera in three acts, music by Franchetti, words by Castelnovo, produced in Milan, 1894.

Fiorella — Comic opera in three acts. Music by Auber, text by Scribe, produced at Paris, 1826. A love story in which Fiorella nearly gives up her plainer lover for the false promises of a grand gentleman, but she repents in time and is taken back by her lover.

Flaminio, Il (Flaminius) — Italian comic opera, music by Pergolesi, produced in Naples in the fall of 1735. Flaminius was a Roman general in the Second Century, B. C.

Flaminius à Corinthe (Flaminius at Corinth) — French opera, music by Isouard and Rudolphe Kreutzer, words by Pixérécourt and Lambert, produced in Paris, 1801. Flaminius besieged Philip III. of Macedon, 197 B. C.

Flauto Solo (The Solo Flute) — Opera in one act. Music by D'Albert, text by Hans von Wolzogen. First performed at Dresden, 1906. The story is an amusing take-off on the music of Italy and Germany, and in the Prince and his father, one readily recognizes Frederick the Great and his quick-tempered father. This opera is scoring at present even a greater success than its predecessor, "Die Abreise."

Flavio — English opera by Handel, words by Haym, first performed at London, 1723.

Fleur de Thé (Tea-Flower) — French operetta in three acts, music by Lecocq, words by Chivot and Duru, produced in Paris, 1868. It was the composer's first great success.

Flitch of Bacon, The — English comic opera, music by William Shield, produced in London, 1778. It was Shield's first opera and a great success at the time.

Flora; or, Hob in the Well — English opera by Bates, produced at London, 1791, and one of the ballad operas which appeared in the musical repertory of a company of comedians who played in Philadelphia and New York about 1850 and later.

Flora Mirabilis (The Wonderful Flora) — Italian opera, music by Spiro Samara, words by Ferdinando Fontane, produced in Milan, May 16, 1886. The libretto is legendary and rather fantastic. It is said to have been suggested by the ballet of the flower girls in Parsifal. The opera was immensely popular for a time, but is now no longer sung.

Florestan, ou Le Conseil de Dix (Florestan, or the Council of Ten) — French comic opera, music by Manuel del Popolo Garcia, words by Delrieu, produced in Paris, 1822. The Council of Ten consists of ten Venetian ladies, who decide to teach a lesson to a young gallant, who has compromised one of them, and they accordingly impersonate that terrible tribunal.

Floridante — Italian opera by Handel, text by Rolli, first produced at London in 1721.

Florinda — Italian opera, music by Thalberg, words by Scribe, produced in London in 1721.

Flüchtling, Der (The Fugitive) — German romantic comic opera, music by Edmund Kretschmer, produced in Ulru in 1881.

Fohè, Une (A Piece of Folly) — French comic opera in three acts, music by Mèhul, words by Bonilly, produced in Paris, April 4, 1802. It has been sung recently in Germany.

Folies Amoureuses, Les (The Foolish Lovers) — Comic opera in three acts. Words by Regnard with additions by Castil-Blaze, music by Stribbett, Generali, Comarosa, Paër, Rossini, and Mozart; produced at Paris, 1823. Also a comic opera by E. L. Pessard with text by Leneton and Matrat, produced at Paris, 1891.

Folkunger, Die (The Folkungers) — Grand opera in five acts. Music by Edmund Kretschmer, text by S. H. Mosenthal, first performed at Dresden, 1874. This is the first opera by this talented composer. Founded on historical incidents in Sweden at the time when Magnus II. Erikson becomes King of Scandinavia and Finnland in 1333. Music is charmingly suited to the Scandinavian story.

Fomka Douratchok (Fomka the Fool) — Russian opera in one act, music by Rubinstein, produced in St. Petersburg, 1858. The opera is now quite forgotten.

Fortunate mit dem Säckel und Wunsch-Hütlein (Fortunate with the Sack and Wishing Hat) — German fairy opera, music by Wartensee, words by Döring, produced in Frankfurt, 1829.

Fortune — Musical fairy tale in one act, music by Rudolph Baron Prochazka, words by Dr. Theodor Kirchner. This is an allegorical tale of the pursuit of fortune.

Fortune Teller, The — Comic opera by Victor Herbert, produced at New York in 1900; the music is catchy and light and the opera scored a great success.

Forza del Destino (The Force of Destiny) — Italian opera, music by Verdi, words by Piave, produced in St. Petersburg, 1862. The libretto is founded upon a play of de Rivas', a Spanish dramatist. It was slightly changed for its production in Paris in 1876.

Forza della Virtu, La (The Force of Virtue) — German opera, music by Keiser, words by Bressand, produced in Hamburg, 1700. The libretto is adapted from the Italian.

Fosa — Opera by Gomez, first produced at Milan, 1873, where it was unsuccessful. Five years later it was presented in the same city and met with a cordial reception.

Fra i due Litiganti il Terzo Gode (Where Two Quarrel, the Lord Rejoices) — Italian comic opera, music by Sarti, words by Lorenzi, produced in Turin in 1780.

Francesca da Rimini — German opera in three acts, music and words by Herman Götz, produced in Mannheim, 1877. Götz died before completing the opera, which was finished by Ernst Frank, his friend. It is the well known story of Paolo and Francesca.

Francesca da Rimini — Russian opera, music by Napravnik, produced in St. Petersburg in 1903. The libretto is based upon Stephen Phillips' play of the same name. The opera has been given with marked success.

Françoise de Foix — French comic opera, music by Berton, words by Bouilly and Dupaty, produced in Paris, 1809.

Françoise de Rimini — French grand opera in five acts, music by Ambroise Thomas, words by Barbier, and Carré, produced in Paris in 1882. It is the Italian story of the two unfortunate lovers, Paolo and Francesca.

François I., ou La Fête Mystérieuse — French opera in two acts, music by Kreutzer, words by Sewrin and Chazet, produced at Feydeau, 1807.

François Villon — French opera in one act, music by Membrée, words by Got, produced in Paris, 1857. The story deals with an imaginary romance in the life of the famous François Villon.

La Frascatana — Italian opera, music by Paisiello, produced in Venice, 1776.

Lo Frate Innam Orato (The Monk in Love) — Italian comic opera in Neapolitan dialect, music by Pergolesi, produced in Naples in 1732.

Fratelli Nemici, I (The Estranged Brothers) — Italian opera, music by Graun, text by Tagliazucchi, produced at Berlin, 1756. The story of this opera is furnished by the "Bride of Messina."

Frauenlob (Praise of Women) — Opera in three acts, music by Reinhold Becker, text by Koppel-Ellfeld, first produced at Dresden, 1892. Libretto is fine. Time of story, early in the Fourteenth Century; place, Mainz, Germany. Frauenlob is the old German minstrel who got his name by his songs in praise of women. Some of the songs are irresistibly sweet.

Frédégonde — French opera in five acts, music by Ernest Guirand, but finished by Saint-Saëns, produced in Paris in 1895. It was first sung after Guirand's death and was only moderately successful.

Free Lance, The — Comic opera, music by John Philip Sousa, words by Harry B. Smith, produced in New York, in 1906.

French Maid, The — Musical comedy in two acts, music by Walter Slaughter, words by Basil Hood, first produced at Terry's Theatre, London, April 24, 1897.

Frivoli — Comic opera in three acts, music and words by Hervé, English version by William Beatty-Kingston, first produced at Drury Lane Theatre, London, June 29, 1886.

Fronde, La — French opera in five acts, music by Neidermeyer, words by Maquet and Lacroix, produced in Paris, 1853. The plot is founded upon love and political intrigue in the court of Louis XIV.

Fuorusciti di Firenze, I (The Exiles from Florence) — Italian opera, music by Paër, produced in Vienna, 1800. An English version is called "The Freebooters."

G

Gabriella di Vergy — Italian tragic opera by Carafa, produced at Naples in 1816. A fabled love story of the Twelfth Century. Gabriella, the wife of Endo of Fayel, is loved by the troubadour knight, Raoul de Loncy, He is killed in battle but has previously commissioned his servant to send his heart to Gabriella. Her husband intercepts the messenger, has the heart roasted and served to his wife. After she has partaken of it he tells her what it is. She refuses to eat again and starves to death.

Gabrielle d'Estrees; or, The Love Affairs of Henry IV.— Opera in three acts. Music by Mèhul, text by Saint-Just, produced at Paris, 1806. Story has as its foundation the love affair between Henry IV. of France and Gabrielle d'Estrees for whom he had intended to get divorced from Margaret of Valois.

Garibaldi — English operetta, music by F. H. Cowen, produced in London, 1860. Garibaldi was the great Italian patriot.

Gastibelza — French grand opera, music by Maillart, libretto by Cormon and Dennery, produced at Paris in 1847. Monpou's very popular ballad "Le Fou de Tolède,' forms the basis of the opera.

Gay Parisienne, The — A musical comedy in two acts, music by Ivan Caryll, words by George Dance, produced at the Duke of York's Theatre, April 4, 1896.

Gazza Ladra, La (The Cats in the Larder) — Italian comic opera in two acts, music by Rossini, words by Gherardini, produced in Milan, 1817.

Geheimnis, Das (The Secret) — Czechish comic opera in three acts, music by Smetana, produced in Prague in 1878.

Geigenmacher von Cremona, Der (The Violin Maker of Cremona) — Opera in two acts, music by Jenö Hubay, words by François Coppée and Henry Beauclair, German words by Max Kalbeck. The libretto is founded upon Coppée's "Luthier de Crémone." The time of the action is 1750, and a contest for a prize to be given the maker of the best violin forms the basis for the plot.

Geiger aus Tyrol, Der (The Tyrolean Fiddler) — A comic opera with music and text by R. Genée, produced at Danzig, 1857.

Geisha, The — A Japanese musical play in two acts, music by Sidney Jones, book by Owen Hall, lyrics by Harry Greenbank, produced at Daly's Theatre, April 25, 1896. The plot of this opera is based upon the adventures of an English girl who visits Japan disguised as a Geisha girl.

Geisterinsel, Die (The Enchanted Island) — Romantic opera in three acts; music by Franz Fleischmann, text by Gotter, produced at Regensburg, 1796. Based on Shakespeare's "Tempest."

Gelmina, od Col Fuoco Non si Scherza (Gelmina, or No Playing with Fire) — Italian comic opera, music by Pedrotti, words by Peruzzini and Poniatowski, produced in Milan in 1853.

Gelosie Villane, Le (The Jealous Country Women) — Italian comic opera, music by Sarti, words by Grandi, produced in Venice in 1776.

Geloso in Cimento, Il — Italian opera in three acts, music by Anfossi, produced in Rome in 1775.

Gelübde, Das (The Oath) — German opera in one act; music by A. Eberhardt, text by Dr. Gustav Weinberg, first produced at Aachen in 1905. The story is laid in a village in Southern France in the Eighteenth Century. Cleo, a young girl of the Carnern type, is the cause of an impending duel between a smuggler and a rich peasant. The latter is loved by Eleni, a gentle girl who has sworn not to disclose her love, but when she hears of the coming duel she breaks her oath and tries to avert the duel. Unmindful of her the peasant insists on fighting when the smuggler pursued by officers rushes upon the stage and is killed by a well directed bullet. A prayer for the dead into which mingles the frenzied song of Cleo closes the play. The opera has been well received.

Gemma di Vergy—Italian opera, music by Donizetti, presented at Milan in 1835.

Genesius—German opera in three acts. Music and text by F. E. von Weingartner, Imperial opera director at Vienna since 1907. Time of the story, Third Century; scene, laid in Rome. Genesius, actor at the court of the heathen emperor, Diocletian, becomes a Christian and suffers a martyr's death. The opera contains excellent music, among the notable numbers are: "Hear My Confession," soprano, by the young Christian Pelagio; "I Am a Heathen," tenor, by Genesius; "A Miracle Has Happened Unto Me," same. Is being presented in all the leading cities of Germany.

Geneviéve de Brabant—French opera in two acts and seven tableaux, music by Offenbach, words by Jaime and Tréfeu, produced in Paris, 1859.

Genoveva—Opera in four acts. Music by Robert Schumann, text after Herbel and Tieck, first produced at Leipzig in 1850. The text is based upon the well known legend of Genevieve, daughter of the Duke of Brabant, who for unjust suffering later became Saint Genoveva.

Gentile di Varano, Il (A Noble Family of Verona)—Italian opera, music by Marchetti, words by Raffaelo Marchetti, brother of the composer, produced in Turin, 1856.

Gentleman Joe, the Hansom Cabby—Musical farce in two acts, music by Walter Slaughter, words by Basil Hood, first produced at the Prince of Wales' Theatre, London, March 2, 1895.

Germania—Italian opera, music by Franchetti, produced in Milan, 1902.

Gernot—Tragic opera in three acts. Music by d'Albert, text by Gustav Kastropp. First performed at Mannheim in 1897. Time of the story, before the Roman wars; scene laid in the regions around Lake Constance. Gernot has made himself King of the Seuvi by murdering their King Wulf, and is himself killed by Wulf's son who seizes Helma, the beautiful fiancée of Gernot.

Gerusalemme Liberata (Jerusalem Delivered)—Italian opera in two acts, music by Righini, words by Filistri, produced in Berlin in 1803.

Gheist von Wojewoden, Der (Wojewoden's Ghost)—A Polish comic opera in three acts, music by L. Grossmann, text by L. Anczic, produced at Warsaw in 1877. Leon, and the president, Kobierski, both love Helene. At an old castle in the Caucasus Mountains where they are all spending the summer, tradition says that Wojewoden's ghost walks at night. Unknown to each other the two men disguise as the ghost and appear before Helene's terrified aunt and each command her to give Helene to him. Two ghosts are too many, the men are recognized and Leon wins the girl. The Polish title is "Duch Wojwodi."

Ghisèle—French opera in four acts, music by César Franck, produced at Monte Carlo in 1896. The libretto is based upon a poem by G. A. Thierry. The opera was completed by the composer's pupils after his death.

Ghismonda—A highly dramatic opera in three acts. Music and text by d'Albert, first produced at Dresden in 1895 with overwhelming success. Immermann's poem by same title forms the basis for the libretto. Ghismonda, a princess, in obedience to her father's wishes consents to marry Duke Manfred whom she does not love. To the engagement festivities comes young Guiscardo, the son of a noble family, and he falls in love with Ghismonda at first sight. Remembering her promise, she flees from him to the garden. Here he finds her, she confesses she loves him, and they promise to keep their sacred love a secret, and separate. Ghismonda's father however witnesses this garden scene, and when he confronts Guiscardo, the latter, true to his promise of silence, denies their love. Then the father stabs him. When Ghismonda learns this, she orders her lover's body to be brought before her, and in the presence of all the guests she tells their secret, then drains a cup of poison and dies beside her lover. This splendid opera is scoring a wonderful success in many cities. Ghismonda's song "Oh, Foolish Beginning," and Guiscardo's "I Swore the Oath of Faith," are two of the best numbers.

Giacinta and Ernesto—Italian opera, music by Sir Julius Benedict, produced in Naples, 1829. It was the composer's first opera.

Giasone (Jason) — Italian opera, music by Cavalli, words by Cicognini, produced in Venice in 1649. Jason is the well known mythological hero.

Gilana, La — French opera in four acts, music by Rey, words by Chareau, produced in Bordeau, 1864.

Gille et Gillotin — French comic opera in one act, music by Ambroise Thomas, words by Sauvage, produced in 1874, though it was written several years before.

Gillette — Comic opera, music by Audran, words by Chevot and Duru, first produced in Paris at the Bouffes Parisienes, November 11, 1882. English version by Saville Clarke, first produced at the Royalty Theatre, London, November 19, 1883. The plot is taken from Boccaccio's "Gillette de Narbou," and was also used by Shakespeare in "All's Well That Ends Well."

Giosse, Ré di Ginda (Joshua, King of Judah) — Italian sacred opera, music by Karl Reutter, words by Métastase, produced in Vienna in 1735. The libretto is founded upon Racine's drama "Athalie."

Giovanna II., Regina di Napoli (Johanna II., Queen of Naples) — Italian opera in four acts, music by Petrella, words by Ghislanzoni, produced in Naples, February 27, 1869. Johanna II. was a figure of the Fifteenth Century, ambitious, passionate and desirous of power.

Giovanna Shore (Jane Shore) —An Italian opera, music by V. Bonnetti, text probably by Romani, produced at Barcelona in 1853. Jane Shore is the famous beauty who is the heroine of a splendid English tragedy by N. Rowe.

Giove de Grasso, Il (Thursday before Shrove Tuesday) — Italian opera by Donizetti, produced at Naples in 1827.

Gipsy, La (The Gypsy) — French ballet in three acts, music by Ambroise Thomas, Benoist and Marliani, produced in Paris in 1839. The second act only was written by Thomas.

Gipsy's Warning, The — English romantic opera, music by Sir Julius Benedict, words by Linley, produced in London in 1838. It is only remembered to-day as containing the song, "Rage, Thou Angry Storm."

Giralda, The New Psyche — French comic opera in three acts, music by Adam, text by Scribe, produced at Paris in 1850. A popular opera.

Girl from Paris, The — Opera in two acts by Caryll. Libretto by George Dance. Place, England and Switzerland. Time, Nineteenth Century. First produced at London in 1896.

Giulietta e Romeo (Romeo and Juliet) — Italian opera in three acts, music by Lingarelli, words by Foppa, produced in Milan, January 30, 1796. Shakespeare's tragedy formed the basis for the libretto.

Giulietta e Romeo (Romeo and Juliet) — Italian opera in three acts, music by Vaccai, words by Romani, produced in Milan, October 31, 1825. Shakespeare's tragedy formed the basis for the libretto.

Giulio Sabino (Julius Sabinus) — Italian opera, music by Sarti, words by Métastase, produced in Venice in 1781. Julius Sabinus was a Gaul, who headed an insurrection against the Romans in the First Century, A. D. He was captured and executed.

Giuoco della Cieco, Il (Blind Man's Buff) — Italian opera, music by Emilio del Cavalieri, produced in Florence in 1595. This is historically important as being one of the first real operas.

Giuramento, Il (The Oath) — Italian opera in four acts, music by Mercadante, words by Rossi, produced in Milan, 1837. It is a tragedy somewhat after the manner of "Romeo and Juliet," and is Mercadante's finest work.

Giustino — Lyric tragedy in three acts, words by Métastase, music probably by Caldora about 1730.

Giustino (Justinus) — Italian opera by Handel. Produced at London in 1736. Justinus was a Byzantine Emperor in the Sixth Century.

Glücksritter, Der (The Fortunate Knight) — Operetta in three acts with music by Alfons Czibulka, text by Genée. Produced at Vienna, 1887.

Godolphin — English opera by C. E. Horn, produced at London in 1813. Sidney, Duke of Godolphin, called the Lion of the North, is the hero.

Goldene Kreutz, Das (The Golden Cross) — Comic opera in two acts. Music by Ignaz Brüll. Text based upon the French by H. Mosenthal. First produced at Berlin, 1875. Time of story, 1812-1815; scene laid in Milan. Napoleon is recruiting soldiers for his Russian invasion, and Christine, the beautiful sister of a miller, promises to marry that soldier who shall go in her brother's stead. As a pledge she gives her golden cross. Her lover goes, and wins.

Gondoliers, The; or, the Ring of Barataria — English comic opera in two acts, music by Sullivan, words by Gilbert, produced in London in 1889. The scene is Venice in the year 1750. This is the last joint opera by Gilbert and Sullivan.

Goti, I (The Goths) — Italian opera, music by Stefano Goboti, produced in Bologna in 1873. The scene is laid in Italy in the Sixth Century, and the story deals with Amalasuntha, daughter of Theodorich the Great.

Götz von Berlichingen — Historical opera in five acts. Music by Goldmark. Text by A. M. Willmer, first performed at Frankfurt A/M in 1903. Story follows Goethe's drama by the same title.

Gouverneur und Müller (Governor and the Miller) — A comic opera by Alfred Ernst, produced at Halle in 1908. The text is based upon a Spanish story.

Gräfin, Die (The Countess) —Polish opera, music by Moninszko, produced in Warsaw in 1859. This opera with the "Paria" is the composer's best work.

Grand Duke, The; or, The Statutory Duel — Comic opera in two acts, music by Sir Arthur Sullivan, words by W. S. Gilbert, first produced at the Savoy Theatre, London, March 7, 1896.

Grand Mogul, The — Comic opera in three acts, music by Edmond Audran, words by Chivot and Duru, first produced in Marseilles in 1876, later at the Gaîte, Paris, on September 19th, 1876. An English version by H. B. Farnie was performed at the Comedy Theatre, London, November 17, 1884.

Grand Prix, Le (The Grand Prize) — French comic opera, music by Adam, text by Masson and Gabriel, produced at Paris in 1831. Hoping to be near his sweetheart who lives in Rome, a young musician tries for the Roman grand prize. He fails, but leaves for Rome anyway. On the way he meets another suitor for the girl's hand, he hastens ahead and succeeds in getting the girl.

Grand Tante, La (The Great Aunt) — French comic opera in one act, music by Massenet, words by Adenis and Grandvalet, produced in Paris, 1867. It is an early work of this composer.

Graziella — English opera, music by Sir Julius Benedict, produced in London, 1833. It had previously been presented as a cantata at the Birmingham Festival of 1832.

Grille, Die — German opera in three acts, music by Johannes Doebber, produced in Leipzig in 1897. The libretto is adapted from George Sands' novel "La Petite Fadette." The scene is Elsass at the present time. The Grille is the granddaughter of the old Fadette, who has the power to foretell the future.

Gringoire — Opera in one act. Music by Brüll, text by Leon, first produced at Munich in 1892. The scene is laid in France in 1469. The barber of King Louis XI. wishes to marry Loyse, the daughter of a French merchant, but she will not have him. She loves Gringoire, a singer, who nearly loses the girl and his head too through the cunning of the barber. But the King discovers the barber's treachery and aids the lovers. The opera has been very successful.

Griselda, La Virtu al Cimessto (Virtue on Trial) — Italian opera by Paër, words by Anelli, produced in Parma, 1796. Griselda, the daughter of a peasant, was chosen because of her beauty by Walter of Salnzzo, who submitted her to every possible trial to prove her fidelity. The tale is first found in Boccaccio.

Grisélides — Opera in three acts and prologue by Massenet. Libretto by Armand Sylvestre and Eugene Morand. Adapted from Boccaccio. Place, Provence. Time, Middle Ages. First produced in Paris in 1901.

Guarany — Italian opera, music by Antonio Gomez, a Brazilian, words by Scalvini, produced in Milan in 1870.

Guerillero, Le (The Guerilla) — French opera in two acts, music by Ambroise Thomas, words by Theodore Anne, produced in Paris in 1842. The action is laid at the time of the separation of Portugal from Spain in the year 1640.

Gugeline — Opera in five acts; music by Ludwig Thuille, words by

Gugeline

O. J. Bierbaum. An old time story. A young prince has never been allowed to hear the word "woman," but one day it slips the jester's mouth, and the prince immediately becomes interested. So eligible princesses are brought to the house and each one tries to win him but in vain. So he leaves home and finds Gugeline, a simple little peasant girl, but it is only after much trouble that he receives the King's consent to marry her. This opera has been well liked.

Guglielmo Ratcliff — Italian opera, music by Mascagni, produced in Milan in 1895. The libretto is founded upon Heine's tragedy "William Ratcliff."

Guido et Ginevra; ou, La Peste de Florence (Guido and Ginevra; or, The Plague of Florence) — French opera in five acts, music by Halévy, words by Scribe, produced in Paris, 1838. Ginevra, supposedly dead from the plague, comes to life and, leaving her tomb, falls in love with a young man who protects her and whom she afterward marries.

Guitarrero, La (The Guitar Player) — French comic opera in three acts. Music by Halévy, text by Scribe, produced at Paris, 1841. A Portuguese love story with the Revolution of 1640 as a background.

Gulistan, ou Le Uhlan de Samarcande — French comic opera in three acts, music by Dalayrac, words by Etienne and La Chabeaussière, produced in Paris, 1805. The plot is taken from the "Arabian Nights."

Gundrum — Famous heroine of the Norse Gundrum legend. This picturesque figure closely rivals Wagner's heroines of Niebelungen fame. Among the German operas on this subject are those by K. A. Mangold, 1851; August Klughardt with text by Niemann, 1882, and by Felix Draeseke with his own text, produced at Hanover in 1884.

Gunnlöd — German opera, music by Peter Cornelius, words by Edda, produced in Weimar in 1891. The opera was completed after the composer's death by Hoffbauer and Lassen.

Günther von Schwarzburg — The only German opera written by I. Holzbauer, text by A. Selein, produced at Mannheim, 1776. Holzbauer preferred Italian operas.

Guntram — Musical drama in three acts. Music and words by Richard Strauss, first produced at the court theatre in Weimar, 1894. Time of story, about 1250; scene laid in Germany. Story: Religious knights have formed a society which aims to establish brotherly love throughout the country, and music is to be its medium. Among them is young Gundrum, a singer. He sets out on his mission but learns that brotherly love becomes secondary when he finds the woman of his heart, Freihild. Interest is attached to this opera in that in 1904 Strauss married the singer Pauline de Ahne who created "Freihild" so successfully in Guntram.

Gustav Basa — Swedish opera, music by J. G. Naumann, words by Kellgren, produced in Stockholm in 1786. The hero of the opera, Gustav I., was the founder of the Swedish monarchy in the early part of the Sixteenth Century.

Gustavus III., or The Masked Ball — Grand opera in five acts. Music by Auber, text by Scribe, first produced at Paris in 1833. Soon after in England. The story is historical; place, Stockholm; time, 1792. Verdi's "Masked Ball" appeared twenty-six years later with place and characters changed. Auber's opera was so popular that it literally took Europe off its feet, and the famous Gustavus gallop has been danced all over the world.

Guy Mannering — English opera, music by Sir Henry Bishop, produced in London in 1845.

Gwendoline — Opera in two acts, music by Chabrier, words by Catulle Mendés, first produced in Brussels, April 10, 1886.

Gypsy Baron, The — Comic opera in three acts. Music by Johann Strauss, libretto by Schnitzer after Jokai's story of the same name. First produced at Vienna in 1885. The hero ran away from home when a lad and comes back to find it deserted and in the possession of gypsies. His sweetheart rejects him, he leaves her and goes over to the gypsies who make him their baron. With his followers he renders the government aid and is made a real Baron. Forgetting his old love he marries the gypsy Suffi who turns out to be of royal blood. The music is lively and is bright with gypsy melodies and dance music. For a light opera it has a well sustained plot.

H

Habanera, La — Lyric drama in three acts, music and words by Raoul Laparra, first produced at the Theatre Royal de la Monnaie in Brussels, March 25, 1909.

Haddon Hall — Light opera, music by Sir Arthur Sullivan, words by Sydney Grundy, produced at the Savoy Theater, London, September 4, 1892.

Hagar in der Wüste (Hagar in the Desert) — A musical drama, with music by Rubinstein, and text by F. von Saar, produced in 1873.

Hagbarth and Signe — German romantic opera in three acts, music by Michalovich, words by Stern, produced in Dresden, 1882. The libretto is adapted from Ohlenschlager's drama. The theme is a Scandanavian legend.

Haideschacht, Der (The Shaft on the Heath) — Opera in three acts. Music and text by Franz von Holstein, first produced in Dresden, 1868. Time of story, end of the Thirty Years War; scene, Faulun in Dalekarlien. Story is one of rough miners in a little mountain town. This opera was very popular in Dresden and especially in Leipzig. After an obscurity of twenty years, it was revived in Berlin in 1903 and enthusiastically received. It is based on a legend that the bodies of those who lose their lives in this shaft do not perish.

Halka — Polish opera in two acts, music by Moninszko, words by Wolski, produced in Wilna, 1851. In 1858 it was enlarged to four acts and given in Warsaw. The story of Halka is taken from Bohemian history.

Halling, Der — A German opera in three acts; music by Eberhardt; text by Dr. Weinberg; produced at Stettin in 1904. The text is adapted from a novel by Karl Bleibtren. "Der Halling" is a much finer opera than the composer's "Das Gelübde" and it has justly been very cordially received.

Halte du Roi, La (The King's Halt) — A French comic opera in two acts; music by Boieldieu, Jr., and text by Nuitter, produced in Rouen in 1875. Henry III. of France is the central figure. Nuitter wrote the text to commemorate the one hundredth anniversary of his father's birth.

Hamlet — French grand opera in five acts, music by Ambroise Thomas, words by Carré and Barbier, produced in Paris, 1868. The libretto was adapted from Shakespeare's tragedy, which is followed fairly closely till the end, when Hamlet kills Claudius at the grave of Ophelia, and is then at once chosen King of Denmark. This opera with Mignon is Thomas' best work.

Hannibal (Annibale, It.) — Opera by many Italian composers, among them Porpora (Venice, 1731), Zingarelli (Tunu, 1787), Farinelli (Milan, 1810). Earliest mentioned is one by Franck, a German composer, whose Hannibal appeared in Hamburg, 1681. Subject is the great Carthaginian general Hannibal.

Hänschen and Gretchen — German operetta, music by Reichardt, produced in Königsberg, 1772.

Hans der Fahnenträger (Hans the Standard Bearer) — German musical drama in four acts. Music and text by Gustav Dippe, first produced at Cassel in 1907. A tragic love story of the Sixteenth Century. The scene is laid in middle Germany. Hans is a handsome young soldier who falls in love with the beautiful Irmengard. She loves him ,and while they are together in the courtyard of Irmengard's castle they are spied upon. Hans kills the spy, a fellow soldier, and is sentenced to death Irmengard hears he is killed and becomes a nun. Too late she learns that he has been spared. He seeks death and is brought to the convent sorely wounded, where he dies in Irmengard's arms.

Hans Max von der Humpenberg — An operetta in one act; music by Lindpainter, produced at Munich in 1816. The text is by Kotzebue.

Hans Sachs — German comic opera in four acts by Lortzing; produced at Leipzig in 1840. The hero is the famous cobbler, and mastersinger of Nürnberg whom Wagner has immortalized in his "Meistersinger von Nürnberg."

Happyland—Comic opera in two acts, music by Reginald de Koven, words by Frederic Ranken, produced in New York, 1905.

Harlequin Freemason—A musical funmaker by Dibbin, appeared in London in 1780.

Harold—English opera, music by F. H. Cowen, produced in London, 1895. The hero is Harold, the last of the Saxons.

Harold der Wiking (Harold the Viking)—A Swedish opera; music by Andreas Hallén, text by Lindgren, produced at Stockholm in 1883. The text is similiar to that of "Hagbarth and Signe" by Michalovich.

Harold und Treano—German opera in four acts; music by K. A. Lorenz, libretto by Felix Dahn, produced at Hanover in 1893. The scene is laid on the Island of Cypress in the Fourth Century. The Governor of Cypress and his heathen followers are celebrating in honor of the Goddess Aphrodite. Not far away in a grotto is an assemblage of Christians; their leader, Josephus, is lingering there in danger of his life, hoping to convert Theano, the niece of the governor. All are taken prisoners when Harold the Saxon chieftain appears, kills the governor and frees the Christians. The opera has received a warm reception whenever it has appeared.

Hasheesh—Opera in one act. Music by Askar von Chelius, words by Axel Delmar, first produced at Dresden, 1897. Characters are Omar, Bey of Tunis (bass), Paolo, Italian painter (tenor), Hama, one of the Bey's wives (soprano). When Omar finds that Paolo and Hama love each other, he decides that fate shall tell who is to blame. He orders his servant to bring three goblets of wine, and to put Hasheesh in one. All three drink. Hama draws the poison cup and expires singing her death song, and while Paolo pours forth his agony, the Muezzin calls to prayer.

Haste to the Wedding—Comic opera, music by George Grossmith, words by W. S. Gilbert, produced at the Criterion Theater, London, July 27, 1892. It is a new version of "Le Chapeau de Paille d'Italie" and the same story was used twenty years before in the "Wedding March," at the Court Theater, London.

Haunted Tower, The—English comic opera by Storace, first produced at London, 1789.

Hausierer, Der (The Peddler)—Opera by Onslow with German text by Ludwig von Lichtenstein, produced at Berlin in 1828. Text is taken from the composer's "Colporteur" (The Hawker), a great favorite and it appeared often.

Havana—Opera in two acts by Stuart. Libretto by Grossmith. Place, Havana and environs. Time, the present. First produced in England in 1908; at New York in 1909.

Heimkehr aus der Fremde (Return from Foreign Lands)—German musical play in one act, music by Mendelssohn.

Heinrich, der Löwe (Henry the Lion)—German opera, music and words by Edmund Kretschmer, produced in Leipzig, 1877. Henry, Duke of Saxony and Bavaria, who lived in the Twelfth Century is the hero of the opera.

Heinrich der Vogler (Henry the Fowler)—German opera; music by G. Schürrmann, text by König, produced at Braunschweig and Hamburg in 1719. The hero is the German Emperor who reigned from 919-936.

Heirath Wider Willen, Die (The Forced Marriage)—German comic opera in three acts; music by Humperdinck; text adapted from Dumas' comedy, "Demoiselles de père Saint-Cyr," first produced at Berlin in 1905. Story is laid in Paris and Madrid early in the Eighteenth Century. Count Montfort enters the Park of St. Cyr in order to meet his sweetheart Hedwig. His friend Duval in the meantime walks with Hedwig's friend Louise. The two couples are captured by the watch and taken to the Bastile, and the young men are forced to marry the young ladies. Believing their wives to have duped them and fearing the raillery of friends, the husbands flee to Spain. But court life then becomes dull, and they return to Paris to learn that their wives had no hand in the forced marriage, that they really loved their husbands and are in return loved by them.

Heisze Liebe (Ardent Love)—Danish opera in two acts. Music by Enna, text by P. Rosenberg. The libretto is adapted from a story by the Hungarian novelist, Kalman

Mikszath. The scene is laid in a Slavic village in the Nineteenth Century. A young peasant girl, in spite of her father's protests and the threats of her lover, gives her heart to a young nobleman. She and the Duke are about to flee from the village when they are discovered by the girl's former lover. He kills them, believing he has saved the girl from a life of disgrace. This opera has won favor in Denmark and in Germany.

Heksen (The Witch) — Danish opera, music by August Enna, produced in Copenhagen in 1892. It was a brilliant success.

Hélène — Opera in three acts by Gyrowetz. Produced at Vienna, in 1816. Though this opera was successful at its time, it has long since been forgotten.

Helle — An opera in four acts, music by Victor Alphonse Duvernoy, words by Camille du Locle and Charles Nuitter, first produced in Paris at the Grand Opera in 1896. Helle is a priestess of Diana in Thessaly. Her abduction by Gautier, ex-Duke of Athens, and the tragic consequences of his act form the basis of the plot.

Helvellyn — English opera, music by Sir George Alexander Macfarren, words by Oxenford, produced in London, 1864. The libretto is based upon Mosenthal's "Sonnenwendhof" (Sonnenwend Court.)

Henrico Leone (Henry the Lion) — Italian opera, music by Steffani, produced in Hanover, 1689. It was translated into German and given in Hamburg, 1696. Henry was Duke of Saxony and Bavaria and lived in the Twelfth Century.

Henry VIII. — Opera in four acts; music by Saint-Saëns, libretto by Detroyat and Silvestre, produced at Paris in 1883. Henry VIII. was king of England from 1509 to 1547. His political life as well as his domestic affairs with his six unfortunate wives make interesting history. This opera is considered by many to be Saint-Saëns' best work; the music is extremely dramatic.

Herbort und Hilde — A jolly opera in three acts. Music by Waldemar von Baussnern, words by Eberhard König, first produced at Mannheim, Germany, in 1902. Story: Dietrich von Beru sends Herbort, a young knight, to woo the Princess Hilde for him. But, as usual, Hilde and Herbort fall in love, and Dietrich von Beru finally generously forgives the lovers. The two songs, "In My Heart I Sorrow" (tenor), Herbort; "Now I'll Sorrow Never" (duet), Herbort and Hilde, have gained some prominence.

Herculaneum — French opera in four acts, music by Félicien David, words by Mery and Hadot, produced in Paris, 1859. The action takes place just before the destruction of Herculaneum and Pompeii. The opera was very popular in its day.

Herkules — German opera, music by Hasse, text adapted from one by Métastase, produced at Vienna in 1760. This opera was composed for the wedding of Archduke Joseph with Isabella of Bourbon. Hercules, the great mythological hero, is the subject of no less than fifty operas by German, English, French and Italian composers.

Hermann; or, The Broken Spear — English opera, music by John Thomson, produced in London, 1834.

Hermione — German opera in four acts. Music by Max Bruch, text by Emil Hopffer, produced at Berlin in 1872. Text is based on Shakespeare's "Hermione." Rossini's opera "Ermione," the daughter of Menelaus and Helen, appeared at Naples in 1819.

Hero und Leander — German opera in three acts; music by Ernst Frank, text by Ferdinand Vetter, produced at Berlin in 1884. Leander is the beautiful youth who swam across the Hellespont every night to visit his beloved, Hero. One night, when the light that guided him was out, Leander drowned; and Hero, unable to live without her lover, sought a similar death.

Herrat — Grand opera in three acts, music and libretto by Felix Draeseke. First produced at Dresden, 1892. Draeseke's operas, like Wagner's, are serious and are founded on the old hero legends. In "Herrat," Draeseke has introduced to us the splendid German hero, Deitrich von Beru, a less familiar though a much more real hero than Wagner's Siegfried.

Herzog Magnus und die Seejungfer (Duke Magnus and the Mermaid) — Swedish opera by Ivar Hallström, produced at Stockholm in 1867.

Hésione — French grand tragic opera in five acts and a prologue, music by André Campra, words by Danchet, produced in Paris, 1700. Hésione was the daughter of King Laomedon of Troy.

Heure de Mariage, Un (An Hour of Marriage) — French comic opera in one act; music by Delayrac and text by Etienne; produced at Paris in 1804.

Hexe, Die (The Witch) — Opera in three acts. Music by August Enna, text based on the drama of the same title by A. Fitger, first produced at Copenhagen in 1892. Time of story, about 1650; scene, Greenland. When this opera first appeared in Copenhagen it had four acts; a year later, 1893, at Prague, it was re-arranged to three acts.

Hieronymus Knicker (Jerome Knicker) — German comic opera in two acts. Music by Dittersdorf, text by Stephanie, produced at Vienna, 1789.

Hippolyte et Aricie — Grand opera with prologue. Music by Rameau, text by the Abbé Pellegrin, first produced at Paris, 1733. Story is identical with that in Racine's tragedy, "Phédre."

His Excellency — Comic opera, music by Frank Osmond Carr, libretto by Gilbert. Produced in England in 1894.

His Majesty — Comic opera in two acts, music by Sir A. C. Mackenzie, book by F. C. Burnand, lyrics by R. C. Lehmann and Adrian Ross, first produced at the Savoy Theater, London, February 20, 1897.

Hippomène et Atalante — French opera, music by Louis Piccinni, words by Lehoc, produced in Paris, 1810.

Hjarne der Sängerkönig (Hjarne the Minstrel King) — German grand opera in four acts, music by Marschner, text by W. Grothe, first produced at Frankfurt A/M in 1863. In 1883 this opera appeared in Munich under the title "König Hjarne und das Tyrfingschwert." The latter title describes the text better. The magic Tyrfing sword aids only him who wields it in the right cause. It helps Hjarne to win Asloga, the daughter of the Norse king, Frotho III., but, when Hjarne turns the sword against Asloga's brother, it paralyzes his arm and he is forced to flee. Later he returns to court disguised as a minstrel and sings of Hjarne's love for his wife. Asloga's uncle recognizes Hjarne and raises the magic sword to kill him, but the sword turns in his hand and the uncle falls dead to the floor. Hjarne and Asloga are happy again.

Hochländer, Die (The Highlanders) — German opera in four acts. Music and text by Franz von Holstein, produced at Mannheim in 1876. A romantic opera drawn from Scotch history in 1746. The hero is Reginald who at the last uprising of the Stuarts is forced for a while to turn against his old friend Macdonald.

Hochzeit des Gamacho, Die (Gamacho's Wedding) — German comic opera in two acts, music by Mendelssohn, words by Klingemann, produced in Berlin, 1827.

Hochzeitsglocken (Wedding Bells) — An opera in one act. Music by Emanuel Moor, first produced at Kassel in 1908. The scene is laid in a village of the Bernese Alps in the present time. Gottfried, a wealthy young farmer, is engaged to Agnes, not because he loves her but because she saves his life; he loves instead her sister Berta. On the evening before the wedding their house is set on fire, Agnes and her sister Berta are in the house. Gottfried enters the house to save them and rescues Agnes, but Berta refuses to be saved; both she and Gottfried choose to die in the flames and the fire bells become their wedding bells. The opera is the first by this young Hungarian composer; it lacks coherent, dramatic force but is a promise of better work to come.

Hochzeitsmorgen (Wedding Morning) — Opera in one act. Music by Karl von Kaskell, text by Franz Koppel Ellfeld, first produced at Dresden, 1893. The scene is laid in a little Italian frontier fortress and is full of local coloring. This opera is the first one by the gifted composer and is full of music.

Holger Danske — Danish romantic opera in three acts, music by Kunzen, words by Baggesen, produced in Copenhagen in 1789. The subject of the opera is Oberon.

Holstgildet (The Harvest Festival) — Danish operetta in one act, music

Holstgildet by Schulz, produced in Copenhagen, 1790.

Holzdieb, Der (The Wood-Thief) — German comic opera in one act. Music by H. Marschner, text by F. Kind, produced at Dresden in 1825. This little poem was a great favorite for amateur performances.

Homerische Welt — A hexology, music by August Bungert. The work is divided into two parts, "Die Ilias," consisting of the two operas, "Achilles" and "Klytemnestra"; and "Die Odyssee," containing "Kirke," "Nausikaa," "Odysseus Heimkehr," and "Odysseus Tod."

Horaces, Les — Lyric tragedy in three acts, music by Salieri, produced in Vienna, 1786. The libretto is adapted from Corneille's drama.

House that Jack Built, The — An operetta in two acts. Music by Mrs. Jesse L. Gaynor, libretto by Mrs. A. C. D. Riley; both ladies are from Evanston, Ill. First produced at Chicago at the Studebaker Theatre, December 21, 1900. The general plan of the opera is a birthday party which Mother Goose gives her son Jack, and all the familiar nursery people are invited. The music is catchy and rythmic and full of originality and a great credit to its very able composer. The whole affair is charming.

Hoyden, The — Musical comedy, music by John L. Golden and Robert Hood Bowers, words by Cosino Hamilton, produced in New York, 1907.

Incognita The libretto is taken from a French comedy, "La Soeur," by Tristan Bernard.

Hubicka (The Kiss) — Czechish opera in three acts by Smetana, produced at Prague in 1876.

Hughes de Somerghem — French grand opera in three acts, music by Gevaert, words by Prilleux, produced in Ghent, 1848.

Hulda — French opera in four acts, music by César Franck, words by Grandmougin, produced in Monte Carlo in 1894. The libretto is based upon a work of Björnsen, the Norwegian writer.

Hunyadi Laszeo (Ladislaus Hunyady) — Hungarian grand opera in four acts; music by Franz Erkel, text by B. Egressi, produced at Buda Pest in 1844. Ladislaus II., King of Poland, the hero, was killed at the battle of Vana in 1444.

Huron, Le — Comic French opera in two acts. Music by Grétry and text by Marmontel, first produced at Paris, 1768. Text after Voltaire's "Ingenu." "Le Huron" is the beginning of Gretry's brilliant success in France.

Husar, Der — German comic opera, music by Ignaz Brüll, produced in Vienna, 1898. It was a decided success.

Hydaspes — Opera, music by Mancini, produced in London, 1710. This was one of the first operas performed in England wholly in Italian.

I

Idomeneus — Opera in three acts with a ballet. Music by W. A. Mozart, text by the Abbé Varesco, first produced at Münich in 1781. In accordance with his promise given to Neptune, Idomeneus, King of Crete, is about to sacrifice his son when the water god appears and releases him from his unhappy promise. This opera is one of Mozart's earliest operas, and has never been received with any favor, though its melody should make it a favorite to any music lover.

Ifegenia in Aulide (Iphegenia in Aulis) — Italian opera, music by Scarlatti, produced in Rome, 1713.

Ilias, Die — One of the two main divisions of August Bungert's hexology "Homerische Welt." "Die Ilias" comprises the two operas, "Achilles" and "Klytemnestra."

Imeneo — Italian opera by Handel with text by Zeno, produced at London in 1740.

Improvisator, Der (The Improvisor) — Opera in three acts. Music by Eugen d'Albert, text by G. Kastropp. First produced at Berlin, 1902. Time of story, about 1540; scene laid in Padua, Italy.

Incognita — Comic opera, music by Charles Lecocq, book by F. C. Burnand, lyrics by Harry Greenbank, first produced at the Lyric Theatre, London, October 6th, 1892. A royal love affair forms the basis of the plot.

Indiana — Comic opera in three acts, music by Audran, words by Farnie, produced at the Avenue Theater, London, October 11, 1886.

Indra — Opera in three acts. Music by Flotow, text by Putlitz, first produced at Vienna in 1852. Scene opens at Sofala, a town in East Africa. Here the Portuguese poet, Camoens, is doing guard duty and meets and loves a beautiful Indian slave girl named Indra. He deserts, and flees to Lisbon, she goes with him. At Lisbon Camoens is discovered and brought before the King, but Indra pleads for her lover's life. When the King learns that the prisoner is the author of the verses that have been charming all Portugal, he bows before the poet, frees him, and unites the lovers. At its first performance the opera was brilliantly staged, and it has been very well received since.

Inez di Castro — Opera, music by Bianchi, produced in Naples, 1791. The composer wrote this especially for the famous singer, Mrs. Billington.

Ingo — Grand opera in four acts, music by Philipp Rüfer, text by Martha Friedmann, first produced at Berlin in 1896. The text is based upon Freytag's novel by the same title. Time of story, 357; place, Thüringen, Germany.

Ingrid — Opera in two acts. Music by Karl Gramann, text by J. Kersten. The scene is laid in Norway. Ingrid, a supposed waif, is brought up in the home of Wandrup, a Norwegian peasant. She falls in love with a German tourist whom she rescues from an accident. But he loves Godila, Wandrup's daughter, and Ingrid unselfishly helps the lovers to marry. It is then discovered that the traveller is her brother and Wandrup is her father. Music is full of local color and well adapted to the text.

Ingwilde — Opera in three acts, music by Max Schillings, words by Ferdinand, Count Sporck, first produced at Karlsruhe, 1894. This is a tale of a bloody feud in Norway, in Viking days.

Inkle and Yarico, or The Benevolent Maid — English opera, music by Dr. Samuel Arnold, words by George Coleman, produced in London, 1787.

Inquisitive Women, The — Italian musical comedy in three acts, music by Ermanno Wolf-Ferrari, words by Lugana, translated into German by Teibler, produced in Münich, November 17, 1903. The action centers about a club formed by some honest Venetian citizens, from which their wives are excluded.

Ione — Italian opera in three acts, music by Petrella, words by Peruzzini, produced in Milan, January 21, 1858. Bulwer Lytton's novel, "The Last Days of Pompeii," gave the basis for the libretto. It is regarded by many as Petrella's masterpiece.

Ipermestra (Hypermnestra) — Tragic Italian opera by Giacomelli, with text by Métastase. Produced at Venice, 1724. Ipermestra, the only one of Danao's daughters who failed to carry out her father's command to murder her husband on the wedding night, is a favored theme for operas of the Eighteenth Century. Métastase's most excellent text was generally preferred.

Ippolito and Aricia — Italian opera, music by Traetta, produced in Parma in 1759. The story is mythological. The opera was very successful and was revived at least once after the first productions.

Irene — German opera, music by Keiser, produced at Hamburg, 1697.

Iris — Opera in three acts, music by Pietro Mascagni, words by Luigi Illica, first produced in Rome, November 22, 1898. Iris, an innocent Japanese girl, is sacrificed to wicked men, but through all her trouble she remains pure, and at last becomes one with the flowers.

Iron Chest, The — English opera by Stephen Storace, text by G. Coleman, Jr., first produced at London, 1796.

Irrlicht (Will o' The Wisp) — Opera in one act. Music by Karl Gramann, text by Kwit Geucke. Scene is laid at light-house station in Normandy, and tells the tragic story of the young, beautiful daughter of a ship captain who has been abandoned by her French lover. Irrlicht is the name of the Frenchman's yacht.

Isabelle and Gertrude; or, The Supposed Sylphs — French comic opera in one act. Text by Favert. Both Blaise and Grétry used this text. Blaise's opera appeared at Paris in 1765; Grétry's at Geneva in 1767. Text

Isabelle and Gertrude is after Voltaire's "L'Education des Filles."

Isis — French ballet opera in five acts, and a prologue, music by Lully, text by Quinault, produced in Paris, 1677. Subject is mythological, being the love of Jupiter for the nymph Io.

Isle of Champagne, The — Opera in three acts by W. W. Furst. Libretto by Charles A. Byrne and Louis Harrison. Place, Isle of Champagne, unmapped. Produced at Buffalo, 1892.

Isle of Spice, The — Musical extravaganza, music by Paul Schindler and Ben Jerome, words by Allen Lowe and George E. Stoddard, produced in New York, 1904.

Ismalia — Italian grand opera, music by Mercadante, words by Romani, produced in Milan in 1832.

Isola Incantata (The Enchanted Isle) — Italian opera, music by Bruni, was produced at Paris, in 1792. Subject identical with Shakespeare's "Midsummer Night's Dream."

Isse — Pastorale in three acts with a prologue. Music by Detouches, text by La Mothe, first produced at Versailles, 1697. In 1708 it was extended to five acts. This mythological medley was a great favorite with the French, and Louis XIV. highly complimented Detouches upon it.

Jardinier et Son Seigneur, Le

I'Italiana in Algeri (The Italian Woman in Algiers) — Italian comic opera in two acts, music by Rossini, produced in Venice, in 1813.

I'Italiana in Londra (The Italian Woman in London) — Italian comic opera in two acts, music by Cimarosa, produced in Rome in 1779.

Italian Monk, The — English opera, music by Dr. Samuel Arnold, produced at London in 1797.

It Happened in Nordland — Musical extravaganza, music by Victor Herbert, words by MacDonough, first produced in New York in 1904.

Ivanhoe — An opera by Sir Arthur Sullivan, produced at the Royal English Opera in London, in 1891. It is founded upon Scott's novel, "Ivanhoe," and is of a more serious nature than Sullivan's other operas. In 1895 it was played with great success at the Royal Opera House, Berlin.

Ivan Lusannino — Russian opera, music by Cavos, words by Schaschowskoi, produced in St. Petersburg in 1799. Lusannino is a peasant who sacrifices his life to save the Czar.

Iwein — A German grand opera in three acts; music by A. Klughart, text by K. Niemann, produced at Neustrelitz in 1879. The hero is a knight of the middle ages.

J

Jacquerie, La (The Insurrection) — French grand opera in four acts, music by Joseph Mainzer, words by Langle and Alboize, produced in Paris, 1839. The subject is a peasant uprising in Northern France in 1358.

Jadis et Aujourd'hui (Yesterday and To-day) — French comic opera in one act; music by Kreutzer; words by Sewrin, produced at Paris in 1808.

Jagd, Die (The Chase) — German musical comedy in three acts. Music by Johann Adolph Hiller, text by C. F. Weisse, produced at Leipzig, 1771.

Jagiello Wietki (Jagello the Great) — A Polish grand opera in three acts, by Joseph Elsner, produced at Warsaw in 1820. The hero, who mounted the throne in 1386, is the founder of the Lithuanian dynasty in Poland.

Jaguarita l'Indienne (The Jaguarita Indian) — French comic opera in three acts, music by Halévy, words by Saint-Georges and Leuven, produced in Paris, 1855. Jaquarita is queen of a tribe of Indians, upon whom the Dutch are making war. She falls in love with one of the officers of the enemy and marries him.

Jane Annie, or the Good Conduct Prize — A comic opera, music by Ernest Ford, words by the novelists, J. M. Barrie and A. Conan Doyle, first produced at the Savoy Theatre, London, May 13, 1893. This is a story of a girls' seminary close to a university city.

Jardinier et Son Seigneur, Le (The Gardener and His Master) — French comic opera in one act; music by F.

A. D. Philidor, text by Sedaine, produced at Paris in 1761. Text is based upon Fontaine's pretty fable, and the music forms one of Philidor's best operas.

Jason — A French grand opera in five acts; music by P. Colasse, libretto by J. B. Rousseau, produced at Paris in 1696. Jason is the Greek hero, son of Æson, who led the Argonauts in their expedition to recover the Golden Fleece.

Jean de Nivelle — French comic opera in three acts, music by Delibes, words by Goudinet and Gille, produced in Paris, 1880. The theme is historical, the scene being laid in France in the Fifteenth Century.

Jean de Paris (John of Paris, Dauphin of France)—French comic opera in two acts. Music by Boieldieu, text by Saint Just, first produced at Paris in 1812 and a year later at Berlin. Plot is a lively story of the Dauphin's traveling incognito to meet his fiancée, the Princess of Navarre, who is also disguised. They meet at an inn, where she recognizes him in spite of his dissemblance and they have a merry time. This opera was extremely popular. Schumann ranks it with "Figaro" and "The Barber of Seville, as the best three comic operas of the world. Recently the opera has reappeared.

Jeanie Deans — English opera in four acts, music by Hamish MacCunn, words by Joseph Bennett, produced in Edinburgh, 1894. The libretto is based upon a novel of Walter Scott's "Heart of Midlothian."

Jeanne la Foile (Jean, the Demented) — A French grand opera in five acts; music by A. L. Clapisson, libretto by Scribe, produced at Paris in 1848. Jean of Castile murders her husband, Philip I., through jealousy. The deed preys upon her mind till she loses her reason.

Jeannot et Colin (Jeannot and Colin) — French comic opera in three acts. Music by Nicolo Isouard, text by Etienne, produced at Paris, 1814. A favorite opera with the French, and produced at different periods throughout the Nineteenth Century.

Jenny — French comic opera in three acts. Music by M. Carafa, text by Saint-Georges, produced at Paris, 1829. Some of the songs were very popular for a while.

Jenny Bell — A French comic opera in three acts; music by Auber, text by Scribe, produced at Paris in 1855. Jenny Bell is an actress with whom the son of Lord Mortimer is madly in love.

Jerusalem Delivrée (Jerusalem Delivered) — French opera in five acts, music by Persuis, words by Baour Lormain, produced in Paris, 1812.

Jery and Bately — German comic opera in one act, music by Kreutzer, words by Goethe, produced in Vienna, 1803.

Jessonda — German grand opera in three acts by Louis Spohr, text by Henry Gehe, first produced at Cassel in 1823. Place, Goa on the coast of Malabar; time, early in the Sixteenth Century. Jessonda, the young widow of the aged Rajah, is doomed by custom to be burned with her husband. She is rescued from this fate by the arrival of her early Portuguese lover, Tristan. Music of opera added much to Spohr's fame. This opera is still occasionally heard in Germany.

Jeune Femme Colere, La (The Young Shrew) — French comic opera in one act. Music by Boieldieu, text by Claparede, produced at St. Petersburg, 1805. Text is based upon Etienne's comedy by the same title. Music is excellent and in many respects equal to the composer's "Calife de Bagdad."

Jeune Henri, Le (The Young Henry) — Comic opera in two acts, music by Mèhul, words by Bouilly, produced at Favart, 1797. The overture, a beautiful piece of descriptive music, has become famous.

Joanita — French grand opera in three acts, music by G. Duprez, words by E. Duprez, produced in Paris, 1852. This opera had been presented in Brussels in 1851, under the title, "l'Abime de la Maladetta."

Joan of Arc — English opera in three acts, music by Balfe, words by Bunn, produced in London, 1837. The composer sang the part of Theodore in the first performance of the opera.

Jocelyn — French opera in four acts; music by Benjamin Godard, words by A. Sylvestre and Vic. Capoul, produced at Brussels, 1888. This opera attained only moderate success.

Jockei, Le (The Jockey) — French musical comedy in one act; music by Solié, text by Hoffmann, produced at

Paris in 1796. This little opera appeared several times annually for a number of years.

Jaconde — French comic opera in three acts, music by Isouard, words by Etienne, produced in Paris, 1814, revived later in Germany.

Johann von Lothringen (John of Lorraine) — Opera in four acts; music by Victorian Joncières, words by Gallet and Blau. First produced at Paris in 1885. A story of the Rhine country in the Twelfth Century.

Jolie Persane, La (The Beautiful Persian) — An opera in three acts, music by Lecocq, words by Leterrier and Vanloo, first produced in Paris, October 28, 1879.

Jolanthe — Lyric opera, music by Tschaikowsky, libretto by his brother Modiste, produced in Russia in 1893. It appeared in Bremen in 1907. Text is based on a story by Henrik Hertz entitled "King Rene's Daughter." This daughter flees from the realities of life and revels in moonshine romance. The music is dreamy and enchanting.

Jolie Fille de Perth, La (The Fair Maid of Perth) — French comic opera in three acts. Music by Bizet, words by Saint-Georges and J. Ademis, produced at Paris, 1867. Scott's novel by this title is well known.

Joseph in Egypt — French opera in three acts, music by Mèhul, words by Alexander Duval, produced in Paris, 1807. The text follows the Bible story fairly accurately. The opera has disappeared from the French stage but is still sung in Germany.

Josephine Sold by Her Sisters — French comic opera in three acts, music by Victor Roger, words by Ferrier and Carré, English adaptation of the libretto by William von Sachs, first English production in New York, 1886. It had been previously sung in Paris.

Journée aux Aventures, La (The Adventurous Journey) — French comic opera in three acts, music by Mèhul, words by Chapelle and Mezieres, produced in Paris, November 16, 1816. It remained upon the stage for some time but is now no longer sung.

Jovial Crew, The — English opera, music by Arne, words by William Bates, produced in London, 1760.

Judgment of Paris, The — English opera, music by Arne, words from a masque by Congreve, produced in London, 1740.

Judith — Russian grand opera in five acts, music and words by Serov, produced in St. Petersburg, 1863. The story is a Biblical one. Judith murdered Holofernes and freed her native city of Bethulia. "Judith" is still in the repertory of Russian opera and fairly popular. It was Serov's first work for the stage.

Jugement de Dieu, Le (The Judgment of God) — French opera in four acts, music by August Morel, words by Carcassone, produced in Marseilles, 1860.

Jugement de Midas, Le (The Judgment of Midas) — French opera in three acts, music by Grétry, words by d'Hele, produced in Paris, 1778.

Jugend Peter des Grossen, Die (The Youth of Peter the Great) — German operetta in two acts, music by Weigl, words by Treitschke, produced in Vienna, 1814.

Juif Errant, Le (The Wandering Jew) — French opera in five acts music by Halévy, text by Saint-Georges and Scribe, produced at Paris in 1852. Text is based on Eugene Sue's novel by the same title.

Julie — French operetta; music by Dezede, text by Monvel, produced at Paris in 1772. "Julie" appears in both German and French texts with the title "The Flowerpot."

Julius Cæsar — Italian opera by Handel, first produced at London, 1723. Subject is the great Roman.

Jungfrau von Orleans, Die (The Maid of Orleans) — Opera by Reznicek, produced in Prague, 1887. While the story is of French origin, the opera is distinctly Czechish.

Junker Heinz (Sir Henry) — Opera in three acts. Music by Karl von Perfall, text by Franz Grandour. First produced at Münich. Time, early part of the Eleventh Century; place, Swabia. Story is based upon Hertz's pretty poem, "Henry of Swabia." Libretto and music both excellent and popular in Germany at present time.

Justinus — Italian opera by Handel, produced at London in 1736. The hero was probably Justinian the Great, Byzantine emperor in the Sixth Century. The chief event of his reign was the publication of the Justinian code.

K

Kain and Abel — German opera in three acts, music by J. P. Förtsch, text by Postel, produced at Hamburg in 1689. The story is the Bible story of the fratricide with some additions.

Kais — English opera, music by Reeve and Braham, produced in London, 1808.

Kalasch ni Koff (The Merchant of Moscow) — Russian opera in three acts, music by Rubinstein, words by Kulikoff, produced in St. Petersburg, 1880. The libretto is adapted from "Lermontoff." The scene is laid in the time of Ivan the Terrible.

Kamennoi Gost (The Stone Guest) — Russian opera in three acts. Music by Dargomyski, text after that by A. Puschkin, produced at St. Petersburg, 1872. Text is the well known story of Don Juan. The instrumentation, unfinished at the death of the composer, was added by Rimsky-Korsakov. It has never been popular, although its music has had a marked influence on Russian composition.

Kanonikus von Mailand, Der (The Canon of Milan) — An operetta with music and text by E. J. A. Hoffmann, produced at Warsaw in 1805. Text is adapted from a story by Alexander Duval.

Kara Mustapha — German opera in two parts of three acts each. Music by Johann W. Franck, text by L. von Bostel, produced at Hamburg, 1686. Part first depicts Kara Mustapha, a grand vizier, successful in his attempt to storm the imperial city of Vienna; part second describes the city's joy at his failure to hold the same.

Kaschatschei der Unsterbliche (Kaschatschei, the Immortal) — Russian opera, music and text by Rimsky-Korsakov, first produced at St. Petersburg in 1905. The enthusiasm at this performance is indescribable. Flowers and wreaths were showered upon the stage, addresses were delivered before the raised curtain until the police, stirred by too many words of "Freedom and Justice" closed the celebration.

Kassya — French opera in five acts. Music by Delibes. Produced in Paris, 1893. The opera was completed after the composer's death by Guirand.

Katakomben, Die (The Catacombs) — German opera in three acts. Music by Ferdinand Hiller, words by Moritz Hartmann, produced in Wiesbaden, 1862. A Greek slave, Lucius, is the head of a body of Christians, who hold their meetings in the Catacombs. The jealousy of his mistress, whose love he does not return, causes her to betray them to the Romans.

Katharina, Sainte-Catherine d'Alexandrie — Dramatic legend in three tableaux, music by Edgar Tinel, words by Leo Van Humstede, translated into French by Florimond Van Duyse, and first presented at the Theatre Royal de La Monnaie in Brussels, February 27, 1909. The work is founded upon incidents in the life of St. Katharine, who lived in Alexandria in the beginning of the Fourth Century.

Käthchen von Heilbronn, Das (Kathrine of Heilbronn, or The Magic of Love) — German opera in four acts, music by Karl Reinthaler, libretto by Heinrich Bulthaupt. First produced at the opening of the Opera House at Frankfurt A/M, December 7, 1881. The theme is a romantic love story of the age of chivalry.

Keolanthe — English opera, music by Balfe, words by Fitzball, first produced in London, 1840, and in Vienna, 1853.

Kerim — French light opera in three acts, music by Alfred Bruneau, words by Milliet and Lavedau, produced in Paris, 1887. The story is an eastern one. Before the Emir can win the hand of his beloved, he is compelled to find some genuine tears. "Kerim" was the composer's first opera.

Khovantschina — Russian national music drama in five acts, music by Moussorgsky, finished in 1880 but not performed till later. The instrumentation of the opera was left to Rimsky-Korsakov. The opera is intensely national, the scene being laid in the time of Peter the Great. Some religious music is also introduced into "Khovantschina."

King Arthur — English opera, music by Henry Purcell, words by Dryden, the English poet, produced in London, 1691. The music was revised by Arne in 1770. The theme of the opera is King Arthur and the Knights of the Round Table. It is the composer's finest work.

King Dodo — Comic opera in three acts, music by Gustave Luders, words by Pixley, produced in Chicago, 1901.

Kirke (Circe) — Musical drama in three acts. Music and libretto by August Bungert, first produced in Dresden in 1898. Kirke is the first part of Bungert's "Odyssey" and is based upon the well known mythological story of Ulysses and Circe.

Kirmess, Die (The Kermess) — German operetta, music by Abt Vogler, text by Patrat, produced at Paris in 1783.

Knight of Snowden, The — English opera, music by Sir Henry Bishop, produced in London, 1811. The story is taken from Scott's "Lady of the Lake."

Kobold, Der (The Goblin) — A fairy opera in three acts. Music and text by Siegfried Wagner, produced at Hamburg in 1904. The text is rather loosely connected. Because he is the son of the great Richard Wagner, Siegfried has much to live up to. German audiences are very cordial to him though there is some doubt as to whether his music will live.

König Drosselbart — A fairy opera in three acts, music by Gustav Kulenkampff, text by Axel Delmar. First performed at Berlin in 1889. König Drosselbart is the name a young princess scornfully gives her royal suitor as she rejects him; but she regrets it and he forgives her and they live happily ever afterward.

Königin Mariette (Queen Marietta) — German comic opera in three acts, music by Ignaz Brüll, words by Tell and Genée, produced in Münich, June 16, 1883.

Königin von Saba (The Queen of Sheba) — German grand opera in four acts, music by Karl Goldmark, words by Mosenthal, produced in Vienna, March 10, 1875. It is a Biblical subject. Other characters beside the Queen are Solomon, Assad, and Sulamith. It is Goldmark's first opera.

König Manfred (King Manfred) — German grand opera in five acts. Music by Karl Reinecke, libretto by F. Roeber, produced at Wiesbaden, 1867. The hero is one of the last of the Hohenstaufen kings; he ruled over Sicily and Naples, was excommunicated by the Pope, and fell in battle in 1266.

König, und der Kohler, Der (The King and the Charcoal Man) — Comic opera, music by Dvořák, the Bohemian composer, produced in Prague, 1874.

Korrigane, La — A French ballet in two acts, music and text by C. M. Widor, first produced at Paris in 1880, and has ever since enjoyed a very successful run.

Kosiki — French operetta, music by Lecocq, words by Busnachliveat, produced at Paris, 1876.

Kostchei, the Immortal — Russian opera, music by Rimsky-Korsakov, produced in St. Petersburg, 1902. The subject of the opera is a Russian legend.

Kreuzfahrer, Der (The Crusader) — German opera in three acts. Music by L. Spohr, text by his wife, Marianna Spohr, produced at Cassel, 1845.

Kriegsgefangene, Die (The Prisoner of War) — Opera in two acts, music by Karl Goldmark, words by Emil Schlicht, first produced in Vienna, 1899. The scene is laid at Troy toward the close of the Trojan war.

Kunihild — German opera in three acts, music by Cyrill Kistler, produced in Sondershausen, 1884. The theme is the legend of Kynast in the Riesengebirge.

Kuss, Der (The Kiss) — Opera in two acts by Smetana. Libretto by Krasnohorska. Place, the Bohemian mountains near the frontier. Time, the Nineteenth Century. First produced at Prague in 1876.

Kyffhaüserberg, Der — German opera, music by Marschner, produced at Pressburg, 1817. The libretto is a one-act play written by Kotzebue, the German dramatist.

L

Labyrinth, Das (The Labyrinth) — German opera or song-play in one act, music by Peter von Winter, words by Schikaneder, produced in Vienna, 1794. It was written as a continuation to Mozart's "Magic Flute."

Lac des Fées, Le (The Fairy Lake) — French grand opera in five acts, music by Auber, words by Melesville and Scribe, produced in Paris, 1839.

Lady of the Manor, The — English comic opera, music by James Hook, produced in London, 1778.

Lady Teazle — Comic opera, music by A. Baldwin Sloane, words by John Kendrick Bangs and Roger Penfield, produced in New York, 1905. This is a musical version of Sheridan's famous play "The School for Scandal"

L'Agnese — Italian opera by Paër, produced in Parma, 1810. The heroine is St. Agnes, who was beheaded in 303, because she scorned the love of Symphonius.

Lago delle Fate, Il (The Lake of Faries) — Opera in four acts, music by Augier, libretto derived from that written by Scribe for Auber's "Le Lac des Fées," first produced at Milan in 1878.

L'Ajo Nell Imbarrazzo (The Preceptor in a Perplexity) — Italian comic opera. Music by Donizetti, produced at Rome in 1824. This same opera appears under the title "Don Gregario."

Lalla Rookh — French comic opera in two acts, music by Félicien David, words by Lucas and Carré, produced in Paris, 1862. The libretto is based upon Thomas Moore's poem.

L'Altaque du Moulin — French opera, music by Alfred Bruneau, produced in 1893. The scene is laid during the Franco-Prussian war.

L'Amante Astuto (The Astute Lover) — Opera by Garcia, produced at New York in 1826. The composer, himself a great singer, took part in the production. His operas were all successful, but have since been quite forgotten.

L'Amant et le Mari (The Lover and The Husband) — French comic opera in two acts, music by Fétis, words by Etienne and Roger, first produced in Paris, 1820.

L'Amant Jaloux (The Jealous Lover) — French opera, music by Grétry, worde by d'Hele, produced in Versailles, November 20, 1778. It retained its place on the stage a long time.

L'Amant Statue (The Statue Lover) — French comic opera in one act. Music by Dalayrac; text by Desfontaines, appeared at Paris, 1785. A lover imagines himself to appear before his mistress as an animated statue, and an amusing dialogue follows. Music is dainty and bright.

L'Ambassadrice (The Ambassadress) — French comic opera in three acts, music by Auber, words by Scribe and St. Georges, first produced in 1836.

L'Amitie au Village (Friendship in the Village) — French comic opera, music by Philidor, words by Desforges, produced in Paris, 1785.

L'Amor Contadino (Love in the Country) — Italian comic opera, music by Lampugnani, produced at Lodi in 1766.

L'Amor Marinnaro (A Seaman's Love) — German opera, music by Weigl, produced in Vienna, 1797.

L'Amour et Psyche (Cupid and Psyche) — French opera in one act by August Pilati, produced at Paris in 1856. Cupid forms the subject of countless European operas.

L'Amour Romanesque (The Romantic Love) — A one-act comic opera, music by Wölfl, text by d'Armand Charlemagne. Produced at Paris in 1804.

Landfriede, Der (The Public Peace) — German romantic opera in three acts, music by Ignaz Brüll, words by Mosenthal, produced in Vienna, October 4, 1877. The libretto is adapted from Bauernfeld's comedy by the same name which is followed very closely. The peace was one proclaimed by Emperor Maximilian in the middle of the Sixteenth Century.

Landgraf Ludwig's Brautfahrt (Count Ludwig's Wedding Journey)

Landgraf Ludwig's Brautfahrt — German grand opera in five acts, music by Eduard Lassen, words by Pasque, produced in Weimar, 1857. The hero is Ludwig IV. of Thuringia, the husband of St. Elizabeth.

Langue Musicale, La (The Language of Music) — French comic opera in one act, music by Halévy, words by Gabriel and Moreau, produced in Paris, 1830.

L'An Mil (The Year One Thousand) — French comic opera in one act. Music by Albert Grisar, text by Paul Foucher and Melesville, produced at Paris in 1837. Libretto is based on a revolt of some serfs. Both music and text are poor.

Lanterne Magique, La (The Magic Lantern) — French comic opera in one act. Music by Francesco Bianchi. Produced at Paris early in the Eighteenth Century. Though the music was pleasing it did not last long.

Laodicea et Berenice — Italian opera, music by Scarlatti, produced in Naples, 1701. Laodicea was the wife of Antiochus II. of Syria, put aside that he might marry Berenice.

L'Apparition (The Apparition) — French opera in two acts, music by Benoist, words by Germain Delavigne, first produced in Paris, 1848.

L'Arbore di Diana (The Tree of Diana) — Italian opera, music by Martin y Solar, words by da Ponte, produced in Vienna, 1785.

L'Arbre Enchante (The Enchanted Tree) — Comic opera in one act, music by Gluck, first produced in Vienna, 1759. The plot is taken from a vaudeville by Vade called "Poirier"

L'Arcadia in Brenta — Italian comic opera, music by Galuppi, words by Goldoni, produced in Venice, 1749. It was the first of Galuppi's comic operas and was very successful.

L'Artisan (The Artisan) — French comic opera in one act. Music by Halévy, text by Saint-Georges and Simonnin, produced at Paris, 1827. L'Artisan marks Halévy's debut as a comic opera composer and was a great success.

L'Aspirant de Marine (The Midshipman) — French comic opera in two acts. Music by Theodore Labarre, text by Rochefort and Decomberousse, produced at Paris, 1834. The music of this opera won Labarre great distinction.

L'Assedio di Firenze (The Siege of Florence) — Italian opera, music by Bottesini, words by Manetta and Corghi, produced in Paris, 1856. The libretto is adapted from Guerrazzi's novel by the same name.

L'Assedio di Leyda (The Siege of Leyden) — Italian opera, music by Petrella, produced in Milan, 1856. The title gives the subject of the opera; its heroine is Elnava.

Lasthenu — French opera in one act, music by Hérold, words by Chaillon, produced in Paris, 1823. The plot is taken from "Voyages d'Antenor en Grece," by Lantier.

L'Astuzie Femminili (Women's Deceit) — Italian opera, music by Cimarosa, words by Métastase, produced in Naples, 1793.

L'Auberge de Bagneres (The Tavern of Bagneres) — French comic opera in three acts, music by C. S. Catel, words by Jalabert, produced in Paris, 1807.

L'Avaro (The Miser) — Italian opera, music by C. Brizzi, text by Romania, produced at Bologne in 1877.

L'Avengle de Palmyre (The Blind Man from Palmyra) — French comic opera by Rudolphe, libretto by Desfontaines, produced at Paris in 1767. The blind man of Palmyra recovers his sight and immediately recognizes his sweetheart among all the other girls.

Law of Java, The — English opera, music by Sir Henry Bishop, presented in London, 1822.

Lazarus (The Resurrection) — Religious opera. Music by J. H. Rolle, text by A. H. Niemeyer, produced at Leipzig, 1777.

Lazzarone, Le; ou, Le Bienvient en Dormant — French opera in two acts, music by Halévy, words by St. Georges, produced in Paris, 1844.

L'Eau Merveilleuse (The Miraculous Water) — A French operetta; music by Grisai, text by Sauvage; produced at Paris in 1839. The text is very similar to that of "Der Dorfbarbier."

L'Ebreo — Melodramatic Italian opera by Apolloni, words by Boni, produced in Venice, Naples and Milan in 1855.

L'Eclair (The Lightning) — Comic opera in three acts, music by Halévy, text by Planard and Saint Georges, first produced at Paris, 1835. Place, near Boston, Mass.; time, 1790. Most familiar number in this opera is "Call Me Thine Own." L'Eclair added greatly to Halévy's success.

L'École de la Junesse; ou, Le Barnevelt Français (The School of Youth; or, The French Barnevelt) — French opera, music by Duni, words by Anseaume, produced in Paris, 1765. The plot is taken from Thompson's tragedy, "Barnevelt; or, The Merchant of London." This is one of the first French operas in which the dialogue is spoken and intermixed with songs.

L'Écossais de Chatou (The Scotchman of Chatou) — A French operetta in one act; music by Delibes, text by Gille and Jaime, produced at Paris in 1869. A Scotchman builds a beautiful little palace in Chatou and welcomes all strangers to come and be his guests, but when no one makes use of his hospitality, he investigates and finds that his servants have ordered all visitors away in order that they may live in idleness.

Ledia — Opera, music by Zubiaurre, words by Cardenas, first produced in Madrid, 1877.

L'Education Manquée (An Education Wanting) — French operetta, music by Chabrier, produced May 1, 1879.

Leheman (A Tour of Neustadt) — French comic opera in three acts. Music by Dalayrac, text by Marsollier, produced at Paris, 1801.

Leila — Czechish grand opera in four acts. Music by Karl Bendl, text by Elise Krasnohorski, produced at Prague in 1868.

L'Enfant Prodigue (The Prodigal Son) — French opera in five acts, music by Auber, words by Scribe, produced in Paris, 1850. The Bible story of the Prodigal Son has been greatly elaborated. The Oriental setting presents opportunities for much that is beautiful in music and stage settings.

L'Enfant Roi (The Child as King) — Lyric comedy in five acts, music by Alfred Bruneau, text written by Emile Zola, shortly before his death; produced first at Paris in 1905. Scene is laid in Paris in the present time. The baker suspects his wife of having a youthful lover. This young man turns out to be the woman's illegitimate son. Jealous of her love for this boy he sends the youth away, but the mother leaves too. Her husband grieves so for her that she returns to him. When the young man wishes to leave for America the baker's heart softens toward him, and he adopts him as his son. This opera scored a greater success than "Messidor." Both libretto and music are a credit to their authors. Interest in the play increases with each act.

Léocadie — French comic opera in three acts; music by Auber, text by Scribe and Melesville, produced at Paris in 1824. Léocadie is a young girl who brings up her illegitimate child with great tenderness and care. Her betrayer becomes her lover and marries her.

Leonce (The Adopted Son) — French musical comedy in two acts. Music by Niccolò Isouard, text by Marsollier, produced at Paris, 1805. Libretto is one of Marsollier's best efforts, and many songs of the opera were popular for years.

Leonidas; ou, Les Spartiates (Leonidas; or, The Spartans) — Opera in three acts, music by Persuis and Gresnick, words by Pixerecourt, produced in Paris, 1799.

Leonora — Opera, music by William H. Fry, words by Joseph R. Fry, first produced in Philadelphia, 1845. This is the first American opera worthy of the name.

Léonore; ou, L'Amour Conjugal (Elenore; or, Conjugal Love) — Musical drama in two acts; music by Gaveaux, text by Bouilly, produced at Paris in 1798. A historical incident furnishes the basis for the text. In order to save her husband, Elenore, a French noblewoman, disguises herself and gains entrance to her husband's prison.

L'Épreuve Villageoise (The Village Trial) — French comic opera in three acts. Music by Grétry; text by Desforges, produced at Paris, 1784. The plot is very slight, taking on the character of a vaudeville performance. The music is excellently suited to the text and a credit to the composer.

Lequel (Which One) — French comic opera in one act; music by Aimé Leborne, text by Ancelot and Duport, produced at Paris in 1838. A rich man tries the experiment of having his son and a strange boy brought up together without their knowing which is which. The experiment proves the son to be the weaker character of the two.

Lerment; ou, les Faux Monneyeurs, Le (The Oath of the Counterfeiters) — French grand opera in three acts, music by Auber, words by Scribe and Mazeres, produced in Paris, 1832.

L'Errore Amoroso (A Loving Blunder) — Italian opera, music by Jomelli, produced in Naples, 1737. The opera was first given under the name of Valentino.

L'Esclave (The Slave) — French grand opera in four acts, music by Membrée, words by Foussier and Got; produced in Paris, 1874.

L'Esclave du Camoens (Camoens' Slave) — A French comic opera in one act. Music by Flotow, text by Saint Georges, produced at Paris, 1843. Historically, Camoens, the famous Portuguese poet, had a faithful slave. In the opera the servant becomes a female slave whom the poet loves and marries.

Lestocq (Love and the Intrigue) — French comic opera in four acts. Music by Auber, text by Scribe, produced at Paris, 1834. Story is historic. Lestocq, the French physician, formerly a favorite of the Czar, organizes a conspiracy which places Elizabeth, daughter of Peter the Great, upon the Russian throne. Lestocq is perhaps Auber's poorest effort: the music lacks character.

L'Esuli di Roma — Italian opera, music by Donizetti, words by Gilardoni, presented at Naples, 1829.

L'Étoile (The Star) — French operetta, music by Chabrier, words by Leterrier and Vanloo, produced in Paris, Nov. 28, 1877.

L'Étoile de Seville (The Star of Seville) — French grand opera, music by Balfe, words by Lucas, produced in Paris, 1845. The libretto is adapted from a play of de Vega's.

L'Étoile du Nord — Opera in three acts, music by Meyerbeer, words by Scribe, first presented Feb. 16, 1854, at the Opera Comique, in Paris. The same in Italian was given at Covent Garden, London, July 19, 1855, under the title "La Stella del Nord." It has been produced in English as "The Star of the North." The opera opens in Finland and presents Czar Peter the Great disguised as a shipwright. Peter falls in love with Catharine, a cantiniere and they are betrothed. Her brother, George, has just married, and, to save him from conscription, Catharine disguises herself and goes to the war. There she sees Peter making love to another girl, and is so overcome that she disobeys orders and is about to be shot. She escapes, but goes mad with her grief. At length Peter finds her, restores her to reason by playing upon his flute, and makes her his bride.

L'Étranger — French opera in two acts, music and words by Vincent d'Indy, produced in Brussels, Jan. 7, 1903.

Lettre de Change, La (The Bill of Exchange) — A French comic opera in one act: music by Bochsa, text by Planard; produced at Paris in 1815. The opera is no longer sung.

L'Heritier de Paimpol (The Heir of Paimpol) — French comic opera in three acts. Music by Christian Bochsa, words by Sewrin, produced at Paris, 1814.

L'Heure Espagnole (The Muleteer's Hour) — Comic opera in one act by Ravel. Libretto by Franc-Nohain. Place, Spain. Time, the Nineteenth Century. First produced in Paris in 1909.

L'Homme Sans Facons (The Informal Gentleman) — French comic opera in three acts; music by R. Kreutzer, text by Sewrin; produced at Paris in 1812. The opera has long since been forgotten.

L'Hôtellerie Portugaise (The Portuguese Inn) — French comic opera in one act, music by Cherubini, words by Aignan, first produced in Paris, 1798.

L'Huître et les Plaideurs (The Oyster and the Litigants) — French comic opera in one act. Music by Philidor, text by Sedaine, produced at Paris in 1759. Two people quarrel over an oyster, the first claims it because he saw it first, the second because he picked it up. The high count settles the dispute by giving each one-half of the shell and himself the oyster. It is a comic satire on the great amount of legal process that is wasted over trivial cases. Also known as "Le Tribunal de la Chicane."

Lia — Italian opera, music by Francesco Schira, words by Marcello, produced in Venice during the carnival of 1776. Some regard it as rivalling "La Selvaggia," his best opera.

Liberty Hall — English opera, music and words by Charles Dibdin, produced in London, 1785. It contains the seaman's song "Jack Ratlin," still popular today.

Libussa — German romantic opera in three acts, music by Conradin Kreutzer, words by Bernard, produced in Vienna, Dec. 4, 1822.

Libussa — Czechish opera in three acts, music by Smetana, words by Wenzig, produced in Prague, 1881.

Lichtenstein — German romantic opera in five acts, music by Lindpaintner, words by Dingelstedt, produced in Stuttgart, 1846. The libretto is based upon Hauff's novel by the same name.

Liden Kirsten (Little Christie) — Danish romantic opera in three acts, music by Johann P. E. Hartmann, text by Andersen, produced with success at Copenhagen in 1846.

L'Idol Cinese (The Chinese Idol) — Italian comic opera, music by Paesiello, produced in Naples, 1767.

Liebeskampf Der (Love's Battle) — Opera in two acts, music and text by Meyer-Helmund. First produced at Dresden, 1892. Story of a Corsican sailor who returns after years of absence to find his wife married to another. One of the prettiest songs is a charming love duet "Die Sonne neigt sich" (The Sun is Setting).

Liebestrank Der (The Love Potion) (L'Elisir d'Amore) — Comic opera in two acts, music by Donizetti, text by Romani, translated into German by J. C. Grünbaum. First produced at Milan, 1832. Scene, Italian village at the beginning of 1800. Story same as Auber's "Philtre."

Liebesverbot Das (Love's Prohibition) — German comic opera, music and words by Richard Wagner, produced in Magdeburg, 1836. The libretto is a free adaptation of Shakespeare's "Measure for Measure." The opera was first given under the title "Die Novize von Palermo," (The Novice of Palermo).

Life for the Czar (Zarskaja Skisu) — Russian grand opera in five acts, music by Glinka, text by Jonkowski, first produced at St. Petersburg in 1836. The hero of the story is Ivan Sussanina, a peasant, who forfeits his life to the Poles, whom he has deceived, in order to save the Czar. This opera marks the birth of national opera in Russia, with it and its successor, Glinka justly earned the title, "Father of Russian Music." The text is romantic and full of national color and the music is decidedly Russian, built upon national motifs. The success of this first national opera was immediate and overwhelming. The Czar was present at its first production and sent Glinka a valuable ring as a token of his pleasure. Though such a great favorite in Russia this opera is little known away from its native soil.

Light of Asia, The — Grand opera by Isodore de Lara, produced at Covent Garden, London, June 11, 1892. The libretto is founded upon Edwin Arnold's poem by the same name.

L'Ile Sonnante (The Resounding Isle) — French comic opera in three acts, music by Monsigny, words by Celle, produced in Paris, 1768.

Lili-Tsee — Opera in one act, music by Franz Curti, words by Wolfgang Kirchbach, first produced at Mannheim, in 1896. The story is a Japanese fairy tale in which a hand-mirror, an unknown object to the people in this simple Japanese village, causes many amusing incidents.

Lily of Leoville — Comic opera in three acts, music by Ivan Caryll, words by Felix Remo and Alfred Murray, lyrics by Clement Scott, presented for the first time in London, at the Comedy Theatre, May 10, 1886.

L'Impresario in Augustie (The Director in a Predicament) — Italian comic opera, music by Cimarosa, produced at Naples in 1795. A popular opera in Italy and in France.

Lina — Italian opera, music by Pedrotti, words by Marcello, produced in Verona, 1840. It was Pedrotti's first opera. To its success was due his appointment in Amsterdam as conductor of the Italian opera there.

L'Inconnue Persécutée (The Stranger Persecuted) — Opera in three acts, music by Pasquale Anfossi, words by Rosoy, produced in Rome, 1773. A French adaptation by Rochefort was presented in Paris, 1781.

L'Incoronatione di Poppea (The Coronation of Poppea) — Italian opera, music by Monteverde, produced in Venice, 1642. This is the last great work of the composer and the only one of his operas, except **Orfeo**, which has been preserved.

L'Infante di Zamora (The Prince of Zamora) — French comic opera in three acts, music by Paesiello, text by Framery, produced in Paris in 1789. The text is based upon Paesiello's "Frascatana." The music is charming and was a great favorite in Paris.

L'Inganno Felice, or L'Inganno Fortunato (The Fortunate Blunder) — Comic opera in one act, music by Rossini, produced in Venice during the carnival of 1812. This was one of Rossini's first operas and at once became very popular.

L'Intrigue aux Fenêtres (A Widow's Intrigue) — A French comic opera in one act, music by Niccolò Isouard, text by Bouilly and Dupaty, produced at Paris, in 1805.

Lionel and Clarissa — English opera, music by Dibdin, words by Bickerstaff, produced in London, 1768. The music was partly original and the remainder taken from other composers.

L'Irato; ou, L'Emporté — Comic opera in one act, music by Méhul, words by Marsollier, produced in Paris, 1801.

Lisbeth — French operetta in three acts; music by Grétry, text by Favieres, produced at Paris in 1797.

List Gegen List (Cunning Against Cunning) — German operetta, music by I. von Beeke, text by G. Spaur, produced at Vienna in 1785. The opera was also called "The Bell Has Tolled Twelve."

Little Corporal, The — Opera in three acts by Englander. Libretto by Harry B. Smith. Place, France and Egypt. Time, 1798-1799. First produced at Rochester, N. Y., in 1898.

Lituani, I (The Lithuanians) — Italian opera in three acts, music by Ponchielli, words by Ghislanzoni, produced in Milan, 1874. The libretto is founded upon a poem by Mickiewicz.

Lobetanz (Dance of Praise) — Opera in three acts, music by Ludwig Thuille, words by Otto Julius Bierbaum. A poet-musician restores the princess to health by his music, they fall in love and the poet is sentenced to death as a magician. Again the princess pines away, the musician restores her, and in his happiness the king consents to their union.

Locataire, Le (The Lodger) — French comic opera in one act, music by Gaveaux, text by Sewrin, produced at Paris in 1800. This opera is full of comedy, and the different airs are very musical and were great favorites with French opera singers.

Lock and Key — English opera, music by William Shield, words by Prince Hoare, produced in London, 1796.

Lodoiska — French opera in three acts, music by Cherubini, words by Fillete-Loreaux, produced in Paris, July 18, 1791. The opera was given with great success.

Lodoiska; ou, Les Tartares (Lodoiska; or, The Tartars) — French opera in three acts, music by Rudolphe Kreutzer, words by Dejaure, produced in Paris, August 1, 1791. The overture to the opera and the Tartars' March were for a long time great favorites.

L'Oeil Crève — Opera in two acts, music and words by Hervé, first produced in Paris, 1867. This was presented in London, in 1872. An English version called "Hit or Miss" was given in London, 1868, another in 1872, and still another termed "Shooting Stars," in 1877.

L'Officier Enlevé — French comic opera in one act, music by C. S. Catel, text by Duval, produced at Paris, 1819.

L'Officier et le Paysan (The Officer and the Peasant) — French comic opera in one act, music by C. F. Kreube, text by A. Dartois, produced at Paris in 1824.

L'Offrande à la Liberté (Offering to Liberty) — French revolutionary opera, music by Gossec, produced in Paris, 1792. The air of the Marseillaise with slight changes in the music was introduced into the opera with great effect.

L'Oie du Caire (The Goose of Cairo) — A combination by Victor Wilder of two unfinished operas of Mozart, "L'Ocadel Cairo" (The Goose of Cairo), and "Lo Sposo Deluso" (The Deluded Husband). It was produced in France and England in 1867. The story turns upon an enormous goose, inside of which a lover is introduced into his mistress' garden.

L'Olimpiade — Italian opera, music by Pergolesi, words by Métastase, produced in Rome, 1735. This libretto has been oftener used by composers than any other one of this writer's. The opera was very coldly received and its lack of success is said to have hastened Pergolesi's death.

L'Olimpiade — Italian opera, music by Sarti, words by Métastase, produced in Florence, 1755. The libretto is Métastase's most popular one.

Lombardi Alla Prima Crociata, I (The Lombards in the First Crusade) — Italian opera in four acts, music by Verdi, text by Solera after Grossi's poem, produced at Milan, 1843. The libretto is fervently religious, almost tempestuous, while the music, equally strong, is sweet and charming. This opera appeared at Paris in 1847 in a somewhat changed form, in French, under the title "Jerusalem."

L'Ombre — Comic opera, music by Flotow, words by St. Georges, first produced in Paris, 1870. An English version by Gilbert à Beckett, entitled "The Phantom," was presented in London, 1878. The opera scored a great success in all the capitals of Europe.

L'Oncle Valet — French comic opera in one act, music by D. D. Maria, text by A. Duval, produced at Paris in 1798.

L'Opera Comique — A French vaudeville opera in one act, music by Della Maria, text by Dupaty and Segur, produced at Paris in 1798.

Lord of the Manor — English opera, music by William Jackson, words by General Burgoyne, produced in London, 1780.

Lorelei. Die (The Loreley)— German opera in four acts, music by Max Bruch, words by Geibel, the German poet, produced in Mannheim, 1863. It is based on the famous Rhine Legend of the same name.

L'Orfanella di Ginevra (Orfanella of Geneva)— Italian opera in two acts, music by Luigi Ricci, words by Ferretti, produced in Naples, 1829. It was a success at the time.

L'Oriflamme — French opera in one act, music by Méhul, Paër, Berton, and Kreutzer, words by Etienne and Baour-Lormain, produced in Paris, Jan. 31, 1814, on the occasion of the approach of the allied armies. The oriflamme is the oblong red flag, the royal standard of France.

Lorle — Opera in three acts, music by Alban Foerster, text by Heinrich Schefsky, first produced at Dresden, 1891. Libretto adapted from Auerbach's little Black Forest village story "Die Frau Professorin" (The Professor's Wife.) The songs are sweet and touching and the opera is very popular.

Lorraine — Opera in three acts by Rudolph Dellinger. Libretto by O. Walther. English version adapted by W. J. Henderson. Place, France. Time, Seventeenth Century. First produced at Hamburg in 1886. English version produced in New York in 1887.

Lotario — Italian opera by Händel, first produced at London, 1729. Title is identical with "Lothario," a gay deceiver.

Lottchen am Hofe (Lottie at Court) — German operetta in three acts, music by Adam Hiller, words by Weisse, produced in Leipzig, 1769. It was one of the first of German operettas, and was exceedingly popular when first produced.

Louis IX. en Egypt — French opera in three acts, music by Le Moyne, words by Guillard and Andrieux, produced in Paris, 1790.

Loup Garou, Le (The Werwolf) — French comic opera in one act, music by Mlle. L. A. Bertin, text by Mazères and Scribe, produced at Paris in 1827.

Love in a Village — English opera, music by Arne, partly original and partly selected, words by Bickerstaff, produced in London, 1762.

Love in the East — English opera, music by Linley, produced in London, 1788.

Love Makes a Man, or The Fop's Fortune — An English comedy, music by Gottfried Finger, text by C. Cibberm, produced at London in 1698.

Love's Lottery — Comic opera, music by Julian Edwards, words by Stanislaus Stange, produced in New York, 1904. The opera was especially written for Mme. Schumann-Heink.

Love's Triumph — English opera in three acts, music by William Wallace, words by J. R. Planché, produced in London, 1862.

Lucile — French musical comedy in one act, music by Grétry, words by Marmontel, produced in Paris, 1769. It contains the famous quartet, "Ou pent-ou etre mieux qu-au sein de sa famille," "Where can one be better than in the bosom of one's family?" which has been sung on several historical occasions.

Lucinda ed Artemidoro — Italian opera in three acts by Paesiello, produced at St. Petersburg in 1782.

Lucio Papiro (Lucius Papirus) — Italian operas, music by numerous Italian and German composers. Hasse's opera appeared at Dresden in 1840 and Paisiello's was produced at Naples in 1767. They used the libretto by Zeno which was used by all composers after 1719. Lucio Papiro was the splendid Roman consul, general and dictator who won a victory over the Samnites in 309 B. C.

Lucio Silla (Lucius Sulla) — Italian opera, in three acts, music by Mozart, words by Gamera, revised by Métastase, produced in Milan, 1772. The hero is the famous Roman general and statesman.

Lucio Vero (Lucius Verus) — Opera by Torri, text by Zeno, produced at Münich in 1720. Vero was the adopted son of Emperor Antonius Pius, and was himself the colleague of Emperor Marcus Aurelius.

Lucky Star, The — Comic opera, music by Ivan Caryll, libretto founded upon the French by Leterrier and Vanloo and an American version by Goodwin and Morse, first produced in London, 1899.

Lucullus — Burlesque opera in three acts, music and words by Meyer-Helmund, first produced at Riga in 1905. The libretto is very poorly adapted from a drama by Kotzebue. Lucullus is a wealthy nobleman who lived in the First Century. His life of luxury was spent in revels of all sorts in which he finds his son to be a chip of the old block and the two have some difficulty in escaping the eager eye of Lucullus' wife. This opera has appeared in Italy and in nearly all of the large German cities.

Ludovic — French comic opera in two acts, music by Hérold and Halévy, text by Saint Georges, produced at Paris in 1833. Hero is a young Corsican who convinces his sweetheart of his love by attempting to shoot his rival. Hérold left the music unfinished and Halévy completed it.

Luisa Miller — Italian opera in four acts, music by Verdi, words by Cammarano, produced in Naples, 1849. The libretto is adapted from Schiller's drama, " Kabale und Liebe."

Lully et Quinault; ou, Le Dejeuner Impossible (Lully and Quinault; or, the Impossible Breakfast) — French comic opera in one act. Music by Isouard, text by Gaugvian-Nanteuil, produced at Paris, 1812.

L'Ultimo Giorno di Pompeia (The Last Day of Pompeii) — Italian opera by Giovanni Paccini, produced in Naples in 1825.

L'Une Pour l'Autre (One for the Other) — French comic opera in three acts, music by Isouard, text by Etienne, produced at Paris in 1816.

Luretti — Comic opera in three acts, music by Offenbach, words adapted from the French by Frank Desprez and Alfred Murray, lyrics by Henry S. Leigh, produced at the Avenue Theatre, London, 1883.

Lustige Schuster, Der (The Merry Cobbler) — This comic opera forms the second part of the well known and oft-composed opera "The Devil to Pay." It first appeared in English and there spread to the continent, appearing under different titles. The first part of this opera is known as "The Wives Metamorphosed." See "The Devil to Pay."

Lutheir de Vienna, Le (The Lutemaker of Vienna) — French comic opera in one act, music by Monpou, text by Saint Georges and Leuven, produced at Paris, 1836. Music had little merit and it was short lived.

M

Macbeth — Italian opera in four acts, music by Verdi, words by Cammarano, produced in Florence, 1847. The libretto is based upon Shakespeare's tragedy.

Maccabees, The — Russian opera in three acts, music by Rubinstein, words by Mosenthal, produced in Berlin, April 17, 1875. The text is adapted from Ludwig's drama. The story is the biblical one of Judas Maccabeus.

Macht des Liedes, Die (The Power of Song) — Comic opera in three acts, music by Peter J. Lindpaintner, text by Castelli, produced at Stuttgart, 1836.

Maçon Le (The Mason) — Comic opera in three acts, music by Auber, words by Scribe and Delavigne, first produced at the Opera Comique, Paris, May 3, 1825. The plot is founded upon an adventure of a mason named Robert, in the suburbs of St. Antoine at Paris, in 1788.

Madame Chrysanthème — French lyrical opera, music by Messager, produced in Paris, 1893. The subject is a Japanese one. The libretto is founded upon Pierre Loti's novel by the same name.

Madame Favart — Comic opera in three acts, music by Offenbach, words by Chivot and Durn, first produced at the Folies-Dramatiques, Paris, Dec. 28, 1878. An English version by H. B. Farme was performed at the Strand Theater, London, April 12, 1879, and the opera was revived at the Avenue Theater, London, March 11, 1882. Madam Favart was the wife of a composer who lived in the latter part of the Eighteenth Century. The opera is one of Offenbach's best.

Madame Gregiore, ou La Nuit du Mardi-Gras (Madame Gregiore, or The Night of Mardi-Gras) — French comic opera in three acts, music by A. L. Clapisson, text by Scribe and Boisseux, produced at Paris in 1861.

Madcap Princess, A — Comic opera, music by Ludwig Englander, words by Harry B. Smith, produced in New York, 1904. The plot is taken from "When Knighthood Was in Flower."

Mädchenherz, Das (The Heart of a Lass) — Opera in four acts, music by Crescenzo Buongiorno, German text by Ludwig Hartmann after the Italian by Luigi Illica, produced at Cassel in 1901. Its first production attracted a large audience from different parts of Germany and Italy and it was accorded the greatest enthusiasm.

Mädchen vom Lande, Das (The Country Girl) — Romantic comic opera in three acts, music by Suppé, words by Karl Elmar, produced in Vienna, 1847.

Mademoiselle de Belle-Isle — Opera by Samara, text by Paul Milliet, first produced at Genoa in 1905. Libretto is adapted from Alexandre Dumas père, and the story is enacted at Chantilly on June 25 and 26, 1726. The Marchioness of Prie loves the Chevalier d'Aubigny who is affianced to Mlle. Belle-Isle. Richelieu, a former lover of the Marchioness, makes a wager that he can win the first lady who appears in the park, provided she is young and beautiful. It happens that Mlle. de Belle-Isle is the first to pass by. Then comes the terrible duel between the Chevalier and Richelieu. This opera is by far the best Samara has written; it is an excellent production and is deservedly popular.

Mademoiselle de Guise — French comic opera in three acts, music by Solié, text by Dupaty, produced at Paris in 1808. The libretto is part fiction and part fact, the historical color being taken from the history of Charlemagne.

Mademoiselle Modiste — Comic opera in two acts, music by Victor Herbert, words by Henry Blossom, produced in New York, 1906. A great hit with Fritzi Scheff in the title role.

Madone, La (The Madonna) — French comic opera in one act, music by L. B. Lacombe, words by Carmonche, produced in Paris, 1861.

Maestro di Musica, Il (The Music Master) — A famous Italian opera buffa for three persons, by G. B. Pergolesi, produced at Naples in 1731. The music master attempts to prepare Lauretta for the stage and during the preparation many a thrust is made at the screaching method of singing. A theatre manager proposes to Lauretta but she refuses him and accepts the music master, much to the chagrin of the theatre manager.

Mage, Le (The Philosopher) — French opera in five acts, music by Massenet, produced in Paris, 1891. It is inferior to Massenet's best work.

Magellone — German opera, music and text by Dr. Krönlein, produced at Karlesruhe in 1874. The text is based on the tale in which the Princess Magellone of Naples flees with her lover Peter of Province, in order to escape marrying a man whom she did not love. In their fright they lose each other, but after long wandering the lovers are united.

Magicienne, La (The Magician) — French opera in five acts, music by Halévy, words by St. Georges, produced in Paris, 1858. The plot is derived from an old legend.

Magic Opal, The — Light opera in two acts, music by Senor Albemz, words by Arthur Lau, first produced at the Lyric Theater, London, Jan. 19,

1893. This play was revised and rechristened "The Magic Ring," under which title it appeared at the Prince of Wales' Theatre, London, April 11, 1893.

Magnelone — Musical drama in one act, music by Edmond Missa, text by Michel Carré, first produced at Paris, 1908. In order to protect her lover, the smuggler, from the watchful eye of the guard, Magnelone coquettes with the latter. The smuggler sees the two together, and ignorant of Magnelone's intention, he becomes jealous and kills the watchman. Missa is an apt pupil of Massenet and has very pleasingly employed the provincial folk music.

Mahmoud — English opera, music by Storace, words by Prince Hoare, produced in London, 1796. Storace was engaged in writing this when he died and the work was completed by Kelly.

Mahomet II. — French opera, music by Jadin, words by Saulmér, produced in Paris, 1803. Mahomet II. was Sultan of Turkey from 1444 to 1453.

Maidens of Schilda, The — German comic opera, music by Förster, words by Bunge, produced in Neu-Strelitz, 1887. The scene is laid in the Eighteenth Century in Schilda, which in Germany is synonymous with narrow mindedness.

Maid Marian — English comic opera in three acts, music by Reginald de Koven, words by Harry B. Smith, produced in Philadelphia, Nov. 4, 1901. The opera is a sequel to Robin Hood. The scene is laid in Palestine and Sherwood Forest in England in the time of Richard Cœur de Lion.

Maid of Artois, The — English grand opera in three acts, music by Balfe, words by Bunn, produced in London, 1836. The song "The Light of Other Days," occurs in this opera. It is still sung and at the time it appeared was one of the most popular in England.

Maid of Honor, The — English opera in three acts, music by Balfe, words by Fitzball, produced in London, 1847. The libretto is adapted from "Lady Henriette" by Saint Georges.

Maid of the Mill, The — English opera, music by Dr. Samuel Arnold, words by Bickerstaff, produced in London, 1814.

Mainacht, Die (May Night) — Russian opera, music and words by Rimsky-Korsakov, produced in St. Petersburg, 1880. The opera has never been sung outside of Russia, but it is highly regarded there.

Maison à Vendre (A House for Sale) — French comic opera in one act, music by Dalayrac, words by Alexander Duval, produced in Paris, 1800.

Maître Chanteur, Le (The Meistersinger) — French opera in two acts, music by Limnander, words by Henri Frianon, produced in Paris, 1853. The Meistersinger is the Emperor Maximilian, who thus disguises himself to right the wrongs of his people.

Maître Claude (Master Claude) — Comic opera in one act, music by Cohen, words by St. Georges and Leuven, produced in Paris, 1861. The plot is founded upon a supposed incident in the life of the painter, Claude Lorrain.

Maître de Chapelle, Le — French comic opera in two acts, music by Paër, words by Madame Gay, produced in Paris, 1821.

Maître de Musique, Le (The Music Master) — French comic opera in one act, music by F. Horzizki, produced at Rheinsberg about 1790.

Maître en Droit, Le (The Master in the Right) — French comic opera in two acts, music by Monsigny, words by Lemonnier, produced in Paris, February 13, 1760.

Maître Griffard — French comic opera in one act, music by Delibes, words by Mestepès, produced in Paris, 1857.

Maître Peronilla — Comic opera in three acts, music by Offenbach, first produced in Paris, 1878. The matrimonial complications of Manoela, who is united to one husband by a civil marriage, and to another by the church, form the basis of the plot.

Maître Wolfram — French comic opera in one act, music by Ernest Reyer, words by Méry and Gautier, produced in Paris, 1854. It has been revived since, but is now no longer sung.

Major Palmer, Le (Major Palmer) — French comic opera in three acts, music by Bruni, text by Piqualt-Lebrun, produced at Paris in 1797. "Major Palmer" is made up of a series of improbabilities.

Mala Vita (A Misspent Life) — Italian dramatic opera in three acts, music by Humbert Giordano, text by Daspero, first produced at Rome in 1892. Story is based upon a strangely repulsive play by the same name. At the time this opera was written the Italian public had a craving for morbid melodramatic stuff, and this opera made an immense hit. In 1897 it appeared in a revised form at Milan under the title "Il Voto" (The Religious Vow).

Malek-Adel — Italian opera by G. Niccolini, produced at Verona in 1830. The hero, Malek-Adel, was a Saracen general during the Third Crusade. He fell in love with Mathilde, sister of Richard the Lion-hearted. She was, however, engaged to marry another, but both she and Malek-Adel died before their love affair could be adjusted.

Malhem d'être Joie, Le (The Misfortune of Being Pretty) — French comic opera in one act, music by François Bazin, text by C. Desnoyers, produced at Paris in 1847. A pretty young girl, in love with a young page, resorts to an elixir which renders her unattractive in the eyes of the old baron to whom she has been promised in marriage, thus gaining her release from him.

M'Amie Rosette (My Sweetheart Rosette) — Romantic opera in two acts, music by Ivan Caryll, words by George Dance, taken from the French libretto of Preval and Liorat with music by Paul Lacome. First produced in English at the Globe Theater, London, Nov. 7, 1892. This is a tale of a village beauty, Rosette, with whom Henry IV. falls in love.

Mamzelle Fifi (Miss Fifi) — A Russian opera in one act, music by César Cui, text after Maupassant's novel by same title, produced at St. Petersburg in 1900 with success and is still before the public.

Mandanika — German romantic opera in one act, music by Gustav Lazarus, text by Julius Freund, published at Münich in 1900; text is based on an Indian Legend.

Mandarin, The — Comic opera by De Koven. Libretto by Harry B. Smith. Place, the Middle Kingdom, a region in China. Time, the Nineteenth Century. First produced at New York in 1896.

Maniac, The — English opera, music by Sir Henry Bishop, produced in London, 1810.

Mannequin de Bergame, Le — French comic opera in one act, music by Fétis, words by E. and P. Dupont, produced in Paris, 1832. This was written in imitation of the Italian style.

Manola — Comic opera in three acts, music by Charles Lecocq, English version by H. B. Farnie. Under the title "Le Jorie et La Nuit," Day and Night, the opera was first produced at the Nouveautée, Paris, Nov. 5, 1881. Manola was first performed at the Strand Theater, London, Feb. 11, 1882.

Manan Lescaut — French opera, music by Auber, text by Scribe, produced at Paris in 1856. Auber and Scribe, like Puccini, carry Manon across the sea and have her die in America. This gives them a chance to use local color and they introduce creole and negro melodies and dances. See "Manon Lescaut," by Puccini, and "Manon," by Massenet.

Manteaux Noirs, Les (The Black Mantles) — Comic opera in three acts, music by Bucalossi, words by W. Parke and Harry Paulton after Scribe's story "Giralda, ou La Nouveau Psyche" produced at the Avenue Theater, London, June 3, 1882.

Manto la Fée (Manto, the Fairy) —French grand opera in five acts and a prologue, music by Battistin Struck, words by Menesson, produced in Paris, in 1711.

Mara — Opera in one act, music by Ferdinand Hummel, words by Delmer, first produced in Berlin, 1893. The opera relates the tragic tale of a Circassian feud.

Marco Spada — French comic opera in three acts, music by Auber, text by Scribe, produced at Paris in 1852. Marco Spada is a brigand. Later this opera was extended to a grand ballet.

Marechal-Ferraut, Le (The Farrier) — French operetta in two acts, music by Philidor, words by Quétant and Anseaume, produced in Paris, Aug. 22, 1761. Philidor introduced into The Farrier an "air descriptiv," the first instance of this sort in opera.

Marga — Opera in one act, music by Georg Pittrich, text by Arnd Spiess, produced for the first time at Dresden in 1894. Marga is a Roumanian peasant girl, who wanders through the world in search of her sister's seducer in order to avenge her wrong. The coloring is decidedly Bulgarian, and the opera was such a success that it immediately aroused the keenest interest in the composer. The music is excellent.

Margherita d'Anjou — Opera, music by Meyerbeer, words by Romani, produced in Milan, 1820. This belongs to the first, or Italian, period of the composer's activity.

Maria di Rohan — Italian opera in three acts, music by Donizetti, produced in Vienna, 1842. This opera contains some of Donizetti's best work.

Mariage Extravagant, Le (The Extravagant Marriage) — French operetta in one act, music by S. Champein, text by Valory and Desangiers, produced at Paris in 1812. A popular operetta and revived later.

Mariages Semnites, Les (The Samnities Marriages) — French comic opera in three acts, music by Grétry, text by Rosoy, first produced at Paris, 1776. In 1768 Grétry had tried this same subject as a grand opera, but it failed.

Maria Tudor — Italian opera in four acts, music by Antonio Gomez, words by Braga, produced in Rome, 1877. Mary Tudor was Queen of England from 1553 to 1558.

Maria von Montalban — Grand opera in four acts, music by Peter von Winter, text by Reger, produced at Münich in 1798..

Mari de Circonstance, Le (The Husband of Chance) — French comic opera, music by C. H. Plantade, with text by Planard, produced at Paris, 1813.

Marie — French comic opera in three acts, music by Hérold, words by Planard, produced in Paris, 1826. The opera is still upon the stage.

Marie Stuart — Opera in five acts, music by Niedermeyer, words by Théodore Anne, produced in Paris, 1844. The selection "Adieu à la France" is well known.

Marie Thérèse — French opera in four acts, music by Nicolas Louis, text by Cormon and Dutertre, produced at Lyons in 1847. The heroine of this opera is the well known Empress of Germany, mother of the unfortunate Marie Antoinette. The text is not entirely true to history. The opera was a great success.

Marietta — Comic opera in one act, music by Alexander E. Fesca, produced at Karlsruhe in 1838. This opera is the composer's first production.

Marino Faliero — Opera in three acts, music and text by Wilhelm Freudenberg, first produced at Regensburg, 1889. Place, Venice; time, 1355. Marino Faliero, Doge of Venice, is the tragic hero of the story.

Marino Faliero — Italian opera, music by Donizetti, words by Bidera, produced in Paris in 1835.

Marion Delorme — Italian opera in three acts, music by Ponchielli, produced in Milan, 1882. The libretto is based upon Victor Hugo's drama.

Marito e l'Amante, Il (The Husband and the Lover) — Italian opera in three acts, music by F. Rucci, words by Rossi, produced in Vienna, June 9, 1852. It was exceedingly well received.

Marietto, oder Die Madonna mit dem Kreuze (The Madonna with the Cross) — An opera, music by Karl Aggházy, text by Irene Fuhrmann, first produced at Budapest in 1897. The opera was received with most marked enthusiasm.

Marjolaine, La — Comic opera in three acts, music by Lecocq, words by Vanloo and Leterrier, first produced in Paris, Feb. 3, 1877, and in London, October, 1877. The English version is by H. Sutherland Edwards, who has purified the original French plot.

Marjorie — Comic opera, music by Walter Slaughter, words by Lewis Clifton and Joseph J. Dilley, first produced at the Prince of Wales Theatre, London, July 18, 1889.

Marlborough S'en Va-t-en Guerre (Marlborough Goes off to War) — A French operetta in four acts, music composed jointly by G. Bizet, L. Delibes, Bernardin, E. Jonas and J. E. Legouix. Produced at Paris in 1867. This famous operetta with text by Busnach and Sirandin was written for the opening of the Théâtre de l'Athénée. The old march Melody was very prominent in the composition.

Marquise, La (The Marchioness) — French comic opera in one act, music by Adam, text by Leuven and St. Georges, produced at Paris in 1835.

Marquise des Rues, La (The Marquise of the Streets) — Comic opera in three acts, music by Hervé, words by Siraudin and Gaston Hirsch, produced at the Bouffes-Parisiens, Feb. 22, 1879.

Marthésie, Première Reine des Amazones (The First Queen of the Amazons) — Grand opera in five acts with a prologue, music by Andrè Destouches, text by Lamothe, produced at Fontainbleau in 1699.

Martyrs, Les — Opera in four acts, music by Donizetti, words by Scribe, produced in Paris, 1840. This is a version of the story of Polyeucte used by Corneille and so many others.

Maschere, Le (The Masqueraders) — Italian opera in three acts, music by Peitro Mascagni, produced simultaneously in Milan, Venice, Verona, Naples, Turin, Genoa and Rome on Jan. 17, 1901. It soon passed into oblivion.

Masnadieri, I (The Robbers) — Italian grand opera in four acts, music by Verdi, words by Maffei, produced in London, 1847. The libretto is an adaptation of Schiller's "Raüber."

Master-Thief, The — Comic opera by Eugen Lindner, libretto by the composer and his friend, Gustav Kestropp, after Fitzger's poem, first produced at Weimar, 1889. The story is founded on a German legend of the Rhine. The Master-Thief is a young nobleman in love with the count's daughter. In order to win the count's consent, he must perform three great thefts. First, he must steal the count's greatest treasure; second, he must steal the count; third, he must steal the count's personality. The opera at once touched the lovers of music and romance and it has been a great favorite on the German stage.

Matador, Der — German operetta, in one act, by Heinrich Hofmann, words by Sivinel, produced in Berlin, April 13, 1872.

Ma Tante Aurore; ou, Le Roman Impromptu (My Aunt Aurore; or, The Impromptu Romance) — French comic opera in two acts, music by Boieldieu, words by Longchamps, produced in Paris, 1803. The plot of this popular opera deals with a romantic old lady who is willing to marry her niece only to the hero of many adventures.

Mataswintha — German opera by Xavier Scharwenka, first produced at Weimar in 1906 with great success. The story is drawn from Felix Dahn's historical novel "Ein Kampf um Rom" (A Fight for Rome). This is an extremely interesting opera. It was produced in New York in 1907 under very unfavorable circumstances and deserves to be brought out again.

Matchmaker, The — Russian opera dialogue, music by Moussorgsky, written in 1868. The composer attempted to set to music Gogol's Russian comedy in prose without making any changes in the text. But one act was completed. It is important and significant, as showing the realistic trend of the Russian school at that time.

Mathilde — A German grand opera in three acts, music by M. Hauptmann, libretto by Caroline Pichler, produced at Cassel in 1826.

Matilda di Sabran — Italian opera in two acts, music by Rossini, produced at Rome during the carnival of 1821.

Matilda of Hungary — English opera, music by Wallace, words by Alfred Bunn, produced in 1847.

Matrimonio per Sussuro, Il (The Marriage Through Calumny) — Italian comic opera, music by Cimarosa, produced in Paris, 1802, but written in 1794.

Matrose und Sänger (Mariner and Singer) — German comic opera in three acts, music by Hentschel, words by J. C. Heinrich, produced in Leipzig, 1857.

Mattia Corvino — Opera in prologue and three acts, music by Ciro Pinsuti, words by Carlo d'Ormeville, first produced in Milan, 1877. The plot is founded upon an incident in Hungarian history, in the Fifteenth Century.

Mazeppa — Russian opera in three acts by Tchaikovsky, produced at Moscow in 1884. Mazeppa was a Polish youth who fell in love with the wife of a nobleman. The enraged husband had the youth bound to a horse and whipped out of the country. Captured by the Cossacks, he became their prince, and strove to free them from Russian rule. Disappointed in his endeavor, he committed suicide. The opera is full of the local color so characteristic of Tchaikovsky's music.

Medea — Well known tragic daughter of King Ætes, who helps Jason obtain the golden fleece, has been chosen by many composers as subject for operas. With Jason she appears under many different titles, some of which are: "Medée et Jason" — French grand opera by Salomon (Paris, 1713); "Medea e Giasone"— Italian opera by Brusa (Venice, 1726); "Die Argonauten" by Bach (1870); "Medée" by Cherubini, Paris, (1797).

Médecine Sans Médicin, La (A Cure Without Medicine) — French comic opera in one act, music by Hérold, text by Bayard and Scribe, produced at Paris in 1832. Without medicine the doctor saves two people. By bringing about a marriage between the daughter of an insolvent merchant and a rich Englishman, he saves the merchant from bankruptcy and the young man from suicide, which he was about to commit in a fit of ill humor.

Médecin Malgré Lui, Le (The Doctor Against His Will) — French comic opera, music by Gounod, produced in Paris, 1858. The libretto is Moliere's comedy by the same name. It has been given in England under the title "The Mock Doctor," first performed there in 1864.

Médecin Turck, Le (The Turkish Doctor) — French comic opera in one act, music by Niccolò Isouard, text by Gouffé and Villiers, produced at Paris in 1803. A young French lieutenant and his wife are captured by some Corsairs. The lieutenant is sold as a slave to the grand vizier of Constantinople, while his wife is carried off to the harem of an old Turkish doctor. Hearing by chance that the old doctor is enamored of a beautiful French slave in his harem and suspecting she is his wife, he has himself sent to the doctor's and after much difficulty gains her release and they leave for France. This is regarded as one of Isouard's best operas, and he probably considered it so himself since he dedicated it to the Princess Louise.

Medée (Medea) — French grand opera in three acts, music by Cherubini, words by Hoffmann, produced in Paris in 1797. All the operas by this name are adapted more or less freely from Euripides' tragedy.

Medico per Forza, Il (A Doctor by Force) — Italian comic opera, music by Lavinga, produced in Milan, 1802.

Medo, Il — Italian opera, music by Scarlatti, words by Frugoni, produced in Venice in 1708. Medo is Medus, King of Media.

Medonte — Italian opera in three acts, music by Guiseppe Sarti, produced in Florence in 1753.

Meister Martin und Seine Gesellen (Master Martin and His Apprentices) — German comic opera in three acts, music by W. Weissheimer, text by August Schricker, produced at Karlsruhe in 1879. Libretto is adapted from Hoffmann's story. Martin is a master cooper and he has a beautiful daughter, Rose. The comedy is furnished by her three suitors, a painter, a goldsmith and a knight, who all become Martin's apprentices because an old tradition has decreed that Rose shall marry only a cooper. This opera reminds one very much of "Die Meistersinger von Nürnberg."

Méléagre (Meleager) — French grand opera in five acts and a prologue, music by Battistin Struck, words by Jolly, produced in Paris in 1709. The story is a mythological one. Meleager, with Atalanta, slew the Calydonian boar.

Mélidore et Phrosine — French grand opera in three acts, music by Méhul, words by Arnault, produced in Paris, May 4, 1794. A novel of Gentil Bernard's is the basis for the text.

Melomanie, La (The Music Lover) — French comic opera in one act, music by Stanislaus Champein, text by Grenier, produced at Paris in 1781. A love story in which Saint-Real impersonates a musician, and by his song he charms the old music lover so that he consents to give him his daughter, Elise.

Melusine — Fanciful opera in three acts, music and libretto by Karl Grammann; text is based upon C. Camp's poem "Melusine." Produced in its present form at Dresden, 1891. Scene is laid in a French province on the upper Rhine about the year 100, and is a sad but picturesque little romance of the Mermaid princess, Melusine, and her lover, Count Raymond of Lusignau. Neither music nor libretto offer any marked originality and are Wagnerian in their composition.

Memnon — French comic opera in two acts, music by Charles Grisart, text by Cadoe and Bocage, produced at Paris in 1871. Memnon is the mythological king of Euthopia, who came to the aid of Priam at the siege of Troy, and who was killed by Achilles.

Merlin — Opera in three acts, music by Goldmark, text by S. Lipiner, first produced at Vienna, 1886. Text based on story of the ancient magician, Merlin. Time, Seventh Century; place, Wales.

Merope — Italian opera, music by Jomelli, words by Apostolo Zeno, revised by Métastase, produced in Venice, 1747. The theme is a mythological one and forms the subject of one of Euripides' tragedies "Cresphontes."

Merrie England — Comic opera, music by Edward German, words by Captain Basil Hood, first produced in London in 1902. The plot is laid in Elizabethan times.

Merry Duchess, The — Comic opera in two acts, music by Frederic Clay, words by George R. Sims, produced at the Royalty Theater, London, Aug. 23, 1883.

Merry Monarch, The — Comic opera by Chabrier and Morse. Libretto by J. Cheever Goodwin. Place, India. Time, the Nineteenth Century. First produced at New York in 1890.

Merry Sherwood — English opera, music by William Reeve, produced in London, 1795. It contains the well-known song, "I am a Friar of Orders Gray." The characters are Robin Hood and his band.

Merry Widow, The (Die Lustige Witwe) — Music by Franz Lehar, words by Victor Leon and Leo Stein, two Viennese journalists, first produced in Vienna, Dec. 30, 1905, English version by Edward Morton, lyrics by Adrian Ross, first produced in London, June 8, 1907, and in the United States at Syracuse, Sept. 23, 1907. The main plot deals with a love affair between Sonia, widow of a multi millionaire, and Danilo, Crown Prince of the impecunious State of Marsovia. The sub-plot, founded upon an intrigue between Natalie, wife of Baron Popoff, and the Vicomte Camille de Jolidon, is made more important in the English version. The opera has been extremely popular, particularly for its waltz-song.

Messalina — Opera in four acts, music by Isidore de Lara, text by Sylvestre and Morano, first produced at Cologne, 1907. Time, about 40 A. D.: place Rome, the imperial gardens and the circus. The story concerns the love affairs of the Empress Messalina during the absence of the Emperor. German libretto by Otto Rupertus.

Messenzio, Il — Italian opera in three acts, music by Cherubini, first presented in Florence, 1782.

Michel Angelo e Rolla — Italian opera, music by F. Ricci, produced in Florence, March 30, 1841. The Florentine painter and sculptor is the hero of the opera.

Michele Perrini — Italian opera in three acts, music by Cagnoni, words by Marcello, produced in Milan, 1864.

Mietje — A light opera with words and music by Benoit Hollander, first produced in London, May 11, 1909, at the Hampstead Conservatoire of Music.

Miller and His Men, The — English opera, music by Sir Henry Bishop, produced in London, in 1813.

Milton — French comic opera in one act, music by Spontini, words by Jouy and Dieulafoy, produced in Paris, November 27, 1804. The hero of the opera is the English poet, John Milton. It was dedicated to the Empress Josephine.

Miltiade à Marathon (Miltiades at Marathon) — French opera in two acts, music by Le Moyne, words by Guillard, produced in Paris, 1793.

Mina — French comic opera in three acts, music by Ambroise Thomas, words by Planard, produced in Paris, October 10, 1843. The opera did not long remain upon the stage.

Mirandolina — A German comic opera in three acts; music by Bernhard Scholz, text after Goldoni by Th. Rehbaum. First produced at Darmstadt in 1907. The scene takes place at a Florentine town, where a count, a marquis, a baron and a servant of the house all strive to win the hand of Mirandolina, the wealthy young hostess. The faithful butler wins. A successful opera.

Mireille — Pastoral opera in three acts, music by Gounod, words by M. Carré, taken from "Mireio" a Provencal poem by Mistral, and first given March 19, 1864, in the Théâtre Lyrique, Paris. As originally written the ending was unhappy, but this part has since been changed and the whole abridged. The English version has for its title "Mirella." Mireille, daughter of the rich farmer, Raymond, is in love with a poor young basket-maker, Vincent, though her father has promised her hand to Ourrias, a herdsman. After much unhappiness, Mireille is almost overcome by a sunstroke while on her way to meet her lover. At the sight of his daughter in an almost dying condition, the father relents and all ends happily.

Misé Brun — A lyric drama in four acts, music and text in four acts, first produced at Stüttgart in 1908. It is the struggle of a noble, pure woman to remain true to her husband, though she has ceased to love him. The opera was greatly appreciated.

Miss Decima — Operatic comedy in three acts, music by E. Audrau, English words adapted from the French of Boucheron by F. C. Burnand. Under the title "Miss Helyett," the piece was originally produced in Paris, at the Bouffes Parisiens, November 12, 1890. The English version appeared first at the Criterion Theatre, London, July 23, 1891. It was a great success in both countries.

Miss Innocence — Opera by Englander. Libretto by Harry B. Smith. Place, Paris and the country in France. Time, the present. First produced at New York in 1908.

Mitridate — Italian opera in three acts, music by Gasparini, text by Parmi, produced at Turin in 1767. Revised in 1770 by Amadeo and Mozart; libretto adapted from Racine's tragedy. Mitridates V. was the great King of Pontus, who was overcome by Pompey in 66, B. C.

Mitridate Eupatore, Il — Italian opera in three acts, music by Scarlatti, words by Roberti, produced in Venice in 1707.

Molinara, La (The Miller's Wife) — Italian opera, music by Paisello, produced at Naples, 1788.

Moloch — German tragic opera in three acts, music by Max Schillings, words by Gerhäuser, produced in Dresden, 1906. The libretto is founded on the fragment "Moloch," by the German dramatist, Hebbel. The scene is Thule, supposedly the Island of Rügen, in the Baltic Sea, and the time shortly after the destruction of Carthage.

Mönch von Sendomir, Der (The Monk of Sendomir) — A German opera in three acts with a prologue and an epilogue, music by Alfred Lorenz, libretto by Franz Kaibel, first produced at Karlsruhe in 1907. The libretto is adapted from Grillparzer's novel, "The Convent of Sendomir." Hauptmann had previously drawn his drama, "Elga," from the same source. Elga's relation to her brother is more repulsive in the opera than it is in the novel. The opera is impressive and scored a success.

Monks of Malabar, The — Three-act opera by Englander. Libretto by J. Cheever Goodwin. Place, Malabar, India. Time, the Nineteenth Century. First produced at New York in 1900.

Monna Vanna — Opera in three acts, music by Emil Abrányi, Jr., text by Emil Abrányi, Sr., first produced at Budapest in 1907. Libretto is drawn from Maeterlinck's drama with the same title. The opera deserves success.

Monna Vanna — Maeterlink's drama set to music by Février and presented at the Opéra in Paris and later at the Théâtre Royal de la Monnaie in Brussels early in the year 1909.

Monsieur de Pourceaugnac — French comedy with a ballet, music by Lully, text by Molière, produced at the Castle of Chambord in 1669, and at Paris in 1716 and again in 1730.

Monsieur Deschalumeaux — French comic opera in three acts, music by Gaveaux, text by Auguste under the pseudonym Crenzé de Lesser, produced at Paris in 1806. A rollicking comic opera, full of amusing incidents that happen to Monsieur Deschalumeaux on his trip to Marseilles. Music is not on a par with the text; reproduced in 1843.

Monsieur et Madam Denis (Mr. and Mrs. Denis) — French operetta in one act, music by Offenbach, text by Delaporte and Laurencin, produced at Paris in 1862.

Montano and Stéphanie — French comic opera in three acts, music by H. M. Berton, words by Dejaure, produced in Paris, April 15, 1799. It is the composer's best work. The song, "Oui, c'est demain que l'hymenée," is still sung.

Monte Carlo — Musical comedy in two acts, music by Howard Tallot, lyrics by Henry Greenbank, words by Sidney Carlton, first produced at the

Avenue Theatre, London, August 27, 1896. The comedy deals with certain visitors at Monte Carlo, notably a Mrs. Carthew, who, intent upon securing a new husband, finds her former spouse, whom she supposed to be dead, a waiter at Monte Carlo.

Monténégrins, Les — Lyric drama in three acts, music by Limander, words by Alboize and Gerard de Nerval, produced in Paris, 1849. In 1858 the work was again presented, reduced to two acts.

Montesuma — German opera, music by C. H. Graun, presented in Berlin, 1755. French text by King Frederick II., Italian text by Tagliazucchi.

Mort de Cleopatre, La (The Death of Cleopatra) — Opera by Victor Massé. Produced at Paris in 1885. This is Massé's last opera. He composed it during his last years of suffering and it was produced in his honor the year after he died. It falls far short of his best work. Its aim is too pretentious and it lacks the charm and ease which characterized Massé's earlier productions.

Mort du Tasse, La (The Death of Tasso) — French grand opera in three acts, music by Garcia, text by Cuvelier and Helitas de Meun, produced at Paris in 1821. Hero is the well known poet, Tasso, in love with the Princess Leonore.

Moses — German sacred opera in eight tableaux, music by Rubinstein, written in 1887.

Moudo della Luna, Il (The Inhabitants of the Moon) — Italian opera, music by Baldassare Galuppi, produced in 1750.

Mountaineers, The — English comic opera, music by Dr. Samuel Arnold, words by George Colman, Jr., produced in London, 1795.

Mountain Sylph, The — English romantic opera, music by John Barnett, words by Thackery, produced in London, 1834. It was the first real English opera since Arne's "Artexerxes," in 1762, and was the signal for a great development in dramatic music in England.

Mountebanks, The — Comic opera, music by Alfred Cellier, words by W. S. Gilbert, first produced at the Lyric Theatre, London, January 4, 1892. The plot turns upon the power of a mystic potion to cause the person drinking it to really become that which he is pretending to be.

Mousquetaires au Couvent, Les — Comic opera in three acts, music by Varney, words by Prevel and Fevrier, first produced in Paris at the Théâtre des Bouffes, March 16, 1880, it being a modification of Saint-Heliare and Duport's "l'Habit ne Fait Pas le Moine," (The Habit Does Not Make the Monk). An English version by H. B. Farnie was presented at the Globe Theatre, London, October 30, 1880.

Mousquetaires de la Reine, Les — French comic opera in three acts, music by Halévy, words by Saint-Georges, produced in Paris, 1846. The Queen is Anna, wife of Louis XIII. of France. The opera is still occasionally sung in France.

Mozart and Salieri — Russian opert, music by Rimsky-Korsakov, produced in St. Petersburg. The libretto is adapted from a dramatic duologue by Poushkin, the Russian poet. Salieri was a composer and court musician of Austria and a bitter enemy of Mozart.

Mozart and Schickaneder, the Theatrical Manager — Vocal comedy in one act, first produced at Schönbrunn, 1786. This opera consists of music collected from older operas. Mozart wrote one overture and one terzett for the original, but in a revision of it made by Louis Schneider and W. Taubert in 1861, all the songs are by Mozart.

Much Ado About Nothing — An English opera, music by Sir Charles Stanford, libretto by Julian Sturgis, produced at London in 1900. It was produced for two nights with great success and then dropped. One can hardly understand why so excellent a composition should have been so short lived. One of the best songs is the pathetic dirge to "Hero."

Mule de Pedro, La (Pedro's Mule) — French comic opera in two acts, music by Victor Massé, words by Dumanior, produced in Paris, 1863.

Muletier, Le (The Muleteer) — French comic opera in one act, music by L. J. F. Hérold, text by Paul de Kock, produced at Paris in 1823. The text is not as refined as it might be, but the music is very pretty.

Müller und Sein Kind, Der (The Miller and His Child) — A folk opera in four acts, music by Bela von Ujj, libretto by Karl Shreder and Robert Prosl, produced at Graz in 1907. An old tradition states that at midnight on Christmas the spirits of those who are to die in the following year can be seen wandering over the cemetery. The miller and his daughter, Marie, have been seen in the ghostly procession by Marie's lover, and father and child die the following year. This opera bears promise of better things to come from the hands of its blind composer.

Murillo — A romantic opera in three acts, music by Ferdinand Langer, text by Elise Henle, produced at Mannheim in 1887.

Muses Galantes, Le (The Gracious Muses) — A ballet opera in three acts, by J. J. Rousseau, produced in 1745 at a private performance. Each act has a separate hero. In the first act Tasso holds the stage, in the second Ovid, and in the third Anacreon. Two years later this subject was rehearsed as an opera, but was found unsuitable.

Musketeers, The — Two-act opera by Varney. Libretto by Ferrier and Prevel. Place, France. Time, Seventeenth Century. First produced at Paris in 1880.

Muza Haireddin — German grand opera in four acts, music by Conradi, words by Gustav Bouillon, produced in Berlin in 1852. Haireddin was the last of the Moorish princes.

Muzio Scevola — English opera in three acts, produced in London, 1721. The music for the first act was written by Ariosti, second by Buononcini, third by Handel. A warm discussion as to the merits of the latter two resulted.

Myrtia — German opera in two acts, music and text by Ludwig Rochlitzer, first produced at Prague in 1907. Rochlitzer has drawn his material from Felix Dahn's "A Struggle for Rome." The scene is laid on the Island of Delos in 520. Myrtia is the niece of a wealthy merchant in Delos. Among her uncle's slaves she sees Teja, a young Goth, who served King Theodoric and has been taken prisoner by the Greeks. She realizes that Teja is no slave by birth, loses her heart to him, and their tragic story forms the opera. "Myrtia" is the composer's first opera.

Mystères d'Isis, Les (The Mysteries of Isis) — Opera in four acts, music by Mozart, words by Morel de Chedeville, presented at Paris, 1801. The music for this opera was arranged by Lachnith from "Die Zauberflötte," part of which was omitted and pieces from the "Nozze di Figaro," "Don Giovanni," and Haydn's symphonies substituted.

Mysteries of the Castle, The — English opera, music by Shield, produced in London, 1795.

N

Nabucodonoser (Nebuchadnezzar) — Italian grand opera in four acts, music by Verdi, words by Solera, produced in Milan, 1842.

Nacht auf Paluzzi, Die (The Night on Paluzzi) — German romantic opera in three acts, music by Pentenrieder, words by Forst, produced in Munich, 1846.

Nachtigall und Rabe (Nightingale and Raven) — German operetta in one act, music by Weigl, words by Treitschke, produced in Vienna, 1818. The libretto is adapted from Etienne.

Nadeshda — Grand opera in four acts, music by Arthur Goring Thomas, words by Julian Sturgis, first produced at the Drury Lane Theatre, London, April 16, 1885. The scene is laid in Russia in the time of Catherine II.

Nadgy — Comic opera in three acts, music by F. Cassaigne, words by Alfred Murray, first produced in Paris, February 13, 1886, under title, "Les Noces Improvisus." Later it was put on in New York, and then in London at the Avenue Theatre, Nov. 7, 1888. The English version was much more popular than the French.

Nais — French opera-ballet in three acts, music by Rameau, words by Cahusac, produced in Paris, 1749. The prologue celebrates the peace following the War of the Austrian Succession.

Naissance de Venus, La (The Birth of Venus)— French opera in prologue and five acts, music by Colasse, words by the Abbé Pic, produced in Paris, 1696.

Narcisso — Italian opera by Domenico Scarlatti, produced at Rome in 1714. Narcissus is the beautiful young hunter of Grecian mythology who scorns Echo's love. As a punishment for this he falls in love with himself and pines away till he is turned into the beautiful little flower which bears his name.

Narciss Rameau — German opera in four acts, music by Julius Stern, text by V. Hirschfeld, first produced at Breslau in 1907. The libretto is based upon Emil Brachvogel's tragedy, "Narciss," and contains the history of Madame Pompadour. The latter, and not Narciss Rameau, the nephew of the composer, Jean Philippe Rameau, is the real hero of the opera. This opera is a splendid achievement, and will doubtless remain on the stage for some time.

Natalie; ou, La Famille Russe (Natalie; or, The Russian Family) — French opera in three acts, music by Reicha, words by Guy, produced in Paris, 1816.

Naufrage de la Meduse, Le (The Shipwreck of Medusa) — French opera in four acts, music by Flotow with Pilati and Grisar, words by the brothers Cogniard, produced in Paris, 1839. The score was burned later in Hamburg and Flotow wrote the opera once more under the title, "Die Matrosen," ("The Seamen").

Nausikaa — German tragic opera in three acts and a prologue, music and words by Bungert, produced in Dresden, 1901. The story is taken from the second part of the "Odyssey." Nausikaa, a King's daughter, loves Odysseus, and saves his life by offering herself a sacrifice to Poseidon. This opera is one of a series of four.

Nautch Girl, The; or, The Rajah of Chutneypore — Comic opera in two acts, music by Edward Solomon, book by George Dance and Frank Desprez, first produced at the Savoy Theatre, London, June 30, 1891.

Neaga — Swedish opera, music by Ivar Hallström, text by Carmen Sylva, produced in Stockholm, 1885.

Nebenbuhler, Die (The Rivals) — A romantic opera in three acts, music by Wilhelm Frendenberg, text by Gustav Gurski, produced at Wiesbaden in 1879. This opera is also known as "The Flight to Syracuse," and it is adapted from Wieland's "Clelia und Sinibald."

Neger, Die (The Negroes) — German opera in two acts, music by Lalieri, words by Treitschke, produced in Vienna, 1802. It was the composer's last opera.

Neige, La; ou, Le Nouvel Eginhard (The Snow; or, The New Eginhard) — French comic opera in four acts, music by Auber, words by Scribe and Germain Delavigne, produced in Paris, 1823.

Nell Gwynne — Comic opera in three acts, music by Robert Planquette, words by H. B. Farnie, first produced at the Avenue Theatre, London, February 7, 1884. The plot is founded upon the romantic story of Nell Gwynne, who rose from the position of humble orange girl to be the greatest actress of her time and the mistress of Charles II.

Nephtali; ou, Les Ammonites — French opera in three acts, music by Blaugini, words by Aignan, produced in Paris, 1806.

Neptune and Amphitrite — English opera by Thomas A. Arne, produced at London in 1746. In Roman mythology Neptune was the god of the sea; and Aphrodite, his wife, was supposed to have been born of the sea foam.

Nerone (Nero) — Italian opera, music by Duni, produced in Rome, 1735. The story centers about the person of the Roman Emperor Nero.

Ne Touchez pas à la Reine (Do Not Offend the Queen) — French comic opera in three acts, music by Xavier Boisselot, text by Walz and Scribe, produced in Paris in 1847. Text is replete with improbable incidents which cater to an unrefined taste in their hits at royalty. Music is of an excellent character.

Neue Don Quixote, Der (The New Don Quixote) — Polish comic opera by Stanislaus Moninszko with text by Count Fredro, produced at Wilna in 1847; also called the "Inn in the Apennines."

Neue Krumme Teufel, Der (The New Crooked Devil) — German comic opera, music by Haydn, words by Joseph Kurz, produced in Vienna, 1751. The libretto is adapted from Lesage's "Diable Boiteux."

Nicolo de Lapi — Italian opera in four acts, music by Frencesco Schira, words by Pinto, produced in London, 1863. The story has a historical foundation, the scene being laid during the Siege of Florence in 1529.

Night Dancers, The — English romantic opera, music by E. J. Loder, produced in London, 1846. Since that date it has been twice revived. It is Loder's finest work.

Niji-Novgorodians, The — Russian grand opera in four acts, music by Napravnik, words by Kalaschnikoff, produced in St. Petersburg, 1868, revived again in 1888. Niji-Novgorod is a great commercial city of Russia.

Nina — Italian opera in three acts, music by Paesiello, words by Lorenzi, produced in Belvedere, near Naples, 1789. The libretto is adapted from an earlier one by Marsollier.

Nina; or, La Folle par Amour (Nina; or, Insanity Through Love) — Operetta by Delayrac, text by Marsollier, produced at Paris in 1786. This was a popular opera subject. Nina, on her way to meet her lover, is told that he has been killed in a duel. She loses her mind and day after day she walks this same path, till one day her lover appears before her safe and well. This happily restores her reason. This was one of the earliest operas, popular in America in the last decade of the Eighteenth Century.

Ninette à la Cour (Ninette at Court) — French comic opera, music by Duni, words by Favart, produced in Parma and Paris, 1755. It was Duni's first attempt at comic opera and was a great success.

Ninion — A musical drama by Mojsisovics, original French text by Rolf Raymond, translated by Eder May-Lucey and Alfred Hagen, produced at Pressburg in 1907. Ninion is a Bohemian Parisienne. She becomes the wife of a splendid man, but tires of married life, and when he becomes insane she goes back to her old life and sinks lower and lower every day. She realizes too late what her blessings were and when her husband returns she finds she has forfeited his love. A splendid opera which will surely be produced on the best stages.

Nino (Ancient Island of Ios.) — Italian opera, music by Francesco Courcelle, text by Zanella. First produced at Reggio, 1720, and at Venice in 1732.

Ninon Chez Madame de Sevigne (Ninon at the Home of Madame de Sevigne) — One act opera, music by H. Berton, words by Emanuel Dupaty, first produced at the Théâtre Feydeau, Paris, September 26, 1808.

Niobe — Italian opera by Giovanni Pacini, produced at Naples in 1826. "Niobe" is one of Pacini's best compositions, the music is charming. Text is taken from the tragic story of this Queen of Thebes.

Nitetti — An Italian opera by Nic. Jomelli. Libretto is based upon a three-act text by Métastase, produced at Stuttgart in 1753. Nitteti was an Egyptian princess.

Nitocri — Opera by Saverio Mercadante, text by Piosasco, produced at Turin in 1825. Nitocri was the wife of Nebuchadnezzar.

Nixe, Die (The Nymph) — German opera by Müller von der Ocker, produced at Magdeburg in 1907. The text is based on Baumbach's little fairy tale. It is a charming musical production and very well liked.

Noces de Pelée et de Thetis, Les (The Nuptials of Paleus and Thetis) — Celebrated ballet by Benserade, first produced at Paris, 1654. Subject of this ballet and many operas is taken from the mythological story of the marriage feast at which Juno, Minerva and Venus quarrel for the prize of beauty. Benserade's ballet, taken from the Italian, was often danced by Louis XIV. and the ladies of the court.

Noite do Castello, A — Portuguese opera in three acts, music by Antonio Gomez, produced in Rio de Janeiro, 1861. It was the composer's first work for the stage.

No Magic Like Love, or The British Enchanters — An English opera by Lord Lansdowne, produced at London in 1706. Lord Lansdowne strove to improve the quality of operatic librettos, and his efforts were cordially approved of.

Normandy Wedding, A — Three-act opera by Furst. Libretto by J. Cheever Goodwin and Charles Alfred Byrne. Place, Normandy. Time, the Eighteenth Century. First produced at Boston, Mass., in 1898.

No Song, No Supper — English comic opera in two acts, music by Storace, words by Prince Hoare, produced in London, 1790. Later it became quite popular in America.

Notre Dame de Paris — Opera, music by William H. Fry, words by J. R. Fry, first produced in Philadelphia, 1863, later given in New York.

Noune Saglante, La (The Bleeding Nun) — French grand opera in five acts, music by Gounod, words by Scribe and Delavigne, produced in Paris, 1854. The libretto is adapted from Lewis' "Le Moine." The scene is an old Bohemian castle, which is haunted by the "Noune Saglante."

Nourjahad — English opera, music by Loder, words by Arnold, produced in London, 1834.

Nouveau Seigneur du Village, Le (The New Village Magistrate) — French comic opera in one act, music by Boieldieu, text by Favieres and Greuze de Lesser, produced at Paris in 1813.

Nouvelle École des Femmes, La (The New School for Women) — French comic opera in three acts, music by Philidor, words by Moissy, produced in Paris, January 22, 1770.

Nozze di Dorina, Le (The Wedding of Dorina) — Italian opera, music by Sarti, produced in Venice, 1782. It was revived in Paris later on.

Nozze di Teti e Peleo, Le (The Marriage of Teti and Peleo) — Opera in three acts, music by Cavalli, words by Persiana, produced in Venice, 1639. This was the composer's first opera.

Nuits d'Espagne, Les (The Nights of Spain) — French comic opera in two acts, music by Lemet, words by Carré, produced in Paris, 1857.

Numitor — Italian opera, music by Giov. Porta, text by A. Rolla, first produced at London, 1720. Hero is Numitore, King of Alba, who was dethroned by his brother, but whose grandsons, Romulus and Remus, helped him to regain the throne.

Nurmahal — German grand opera in two acts, music by Spontini, words by Herklots, produced in Berlin, May 27, 1822. The subject is taken from Moore's "Lalla Rookh." The oriental setting is the only thing that lends it any interest, and it was never sung outside of Berlin.

Nydia, the Blind Girl of Pompeii — Grand opera by George Fox, first produced at the Crystal Palace, London, May 11, 1892. The story is that of Bulwer Lytton's novel, "The Last Days of Pompeii."

O

Oberon, König der Elfen (Oberon, King of the Elves) — Operetta in three acts. German music by Paul Wranitzky, appeared at Frankfort A/M in 1790. This romantic little operetta was produced in honor of the coronation of Leopold II.

Oberto, Count di San Bonifazio (Hubert, Count of St. Boniface) — Italian opera in two acts, music by Verdi, words by Solera, produced in Milan, 1839.

Ochsenminuett, Das (The Oxen Minuet) — An operetta. Text is by Hoffmann, the music was compiled by Seyfried from various Haydn compositions. Produced at Vienna in 1823.

Octavia— Italian opera by Scarlatti, produced in 1715. Octavia, the wife of Emperor Nero, is the heroine of this opera.

Œdipe à Calone (Œdipus at Colonus) — French grand opera in three acts, music by Sacchini, words by Guillard, produced in Paris February 1, 1787. The first dramatization of Œdipus was by Sophocles, and all later attempts are based upon his great work.

Oddities, The — English opera, music and words by Charles Dibdin, produced in London, 1789. The opera contained many sea songs, which are still sung by English sailors, among them "Ben Backstay" and "Tom Bowling."

Odysse, Die — One of the two main divisions of August Bungert's hexology, "Homerische Welt," comprising the operas, "Kirke," "Nausikaa," "Odysseus," "Heimkehr," and "Odysseus' Tod." It was completed in 1896.

Odysseus' Heimkehr (Odysseus' Return)— German tragic opera with prologue and three acts, music and text by August Bungert, first produced at Dresden in 1903. Well-known story of Ulysses' return to

Penelope, his patient wife, and the slaying of the suitors. This opera is the third in a series of four.

Odysseus' Tod (Odysseus' Death) — Musical drama with prologue and three acts, music and libretto by August Bungert, first produced at Dresden, 1903. Last part of the Odyssey. Scene is laid in Ithaca. Bungert changes the story some by denying Ulysses a peaceful death in his old age. Music of this opera bears marked resemblance to Wagner.

Old Guard, The — Comic opera in three acts, music by R. Planquette, words by H. B. Farnie, first produced at the Grand Theatre, Birmingham, October 10, 1887, then at the Avenue Theatre, London, October 26, 1887. The scene is in the time of the first Napoleon.

Olga — Russian opera in three acts by Moritz Bernhard, produced at St. Petersburg in 1845. Plot is the story of Olga, who is the daughter of a Russian exile.

Olympie — French opera in three acts, music by Kalkbrenner, words by Guillard, produced in Paris, December 18, 1798. The libretto is adapted from a tragedy by Voltaire. Olympia was the daughter of Alexander the Great.

Olympie — French opera in three acts, music by Spontini, words by Briffault, Dieulafoy, and Bujac, produced in Paris, December 20, 1819. The libretto was based upon Voltaire's tragedy.

Omar und Leila — Opera in three acts by F. E. Fesca, libretto by Ludwig Robert, produced at Karlsruhe in 1823. A love story full of romance.

Omphale — French grand opera in five acts with a prolo, ue. Music by Destouches, text by La Motte, produced at Paris i. 1701. Omphaleis the widow of Tmolus, King of Lydia, in whose service Hercules labored three years.

Ondines au Champagne, Les — Comic opera, music by Lecocq, first produced in Paris, 1865. An English version by Farnie, called "The Sea Nymphs," was presented in London, 1877. The love affairs of two mermaids who went to a young ladies' seminary to finish their education, form the basis of the plot.

One o'Clock, or The Wood Demon —An English opera by Michael Kelly and Matthew King, produced at London in 1807.

On ne s'Avise Jamais de Tout (One Never Knows Everything) — French comic opera in one act, music by Monsigny, words by Sedaine, produced in Paris, September 17, 1761. The libretto was adapted from a fable of Lafontaine's.

Opera of Operas, The; or, Tom Thumb the Great — English opera, music by Arne, words by Fielding, the English novelist, produced in London, 1733. It is merely an adaptation from Fielding's "Tragedy of Tragedies," and is a severe satire upon the opera of the time.

Opernprobe, Die (The Rehearsal) — German comic opera in one act, music and text by A. G. Lortzing, produced at Berlin in 1851. Lortzing got the material for his libretto from an old comedy. The story is cleverly told and depends upon disguises for its wholesome, simple fun. The music is genuine Lortzing and equal to that of his larger operas. When first produced, it did not seem to be appreciated, but in 1899 it reappeared and it has since been received with a great deal of favor.

Opritschnick, Der (The Russian Body Guard) — Russian opera in four acts by Tschaikowsky, produced at St. Petersburg in 1874. The text is taken from a Russian tragedy by Layetschnikoff. The Opritschnicks were the well-known historical body guards of Ivan the Terrible, first to call himself "Czar" of Russia, who lived in the Sixteenth Century.

Orakel in Delphi, Das (The Delphine Oracle)— German grand opera in three acts, music by J. N. K. Götze, text by Sonderhausen, produced at Weimar in 1822.

Orazzi e Curiazzi, Gli (The Horatii and Curiatii) — Italian opera in two acts, music by Cimarosa, words by Sografi, produced in Venice in 1797. The story is from Roman legendary history.

Order of His Holiness, By (Auf Hohen Befehl)— Comic opera in three acts, music by Carl Reinecke of Leipzig, with words written by the composer from Rhul's novel, "Ovidius at Court." The scene is laid in a small German capital during the Eighteenth Century.

Orestes — A trilogy by Felix Weingartner, adapted from the "Oresteia" of Æschylus, first produced in Leipzig in 1902.

Orfeo (Orpheus) — Italian opera, music by Monteverde, produced in Mantau, 1607. The theme is a mythological one.

Orion — French grand opera in five acts with a prologue; music by Lacoste, libretto by Lafont, produced at Paris in 1728. Orion, the great hunter in Greek mythology, pursued the Pleiades till they were turned to stars, then he turned his attention to Diana, but as punishment for his audacity he was turned into a constellation and is now one of the finest winter constellations of the north.

Orlando — Italian opera, music by Handel, first produced at London, 1732. Orlando was the same as Roland in French romance.

Orontea, Regina d'Egitto (Queen of Egypt) — Italian opera by Cesti, words by Cicognini, produced in Venice, 1649. The opera was sung in Venice till 1683.

Ostralenka — Opera in four acts, music by Bonawitz, words by Haimbach, produced in Philadelphia, 1874.

Othello — Tragic opera in three acts, music by Rossini, text by Berio, first produced at Naples, 1816. Based upon Shakespeare's tragedy by same title. Verdi's "Othello" appeared seventy years later.

Otto, der Schütz (The Archer) — German opera in four acts, music by K. H. A. Reis, text by Pasque, produced at Mainz in 1856. Otto, the Hunter, is the hero of a Rhine legend.

Ottone — Italian opera, music by Pollaroli, text by Frigimelica Roberti, first produced in 1696, and twenty years later, with some changes, at Venice; appeared in London, 1722, with music by Handel.

P

Padlock, The — English opera, music by Charles Dibdin, words by Bickerstaff, produced in London, 1768. The composer sang the part of Mungo in the opera.

Pagode, La (The Pagoda) — French comic opera in two acts, music by Fauconnier, words by St. Georges, produced in Paris, 1859.

Paladins, Les (The Knights Errant) — French opera ballet in three acts, music by Rameau, words by Monticour, produced in Paris, 1760.

Palma — French comic opera in two acts, music by C. Henry Plantade, libretto by Lemontey, produced at Paris in 1798. Subject tells of funny incidents in a trip to Greece.

Palmira — An Italian opera in two acts, music by Antonio Salieri, libretto by Gamera, produced at Vienna in 1795. The heroine was the Persian Queen Palmira.

Paludier du Bourg-de-Batz, Le (The Saltmaker of Bourg-de-Batz) — French comic opera in two acts, music by Lefebore, words by Tanguy, produced in Angers, 1876.

Panier Fleuri, Le (The Flower Basket) — French comic opera in one act, music by Ambroise Thomas, words by Leuven and Brunswick, produced in Paris, May 6, 1839. It is one of the first of Thomas' compositions.

Panjandrum — Two-act opera by Morse. Libretto by J. Cheever Goodwin. Place, Subaya, a suburb of Manila, and the Island of Borneo. Time, the present. First produced at New York in 1893.

Pantagruel — French opéra-bouffe in two acts by Labarre, words by Henri Trianon, produced in Paris, 1855.

Panurge — A comic opera in three acts, music by Hervé, words by Clairville and Gastineau, represented at the Bouffes-Parisienes, September 10, 1879. It is founded upon the third book of Rabelais' "Pantagruel."

Paolo Emilio — Italian grand opera, music by Romolo Pignatta, words by Rossi, produced in Venice, 1699.

Papa Martin — Italian comic opera, music by Cagnon, words by Ghislanzoni, produced at Genoa, 1871.

Paquerette — French comic opera in one act, music by Duprato, words by Grange and Laronnat, produced in Paris, 1856.

Paria, Der (The Outcast) — Polish opera in three acts, music by Moninszko, words by Checinski, produced in Warsaw, 1869.

Paride (Paris) — Italian opera, music and words by Bontempi, produced in Dresden, 1662. The story is the mythological one of Paris and Helen.

Paride ed Elena (Paris and Helen) — Italian opera, music by Gluck, words by Calzabigi, produced in Vienna, 1770.

Parisiana — Opera in three acts, music by Donizetti, words by Romani, produced in Florence, 1833. Lord Byron's tragic poem is the source of the plot.

Part du Diable, La (The Devil's Share) — French comic opera in three acts, music by Auber, words by Scribe, produced in Paris, January 16, 1843. The scene of the story is Spain in the Eighteenth Century. Philip V. is cured of his melancholy by the sweet singing of Carlo Broschi.

Partenope — Italian opera, music by numerous composers: Caldara (Venice, 1707, popular); Don Serri (Métastase's text, Naples, 1722); Handel (London, 1730); Rossini (Naples, 1819). Parthenope was a siren who drowned herself for Ulysses' sake.

Pastorale en Musique, La (The Pastoral in Music) — The first French opera. Music by Cambert, words by the Abbé Perrin, first produced at Issy, near Paris, 1659, at the château of M. de la Haye. All operas before this were Italian operas or arrangements of them.

Pastor Fido (The Faithful Shepherd) — Famous Italian tragi-comic pastorale, music by Sir Richard Fanshaw, text by the poet, Batiste Guariri. First appeared in London under its English title, 1646. The poem was translated into nearly all the European languages, almost as soon as it appeared, and became popular with composers.

Patrie (Native Land) — French grand opera in five acts, music by Emilé Paladilhe, words by Gallet, produced in Paris, 1886. The libretto is founded upon Sardou's drama by the same name.

Paul and Virginia — French romantic pera in three acts and even tableaux, music by Massé, words by Carré and Barbier, produced in Paris, November 15, 1876. The libretto is adapted from Saint-Pierre's novel by the same name. The scene is an island off the African coast in the Eighteenth Century. The ship bringing Virginia back from France is wrecked and her body is cast upon the shore, where her lover is waiting for her return.

Pauline, the Lady of Lyons — English opera in three acts, music by F. H. Cowen, words by Hersee, produced in London, 1876. This was Cowen's first opera.

Paul Jones — Comic opera in three acts, originally produced under the title "Surcouf," at Folies Dramatiques, Paris, October 6, 1887; adapted into English by H. B. Farnie and first produced at the Prince of Wales' Theatre, London, January 2, 1889.

Pavillon du Calife; ou, Almanzor et Zobeide (The Pavilion of Calif; or, Almanzor and Zobeide) — French opera in two acts, music by Dalayrac, words by Despres, Deschamps and Morel; produced in Paris, 1804. It was later revised under the title, "Le Pavillon des Fleurs; ou, Les Pecheurs de Grenade."

Paysan, Le (The Countryman) — French comic opera in one act, music by Ch. Poisot, text by Alboize, produced at Paris in 1850. A young officer of peasant birth loves the daughter of a proud baron, but the latter objects to the marriage. Emperor Joseph II. comes to the rescue of the lovers by knighting the officer's father.

Pazzia Senile, La (Senile Folly) — Italian intermezzo, music by Banchieri, produced in Venice, 1598. Grove says it may almost be called the first comic opera, though that title is usually given to "La Lerva Padrona," 1733.

Pêcheurs, Les (The Fishermen) — French operetta in one act, music by Gossec, words by the Marquis de la Salle, produced in Paris, 1766.

Pêcheurs de Catane, Les (The Fishermen of Catane) — French comic opera in three acts, music by A. Maillart, text by Carré and Cormon, produced at Paris in 1860. Fernand, a young nobleman, betrays Nella, a peasant girl. When she learns of his engagement to a woman of his own station, she enters a convent. Fernand regrets having deceived Nella, breaks his engagement and offers to marry her, but it is too late; the girl dies of a broken heart.

Pêcheurs de Perles, Les (The Pearl Fishers) — French opera in three acts, music by Bizet, words by Carré and

Cormon, produced in Paris, September 30, 1863. The story is an Indian one. The heroine of the opera is Leila, a priestess on the Island of Ceylon.

Peggy from Paris — Musical play in a prologue and two acts, music by William Loraine, words by George Ade, first produced in Chicago, 1902.

Peines et les Plaisirs d'Amour, Les (The Pains and the Pleasures of Love) —French pastoral opera in five acts and a prologue; music by Cambert, words by Gilbert, produced in Paris, 1672.

Peintre Amoureux de son Modele, Le (The Painter in Love with His Model) — French operetta in two acts, music by Duni, words by Anseaume, produced in Paris, July 26, 1757. The libretto was translated from an Italian one called "Il Pittor Innamorato" (The Painter in Love).

Pelage; ou, Le Roi de la Paix (Pelage; or, The King of Peace) —French opera in two acts, music by Spontini, words by Jouy, produced in Paris, 1814, to celebrate the return of Louis XVIII.

Pelope (Pelops) — Italian opera, music by Jomelli, words by Verazi, produced in Stuttgart, 1755. The story is from mythology. Pelops was the son of King Tantalus and Dione.

Penelope — French opera in three acts, music by Piccinni, words by Marmontet, produced in Paris, 1785.

Penelope, La — Italian opera in two acts, music by Cimarosa, produced in Naples in 1795. Penelope was the wife of Ulysses, and the opera deals with the hero's return from his long wandering.

Pepita — Comic opera in three acts, music by Charles Lecocq, words adapted from the French of Durn and Chivot by "Mostyn Tedde." Under the title "La Princesse des Canaries" the opera first appeared in France, then made a tour of the English provinces and was put on at Toole's Theatre, London, August 30, 1888.

Pepita Jiminez — Spanish opera, music by Isaac Albeniz, produced in Barcelona, 1895. The libretto is adapted from Juan Valera. The scene is laid in a village of Andalusia in Spain.

Père Gaillard (Father Gaillard) — French comic opera in three acts, music by Napoleon Henry Reber, libretto by Sauvage, produced at Paris in 1852. Opera was not a success; one had to be educated up to it to enjoy it.

Perichole, La — A comic opera in three acts, music by Offenbach, words by Henri Meilhac and Ludovic Halévy, first produced at the Théâtre de Varieties, Paris, October 6, 1868. This popular opera has been revived several times, notably at Paris in 1874, and in London at the Garrick Theatre in September, 1897. The English version was written by Alfred Murray. The plot is founded on the true story of a Spanish Indian opera singer who lived in Lima, Peru, in the latter half of the Eighteenth Century, and captured the heart of its old Viceroy.

Perle du Bresil, La (The Pearl of Brazil) — French opera in three acts, music by Félicien David, words by Gabriel and Sylvain St. Etienne, produced in Paris, 1851.

Peronne Sauvée (Peronne Saved) — French opera, music by Dezède, words by Billardon de Sauvigny, produced in Paris, 1783.

Perruche, La (The Parrot)—French comic opera in one act, music by A. Louis Clapisson, libretto by Dumanoir and Dupin, produced at Paris in 1840. This little opera enjoyed a long popularity and for years it was a favorite curtain raiser.

Perruquier de la Regence, Le (The Wigmaker of the Regency) —French comic opera in three acts, music by Ambroise Thomas, words by Planard and Dupart, produced in Paris, March 30, 1838. The music is still occasionally sung.

Persée (Perseus) — French grand opera in three acts, music by Philidor, words by Quinault, revised by Marmontel, produced in Paris, October 24, 1780. The story is from Greek mythology.

Peters Bryllup — Danish opera in one act, music by Schulz, words by Tharup, produced in Copenhagen, 1791.

Peter Schmoll und Seine Nachbarn (Peter Schmoll and His Neighbors) — German comic opera, music by Weber, words by Turk, produced in Augsburg, March, 1803. It had been rehearsed in Salzburg, June, 1802, and there is a possibility that it was performed there. The libretto was adapted from Cramer's novel of the same name.

Petit Chaperon Rouge, Le (Little Red Riding Hood) — French comic opera in three acts, music by Boieldieu, words by Theaulon, produced in Paris, 1818.

Petit Duc, Le (The Little Duke) — Comic opera in three acts, music by Lecocq, words by Meilhac and Halévy, first presented at Paris, 1878. Later in the same year an English version by Saville and Bolton Rowe was presented in London.

Petite Mariée, La (The Little Bride) — French comic opera in three acts, music by Lecocq, words by Leterrier and Vanloo, produced in Paris, 1875. This has been translated into English and is one of Lecocq's most popular operas.

Petit Faust, Le (The Little Faust) — French opéra bouffe in three acts and four tableaux, music by Hervé, words by Cremieux and Jaime, produced in Paris, 1869. This has been translated into English and is the composer's most successful work.

Petite Mademoiselle, La — Comic opera in three acts, music by Lecocq, words by Meilhac and Halévy, produced at the Renaissance Theatre, Paris, April 12, 1879, and at the Alhambra Theatre, London, in 1879. A German version called "Die Feindin des Cardinals" (The Enemy of the Cardinals), was presented at Berlin, March 20, 1880.

Petit Matelot, Le (The Little Sailor) — French comic opera in one act, music by Pierre Gaveaux, libretto by Pigault-Lebrun, produced at Paris in 1796. It reappeared eight years later under the title, "The Impromptu Marriage."

Petruchio —English opera in one act, music by Alick Maclean, written in 1895. It won a prize offered in that year by Madame Fanny Moody and Mr. Charles Manners.

Pfauenfest, Das (The Peacock Festival) — German grand opera in three acts, music by Zumsteeg, words by Werthes, produced in Stuttgart, 1801.

Pfeiferstag, Der (The Piper's Festival) — German opera in three acts, music by Max Schillings, words by Sporck, produced in Schwerin, 1899. The Piper's Day was a custom peculiar to upper Elsass. Once a year all the pipers gathered at Rappoltsweiler under the protection of the Piper King, the master of Rappoltsweiler.

Pfeifer von Hardt, Der (The Piper from Hardt) — A romantic folk opera by Ferdinand Langer, first produced at Mannheim in 1894. Very successful and still very popular.

Phaon — French opera in two acts, music by Piccinni, words by Watelet, produced before the French court in Choisy, 1778. The story is the well known one of Sappho and Phaon.

Pharamond — French opera in three acts, music by Berton, Kreutzer and Boieldieu, words by Ancelot, Guirand and Soumet; produced in Paris, 1825.

Pharao — Opera, music by C. H. Graun, produced in Brunswick, 1733. This is a German version of "Gianguir," by Apostolo Zeno. The recitatives are in German, the airs in Italian.

Philemon and Baucis — This mythological subject is the text of many operas. Among them the earliest is by Gluck (Parma, 1769). Gounod's opera with text by Barbier and Carré, produced at Paris, 1860, is perhaps the best.

Philtre, Le (The Love Charm) — French opera in two acts, music by Auber, words by Scribe, produced in Paris, 1831. This has been translated into English and has had many performances.

Phryne — French comic opera in two acts, music by Saint-Saëns, produced in Paris, 1893.

Picaros et Diego; ou, La Polle Soirée — French comic opera in one act, music by Dalayrac, words by Dupaty, produced in Paris, 1803. This opera had been presented the preceding year as "L'Antichambre; ou, Les Valets Entré Eux."

Piccolino — Comic opera in three acts, music by Ernest Guirand, words by Nuitter, adapted from Sardou; first produced in Paris, April 11, 1876, and in 1879 at Her Majesty's Theatre, London.

Piccolo Haydn, Il (Young Haydn) — An Italian lyric comedy in one act, music by Gætano Cipollini, text by Sociale, produced first at Como in 1893. The text is founded on an incident in the youth of Haydn. The opera is a charming little thing and has been very popular in Italy and Germany.

Pierre de Medicis — Opera in four acts and seven tableaux, music by Prince Poniatowski, words by St. Georges and Pacini, produced in

Paris, 1860. The rivalry of Julien and Pierre de Medicis for the hand of Laura Salviati is the basis of the plot.

Pierre et Catherine (Pierre and Catherine) — French comic opera in one act, music by Adolphe Adam, libretto by F. Flotow and Saint-Georges, produced at Paris in 1829. This opera is one of Adam's earliest compositions and contained indications of his ability.

Pierrette and Jaquot — French operetta in one act, music by Offenbach, words by Noriac and Gille, produced in Paris, 1876.

Pietra del Paragone, La (The Touchstone) — Italian opera buffa in two acts, music by Rossini, words by Romanelli, produced in Milan, 1812. This was one of Rossini's first operas. He later used parts of it in his "Cenerentola."

Pietro il Grande (Peter the Great) — Musical drama in five acts, music by L. G. Jullien, produced in London, 1852.

Pietro von Albano — German opera in three acts, music by L. Spohr, libretto by Karl Pfeiffer, produced at Cassel in 1827.

Pigeon, Vole! (Pigeon, Fly!) — A French opera in one act, music and text by Fr. Castil-Blaze, produced at Paris in 1843. A jealous lover intercepts a dove which is bearing a message from a rival lover to his own sweetheart. He sets the dove free with its message, but has his rival killed.

Pilger von Mekka, Die (The Pilgrims from Mecca) — An operetta by Gluck, produced at Schönbrunn in 1764. The text is translated from Doncourt's "Rencontre Imprévue" (The Unexpected Meeting).

Pipe of Desire, The — A fairy opera in one act, music by Frederick S. Converse, text by G. E. Barton. Iolan, a young peasant, radiant with success and hope, returns to his home after an absence of several years, to claim Naoia, his bride. In the forest he meets the elves and their King; he invites them to the wedding, but because he is rude to the King, the latter plays upon his Pipe of Desire, and poor Iolan sees his bride die before his eyes. Then the King plays more and Iolan finds himself an old man. So bowed is he by grief that he submits and says, "Thy will be done." Feeling that he has curbed the pride

and self-satisfaction of the youth, the King stops playing. Then Iolan sees it was but a dream and before him, in reality, stands his beloved Naoia.

Pique-Dame — Russian tragic opera in three acts, music by Tschaikowsky, words by Modest Tschaikowsky, produced in St. Petersburg, December 19, 1890. The libretto is founded upon Pouschkin's novel.

Piramo e Tisbe (Pyramus and Thisbe) — Italian opera, music by Gluck, produced in London, 1746. It is a parody on the well known story of the two Babylonian lovers. It was a complete failure and is of no significance, were it not for the fact that it is said to have been the means of opening Gluck's eyes to the degradation to which opera had sunk.

Pirata, Il (The Pirate) — Italian opera in two acts, music by Bellini, words by Romani, produced in Milan, 1827. It was a tremendous success when first given and has been often revived since then.

Pirates, The — English opera, music by Storace, words by Cobb, produced in London, 1792.

Pirro, Il — Italian opera, music by Paisiello, produced in Naples, 1876. It is the first serious opera into which are introduced concerted introductions and finales.

Pirro e Demetrio — Italian opera in three acts, music by Alessandro Scarlatti, words by Adriano Morselli, produced in Naples, 1697. An English adaptation, words by McSwiney, and additional music by Nicola Haym, was presented in London, 1708, with great success.

Pittore e Duca (The Painter and the Duke) — Italian opera in three acts, music by Balfe, words by Piare, produced for the carnival in Triest, 1855. The opera was given later in London under the title, "Moro, the Painter of Antwerp."

Pizarro — English opera or song play, music by Michael Kelly, produced in London, 1799. Pizarro was the conqueror of Peru.

Planteur, Le (The Planter)—French comic opera in two acts, music by Hippolyte Monpou, text by Saint-Georges, produced at Paris in 1839. This opera met with some success.

Poete Suppose, Le (The Supposed Poet) — French vaudeville opera in three acts, music by S. Champeign, text by Laujon, produced in Paris in

1782. The comedy is furnished by the preparations for a festival.

Poia — An opera composed by Arthur Nevin, words by Randolph Hartley, first produced at the Royal Opera in Berlin, July, 1909. The libretto is founded on legends of the Blackfeet Indians.

Polyeucte — French grand opera in five acts, music by Gounod, words by Carré and Barbier, produced in Paris, 1878. The libretto is adapted from Corneille's play by the same name. Polyeucte was an early Christian martyr.

Polichinelle — French comic opera in one act, music by Montfort, words by Scribe and Duveyrier, produced in Paris, 1839.

Polifemo — Opera, music by Porpora, first produced in London, 1835.

Polinto, Il — Opera in three acts, music by Donizetti, words by Nourrit and Cammarano, originally written for presentation at Naples in 1838, but forbidden by the authorities. Scribe adapted it for the Grand Opéra at Paris, where it was given April 10, 1840, under the title, "Les Martyrs." Twelve years later it appeared in London as "I Martini." The plot is that of Corneille's tragedy, "Polyeucte," and this story of the early Christian martyrs has supplied Donizetti with many opportunities for dramatic music.

Polly — English song play, music by Pepusch, words by John Gay, produced in London, 1728. It is a continuation of Gay's "Beggars' Opera." It aroused a great deal of criticism and its performance was forbidden, but it appeared later on in print.

Polnische Jude, Der (The Polish Jew) — German opera in two acts, music by Karl Weis, words by Leon and Batka, produced in Prague, March 3, 1901. The libretto was adapted from Erckmann-Chatrian. The story is woven around the murder of a Polish Jew by a Burgomaster of Elsass.

Pomo d'Oro, Il (The Golden Apple) — Italian opera by Cesti, words by Sbarra, produced in Vienna, 1666, upon the occasion of the marriage of Leopold I. of Austria.

Pomone — French pastoral opera in five acts, music by Cambert, words by Perrin, produced in Paris, 1671. It is said to have been the first French opera publicly presented.

Pompeo in Armenio — Italian opera, music by Guiseppe Sarti, produced at Faenza, 1752. This, Sarti's first opera, scored a great success.

Ponce de Leon — French comic opera in three acts, music and words by H. M. Berton, produced in Paris, March 15, 1797. It was performed with great success.

Poor Soldier, The — English comic opera, music by William Shield, words by John O'Keefe, produced in London, 1783. This opera afterwards became popular in America.

Porcherons, Les (The Tea Gardens) — French comic opera in three acts, music by Albert Grisar, text by Lurien and J. Sauvage, produced at Paris in 1850. Scene is laid near and in Paris, and is of the period of Louis XV. The music is some of the best Grisar ever wrote; it is full of grace and melody.

Portefaix, Le (The Porter) — French comic opera in three acts, music by J. M. Gomis, text by Scribe, produced at Paris in 1835.

Porto Basso, A — Lyric drama in three acts. Music by Niccola Spinelli, text based upon Checchi's "Cognetti." Translated into the German by Ludwig Hartmann. First performed at Cologne, 1904. Time, present; scene, Naples. The music soon brought Spinelli prominently before the public.

Portoghesi in Goa, I (The Portuguese in Goa) — Italian opera, music by Sir Julius Benedict, produced in Stuttgart in 1830, and in Naples in 1831, where it was much more successful. Goa is a small Portuguese territory on the west coast of India.

Portrait de Manon, Le (Manon's Portrait) — French operetta in one act, music by Massenet, produced in Paris, 1894.

Porus — German opera in five acts, music by S. Kusser (Cousser), text by Bressand, first produced at Braunschweig, 1693. Porus was King of India in the Fourth Century B. C., and became famous in history as the Indian King who withstood Alexander the Great.

Pounce & Co.; or, Capital vs. Labor — American comic opera in two acts, music and words by Benjamin E. Woolf, first produced in Boston, 1883.

Poupée de Nürnberg, La (The Nuremberg Doll) — French comic opera in one act, music by A. C. Adam, words by De Leuven and Beauplan, produced in Paris, 1852. The motive for the libretto was taken from E. T. A. Hoffmann's "Sandmann" (Sandman). The time is the Nineteenth Century and the place a toy shop in Nuremberg. The opera was quite forgotten, but has recently been revived.

Power of Evil, The — Russian opera, music by Serov, finished by Soloviev, produced after 1871. The libretto is founded on a play by Ostrovsky, the Russian dramatist. The scene is the present time, and the story is exceedingly sordid and realistic. It is still performed on the Russian stage.

Praxitele; ou, La Ceinture — French opera in one act, music by Madame Devismes, words by Milcent, produced in Paris, 1800.

Pré aux Clercs, Le (The Clerks' Meadow) — French comic opera in three acts, music by Hérold, words by Planard, produced in Paris, 1832. The story is historical; the scene is laid at the court of Charles IX. of France in the Sixteenth Century. The opera is sometimes regarded as Hérold's finest.

Preciosa — German musical drama in four acts, music by Charles M. Von Weber, libretto by Alexander Wolff, first produced at Berlin in 1821. The scene is laid in Spain. A young nobleman, Don Alonzo, falls violently in love with Preciosa, a beautiful Bohemian girl whose virtue and charms are on everybody's lips. She does not believe, however, that she should marry so noble a suitor, and remains with the gypsies. But Alonzo loves her dearly. The gypsy chief gets into difficulty, and in order to gain his freedom he confesses that Preciosa was stolen from a noble family when she was a child, and so, of course, the lovers are united. "Preciosa" contains some of Weber's best music; it is a national gem and some of its songs will be popular forever. In 1858 the opera was reduced to one act.

Premier Jour de Bonheur, Le (The First day of Good Fortune) — French comic opera in three acts, music by Auber, words by d'Ennery and Cormon, produced in Paris, 1868.

Prés Saint Gervais, Les (The Meadows of Saint Gervais) — French operetta in three acts, music by C. Lecocq, text by Philip Gille and V. Sardou, produced at Paris in 1874. In 1876 this opera appeared at Vienna under the German title, "Prinz Couti."

Pretendus, Les (The Betrothed) — French grand opera in three acts, music by J. B. Lemoyne, libretto by Rochon de Chabannes, produced at Paris in 1789. This opera was popular for over thirty years.

Prigione d'Edinburgo, La (The Prison of Edinburgh) — Italian opera in three acts, music by F. Ricci, words by Rossi, produced in Triest, March, 1838. The song, "Lulla Poppa del Mio Brick," from this opera, was for a long time one of the most popular in Italy.

Prigionier, Il (The Prisoner); sometimes called "Il Prigionier Superbo" (The Noble Prisoner) — Italian opera in three acts, music by Pergolesi, produced in Naples, 1733.

Prima Donna, La — Comic opera in three acts, music by Tito Mattei, libretto adapted from "The Duke's Dilemma," a story by H. B. Farnie and Alfred Murray; first produced at the Avenue Theater, London, October 16, 1889.

Prince Igor — Russian opera in four acts and a prologue, music by Alexander Borodin, published in 1889. The opera was left unfinished by Borodin and was completed by Rimsky-Korsakov and Glazounov. The libretto is based upon "The Epic of the Army of Igor," one of the most interesting of all the old Russian chronicles.

Prince Methusalem — Comic opera in three acts, music by Johann Strauss, words by Treumann, adapted from Wilder and Delacour, first produced in Vienna, January 3, 1876. An English version with lyrics by Henry S. Leigh was performed at the Folies Dramatiques Theatre, London, May 19, 1883.

Prince of Pilsen, The — Musical comedy in two acts, music by Gustave Luders, words by Pixley, produced in Boston, May 21, 1902. The scene is Nice at the present day. A Cincinnati brewer is taken for the Prince, and he accounts for the honors shown him as a tribute to the excellent Pilsener beer that he makes.

Prince Troubadour, Le (The Troubadour Prince) — French comic opera in one act, music by E. N. Méhul, text by A. Duval, produced at Paris in 1813.

Princesse d'Auberge — Opera by Jan Blockx. Libretto by de Tiere.

Place, Brussels. Time, the Eighteenth Century. First produced at Antwerp in 1896.

Princesse de Babylone (The Princess of Babylon) — French opera in three acts, music by Kreutzer, words by Vigée and Morel, produced in Paris, 1815.

Princesse d'Élide, La — French comedy with ballet, music by Lully, text by Molière, produced at Paris in 1664.

Princesse Jaune, La (The Yellow Princess) — French comic opera in one act, music by Saint-Saëns, text by Louis Gollet, first produced at Paris, 1872. A young Dutchman falls in love with the picture of a Japanese princess, but he recovers, eventually marrying a Dutch girl.

Princess Ida; or, Castle Adamant — Comic opera in a prologue and two acts by Sir Arthur Sullivan, words by W. S. Gilbert, first produced at the Savoy Theater, London, January 5, 1884. This is a most amusing parody on Tennyson's "Princess."

Princess Osra — English opera by Herbert Bunning, produced at London, Covent Garden, in 1902. The music is original and dainty, with a touch of Gallic coloring, and a great credit to the composer.

Princess Toto — Comic opera in three acts, music by Frederic Clay, words by W. S. Gilbert, produced at the Opera Comique, London, October 15, 1881.

Principessa Fedele, La (The Faithful Princess) — Italian opera by Fr. Gasparini, produced at Venice in 1709. The opera was well received and shortly after appeared upon the stage at Vienna.

Prinz Eugen, der Edle Ritter (Prince Eugene, the Noble Knight) — German opera in three acts, music and text by Gustav Schmidt, produced at Frankfort A/M in 1847. Alexander Rost helped the composer in preparing the text.

Prinz Harold's Brautfahrt (Prince Harold's Wooing) — A German comic opera in three acts with a prelude and ballet; music by Heinrich Kratzer, text by Jakob Leeser, first produced at Barmen in 1907. The scene is laid on a northern island in the Thirteenth Century. Prince Harold, on his way north to woo the beautiful Princess Gerda, is waylaid by four ruffians. These exchange their beggars' clothes for those of their royal prisoner and his retinue, go north, impersonate the prince and his ministers, and furnish a great deal of fun. But before Gerda is won over to these strange royal people the Prince appears and the rogues are punished. Moderately successful.

Prinz Wider Willen (A Prince Against His Will) — Comic opera in three acts, music by Otto Lohle, text by Rudolph Seuberlich, first produced at Riga, Italy, 1890. Time, 1870; place, village in southern France. Story one of mistaken identity, and popular in Europe.

Prison d'Edinbourg, La (The Edinburgh Prison) — French comic opera in three acts, music by Prince Michele Carafa de Colobrano, text by Planard and Scott, produced at Paris in 1833. Libretto is taken from Sir Walter Scott's novel.

Prisoner of War, The — Two-act opera by Goldmark. Libretto by Emil Schlicht. Place, the Greek camp before Troy. Time, the end of the Trojan war. First produced at Vienna in 1899.

Prisonnier, Le (The Prisoner) — French comic opera in one act, music by D. D. Maria, text by Alexander Duval, produced at Paris in 1798. Opera was popular and appeared in Germany with the title, "The Arrest." Plot of story is based on a resemblance or double.

Prisonnier d'État, Le (The Prisoner of State) — French comic opera in one act, music by Batton, words by Melesville, produced in Paris, 1828.

Prœris and Cephalus — Russian opera, music by Francesco Araja, words by Soumarokoff, produced in St. Petersburg, 1755. It was written at the desire of the Empress Elizabeth and is said to be the first opera to be performed in the Russian language. The story is taken from Greek mythology.

Promesse, Les (The Promise) — French comic opera in three acts, music by A. L. Chapisson, libretto by Leuven and Brunswick, produced at Paris in 1854. A little love story with Queen Marietta as the heroine.

Promesses de Mariage, Les (The Promise to Marry) — French comic opera in two acts, music by H. M. Berton, words by Desforges, produced in Paris, July 4, 1787. It was given with success, but is no longer sung.

Promessi Sposi, I (The Promised Husbands) — Italian opera in four acts, music by Petrella, words by Ghislanzoni, produced in Secco, October 2, 1869. Manzoni's novel by the same name was the basis for the libretto. This opera is thought by many to be almost equal to "Ione," the composer's masterpiece.

Promessi Sposi, I (The Promised Husbands) — Italian opera, music by Ponchielli, produced in Cremona, August 30, 1856, and revised for Milan, December 5, 1872. Manzoni's novel by the same name was the basis for the libretto.

Proscrit, Le (The Outlaw) — French opera in three acts, music by Adolphe Adam, libretto by X. Saintine and Carmonche, produced at Paris in 1833. An invisible tribunal forms the background for the plot.

Proserpina Rapita (The Ravished Proserpina) — Italian opera, music by Monteverde, words by Strozzi, produced in Venice, 1630. The story is from mythology. Proserpina, the daughter of Jupiter and Ceres, was stolen by Pluto and carried off by him to the lower world.

Proserpine — French lyrical drama, music by Saint-Saëns, produced in Paris, 1887. The story has nothing to do with mythology, but is founded upon a poem by Vacquerie. The scene is Italy in the Sixteenth Century.

Proserpine — Italian opera, music by Peter von Winter, words by da Ponte, produced in London, 1804. The story is from mythology.

Protesilao — Italian opera, music by J. F. Reichartt, libretto by Abbate Sertov, produced at Berlin, 1779. This opera reappeared in Berlin several times after with some changes. Hero was the first Greek to fall in the Trojan war.

Pskovitaine, La (The Maid of Pskow) — An opera composed by Rimsky-Korsakov, first produced in St. Petersburg in 1873, founded upon a poem by Mei. It was re-written in 1894 and is still popular.

Psyche — French comic opera in three acts, music by Ambroise Thomas, words by Carré and Barbier, produced in Paris, January 26, 1857. A revised version was given in 1878. The opera has not kept its place on the stage.

Puits d'Amour (The Lovers' Well) — Comic opera in three acts, music by Balfe, text by de Leuven and Scribe, produced in Paris in 1843. The well is so called because a young girl who had been deceived by her lover threw herself into it. At the bottom, however, it leads to a spacious hall in which a certain King Edward and his jolly companions have a merry time. This opera is perhaps Balfe's best and its success in France was remarkable.

Punition, La (The Penalty) — French comic opera in one act, music by Cherubini, words by Desfaucherets, produced in Paris, 1799.

Puntigli delle Donne, I (The Honor of the Ladies) — Italian comic opera by Gasparo Spontini, produced in Rome, 1796. It was Spontini's first work and a great success.

Puppenfee, Die (The Doll Fairy) — A ballet by F. Gaul and J. Hassreiter, music by Joseph Bayer, produced in New York in connection with "Der Barbier von Bagdad," in 1890.

Puritania — Comic opera, music by Edgar S. Kelley, words by C. M. S. McLellan, first produced in Boston, 1892. It treats of Puritan life at the time of the Salem witchcraft craze.

Puritan's Daughter, The — Grand romantic opera in three acts, music by Balfe, words by J. V. Bridgman, first produced in London, November 30, 1861, at Covent Garden. The scene is laid in England, in 1665, during the struggle between the Puritans and Cavaliers, and involves the story of a Puritan maid and her Royalist lover.

Purse, The — English opera by William Reeve, produced at London in 1794, and soon after in New York.

Pygmalion — French melodramatic opera, music by Jean Jacques Rousseau and Horace Coignet, words by Rousseau, produced in Paris, 1775. There was no singing; the music was entirely orchestral and came in the intervals of the declamation.

Q

Quaker, The — English opera in two acts, music and words by Charles Dibdin, produced in London, 1775.

Quart d'Heure de Silence, Un (A Quarter of an Hour in Silence) — French comic opera in one act, music by Gaveaux, text by Guillet, produced at Paris in 1804. This subject is the same as Weber's "The Wager," which was produced in Germany the following year.

Quatre Fils Hymon, Les (The Four Sons of Hymen) — French comic opera, music by Balfe, text by de Leuven and Brunswick, produced at Paris in 1844. Four intrigues which terminate in four marriages are jestingly referred to as the four sons of Hymen. It was translated into German under the title, "Die Vier Haimonskinder." The music is not as good as that in Balfe's "Puits d'Amour.

Queen Andigo — German comic opera in three acts, music by Johann Strauss, words by Jaime and Wilder, produced in Vienna, February 10, 1871. It is a story of Asiatic Turkey in the Nineteenth Century — an impossible tale, in which the harem of the Sultan arms itself as an Amazon army.

Queen Topaze, or La Reine Topaze — A comic opera in three acts, music by Massé, text by Lockroy and Battu, First produced in Paris, 1856. The scene is laid in France in the Eighteenth Century. Plot is very slight. When a child Topaze is stolen by a band of gypsies and later becomes their queen. She falls in love with Rafall, a captain, who is affianced to a rich noblewoman, but he does not marry Topaze until she discloses to him the secret of her birth. Gypsy by-play supplies color and humor to the situations. The music is excellent and the gypsy melodies are unusually charming.

Quentin Durward — French comic opera in three acts, music by F. A. Gevaërt, text by Carré and Cormon, produced at Paris in 1858. Ten years before an English opera with this title, by Laurent, had appeared in London. Quentin Durward is the well known hero in Scott's novel by this name.

Quinto Fabio — Italian opera in three acts, music by Cherubini, first presented at Alexandrie-de-la-Paille, 1780, and at Rome in 1783. This was Cherubini's first opera.

Quiproquo, Le — French operetta in two acts, music by Philidor, words by Mouston, produced in Paris, March 6, 1760.

R

Rabelais — French comic opera in three acts, music by Presteau, text by Gribouval and Noyer, produced at Rouen in 1883.

Rache, Die (Revenge) — A Russian opera in one act, music by Rubinstein, text by Jemtschetschnikoff, produced at St. Petersburg in 1858.

Radamisto — Italian opera, music by Händel, words by Haym, produced in London, 1720. The hero of the opera was the husband of Zenobia, Queen of Palmyra.

Rajah de Mysore, Le — Comic opera in one act, music by Lecocq, words by G. M. Layton, first produced in 1869, and at the Park Theater, London, in 1875. An Oriental potentate, his mother-in-law, and an elixir of life lead to many amusing incidents.

Rantzan, I — Italian opera, music by Mascagni, words by Menasco and Tozzett, produced in Florence, 1892. The libretto is an adaptation from a novel by Erckmann-Chatrain. It is a village Romeo and Juliet story.

Raoul Barbe-Bleue (Bluebeard) — French opera, music by Grétry, words by Sedaine, produced in Paris, 1789. The subject is the well-known children's story.

Rapimento di Cefalo, Il — A musical drama in five acts with a prologue, music by G. Caccini, text by G. Chiabrera, produced at Florence in

1597. It was written for the marriage of Henry IV. of France with Marie di Medici, and is one of the oldest musical dramas in recitative style.

Rappressaglia, La (The Booty) — Italian comic opera in two acts, music by Stunz, words by Romani, produced in Milan, 1819.

Ratbold — Serious opera in one act. Music by Reinhold Becker, text, a ballad, by Felix Dahn. First appeared at Mains, 1896. Time, about 1200; place, Friesland, Ratbold, a sea rover, unfortunately and unsuccessfully loves the wife of his brother.

Rattenfänger von Hameln, Der (The Piper of Hamelin) — Romantic grand opera in five acts, music by Victor Nessler, words by Hofmann, from Julius Wolff's legend by the same name. First produced in Leipzig, March 19, 1879. An English version by Henry Hersee was first produced at the Queen's Theatre, Manchester, November 16, 1882.

Räuberbraut, Die (The Robber's Bride) — A romantic operetta in three acts by Ferdinand Ries with text by C. W. Häser. Produced at Frankfurt A/M in 1828.

Ravnen (The Raven) — A Danish opera in three acts, music by Johann P. E. Hartmann, text by H. C. Anderson. Produced at Copenhagen in 1832. This popular little fairy opera is based upon a tale by Gozzi.

Raymond (The Queen's Secret) — Lyric drama in three acts, music by Ambroise Thomas, text by Rosier and de Leuven, first produced at Paris in 1851. Text is based on the legend of the iron mask.

Rebe, Die (The Vine) — A ballet in three acts with five tableaux, music by Rubinstein, text by P. Joglioni, Hansen and Grandmongin. Composed in 1883. A love story in which the bridegroom is enticed by the Queen of the Vines. Vines of different nations are personified and perform characteristic dances.

Red Mill, The — Musical comedy in two acts, music by Victor Herbert, words by Henry Blossom, produced in New York, 1906.

Regina; or, The Marauders — Romantic opera in three acts, music by Lortzing, words by Adolf L'Arronge, first performed in Berlin, 1899, forty-eight years after the death of the composer.

Régine; or, Two Nights.—French comic opera, music by A. Adam, text by Scribe, produced at Paris in 1839. Text is a flimsy story of a young noblewoman who marries an ordinary soldier, but is separated from him immediately. The music is much better than the text.

Reine de Chypre, La (The Queen of Cyprus) — Opera in five acts, music by Halévy, words by Saint Georges, first produced in Paris, 1841, and revived there in 1878. The Queen is Catarina Cornarv, a Venetian, who lived in the Fifteenth Century and married the King of Cyprus.

Reine de Saba, La (The Queen of Sheba) — French grand opera in four acts, music by Gounod, words by Carré and Barbier, produced in Paris, February 28, 1862. The opera was not a success, and is no longer sung, but certain numbers in it have survived, notably "Plus Grand Dans Son Obscurite." Goldmark's opera by the same name is much the finer of the two.

Reine Fiametta, La (The Queen of Flame) — A French opera in four acts, music by Xavier Leroux, text by the poet, Catulle Mendes; produced in German at Prague in 1907 as "Königin Fiametta." The translation is by O. Smrŏka, and Joseph Vymĕtal. Orlande, Queen of Bologne in the Sixteenth Century, a woman fond of love adventures, owns some land which Cardinal Sforza is eager to hold. So he delegates a young monk to kill the Queen. The monk finds that the Queen is the woman whom he has been loving in secret and refuses to obey the commands. This is the basis for the libretto. Prague welcomed Xavier's opera very cordially.

Rendezvous Burgeois, Le (The Burgeois Meeting Place) — French comic opera in one act, music by Isouard, words by Hofmann, produced in Paris, 1807.

Reole, La — Comic opera in three acts. Music by Gustav Schmidt, libretto by Charlotte Birch Pfeiffer, produced at Breslau in 1863.

Re Pastore, Il (The Shepherd King) — Italian opera in two acts, music by Mozart, words by Métastase, produced in Salzburg, 1775. Abdolonimus, a shepherd in Sidon, was made a King by Alexander the Great.

Re Pastore, Il (The Shepherd King) — Italian opera. Music by Guiseppe Sarti, text by Métastase. Produced at Venice in 1753. Text is based on Alexander the Great's visit to Sidon where he raised the Shepherd Abdolonino to the vice Kingship. This opera was very successful at its time, but is no longer played.

Re Teodoro in Venezia, Il (King Theodoric in Venice) — Italian opera, music by Paesiello, words by Casti, produced in Venice, 1784. Theodoric was King of the Eastern Goths and conquered Italy in the Sixth Century, A. D.

Revenant, Le (The Ghost) — A fantastic opera in two acts. Music by J. M. Gonies, text by Calvinmont, produced at Paris in 1833. The music is good.

Riccardo (Richard) — Italian opera, music by Handel, produced in London in 1727.

Ricciardo e Zoraide — Italian opera in two acts, music by Rossini, words by Berio, produced at Naples in 1818, and at Paris, 1824.

Richard Cœur de Lion (Richard Lionheart) — French song play in three acts, music by Sedaine, produced in Paris, 1784. The theme of the opera is Richard's crusade in 1190.

Richard in Palestine — French opera in three acts, music by Adolphe Adam, words by Paul Foucher, produced in Paris, 1844. The plot deals with incidents in the Crusades.

Ricimero — Italian opera, music by Jomelli, produced at Rome, 1740.

Rien de Trop; ou, Les Deux Faravents — French comic opera in one act, music by Boieldieu, words by J. Pain, produced at St. Petersburg, 1810, and at Paris, 1811.

Rinaldo — Italian opera, music by Händel, produced in London, 1710.

Rip Van Winkle — Opera by G. F. Bristow, first produced at New York in 1855. It is interesting as being one of the first operas by an American composer based upon a native theme.

Rip Van Winkle — Comic opera in three acts, music by Robert Planquette, words by Henri Meilbrac and Philippe Gille and H. B. Farnie, first produced at the Comedy Theatre, London, October 14, 1882. The plot is similar to that in Washington Irving's story, with some few changes, and the opera scored a great success.

Ritorno d'Astrea, Il (The Return of Astrea) — Dramatic cantata, music by J. Weigl, text by Monti, produced at Milan in 1816. Astrea was the last Greek goddess to forsake the earth at the end of the Golden Age.

Rivali di se Stressi, I—(The Rivals) — Italian opera, music by Balfe, first produced at Palermo, 1831. This was Balfe's first complete opera.

Robert Bruce — Opera in three acts, music by Rossini, words by Alphonse Royer and Gustave Vaëz, produced in Paris, 1846. The libretto is founded upon incidents related in Walter Scott's "History of Scotland." The music was adapted by Niedermeyer, with Rossini's permission, from portions of "Donna del Lago," "Zelmira" and "Armida." It was not a success.

Robert Devereux (The Earl of Essex) — Italian opera in three acts, music by Donizetti, text by Camarano, first produced at Naples in 1836. Text is the familiar story of Queen Elizabeth's love for the Earl of Essex. The latter cannot return her love, but loves the Duchess of Nottingham, and Elizabeth has him beheaded.

Robin des Bois (Robin of the Woods) — Opera in three acts, words by Castil-Blaze and Sauvage, music by Weber, produced in Paris, 1824. When Weber's "Der Freischütz" was presented in Paris, it failed to please. Castil-Blaze remodeled it, and the result, "Robin des Bois," became very popular.

Robin Hood — A German romantic opera in three acts. Music by Albert Hermann Dietrich, produced with great success at Frankfort, Germany, in 1879.

Robinson Crusoe — English operetta by Thomas Linley, produced at London in 1781. The opera is based upon Defoe's world famous story.

Rob Roy — English romantic comic opera in three acts, music by Reginald de Koven, words by Harry B. Smith, produced in New York, 1894. The scene is Scotland in the time of George II. The story is woven about the person of the young Pretender, Charles Edward Stuart. Rob Roy MacGregor is the famous Highland chief.

Rodrigo — Italian opera, music by Händel, produced in Florence, 1708.

Rodrigo is the national hero of Spain, commonly known as the Cid.

Roger de Flor — Opera, music by Ruperto Chapi, Spanish words by Mariano Capdepon. Italian translation by Palermi, first produced in Madrid, 1878.

Roger de Sicile; ou, Le Roi Troubadour (Roger of Sicily; or, The Troubador King) — Opera in three acts, music by Berton, words by Guy, produced in Paris, 1817.

Rognéda — Russian opera in five acts, music and words by Leroy, produced in St. Petersburg, 1865. The story is taken from the legendary history of Russia. The opera has been enormously popular and is still sung in Russia.

Roi de Lahore, Le (The King of Lahore) — French grand opera in four acts and six tableaux, music by Massenet, words by Gallet, produced in Paris, 1877. Lahore is a province of India Abni, the King, loves a priestess, Sita. He is killed in war, but is allowed by the gods to return to earth as a beggar, to remain as long as Sita lives.

Roi des Halles, Le — French comic opera in three acts. Music by Adam, text by de Leuven and Brunswick, produced at Paris in 1853.

Roi d'Yvetot, Le (The King of Yvetot) — French comic opera in three acts. Music by A. Adam, text by de Levoen and Brunswick, produced at Paris in 1842. Story is freely taken from the poem by Biranger. This is one of Adam's best operas and its overture is especially fine.

Roi et le Fermier, Le (The King and The Farmer) — French comic opera in three acts, music by Monsigny, words by Sedaine, produced in Paris, November 22, 1762.

Roi l' à dit, Le (The King Has Said It) — French comic opera in three acts. Music by Leon Delibes, text by Edmond Gondinet, first produced at Paris, 1873. Comedy is full of ludicrous situations brought about by the Marquis de Moncontour's trying to please his King, Louis XIV.

Roi Malgré Lui, Le (A King in Spite of Himself) — French comic opera in three acts, music by Chabrier, words by Najac and Burani, produced in Paris, May 18, 1887. The libretto is based upon a comedy by Ancelot.

Roland (Orlando in Italian) — This Frankish hero, nephew of Charlemagne, has been made the subject of countless French, German and Italian operas. Tasso's furious lover, "Orlando," is supposed to be the same hero. Luli's "Roland," text by Quinault (Paris, 1685), Paccinni's "Roland," text by Marmontel (Paris, 1778), are the best. The subject was also popular through the Nineteenth Century.

Roland à Roucevaux — French opera in four acts, words and music by Mermet, produced in Paris, 1864. The libretto is founded upon incidents taken from Thérould's "La Chanson de Roland," and relates some events in the life of the famous Knight Roland.

Roland von Berlin, Der (Roland of Berlin) — Opera in four acts. Music and libretto by Leoncavallo. First produced at the Imperial Opera House in Berlin, 1904. Text is based upon Willibald Alexis' story by the same title. This opera was composed by Leoncavallo at the request of Emperor William II. and was produced in the presence of the royal family under the direction of the composer. It was given a magnificent setting.

Romance, La — French comic opera in one act. Music by H. M. Berton, text by Lesur and Loraux, produced at Paris in 1804.

Romance de la Rose, La — A French operetta in one act. Music by Offenbach, text by Prevel and Jréfeu, produced at Paris in 1869. A young widow becomes infatuated with the beautiful Irish folk song, "The Last Rose of Summer," but before the operetta is ended the song becomes repugnant to her.

Roman d'Elvire, Le (Romance of Elvira) — Comic opera in three acts. Music by Ambroise Thomas, text by Alexandre Dumas and de Leuven, first produced at Paris, 1860.

Romea di Montfort (Romea of Montfort) — Italian opera in three acts, music by Pedrotti, words by Rossi, produced in Verona in 1845.

Roosje Sonder Doornen, De (The Rose Without Thorns) — A Flemish vaudeville with music by H. von Perne, produced at Ghent in 1842.

Rosamonde — English opera, music by Clayton, words by Addison, produced in London, 1707. The music was poor, and in 1733 Arne composed new music which was better received.

Rosaura, La — Italian opera, music by Scarlatti, words by Lucini, produced in Naples, 1690. La Rosaura has some music which has survived to the present day.

Rose de Florence, La — Opera in two acts, music by Biletta, words by St. Georges, produced in Paris, 1856.

Rose de Peronne, La — French opera in three acts. Music by Adam, text by de Leuven and D'Ennery, produced at Paris in 1840.

Rose et Colas — French operetta in one act. Music by Pierre A. Monsigny, text by Sedaine, produced at Paris in 1764. This is one of Monsigny's best compositions; it was extremely popular and with Rousseau's "Devin du Village" it shares the distinction of being a pioneer French operetta.

Rosenhütchen, Das (The Rose Hat) — German comic fairy opera in three acts, music by Karl Blum, words by Hoffmann, produced in Vienna, 1815.

Rosenthalerin, Die — German opera in three acts. Music by Anton Rückauf, text by Lemmermayer, first produced at Dresden in 1897. Scene is laid in Nuremberg at the time of Albrecht Durer, whose adopted daughter, because of her illegitimate birth, cannot marry the nobleman who is in love with her. But Emperor Maximilian helps the lovers out. Rückauf's composition reminds one of Lortzing and Brüll, and while its success has been brilliant it is a question if the opera will live long.

Rose of Castile, The — A comic opera in three acts. Words by Harris and Falconer, and music by Balfe. It was first performed in London at the Lyceum Theatre in 1857. The story is taken from "Muletier de Toledo," by Adolph Adams. The story is very complicated and sometimes it is tedious to follow, but the music is brilliant and some of the songs equal the best ever written by an English composer. The scene of the opera is laid in Spain. Queen Elvira, the Rose of Castile, has just ascended the throne when the King of Castile demands her hand for his brother Don Sebastian. Elvira learns that Don Sebastian is about to enter her domains disguised as a muleteer, in order to satisfy his curiosity about her. She in turn decides to disguise as a peasant girl and goes out to intercept him. She and her maid are rudely treated by the innkeeper at a neighboring village and are protected by Manuel, the muleteer, who suddenly appears. She believes she recognizes Don Sebastian in the muleteer and returns to her castle, sure that he will follow. Soon word is brought of Don Sebastian's marriage and the Queen is enraged since she has lost her heart to the muleteer. But the muleteer is not Don Sebastian but the King of Castile himself and so all ends happily.

Rose of Persia, The; or, The Story-Teller and the Slave — Comic opera, music by Sir Arthur Sullivan, words by Captain Basil Hood, first produced in London, 1899. The plot is a blending of two stories from "Arabian Nights," and relates the troubles of Hassan, a wealthy philanthropist, who prefers the society of beggars to the beggars of society.

Rose vom Liebesgarten, Die (The Rose from the Garden of Love) — Opera in two acts, a prologue and a conclusion, music by Hans Pfitzner, words by James Bruno, first produced at Elberfeld, 1901.

Rosière, La — Comic opera in three acts, music by E. Jakobonski, words by H. Monkhouse, first produced at the Shaftesbury Theatre, London, January 14, 1893.

Rosière Republicane, La; ou, La Fête de la Raison (The Republican Rosière; or, The Feast of Reason) — French opera in one act, music by Grétry, words by Sylvain Marichal, produced in Paris, 1793.

Rosières, Les — Comic opera in three acts, music by Hérold, words by Theaulon, produced in Paris, 1817. This is Hérold's first opera and it scored a great success. The Rosières are young women who have received a prize for virtuous conduct.

Rosina — English comic opera in two acts, music by William Shield, words by Mrs. Brooke, produced in London, 1783. Later it was presented in America.

Rosine; ou, L'Epouse Abandonée (Rosine; or, The Abandoned Wife) — Opera in three acts, music by Gossec, words by Gersin, produced in Paris, 1786.

Röslein im Hag (The Little Hedge Rose) — German opera, music by Cyrill Kistner, produced at Elberfeld in 1903. The opera did not attract much attention.

Rossignol, Le (The Lark) — French opera in one act, music by Lebrun, words by Etienne, produced in Paris, 1816.

Rothkäppchen, Das, sometimes "Die Rothkappe" (Red Ridinghood) — German operetta in two acts by Dittersdorf, words by Stephanie, produced in Vienna, 1788.

Round Tower, The — English opera, music by William Reeve, produced in London, 1797. This is the best of Reeve's operas.

Royal Middy, The (Der Seekadett) — Three-act opera by Genée. Libretto by Zell. English adaptation by Frederick Williams and Edward Mollenhauer. Place, Portugal. Time, 1702. First produced at Vienna in 1876.

Rubezahl and the Bagpiper of Meisse — Opera in four acts, music by Hans Sommer, words by Eberhard König, first produced at Brunswick, 1904. Rubezahl, the beneficent spirit of the mountains, assumes the guise of a piper and assists Widv, a young painter, to free his town from the tyrannical rule of its bailiff and also unites him to his sweetheart.

Rubin, Der (The Ruby) — An opera in two acts by Eugen d'Albert, first produced at Carlsruhe in 1893. The libretto is adapted from the tale by Hebbel.

Ruddygore, or The Witch's Curse — English comic opera, music by Sir Arthur Sullivan, words by Gilbert, produced in London, January 22, 1887. The scene is Cornwall, England, in the Nineteenth Century and the opera is a satire upon the old English melodrama.

Ruggiero — Italian opera, music by Hasse, produced in Venice, 1771, for the marriage festivities of the Archduke Ferdinand. It was the last dramatic work of the composer.

Runenzauber (The Magic of The Runes) — Danish opera in one act by Emil Hartmann, Jr., produced at Hamburg in 1896 with great success. Text is based on a Danish story by H. Hertz.

Russlan and Ludmilla — Russian grand opera in five acts. Music by Glinka, text after a poem by the great poet, Puschkin, produced at St. Petersburg in 1842. The scene of the poem is laid in Kieff, in the time of Vladimir, who is the bright sun in Russian legends. This opera is the second one of Glinka's two great national operas, and ever since its first appearance it has been a great favorite in its own country. Both music and text have a strong local coloring, rugged, strange and fascinating. The music is almost barbarous at times, and the melodies have a haunting power. This opera portrays Glinka's personality and strongly foreshadows the revolutionary effect it produced on his countrymen, and is regarded as Glinka's masterpiece.

Russulka (The Water Nymph) — Russian grand opera. Music by Alex. Dargomyzski, text based on a poem by Puschkin, produced at St. Petersburg in 1856. In this Undine legend, Natacha, in despair because her lover has deserted her, casts herself into the Dnieper, where she is welcomed by the water nymphs and becomes their queen. The music is dramatically realistic, and is interspersed with melodious recitative. "Russulka" has been phenominally successful. It is even now the most popular opera on the Russian stage, but its character is so local that it finds few friends outside of Russia.

Ruth — An English opera by Felice Giardini, produced at London in 1772. The text is based on the Biblical story of Ruth.

Ruy Blas — Italian opera in four acts, music by Marchetti, words by d'Ormeville, produced in Milan, 1869. The libretto is adapted from Victor Hugo's work by the same name.

Ryno — A Swedish opera, music by King Oscar of Sweden, text by Bernhardt von Beskow, produced at Stockholm in 1834. The hero is Ryno, the wandering knight.

S

Sabinus — French opera, music by Gossec, words by Chabanon de Mangris, produced in Paris, 1774. Julius Sabinus was a Gaul, who headed an insurrection against the Romans, 69 A. D. He was finally captured and executed, after having lived nine years in concealment.

Sabots et le Cerisier, Les (The Sabots and The Cherry Tree) — French operetta in one act. Music by F. J. Gossec, text by Sedaine and Cazotte, produced at Paris in 1803.

Sacerdotessa d'Irminsul, La (The Priestess of Irminsul) — Italian opera by Giovanni Pacini, produced in Trieste, 1817. The story is of the Prophetess Norma, a Druid priestess.

Sacountala — French ballet, music by Ernest Reyer (real name Rey), words by Theophile Gautier, produced in Paris, 1858. The libretto is founded upon a play by Kalidasa, an East Indian poet, who lived at the beginning of the Christian era.

Sacrifizio d'Abramo (The Sacrifice of Abraham) — Italian opera, music by Amarosa, produced in Naples, 1786.

Sacrifizio d'Epito, Il — Italian opera in two acts, music by Carafa, libretto by Dalmiro Tindario, produced at Venice in 1819. King Epito becomes blind as a punishment for having entered the temple of Poseidon.

Sadko — Russian opera, music by Rimsky-Korsakov, produced in 1896.

Sakuntala — German opera in three acts; music and text by Felix Weingartner, first produced at Weimar in 1884. An Indian fairy tale by the Hindoo poet, Kalidasa, forms the basis for the libretto. Sakuntala is the daughter of an Indian patriarch. The King finds her while out hunting, they love each other at sight and wish to marry, but the old father begs for time. Sakuntala remains true to the King, but he becomes faithless; broken hearted she remains with her grief stricken father. But repentance overcomes the King, he seeks Sakuntala and her father, they forgive him, and he marries the girl. This is Weingartner's first opera and at its performance the Weimar public presented the young composer with a crown of laurel. It has been successful, though not to such an extent as his later productions.

Salambo — A French grand opera in five acts, music by Ernest Reyer, text by Du Locle, produced at Brussels in 1890. The libretto was adapted from Flaubert's Carthaginian romance by the same title. Salambo is the daughter of Hamilcar, the great Carthaginian general who lived in the Third Century B. C. She is an enigmatic character. Wrapped up in an almost frenzied idolatry of her religion, she seems insensible to the world around her. Matho, an African Hercules, general of the Barbarians, fighting against the Carthaginians, sees her and immediately idolizes her. For her sake he invades the temple, steals the sacred veil of the Goddess Tanith and offers it to Salambo as the only gift fitting his ideal of her. She is horrified at the sacrilege, calls up her servants and Matho is forced to flee, taking the veil with him. Carthage suffers, and the recovery of the veil, it is believed, is all that will save the city. At the risk of her life Salambo goes to the Barbarians' camp, and demands the veil of Matho. Just then the war cry sounds, duty calls him, and she escapes with the veil. Carthage wins; and Matho, a truly splendid figure, is put to death at Salambo's demand on her wedding day. At sight of his suffering her heart seems to be touched and she sinks back among her cushions, dead. This splendid opera has been revived many times since its first production.

Sallustia, La — Italian opera in three acts; music by Giovani Pergolesi, produced at Naples in 1731.

Salvator Rosa — Italian opera music by Antonio Gomez, words by Ghislanzoni, produced in Genoa, 1874. Salvator Rosa was a famous Italian painter, poet, and musician of the Seventeenth Century.

Sancio Pansa, Governatore dell' Isola Barataria (Sancho Panza, Governor of the Island of Barataria) — Italian comic opera, music by Caldara, words by Pariati, produced in Vienna, 1733.

Sanga — Opera by de Lara. Libretto adapted from an Italian story. Place, farm in Italy. Time, the present. First produced at Nice in March, 1906.

Santa Chiara — Romantic German opera, in three acts, music by Ernst II., Duke of Sachsen-Coburg-Gotha, words by Charlotte Birch-Pfeiffer, produced in Gotha, April 2, 1854. The scene is laid in Russia and Italy about the year 1715. The heroine of the opera is Charlotte Christine, wife of Alexis, heir to the Russian throne.

Santa Lucis, A — Opera in two acts, music by Tosca, words by Golisciani, first produced in Berlin, 1892. It is founded upon a work by Cognetti.

Saphir, Le (The Sapphire) — French comic opera in three acts, music by Felicien David, words by Carré, de Leuven and Hadot, produced in Paris, 1865. The libretto is based upon Shakespeare's "All's Well That Ends Well."

Sapphire Necklace, The — English opera, music by Sir Arthur Sullivan, text by Chorley. Libretto lacked dramatic character and caused failure of the opera.

Sapho — Five-act opera by Massenet. Libretto adapted from the novel by Alphonse Daudet by Henri Cain and Arthur Bernède. Place, Paris, Ville d'Avray and Avignon. Time, Nineteenth Century. First produced at Paris in 1897.

Sappho — French grand opera in three acts, music by Gounod, words by Angier, produced in Paris, April 16, 1851. Since then it has been twice revised, but the original form is best. The story is the well known one of Sappho and Phaon.

Saracen, The — Russian opera in four acts, music by César Cui, produced in St. Petersburg, 1889. The libretto is adapted from a novel by Dumas.

Sarah — French opera in two acts, music by Grisar, text by Mélesville, produced at Paris in 1836. The heroine is Sir Walter Scott's witch of Glencoe.

Sardanapal — Russian grand opera in three acts. Music by Alexander S. Faminzin; libretto is based upon Lord Byron's drama. Produced at St. Petersburg in 1875. Sardanapal, the hero, is the weak, sensual Assyrian King who lived in the Ninth Century before Christ.

Sarema — Opera in two acts; music and text by Franz Höfer, first produced at Regensburg in 1907. The libretto is based on Gottschall's "The Rose from the Caucasus." The opera is excellent and has scored splendid success. It is Höfer's first opera.

Satanella, or The Power of Love — English opera in three acts, music by Balfe, words by Harris and Falconer, with a ballet by Taglioni, produced in London, 1858. One of the songs, "The Power of Love," became exceedingly popular. The opera had a very long run, but is no longer given.

Satiro, Il (The Satyr) — Italian pastorale in recitative style by Emilio del Cavalieri, produced at Florence in 1590. This is one of the earliest attempts at recitative. Unfortunately no printed copy of this important work exists.

Saul, König von Israel (Saul, King of Israel) — German Biblical opera, music by Seyfried, produced in Vienna, 1810. The libretto is adapted from the French of Caigviez.

Savonarola — English opera, music by Charles Villiers Stanford, produced in Hamburg, April 18, 1884. The most interesting part of the opera is the prologue, which tells of Savonarola's love for Clarice, and of his renouncement of the world because of her marriage.

Sawitri — Opera in three acts. Music by Hermann Zumpe, text by Count Ferdinand Sporck. First produced at Schwerin, 1907. Sawitri is the idolized daughter of a King of India. This opera was left incomplete at the death of the composer, and was finished by G. von Rossler in Frankfurt A/M. The music is excellent, and places Zumpe among the best of modern composers.

Scaltra Governatrice, La (The Crafty Governess) — Italian burlesque opera in three acts, music by Joachim Cocchi, produced with great success at Venice in 1753.

Scanderbeg — French grand opera in five acts and a prologue, music by Rebel and Francœur, words by Lamotte, produced in Paris, 1735. The text of the prologue was written by Lasèrre.

Scarlet Letter, The — Opera, music by Walter Damrosch, words by

George Parsons Lathrop, first produced in Boston, 1896. The story is founded upon Hawthorne's novel of the same name.

Schach dem König (Check to the King) — Comic opera in three acts. Music by Ignaz Brüll, text by Viktor Leon, first produced in 1892. Text is based on Schauffert's popular comedy by the same title. Its scene is laid in London in 1612 at the time when James I. of England was won over to smoking by the strategy of his court.

Schatzgräer, Der (The Treasure Seeker) — German vaudeville opera by Anton Dimmler, produced at Munich in 1795.

Schauspieldirektor, Der (The Theatre Director) — German comic opera in one act, music by Mendelssohn, words by Stephanie, produced in Schönbrunn near Vienna, 1786. It was written upon the request of the Austrian Emperor.

Schiava, La (The Female Slave) — Italian opera, music by Piccinni, produced at Naples in 1757.

Schiava Fortunata, La (The Fortunate Captive) — Italian opera, music by Cesti, words by Sbarra, produced in Vienna, 1667. It was later revised by Liani and sung in Venice, Bologna and Hamburg.

Schiavi per Amore (Slaves Through Love) — Opera, music by Paesiello, produced in Paris in 1793.

Schiavo, La (The Captive) — Italian opera, music by Antonio Gomez, produced in Rio de Janeiro, 1889.

Schiavo di Sua Moglie, Il (The Slave of His Wife) — Italian opera, music by Provensale, produced in Naples, 1671. Provensale is supposed to be identical with the composer, Francesco della Torre.

Schlafende Prinzess, Die (The Sleeping Princess) — A German comic opera; music by A. von Othegraven, text by Georg Kiesau, first produced at Cologne in 1907. A sea shell into which the Sirens have sung puts the princess to sleep. She can hear everything that goes on about her, can even converse, but the sleep is so sweet that the combined efforts of her lover, her father, and the magician fail to arouse her. Finally her maid piques her through jealousy and the princess wakes up. "This is one of the finest productions we have had in years," says a German critic.

Schneewittchen (Snow White) — Russian opera in three acts. Music by Rimsky-Korsakov, text by Ostrowsky, produced at St. Petersburg in 1882. "Snow White," the children's fairy tale, is the basis for the libretto. Russian title, "Snegorutschka."

Schneider Fips (Tailor Fips) — A song play in one act. Music by Victor Hallander, text by H. von Wentzel, first produced at Weimar in 1909. Text is adopted from a comedy by Kotzebue. The operetta was cordially received.

Schöne Galatea, Die (Lovely Galatea) —Operetta in one act, music by Franz von Suppé, text by Kohl von Kohlenegg, whose pseudonym is Poly Henrion. Produced at Vienna in 1865. In 1884 it was translated into English by Willard G. Day. This mythological comic opera has for its theme the unfortunate love affair between Pygmalion and the beautiful statue Galatea.

Schönen von Forgaras, Die (The Beauties of Fogaras) — Comic opera in three acts. Music by Alfred Grünfeld, text by Viktor Leon, first produced at Dresden in 1907. The story is laid in the little village of Fogaras, Hungary, about the middle of the Fifteenth Century. The women who have lost their husbands in the war go to the King and beg him to supply them with husbands. He consents willingly, sends out for men, and, changing places with his cook, receives the deputation of women. The opera is full of amusements, and the music so simple that it has charmed the public.

Schön Rohtraut — German opera, music by Edmund Kretschmer, produced in Dresden, 1887.

Schönste Mädchen in Städtchen, Das (The Prettiest Girl in Town) — German comic opera in two acts, music by Conradi, words by Winterfeld, produced in Berlin, 1868.

Schwarze Kaschka, Die (Black Kaschka) — Opera in four acts. Music by Georg Jarno, text by Viktor Bluthgen, first produced at Breslau, 1895. The unhappy love story of Kaschka, a peasant girl.

Schweizerfamilie, Die (The Swiss Family) — Operetta by Josef Weigl, text by Castelli, produced at Vienna in 1809. This story is similar to that of "Emeline," a French comic opera by Hérold which appeared in Paris twenty years later. This opera was a great favorite for a long time.

Scipio — Italian opera by Handel, produced at London in 1726. Scipio was the Roman general who defeated Hannibal.

Scipione nelle Cartagena (Scipio in Carthage) — Italian opera, music by Sacchini, words by Grunti, produced in Munich, 1770. The hero of the opera is Scipio Africanus, the great general of the Punic wars.

Scipione nelle Spagne (Scipio in Spain) — Italian opera, music by Galuppi, words by Zeno, produced in Venice, 1746. Scipio, called Africanus, was the famous Roman general.

Scuffiara, La (The Bonnetmaker) — Italian comic opera in three acts, music by Paesiello, produced in Milan, 1790; since then twice revived.

Secret, Le (The Secret) — French comic opera in one act. Music by Solie (Soulier) libretto by Hoffmann, produced at Paris in 1796. A comedy in which a secret panel, a hidden guest, and a suspicious wife furnish a great deal of amusement. The opera was very successful.

Seekadet, Der (The Midshipman) — Comic opera in one act by Hippolyte Chelard, with text by Sondershaufen. Produced at Weimar in 1844.

Seelewig — German opera, music by Sigmund Staden, words by Harsdorffer, printed in Nuremberg in 1644. There is no record of its ever having been produced. It is the first German opera, the score and text of which have been preserved. Dafne was performed in 1627, but the music and words of this opera are lost.

Seher von Khorassan, Der (The Seer of Khorassan) — German romantic opera in three acts, music by Sobolewsky, produced in Königsberg, 1850. The libretto is adapted from "Lalla Rookh," by Thomas Moore.

Seigneur Bienfaisant, Le (The Benevolent Seigneur) — French opera in three acts, music by E. F. Floquet, words by de Chabannes, produced in Paris, 1780. Two additional acts were added in 1781 and 1782.

Sejour Militaire, Le (The Military Abode) — French comic opera in one act, music by Auber, words by Bonilly and Dupaty, produced in Paris, 1813.

Selima and Azor — English song play, music by Thomas Sinley, produced in London, 1776. It is an adaptation of Grétry's "Lemire et Azor," but with some new and original numbers by Linley.

Selvaggia, La (The Savage) — Italian opera, music by Francesco Schira, words by d'Ormeville, produced in Naples during the Carnival of 1875. It is usually regarded as Schira's best work.

Semiramis — French tragic opera in three acts, music by C. S. Catel, text by Desriaux, produced at Paris in 1802. The libretto is adapted from Voltaire. Semiramis was a legendary Queen of Assyria, supposed to have founded Babylon. According to legend, all who enjoyed her love she had killed. When her own son was about to murder her, she escaped in the form of a dove.

Sen Lesa (A Forest Dream) — A Bohemian opera, music and libretto by Ladislav Prokop, text arranged by Karl Masek, first produced at Prague in 1907. The music is good, but the libretto is weak. The text presents a struggle between realism and idealism. The latter is represented by nature, poetry, the satyr, and a sickly music teacher, who scorns humanity. Mankind with its greed for gold represents realism.

Séraphina, La — French comic opera in one act, music by Flotow, text by Soulié, produced at Paris in 1836.

Sergeant Brue — English musical comedy in three acts, music by Elizabeth Lehmann, words by Owen Hall, produced in London, 1904. Madame Lehmann was the first woman to be commissioned to write an opera, and Sergeant Brue was the result.

Serse (Xerxes) — Italian opera by Händel, produced at London in 1738. Hero is the historic warrior King of Persia who lived in the Fifth Century B. C.

Serva Innamorata, La (The Serving Maid in Love) — Italian comic opera, music by Guylielmi, produced in Naples, 1778.

Serva Padrona, La (The Serving Maid a Mistress) — Italian comic opera in two acts, music by Pergolesi, words by Nelli, produced in Naples, 1731. It was composed as an Intermezzo to "Il Prigionier Superba."

Riemann cites it as the first example of real opera buffa. Its production in Paris, 1750, is said to have founded opéra comique there. There are but three parts. Scapin, a valet, disguised as a sea captain, makes love to the little serving maid Serpina, and her master, Pandolfo, is made so jealous thereby that he proposes to her and marries her himself.

Se Sa Minga — Comic opera or operetta, music by Antonio Gomez, produced in Milan, 1867. It was through this opera that Gomez first became known in Europe. It had a phenomenal success.

Sesostrate — Italian opera by Johann A. Hasse, first produced at Naples, 1726. The subject is probably Sesostris, the semi-legendary King of Egypt, supposed by some to be Rameses II.

Sherif, Le (The Sheriff) — French comic opera in three acts, music by Halévy, words by Scribe, produced in Paris, 1839.

She Stoops to Conquer — English comic opera in three acts, music by Sir George Alexander Macfarren, words by Fitzball, produced in London, 1864. The libretto is adapted from Goldsmith's play by the same name.

Sho Gun, The — Musical comedy, music by Gustav Luders, words by George Ade, performed in New York, 1904. The plot is woven around an energetic Yankee who goes to Korea and finally becomes the Sho Gun.

Shop Girl, The — A musical farce in two acts, music by Ivan Caryll, words by H. J. W. Dam, additional numbers by Adrian Ross and Lionel Monckton, first produced at the Gaiety Theatre in London, November 24, 1894.

Siberia — Italian opera in three acts; music by Giordano, libretto by Illica, first produced at Milan in 1904, and in New York in 1908. The text bears a close resemblance to Tolstoi's "Resurrection," but falls far below it. A young Russian lieutenant stabs his superior officer, Prince Alexis, and is sentenced to the mines of Siberia. The cause of the quarrel is a girl, Stephana, who has been living in luxury as the mistress of the Prince. She gives up everything and follows the lieutenant to Siberia to share his fate. Here she meets men whom she had known earlier in her life, they jeer her and life becomes unbearable to Stephana and the lieutenant. They decide to flee but are discovered, and the girl is shot. She thus becomes a martyr to her love and dies "redeemed." Giordano makes excellent use of the Russian folk-music; the effect is very dramatic. The opera scarcely satisfies an artistic temperament. It has had a strong hold on the Italian public and has been repeated many times in New York.

Sibirskije Ochotnikie (The Siberian Hunters) — Russian opera in one act, music by Rubinstein, produced in St. Petersburg, 1852.

Sicilian Bride, The — English opera, music by Balfe, words by St. Georges and Bunn, first produced in London, 1852.

Sicilien, Le (The Sicilian) — French comic opera in one act, music by Jean Levasseur, produced in Versailles, 1780. The libretto is founded upon one of Molière's comedies.

Siège de Corinthe, Le (The Siege of Corinth) — Originally an Italian opera called "Maometto II." (Mohammed II.) by Rossini, and appeared at Naples in 1820 with success. In 1826 it was remodeled and translated into French and produced at Paris. The latter is the favorite title.

Sieben Raben, Die (The Seven Ravens) — German opera in three acts, music by Rheinberger, words by Franz Bohn, produced in Munich, 1869. The story is adapted from Schwind's fables.

Siège de Leyde, Le (The Siege of Leyden) — French grand opera in four acts. Music by C. L. A. Vogel, text by H. Lucas, produced at The Hague in 1847.

Siège de Lille, Le (The Siege of Lille) — French comic opera in one act, music by Rudolphe Kreutzer, words by Bertin d'Antilly, produced in Paris, 1792.

Siege of Belgrade, The — An English opera, music by Storace, text by James Cobb. Produced at London in 1691. Both text and music are after the Italian opera "La Cosa Rara," by Martini. The English version scored a great success.

Siege of Rochelle, The — English opera in three acts. Music by M. W. Balfe, text by Fitzball. Produced in London, 1835; played continuously for three months and immediately made Balfe famous.

Siface, Re di Numidia (Syphax, King of Numidia) — Italian opera in three acts, music by Francesco Feo, words by Métastase, produced in Naples, 1723.

Signa — English opera, music by F. H. Cowen, produced in Milan, 1893. The libretto is adapted from a novel by Ouida.

Silvana — Romantic opera in four acts, music by Weber, text by F. K. Hiemer. This opera was first produced at Frankfurt A/M in 1810 under the title "Des Waldmädchen." (The Forest Maiden). In its new form Weber left it unfinished, and it has recently been completed by Ernest Pasque, librettist, and Ferdinand Langer, composer. The latter introduced into the ballet of the second act some of Weber's favorite compositions. Story is based on an old German legend.

Silvano — Italian opera, music by Mascagni, produced in Milan, 1895. The opera has never been sung outside of Italy.

Silvie — French ballet opera in three acts and a prologue, music by Pierre Montan Berton, with Claude Trial, words by Lanjon, produced in Paris, 1766.

Simon Boecanegro — Italian opera in three acts and a prologue, music by Verdi, words by Piave, produced in Venice, 1856. The story is a Venetian one.

Singspiel auf dem Dache, Das (The Operetta on the Roof) — An operetta by Anton Fischer with text by Treitschke, produced at Vienna in 1806.

Siroe (Queen of Persia) — Italian opera. Music by Vinci, text by Métastase, first produced at Venice, 1726. Subject historical, and a great favorite with Italian composers for nearly a century.

Slave, The — English Opera, music by Henry Rowley Bishop, produced in London, 1816.

Sleepy Hollow — English opera in three acts, music by Max Maretzek, words by Gayler, produced in New York, 1879.

Snegorotchka (The Snow Maiden) — Russian opera in three acts, by Rimsky-Korsakov, words by Ostrowsky, produced in St. Petersburg, March, 1882. The story is a poetical legend of the Spring. It is the one opera of Rimsky-Korsakov's calculated to appeal to any audience other than a Russian one.

Sœur Officieuse, La (The Officious Sister) — French comic opera in one act, music by Bianchi, words by Redon and Dufresnoy, produced in Paris, 1806.

Sofonisba — Italian opera, music by Leonardo Leo, words by Silvani, produced in Naples, 1719. The libretto is founded upon Corneille's tragedy. Sofonisba was the daughter of King Hasdrubal of Numidia; she drank poison rather than appear in Rome in the triumphal procession of Scipio Africanus.

Soixante-Six, Le (Sixty-Six) — French comic opera in one act, music by Offenbach, words by Laurencin, produced in Paris, 1856.

Solange — Comic opera, music by M. G. Salvayre, words by M. Aderer, presented at the Opéra Comique, Paris, in the spring of 1909. This is a love story with all the picturesque settings of the Louis XVI. period.

Soldat Magicien, Le (The Magic Soldier) — French comic opera in one act. Music by F. A. D. Philidor, text by Anseaume, produced at Paris in 1760. Text is furnished by Dancourt's "Good Soldier" (Bon Soldat).

Soliman der Zweite (Soliman II.) — Danish opera by Guiseppe Sarti, produced at Copenhagen in 1770. Soliman II., also called Soliman the Great, was Sultan of Turkey from 1520 to 1566, and a famous warrior.

Solimanno (Soliman) — Italian opera, music by Hasse, words by Migliavacca, produced in Dresden, 1753. Soliman was Sultan of Turkey in the middle of the Sixteenth Century. He made war against Hungary and beseiged Vienna.

Solitaire, Le (The Recluse) — French comic opera in three acts, music by Carafa, text by Planard. Produced at Paris in 1822. This was the most successful of Carafa's operas and it enjoyed a long life.

Songe d'une Nuit d'Été, Le (Midsummernight's Dream) — French comic opera in three acts, music by Ambroise Thomas, words by Rosier and de Leuven, produced in Paris in 1850. It is founded upon Shakespeare's comedy.

Son-in-law, The—English comic opera, music by Samuel Arnold, produced in London in 1779.

Sophie et Moncars (Sophie and Moncars)—French comic opera in three acts. Music by Pierre Gaveaux, text by Guy, produced at Paris in 1797. It is the story of a Portuguese intrigue.

Sophocle—French grand opera in three acts, music by Vincent Fiocchi, words by Morel, produced in Paris, 1811.

Sorcier, Le (The Sorcerer)—French operetta in two acts, music by Philidor, words by Poinsinet, produced in Paris, January 2, 1764. The composer was called before the curtain after the first performance of the opera, which is said to be the first instance of this sort in Paris.

Sorrentine, La—Operetta in three acts, music by Vasseur, words by Moinaux and Noriac, first produced in Paris, 1877.

Sosarme—Italian opera by Handel, produced at London in 1732.

Souvenirs de Lafleur, Les (The Recollections of Lafleur)—A French comic opera in one act, music by Halévy, text by Carmonche and Courcy, produced at Paris in 1833. Text is based on an old comedy entitled "The Old Age of Frontin," (La Viellesse de Frontin). Halévy's music for this successful opera is charming.

Spanish Barber, The; or, A Futile Precaution—An English opera which appeared in New York, Philadelphia, Baltimore and Charleston about 1794. It was undoubtedly an adaptation of Paisiello's "Barbiere di Siviglia."

Spanish Maid, The—English opera, music by Thomas Linley, produced in London, 1783.

Spartaso (Spartacus)—Italian opera, music by Porsile, words by Pasquini, the composer, produced in Vienna, 1726. Spartacus was the leader of the great uprising of the slaves in Italy in the First Century, B. C., which was finally put down by Crassus.

Specter's Bride, The—Cantata, music by Antonin Dvořák, words by Erben, produced in Birmingham, England, in 1885. The story is a Bohemian version of the famous Lenore legend.

Spectre Knight, The—Operetta, music by Alfred Cellier, words by Albery, first produced in London, 1878.

Spia, La (The Spy)—Italian opera by Arditi, produced at New York in 1856. The libretto is adapted from "The Spy," by Cooper. It was very successful.

Spiegelritter, Der (The Knight of the Mirror)—German opera in three acts, music by Ignaz Walter, text by Kotzebue, produced at Mannheim in 1793. Franz Schubert's first opera was written on this text in 1815, but it was never put on the stage.

Sposa Fedele, La (The Faithful Spouse)—An Italian opera buffa, music by G. Pacini, libretto by Rossi, produced at Venice in 1819. A popular opera of the time.

Sposo di Tre, Marito di Nessuna, La (The Spouse of Three, Husband of None)—Italian opera buffa in two acts by Cherubini, produced at Venice in 1783.

Statue, La (The Statue)—French comic opera in three acts by Ernest Reyer, words by Carré, and Barbier, produced in Paris, April 11, 1861.

Stelle die Tanzerin (Stella, the Danseuse)—German comic opera by H. Strobl, text by K. Mattheis, produced at Graz in 1874.

Sternenkönigin, Die (Queen of the Stars)—German operetta by Ferdinand Kauer, produced at Vienna in 1815.

Stiffelio—Italian opera in four acts, music by Verdi, words by Piave, produced in Trieste, 1850.

Stranger at Home, The—English opera, music by Thomas Linley, produced in London, 1786.

Straniera, La (The Stranger)—Italian opera in two acts, music by Bellini, words by Romani, produced in Milan, 1829. The opera was not such a success as Bellini's "Pirata" had been.

Stratonice—French comic opera in one act, music by Méhul, words by Hoffman, recitative by Daussoigne-Méhul, produced in Paris, 1821. Stratonice was the step-mother of Antiochus I. of Syria. She returned her step-son's passionate love, was given to him as wife by her husband, and the two ruled over the lands beyond the Euphrates.

Streichholzmädel, Das (The Match Girl) — Fairy opera in one act. Music by August Enna, text by Enzberg and Rehbaum, first produced at Copenhagen, 1897. Time, early part of 1800. Story after Anderson's fairy tale. This opera has been exceptionally popular in Europe ever since its appearance.

Streik der Schmiede, Der (The Strike of the Smiths) — Opera in one act. Music by Max Josef Beer, text by Viktor Leon, first produced at Augsburg in 1897. Text is based upon a poem by Coppie.

Strollers, The — Musical comedy, music by Ludwig Englander, produced in New York, 1901.

Student King, The — Romantic light opera, music by Reginald de Koven, words by Frederick Rankin and Stanislaus Stange, produced in New York, 1907.

Sultan of Mocha, The — Comic opera in three acts, music by Alfred Cellier, words by W. Lestocq, first produced at the Prince's Theatre, Manchester, England, November 16, 1874, reproduced at St. James' Theatre, London, April 17, 1876, and revived at the Strand Theatre, London, 1887.

Susse Gift, Das (Sweet Poison) — Musical comedy in one act. Music by Albert Goeter, text by Martin Frehse, first produced at Cologne, 1906. Scene, a King's garden where it is discovered that the juice of grapes is not a sweet poison but an exhilirating, golden beverage.

Suzanne — French comic opera in three acts. Music by E. Paladilhe, text by Cormon and Lockroy, first produced at Paris, 1878.

Per Svinaherde (Peter, the Swineherd) — Swedish opera by Ivor Hallström, with text by Christianson; produced with success at Stockholm in 1887 and has since been successful in other cities.

Sylphen, Die (The Sylphs) — German fairy opera in three acts, music by Heinrich Himmel, words by Robert, produced in Berlin, 1806. The libretto is adapted from Gozzi.

Sylvia — French grand mythological ballet in three acts, music by Delibes, words by Barbier and Merante, produced in Paris, 1876.

Symphonie, La (The Symphony) — French comic opera in one act. Music by Clapisson, text by Saint-Georges, produced at Paris in 1839. This opera is also called "Maitre Albert" (Master Albert). The hero is a music master, and the story tells of the suffering and final happiness which came to the musician through this symphony.

Szep Ilon (Beautiful Ilka) — Hungarian opera in four acts, music by Mosonyi, produced in Buda-Pesth, 1861.

T

Tabarin — French comic opera in two acts, music by Georges Bousquet, words by Alboize and André, produced in Paris, 1852.

Tableau Parlant, Le (The Speaking Tableau) — French comic opera in one act, music by Grétry, words by Anseaume, produced in Paris, September 20, 1769. Grétry wrote the score in two months.

Tajewstoi (The Secret) — A Czechish comic opera in three acts by Franz Smetana. It was produced at Prague in 1878.

Talismano, Il (The Knight of the Leopard) — Grand opera in three acts, music by Balfe, original libretto in English by Arthur Matthison, translated into Italian by G. Zaffira, produced at Drury Lane Theatre, London, 1874. The story is taken from Sir Walter Scott's novel, "The Talisman."

Tamerlan — Opera in four acts, words by Morel, music by Winter, produced in Paris in 1802.

Tamerlano (Tamerlane) — Favorite historical subject for many Italian operas in the Eighteenth Century. Text is that by Count Agostino Piovene. Earliest opera by Francesco Gaspanni, with Piovene's text, first produced at Venice, 1710.

Tammany, or The Indian Chief — American opera, music by James Hewitt, words by Ann Julia Hatton, first produced in New York in 1794, under the auspices of the Tammany Society.

Tancrède — French grand opera in five acts and a prologue, music by André Campra, words by Danchet, produced in Paris, 1702. The libretto is adapted from an incident in Tasso's "Jerusalen Delivered," and Voltaire's "Tancred, Prince of Tiberius and Antioch."

Tancredi — Italian grand opera, music by Rossini, words by Rossi, produced in Venice, February 6, 1813. The libretto was adapted from Voltaire's tragedy and Tasso's "Jerusalem Delivered." The hero of the opera is Tancred, Prince of Tiberius and Antioch, who distinguished himself in the first crusade and died in 1112.

Taniousha — Opera, music by Volkov, first produced in 1756. This was the first opera written by a Russian to a Russian libretto.

Tante Schläft, Die (Auntie Asleep) — A bright little German operetta in one act by Henri Caspers, produced at Hamburg in 1903. This vivacious bit of music with its ridiculous text deserves a wide recognition.

Tänzerin, Die (The Dancer) — German opera in three acts; music and text by Arthur Friedheim, first produced at Cologne in 1905. The story takes place in Corinth shortly after Alexander the Great mounts the throne. The young warrior, then only twenty years old, falls in love with Thaïs, a beautiful dancer, who vows to the goddess Artemis that she will remain a virgin all her life. At first she is unapproachable, but the ardent young warrior proves irresistible and with a farewell to her oath she yields to him.

Tarare — French grand opera in five acts and a prologue, music by Salieri, words by Beaumarchais, the French dramatist, produced in Paris, June 8, 1787. The story is founded on an eastern tale, "Sodak and Kalasrade," its theme is the "rights of man" and it had its share in bringing about the great revolution of 1789. The opera is still occasionally performed.

Tatooed Man, The — Comic opera, music by Victor Herbert, words by Harry B. Smith, produced in New York, 1907.

Taucher, Der (The Diver) — German opera in two acts, music by Conradin Kreutzer, produced in Stuttgart in 1813.

Tekeli — English opera, music by James Hook, produced in London in 1808.

Tempesta, La (The Tempest) — Italian opera, music by Halévy, words by Scribe, produced in London, June 14, 1850. Shakespeare's play by the same name is reproduced in part. Avill, Miranda, Caliban and some of the other characters appear in the opera.

Templario, Il (The Templar) — Italian grand opera in three acts, music by Otto Nicolai, words by Girol, produced in Turin, 1840. The libretto is founded upon Scott's novel "Ivanhoe."

Templer und die Jüdin, Der (The Templar and the Jewess) — German opera in three acts, music by Marschner, words by Wohlbrück, produced in Leipzig, December, 1829. The libretto is founded upon Scott's novel, "Ivanhoe."

Templiers, Les (The Templars) — Grand opera in five acts, music by H Litoff, libretto by A. S. Bonnemère and Adenis, produced at Brussels in 1886.

Teodora (Theodora) — Italian opera, music by Scarlatti, words by Marselli, produced in Rome, 1693. Theodora was the wife of Justinian I. This opera is the first in which an accompanied recitative was used.

Teseo (Theseus) — Italian opera, music by Händel, words by Haym, produced in London December 10, 1713. The story is the mythological one of Theseus, rescuer of Ariadne.

Tess — An opera in four acts, music by Frederick d'Erlinger, text by Luigi Illica. First produced in Naples in 1906; first English production, Covent Garden, July 14, 1909. The libretto is founded on Thomas Hardy's novel, "Tess of the d'Urbervilles," and follows the story very closely, there being no change in any but one of the minor characters or their relationship to each other. It has had a favorable reception in both Italy and London.

Testament, Le; ou, Les Billets Doux (The Testament; or, The Love Letters) — French comic opera in one act, music by Auber, words by Planard, produced in Paris, September 18,

1819. Its success was but slight and it is now entirely forgotten.

Teufel ist Los, Der (The Devil to Pay) — German "Singspiel" (Vaudeville), music arranged by Hiller, produced in Leipzig October 8, 1752. The text was adapted from Charles Coffey's farce by the same name. It is hardly to be dignified by the term opera.

Teufel's Lust-Schloss, Des (The Devil's Pleasure Castle) — German opera, music by Johann Friedrich Reichardt, words by Kotzebue, the German dramatist, produced in Berlin in 1802.

Teufelswand, Die (The Devil's Wall) — Czechish opera, music by Smetana, produced in Prague in 1882. It is sometimes called "Teufelsmauer," which has the same meaning.

Thaïs — French lyrical drama in three acts, music by Massenet, words by Gallet, produced in Paris, 1894. The libretto is adapted from Anatole France's beautiful little story.

Tharsis and Zèhe — French grand opera in five acts and a prologue, music by Rebel and Francœur, words by Laserre. produced in Paris, 1728.

Thétis et Pélée (Thetis and Peleus) — French grand opera in five acts and a prologue, music by Colasse, words by Fontenelle, produced in Paris in 1689. Thetis and Peleus were the parents of Achilles.

Thirty Thousand — English opera, music by John Braham and Reeve, produced in London, 1804.

Thomas and Sally — English opera, music by Arne, words by Bickerstaff, produced in London, 1760.

Thomyris, Queen of Scythia — English opera, words by Motteux, produced in London, 1719. The composer is not known.

Thorgrini — English opera in four acts, music by F. H. Cowen, words by Joseph Bennett, produced in London, April 22, 1890. The text is founded upon an Icelandic Saga.

Thürmer's Töchterlein, (Thürmer's Little Daughter) — German comic opera in three acts, music by Rheinberger, words by Max Stahl, produced in Munich, 1873.

Thurm zu Babel, Der (The Tower of Babel) — German religious opera, in two parts, music by Rubinstein, words by Rodenberg, produced in Königsberg, 1870.

Tiefland, Im (In the Valley)— German opera in two acts and a prologue, music by Eugen d'Albert, words by Lothar, produced in Prague, 1903. The libretto is adapted from Guimera. A shepherd comes down from his mountain home to dwell in the valley, but finding there only misery and disappointment, returns to his beloved highlands. It was given in New York during the season of 1908-09.

Tigrane — Italian opera in three acts, music by Scarlatti, produced in Venice, 1715. Tigrane was King of Armenia in the First Century B. C., and ally of Mithridates.

Tilda — Italian opera by Francesco Cilea, first produced at Florence in 1892. An opera which can not please any refined taste.

Till Eulenspiegel — Folk opera by Reznicek, produced in Carlsruhe, Germany, 1901. Eulenspiegel is the well-known comic character of Brunswick. It has since been revived in Berlin.

Timbre d'Argent, Le (The Silver Bell) — French fantastic opera in four acts, music by Saint-Saëns, words by Carré and Barbier, written in 1870, but not produced till February 23, 1877, in Paris. It has very unequal merit and does not occupy an important place among the composer's operas.

Timide, Le — French opera in one act, music by Auber, words by Scribe and Xavier, produced in Paris, 1826.

Timocrate — Italian opera, music by Leonardo Leo, words by Lalli, produced in Venice, 1723.

Toberne; ou, Le Pêcheur Suidois (Tobernem; or, The Swedish Fisherman) — French opera in two acts, music by Bruni, words by Patras, produced in Paris, 1795.

Töchter des Pächters, Die (The Farmer's Daughters) — A Romanian opera by Ad. Caudella, produced at Jassy in 1883.

Tochter Granada's, Die (Granada's Daughter) — A Swedish romantic opera by Ivar Hallström, first produced at Stockholm in 1892. This opera has been very cordially received.

Toinon et Toinette — French opera in two acts, music by Gossec, words by Desboulmiers, produced in Paris, 1767.

Tolommeo — Italian opera, music by Handel, words by Haym, produced in London, April 19, 1728. The hero of the opera is Ptolemy I., King of Egypt in the Third and Fourth Centuries before Christ. He founded the library at Alexandria.

Tom Jones — French comic opera in three acts, music by Philidor, words by Poinsinet, produced in Paris, February 27, 1765. The libretto is based upon the novel of Fielding. This opera was the first to contain an unaccompanied quartet. It is no longer upon the stage.

Tom Jones — Musical comedy, music by Eduard German, book by Alex M. Thompson and Robert Courtneige, lyrics by Charles H. Taylor, first produced in London, 1907. The plot is founded upon Fielding's novel.

Tonelli, La — French comic opera in two acts, music by Ambroise Thomas, words by Sauvage, produced in Paris, March 30, 1853. It is no longer upon the stage.

Tonnelier, Le (The Cooper) — French opera, music by Isouard, words by Debrieau and Quetant, produced in Paris, 1797. The story is somewhat related to one of Boccaccio's.

Töpfer, Der (The Potter) — German song play in one act, music and words by Johann Andre, produced in Frankfurt, 1773.

Torquato Tasso — Lyric drama in four acts, music by Donizetti, words by Ferretti, produced in Rome, 1833.

Totentanz, Der (The Dance of Death) — An operetta by Josef Reiter, first produced at Dessau in 1905. It is a story based on an old Silesian legend, which originated in Germany early in the Sixteenth Century at the time of the "Black Death." Its hero is Rübezahl disguised as an old piper.

Toulon Soumis (Toulon Subdued) — Revolutionary opera, music by Rochefort, words by Fabre d'Olivet, produced in Paris, 1794.

Tragaldabas — A German comic opera in four acts, music by d'Albert, text by Rudolph Lotharo, first produced at Hamburg in 1907. The libretto is based on Vacqueries' French comedy by the same title, which appeared in 1848. Tragaldabas is a plebeian Falstaff, fond of wine, women and gambling, and wholly unrefined. In spite of this, Donna Laura borrows him for a husband, realizing that as a married woman she can more easily win some man. She succeeds in gaining a prince and Tragaldabas is cast off like a worn-out shoe. The public fails to understand how d'Albert lent his genius to such a libretto. The opera has so far been considered a failure.

Trank der Unsterblichkeit, Der (The Drink of Immortality) — German opera in four acts, music by E. T. A. Hoffmann, words by Soden, produced in Bamberg, 1808.

Traum Else (Dream Elsa) — German fairy opera in one act, music by Arpad Doppler, words by Paul Ost. The opera consists of a series of pictures, representing fairy tales, which appear to little Elsa as she sleeps.

Tre Nozze, Le (The Three Weddings) — Italian opera in three acts, music by G. E. A. Alary, text by Berettoni, produced at Paris in 1851. Text is adapted from Molière. An old baron falls in love with the young daughter of the Marchioness, but she loves a young cavalier. The valet and a vivacious soubrette help the lovers by playing all sorts of pranks upon the old baron. The last one sends him into the arms of the Marchioness, who gladly accepts him. Then there comes about three happy weddings.

Trésor Supposé, Le; ou, Le Danger d'Écounter aux Portes (The Supposed Treasure; or, The Danger of Listening at Key Holes) — French comic opera in one act, music by Méhul, words by Hoffmann, produced in Paris, July 29, 1802. It has been sung during the last decade in Germany.

Trial by Jury — English operetta in one act, music by Arthur Sullivan, words by Gilbert, produced in London, March 25, 1875. It is a satire upon English courts of law of the present day.

Tribut de Zamora, Le (The Tribute of Zamora) — French grand opera in five acts, music by Gounod, words by d'Ennery and Bresil, produced in Paris, April 1, 1881. Zamora is a city of Spain, captured in the Tenth Century by the Moors, and forced to send as tribute to the Caliph one hundred maidens.

Trionfo della Libertà, Il (Triumph of Liberty) — Italian opera by Alessandro Scarlatti, produced at Venice in 1707. This is one of the earliest of Scarlatti's more pretentious operas, and he conducted its performance in person. Unfortunately only fragments of it exist and no fair estimate of its value can be formed.

Trionfo di Camillo, Il (Camillo's Triumph) — Italian opera by Gluck, produced at Rome in 1754 The hero is Marcus Furius Camillus, a famous Roman general who earned the title of "Father of His Fatherland."

Trionfo di Clelia, Il (The Triumph of Clelia) — Italian opera, music by Gluck, produced in Bologna in 1762.

Triumph of Bacchus, The — Russian fairy opera, music by Dargomijsky, words by Poushkin, the Russian poet, finished in 1848, but not produced till 1868 in St. Petersburg and Moscow. Story is a mythological one.

Trompette de la Prince, Le (The Trumpeter of the Prince) — French comic opera in one act by François Bazin, text by Melesville, produced at Paris in 1846.

Troqueurs, Les (The Barterers) — French comic opera in one act, music by Daubergne, words by Vade, produced in Paris in 1753. It is usually said to be the first comic opera containing spoken dialogue.

Troubadour, The — English grand opera in four acts, music by Sir Alexander Mackenzie, words by Francis Hueffer, produced in London, June 8, 1886. It was almost a complete failure.

Turandot — Fairy opera in eight scenes, music by Busoni, an Italian composer, words by Gozzi. The foundation for the libretto is the Persian fairy tale, as dramatized by Schiller.

Turk in Italia, Il (The Turk in Italy) — Italian opera, music by Rossini, text by Romani, produced at Milan in 1814 and became a decided success. This opera was written when the composer was only twenty-three years old. It was very popular and found its way to America where it appeared in New York in 1826 and in 1834.

Tutti in Maschera (All in Masks) — Italian comic opera in three acts, music by Carlo Pedrotti, words by Marcello, produced in Verona, 1856.

Twiddle-Twaddle — Comic opera, music by Maurice Levi, words by Edgar Smith, produced in New York, 1906.

U

Ulrich von Hutton — Grand opera in five acts; music by Alexander Fesca; text by A. Schröder, produced at Braunschweig in 1849.

Un'Avventura di Scaramuccia — Italian comic opera, music by L. Ricci, produced in Milan, 1834. It was a very great success. The Scaramuz is a typical figure on the Italian comic stage, where he serves as a foil for the clown.

Un Avvertimento ai Gelosi (A Warning to Jealous People) — Italian opera, music by Balfe, first produced in Pavia, 1831.

Undine — A romantic opera in four acts. Music and libretto by Lortzing, first produced at Hamburg in 1845. This is one of the Undine legends. A young knight, Hugo von Ringstettin, is sent out by his sweetheart to seek adventure. He comes to a fishing village, here he sees Undine, loves her, and marries her. After a while Undine confesses to him that she is a nymph and has no soul. This alarms him, but he loves her and takes her home. There his old sweetheart tries to separate Undine and Hugo and she succeeds, Undine being sent away. Hugo is about to marry her when Undine appears before him. His old love for his nymph wife returns, but as he clasps her in his arms he dies. Undine gains pardon for him and from then on they live together in fairyland. Its brilliant success at Hamburg was one of the few happy moments in Lortzing's life.

Undine (The Water Spirit) — This well-known romantic little fairy tale by Lamotte-Fouquet is popular in all countries and has been set to music by German, French, Russian and Danish composers: Hoffmann (Berlin, 1816), Semet (Paris, 1863), Lwoff (Petersburg, 1846), J. P. Hartmann (Copenhagen, 1842). Lortzing's "Undine" (Leipzig, 1846), is one of the best; the overture is splendid.

Uniform, Die (The Uniform) — German song play in four acts, music by Weigl, words by Treitschke, produced in Vienna, 1803. The libretto is adapted from Carpani.

Un Jour à Paris, ou La Leçon Singulière (A Day in Paris, or The Singular Lesson) — French comic opera in three acts; music by Isouard, text by Etienne, produced at Paris in 1808.

Unmöglichste von Allen, Das (The Most Impossible Thing) — German comic opera in three acts. Music and text by Anton Urspruch, first produced at Carlsruhe in 1897. Text has been freely adapted from a comedy by the same name, ("El Major Imposaible,") by Lope de Vega. The most impossible thing is to manage a woman in love. This opera awakened great interest, the music is original, pure and rather free from Wagnerian influence. It is an acquisition to modern German opera, and has so far been extremely popular everywhere in Europe.

Unterbrochene Opferfest, Das (The Interrupted Sacrifice) — German opera in three acts, music by Peter von Winter, words by Huber, produced in Vienna, 1796. This opera with "Marie von Montalban" was the composer's best work.

Untersberg, Der — German romantic opera in three acts, music by Poissl, words by Schenck, produced in Munich, 1829.

Urvasi — Romantic opera in three acts. Music and text by William Kienzl. One day Urvasi, the princess of the virgins of heaven, comes to earth. She is seen by the King of Persia, he falls in love with her and she returns his love. But, being immortal, she can see him only from time to time. He swears eternal loyalty to her and she promises to be his in heaven and leaves him. In order to test him, she is absent a long time. In despair he doubts her loyalty. This brings great suffering upon both of them, but after years he finds her again and in death becomes hers. The setting is exquisite and the opera is a splendid success.

Uthal — French opera in one act, music by Méhul, words by Saint-Victor, produced in Paris, May 17, 1806. The text is adapted from one of Ossian's legends and in order to give a gray tone to the whole, Méhul left out the vilolins in his score.

Utopia Limited — Comic opera in two acts by W. S. Gilbert and Sir Arthur Sullivan, first produced at the Savoy Theatre, London, October 7, 1893. This opera, founded on the notion of a Utopia run as a limited liability concern, is much heavier and less delightful than the earlier production of this famous pair of writers.

V

Vagabund, Der (The Vagabond) — A German operetta in three acts; music by Karl Zeller, text by M. West and L. Held, produced at Vienna in 1886.

Vakoula le Forgeron (Vakaula the Smith) — Russian opera in three acts, music by Tschaikowsky, words by Polowsky, produced in St. Petersburg, 1876. The libretto is founded upon a novel by Gogol.

Val d'Andorre, Le (The Vale of Andorra) — French comic opera, music by Halévy, words by Saint Georges, produced in Paris, 1848.

Valentine de Milan (Valentine of Milan) — French comic opera in three acts, music by Étienne Méhul, completed by his nephew, Joseph Daussoigne-Méhul, words by Bonilly, produced in Paris, 1822.

Valeria — German opera, music by Gottfried Heinrich Stolzl, produced at Naumburg, 1712. It was very popular at the time.

Valet de Chambre, Le (The Body-servant) — French comic opera in one act. Music by Carafa, text by Melesville and Scribe, produced at Paris in 1823. The music is replete with melody and animation; the Valet's duet has always been a favorite bit of song.

Valet de Deux Maîtres, Le (The Servant of Two Masters) — French comic opera in two acts. Music by

François Devienne, text by Roger, produced at Paris in 1799.

Valet de Ferme, Le (The Valet of the Grange) — French opera, music by César Franck, produced in Paris, 1848.

Vampyr, Der (The Vampire) — Romantic German opera in two acts, music by Marschner, words by Wohlbruck, produced in Leipzig, March 28, 1828. It was very successful notwithstanding its repulsive subject. The Vampire in Slavic legend is the soul that cannot rest peacefully in its grave after its body has died.

Van Dyck — German opera in three acts; music by R. Emmerich, text by E. Pasqué, produced at Stettin in 1875.

Vasall von Szigeth, Der — A German opera by Anton Smareglia, first produced at Vienna in 1889 and in New York in 1890. Szigeth is a little town in Hungary. The story is full of horror, and it quite shocked the American audience. The music is decidedly Hungarian.

Vasco da Gama — Italian opera by F. H. Himmel, text by Filistri, produced at Berlin in 1801. Da Gama was the famous Portuguese navigator, who discovered the route to India, making his voyage in 1499. He has been immortalized by the great Portuguese poet, Camoens, in the national epic "Os Lusiades."

Vaterunser, Das ("Our Father," The Lord's Prayer) — German musical drama in one act; music by H. Röhrs, text by Ernest von Possart, first produced at Cologne in 1905. Text adapted from Coppée's story. A noble-minded young priest is shot by fanatic officers. His sister Rose, who idolized him, is in despair and vows vengeance. In vain does an old priest urge her to find solace in prayer. As she pours over her rosary, her voice chokes at "Thy will be done," she can not say it. She is tortured by her desire for revenge and the knowledge that she should "forgive." In the midst of her troubles one of the young officers who killed her brother seeks refuge at her house. She is tempted to betray him, but her brother's spirit seems to guide her; she takes his cassock and hat from the peg, gives them to the soldier and, grateful to her, he escapes in his disguise. Then Rose kneels and says her prayers, and so well do the text and the music harmonize, so spiritually is the whole constructed that we too say "Amen" with the suffering little girl.

Vecchio Marito, Il (The Old Husband) — Italian comic opera in the Neapolitan dialect, music by Logroscino, produced in Naples about 1735.

Vedova Scaltra, La (The Cunning Widow) — Italian opera buffa by V. Righini, produced at Prague in 1778.

Veiled Prophet, The — A romantic opera, music by Dr. Villers Stanford, words by W. Barclay Squire, first produced at the Court Theatre of Hanover, February 6, 1881, in a German translation by Ernest Frank. Later it was revised and adapted for the Italian opera stage, in which language it was first performed in England at Covent Garden Theatre, July 26, 1893. The libretto is adapted from Moore's well known poem, "Lalla Rookh."

Velleda, Die Zauberin des Brockens (Velleda, The Enchantress on the Brocken) — A German opera, music and text by E. Sobolewsky, produced at Königsberg in 1835.

Venceslao — Italian opera; music by C. F. Pollarolo, text by Zeno, produced at Venice in 1703. The hero is St. Wenceslaus, King of Bohemia, who introduced Christianity into his country and who was murdered by his brother in 935.

Vendatte, La (The Feud) — Italian opera, music by Henry de Ruolz, words by Leon and Adolphe, produced in Paris, 1839.

Vêpres Siciliennes, Les (The Sicilian Massacre) — French grand opera in five acts, music by Verdi, words by Scribe and Duveyrier, produced in Paris, 1855. The massacre was one of the French by the Sicilians, March 30, 1282.

Vera Costanza, La (True Constancy) — Italian opera by Pasquale Anfossi, produced at Rome in 1776. This opera was also popular in Germany.

Verbum Nobile — A national Polish opera in one act by Stanislaw Moninszko, produced at Warsaw in 1860.

Verful Cu Dor (The Summit of Longing) — A Roumanian opera, music by Skibinski (Linbicz), libretto by P. de Lavoc, produced at Bucharest in 1879. This is supposed to be the first Roumanian opera and is all the more interesting since "P. de Lavoc" is the pen name of Princess Elizabeth of Roumania.

Vergine del Sole, La (The Maiden of the Sun) — Italian grand opera, music by Cimarosa, produced in St. Petersburg, 1788.

Verkaufte Braut, Die (The Bartered Bride) — Comic opera in three acts; music by Smetana, text by Sabina, first produced at Prague in 1866. Story is laid in a Bohemian village at the present time. Hans and Marie love each other, but Marie's father, influenced by a marriage broker, insists that she marry Wenzel, the son of Micha. The broker offers Hans three hundred guilders if he will give up Marie, and Hans accepts the money, stipulating that Marie must marry Micha's son. Marie is in tears over this base barter, but Hans reveals himself to Micha, whom he recognizes as his son by a former marriage. Hans knew this and had made a good bargain besides gaining his bride. Fax Kalbeck re-wrote the text in German, and since 1892 this opera has become world famous. The music is charming.

Verlobung zu der Laterne, Die (The Engagement to the Lantern) — Comic opera in two acts. Music by Jacques Offenbach, text after Michael Carré and Leon Batta, first produced at Berlin, 1885. Scene, a little village.

Verlorene Paradies, Das (Paradise Lost) — German opera by Rubinstein, text by J. Rodenberg, produced at Düsseldorf in 1875. Milton's poem by the same title furnished the inspiration for the text.

Vernarrte Prinzess, Die (The Foolish Princess) — A fairy tale in three acts. Music by Oskar von Chelius, text by Bierbaum, first produced in Wiesbaden, 1905. Queen Marguerite of Italy, to whom the charming little opera was dedicated, was present.

Verschwender, Der (The Spendthrift) — A fairy play by Raimund, for which Conradin Kreutzer wrote the incidental music, of which there is a great deal. The play or opera was very successful and is still upon the stage. It is considered one of Kreutzer's best works.

Verschworenen, Die (The Conspirators) — German opera in one act, music by Franz Schubert, text by Castelli. First produced at Vienna in 1861. Like others of Schubert's operas this had been written in 1819 but never produced during the composer's life-time. It is known in French as the "Women's Crusade," and depicts a domestic war.

Versiegelt (Locked Up) — A German comic opera in one act by Leo Blech, first produced at Bremen in 1908. The plot is a simple little intrigue. The Burgomaster is locked up and gains his freedom when he consents to the marriage of his daughter to the son of his bitter enemy. He himself is rewarded by gaining the hand of a lovable widow who has been pining for him. This opera is one of the most wholesome fun-makers on the modern stage. It has run like wildfire all over Germany and it pleases wherever it is heard.

Vestale, La (The Vestal Virgin) — French romantic grand opera in three acts by Gasparo Spontini, words by Jouy, produced in Paris, December 11, 1807. The text was originally written for Cherubini, but not used by him.

Versunkene Glocke, Die (The Sunken Bell) — Musical drama in five acts. Music and text by Heinrich Zöllner, first produced at Berlin, 1899. Libretto based upon Hauptmann's well known drama of same title. A popular opera in Germany, especially in Berlin.

Veuve Indecise, La (The Vacillating Widow) — French operetta in one act, music by E. R. Duni, text by Vade, produced at Paris in 1759. This little operetta is a parody on "La Veuve Coquette," (The Coquettish Widow).

Viaggiatori Ridicoli, I (The Ridiculous Travellers) — Italian comic opera, music by Guylielni, produced in Naples, 1772.

Viaggio a Reims, Il (The Journey to Rheims) — Italian opera in one act, music by Rossini, words by Balocchi, produced in Paris, 1825.

Vicar of Bray, The — Comic opera, music by Edward Solomon, words by Sydney Grundy, first produced at the Globe Theatre, London, on July 22, 1882. A revised version was produced at the Savoy Theatre, London, January 28, 1892. The plot is founded upon the adventures of Sandford and Merton whose youth Mr. Thomas Day depicted in his well known romance.

Vicar of Wakefield, The — Opera, music by Liza Lehmann, lyrics by Laurence Hausman, first produced at Manchester, 1906, and in London, 1907. The plot is that of Goldsmith's romance.

Vieille, La (The Old Woman) — French comic opera in one act, music by Fétis, words by Scribe and Delavigne, produced in Paris, 1826.

Vie Parisienne, La (Parisian Life) — Operatic burlesque in five acts, music by Offenbach, words by Meilhac and Halévy, first produced in Paris, October 31, 1866. An English version by H. B. Farnie was given at the Avenue Theatre, London, October 3, 1883.

Vier Grobiane, Die (The Four Bullies) — Comic opera in three acts. Music by Ermanno Wolf-Ferrari, text by Pizzolato after Goldoni, first produced in Munich, 1906. Translated into the German by Herman Teibler. The four bullies are four husbands who try to lord it over their wives.

Vieux Chateau, Le (The old Castle) — French comic opera in three acts, music by D. Della Maria, text by A. Duval, produced at Paris in 1798. It is a pretty little story of a chance encounter, called also "La Rencontre," but unfortunately the music is not equal to the text.

Vieux Coquet, Le (The Old Beau) — A French comic opera by Papavoine, produced with success in Paris about 1770. "Falstaff," the fat, jovial old beau in Shakespeare's comedy, "The Merry Wives of Windsor," furnishes the amusement.

Viking's Voyage, The — Swedish opera by Ivar Hallström, first produced at Stockholm in 1877. It is of a decidedly national character and was among the first of Hallström's operas to be cordially received.

Village Opera, The — English opera, music by Charles Johnson, produced in London, 1728. It was one of the first of the many imitations of Gay's "Beggars' Opera."

Villi, Le (The Witch Dancers) — Opera in two acts, music by Giacomo Puccini, words by Ferdinando Fontana, first presented at Milan, 1884. The Villi are the spirits of maidens whose lovers have been untrue to them. They dance in the forest, and when one of their faithless lovers appears, whirl him about in their circle until he dies of exhaustion.

Vineta — A German opera in three acts, music by H. Frankenberger, libretto by F. Bohn, produced at Sondershausen in 1851. "Vineta" is a romance of a night on the sea.

Violette, La (The Violet) — French comic opera in three acts, music by Carafa and Anne Leborne, text by Planard, produced at Paris in 1826. Text is based on Count Tressan's novel, "Gerard de Nevers." The music might have been excellent had the composers used a little more care. The opera did not last long, but a popular composition for the piano composed on one of the motifs of "La Violette" keeps the name alive.

Violino del Diavolo (The Devil's Violin) — An opera in three acts, music by A. Mercuri, words by Fontana, first produced at Cagli near Pesaro, September 12, 1878. The plot resembles that of Faust, except that it is the woman who sells herself to the devil.

Virgine (Virginia) — French grand opera in three acts, music by H. M. Berton, words by Desaugiers Sen., produced in Paris, 1823. Virginia was the daughter of Virginius, and was killed by her father to preserve her honor from the attacks of Appius Claudius.

Virtuosi Ambulanti, I (The Traveling Comedians) — Italian comic opera in two acts, music by Fioravanti, words by Balocchi, produced in Paris, 1807.

Visitandines, Les (The Nuns) — French comic opera in two acts; music by Devienne, libretto by Picard, first produced at Paris in 1792. This opera was popular for a long time. It is also known as "The Young Ladies' Seminary."

Vivandière, La — French opera, music by Godard, produced in Paris, 1895.

Voix Humaine, La (The Human Voice) — French opera in two acts, music by Giulio Alary, words by Melesville, produced in Paris, 1861.

Voto, Il — See "Mala Vita."

Voyage Impromptu, Le (The Impromptu Voyage) — French comic opera in one act, music by Pacini, text by Dumersan and Aubertin, produced at Paris in 1866.

W

Waisenhaus, Das (The Orphanage) — Opera by Josef Feigl, text by Treitschke, produced at Vienna in 1808.

Wakula der Schmied (Wakula the Smith) — A Russian opera in three acts; music by Tschaikowsky, text by Polowsky, adapted from that by Gogal; produced at St. Petersburg in 1876.

Wald, Der (The Forest) — A one-act opera, music and words by Miss Ethel Smyth, first produced in Dresden, September, 1901. It was produced at Covent Garden, July 18, 1902, and at the Metropolitan Opera House, New York, in March, 1903, this being the first time that an opera written by a woman had ever been performed in America. A revival at Covent Garden on June 26, 1903, attests its popularity.

Waldemar — A romantic Swedish opera by Andreas Hallén. It was first produced at Stockholm in 1909 and met with success.

Walhalla in Not (Valhalla in Distress) — A German musical satire in three acts; music and libretto by Otto Neitzel, first produced at Bremen in 1905. The "Theft of Thor's Hammer," one of the old Edda stories, forms the background upon which Neitzel satirizes modern man. Over the broad backs of these Norse gods whom he ridicules for their vanity, Neitzel whips us and scorns those of us who think ourselves gods whether by favor of birth, through riches, power or any other cause. The text is original and very witty and is embellished with the most lyrical music. Neitzel deserves great praise for this creation.

Wallace — French grand opera in three acts, music by C. S. Catel, words by Fontanes, revised by Saint-Georges, produced in Paris, 1817. The hero of the opera is William Wallace, the great Scottish apostle of freedom, who was executed in the Tower in 1305.

Wally, La — Opera by Catalani. Libretto by Luigi Illica. Place, Alps of Switzerland. Time, Nineteenth Century. First produced at Turin in 1892.

Walpurgisnacht, Die (Walpurgis Night) — A romantic opera in three acts; music by J. Rümmler, text by E. J. Prochaska, produced at Prague in 1827. This spooky night is well known through Goethe's description in "Faust." It is the night between April thirtieth and May the first.

Waltz Dream, A — Operetta in three acts, music by Oscar Strauss, words by Felix Doermann and Leopold Jacobson, first produced in Vienna. An English version by Joseph W. Herbet was presented in New York, 1908. The plot is founded upon a story taken from Hans Meuller's "Book of Adventures."

Wanda — Grand tragic opera in five acts, music by Dvořák, the Bohemian composer, words by Sumawsky, produced in Prague, April, 1876. The libretto is adapted from the Polish of Sagynsky.

Wang — Two-act opera by Morse. Libretto by J. Cheever Goodwin. Place, Siam. First produced under the title of "Wang" at New York in 1891.

Waterman, The — English song play, music and words by Charles Dibdin, produced in London, 1774. It remained continuously upon the stage for many years, but has now disappeared.

Weinlese, Die (The Vintage) — German operetta by Johann Schenk, produced at Vienna in 1785. This is the composer's first production.

Wem die Krone? (To Whom the Crown?) — German opera in one act, music and libretto by Alexander Ritter. Produced at Weimar in 1800 under the able leadership of Richard Strauss, and scored a success.

Werther — Opera in three acts, music by Massenet, words by Milliet and Blau, completed in 1886 but not produced till 1892 in Vienna; the libretto is founded upon Goethe's "Sorrows of Werther."

Whittington and His Cat — English comic opera in three acts, music by Offenbach, words by G. B. Farnie, produced in London, 1874.

Widerspenstigen Zähmung, Der (The Taming of the Shrew) — German comic opera, music by Götz, words by Widmann, produced in Mannheim, October 11, 1874. The libretto is founded upon Shakespeare's comedy.

Wieland der Schmied (Wieland the Smith) — German romantic opera in four acts, music by Max Senger, words by Allfeld, produced January 18, 1880. The libretto is an adaptation of Simrock's poem of the old legend.

Wilde Jäger, Der (The Wild Huntsman) — German romantic opera in four acts; music by Victor Nesslor, text by Friedrich Hoffmann, produced at Leipzig in 1881. Text is adapted from Wolff's story.

Wildschütz, Der (The Poacher) — German comic opera in three acts, music and words by Lortzing, produced in Leipzig, December 31, 1842. The text is adapted from Kotzebue's "Rehbock."

Wilhelm von Oranien (William of Orange) — German grand opera in three acts by Heinrich Hoffmann, words by Roderich Fels, produced in Hamburg, February 5, 1882.

William Ratcliff — Russian opera in three acts, music by César Cui, produced in St. Petersburg, February 26, 1869. The libretto is a translation by Plechtcheieff of the romantic tragedy by Heine bearing the same name. The opera was very coldly received, but it is still occasionally produced in Russia.

Witch, The — Three-act opera by Enna. Libretto adapted by Alfred Ibsen from Arthur Fitger's tragedy of the same name. Place, Thalea's estate and village. Time, after the Thirty Years' War. First produced at Copenhagen in 1891.

Wittekind — German opera in three acts; music by Josef Wolfram, text by H. Meynert, produced at Dresden in 1838. The hero is Widukind, the great heathen Saxon general who led his army against Charlemagne. He gave up fighting against the latter and accepted the Christian religion. As a reward Charlemagne knighted him.

Wizard of Oz, The — Musical extravaganza by L. Frank Baum and Paul Tietjens, produced in Chicago, 1902.

Wizard of the Nile, The — Opera by Herbert. Libretto by Harry B. Smith. Place, Egypt. Time, 53 B. C. First produced at Wilkesbarre, Pa., in 1895.

Wolkenkind, Das (The Cloudchild) — German comic opera in three acts, music by Titl, words by Told, produced in Vienna, 1845.

Wonder, A; or, The Honest Yorkshireman — An English ballet opera by Henry Carey. It appeared in London in 1735.

Wonderland — Musical extravaganza in three acts, music by Victor Herbert, words by Glen MacDonough, produced in New York, 1905. The plot is founded upon a love philter which causes the eight daughters of the King of Hearts to fall in love with eight princes who live in an enchanted castle.

Woodman, The — An English operetta by William Shield, appeared in London in 1791.

Wreckers, The — Opera in three acts, music by Miss Ethel Smyth, words by H. B. Brewster, first produced in Leipzig, 1906, under the title "Strandrecht," and later in Prague. The first English performance was in London, June 22, 1909. The "Wreckers" are inhabitants of a small Cornish village who make it their business to wreck vessels by extinguishing the lighthouse lantern on stormy nights.

X

Xacarilla, La — Opera in one act and two tableaux; music by Marliani, text by Scribe, produced at Paris in 1839. La Xacarilla is a Spanish song, a kind of bolero, used as a rallying song by some smugglers. This little opera was a favorite curtain raiser.

Xaira — One of Garcia's Spanish operas. In two acts, and produced in Mexico in 1829.

Xerxes — English opera by Handel, produced at London in 1737. Xerxes I., born 465 B. C., was the great Persian king who bridged the Hellespont and marched a devastating army into Greece.

Y

Yelva, or the Orphan of Russia — English opera, music by Bishop, produced in London, 1833.

Yetiva — A Spanish opera by John Arnold, libretto by G. Morgan, produced at San Francisco in 1889.

Yolande — English ballet by G. Jacobi, first produced at London in 1877.

Young Hussar, The — An English operetta by Michael Kelly, produced in London in 1807.

Youth, Love and Folly — An English operetta by Michael Kelly, produced at London in 1805.

Yo, Yea — An English operetta by Dibdin, produced at London in 1776. A nautical theme forms the basis for the text; it is also known as "The Friendly Tars."

Yvonne — A French comic opera in one act; music by Joseph N. Ney, text by Deforges and De Leuven, produced at Paris in 1855.

Z

Zaide, Queen of Granada — A French heroic ballet in three acts. Music by Joseph N. Royer, text by Abbé Delamare, produced at Paris in 1739.

Zaira — Italian opera in three acts; music by Bellini, words by Romani, produced in Parma, 1829. The libretto is adapted from Voltaire's tragedy "Zaire." It was the least successful of Bellini's operas.

Zaire — English opera in two acts; music by Peter von Winter, produced in London, 1805. The libretto is based upon Voltaire's tragedy by the same name.

Zanetta — French comic opera in three acts; music by Auber, text by Saint-Georges and Scribe, produced at Paris in 1840. Zanetta teaches us that "one must not play with fire." A young nobleman tries to pique his sweetheart by making love to Zanetta, the daughter of a servant in the palace, but Zanetta's charms captivate him and he actually falls in love with her.

Zanetto — An Italian opera by Mascagni. It is founded on Coppée's popular one-act play "Le Passant" ("The Traveler"). First produced at Pesaro in 1896. This opera, while not as popular as some of Mascagni's, is of a much finer quality than one usually finds in his compositions.

Zauberbecher, Der (The Magic Cup) — Comic opera; music by Gabriel Pierné, text by Matrat, translated into the German by A. Horlacher; produced at Stuttgart in 1907. The magic cup disclosed the follies of inexperienced youths as well as those of experienced benedicts. The opera is successful.

Zauberschloss, Das (The Magic Castle) — An operetta by Johann Reichardt with text by Kotzebue, produced at Berlin in 1802. This is one of Reichardt's operettas which exercised a considerable influence over German opera.

Zehn Mädchen und Kein Mann (Ten Maids and No Man) — Operetta in one act by Franz von Suppé, produced at Vienna in 1862.

Zelia — Opera in three acts, music by G. Villate, words by T. Solera, first produced in Paris, 1877. The action takes place in Venice in 1553.

Zélisca — A ballet comedy in three acts; music by Jélyotte, text by Sauvé de la Noue, produced at Versailles in 1746. Jélyotte, the famous tenor, composed this music for the Dauphin's marriage.

Zelmira — Italian opera in two acts, music by Rossini, text by Tottola, first produced at Naples in 1822. Text is an imitation of Du Belloy's tragedy "Zelmira." The recitative in this opera is especially admirable. The leading role was sung by Rossini's wife in Italy and London where it was most enthusiastically received. Connoisseurs best appreciate the music of "Zelmira;" it made little impression on the general public.

Zéloide, ou Les Fleurs Enchantées (Zéloide, or The Enchanted Flowers) — French opera in two acts, music by Sebastian Lebrun, text by Etienne, produced at Paris in 1818. The opera achieved only moderate success.

Zemire and Azor — Fairy opera in four acts. Music by Grétry, words by Marmontel, produced in Fontainebleau, November 9, 1771. The opera placed Grétry at once among the foremost composers.

Zemire and Azor — German romantic opera in three acts, music by Ludwig Spohr, words by Shlée, produced in Frankfurt A/M, April 4, 1819. One song from the opera, "Rose Softly Blooming,'" is still occasionally heard.

Zenichove (The Suitors) — A Czechish opera in three acts by Larl Komarowic, produced at Prague in 1884. The text is a comedy.

Zenobia — Opera in three acts. Music by Coerne, text by Oskar Stein, first produced at Berlin, 1907. Zenobia, Queen of the Orient, is conquered by Emperor Aurelian of Rome. He demands that she become his wife, but she prefers death and kills herself.

Zephire et Flore — Opera in three acts with prologue, music by Lully, words by Douboulay, first produced at Paris, 1688.

Zerline, ou La Corbeille d'Oranges (Zerline, or The Basket of Oranges) — French grand opera in three acts by Auber, text by Scribe, produced at Paris in 1851. The text would be better suited to a vaudeville performance. Zerline is an orange seller who succeeds in marrying her daughter, Gemma, to a young officer.

Zerstörung Trojas, Die (The Destruction of Troy) — First part of Berloiz's great opera "Die Trojaner." Æneas is the hero of part one as well as of part two, "Trojene à Carthage" (which see). He is eclipsed however by the magnificent figure of Cassandra. In 1906 the entire opera appeared on two consecutive evenings at Brussels; and in 1907 it appeared again at Munich, both times with great success. It is to be hoped that it will receive the recognition the whole performance merits.

Zerstreute, Der (The Distracted One) — A comedy by Regnard with music by Haydn, produced at Vienna in 1776.

Zierpuppen (The Prims) — German comic opera in one act; music by Anselm Götzel, libretto by Richard Batka, first produced at Prague in 1905. Batka adapted his text from Molière's "Les Precieuses Ridicules" (The Ridiculous Prims) but he changes the ending. In Molière's text the suitors leave in triumph, but Batka has them stay and become reconciled to the girls. Zierpuppen is deservedly popular.

Zilda — French comic opera in two acts. Music by Flotow, text by Saint-Georges and H. Chivot, produced at Paris, 1866. A very light opera and did not last long.

Zirphile et Fleur de Myrthe (Zirphile and Myrtle Blossoms) — French opera in two acts; music by C. S. Catel, text by Jouy and Lefebvre, produced at Paris in 1818. This is one of Catel's last productions and it did not receive the recognition which it merited.

Zoraine et Zulnare — French opera in three acts, music by F. A. Boieldieu, text by Saint Just, produced at Paris in 1798. The text is adapted from Florian's novel "Gonsalve de Cordoue" (Gonzola of Cordova), the great Spanish captain who lived in the Sixteenth Century. This opera was Boieldieu's first real success and added greatly to his reputation.

Zoroastre (Zoroaster) — French grand opera in five acts and a prologue, music by Rameau, words by Cahusac, produced in Paris, 1749. Zoroaster was the Persian philosopher.

Zwarte Kapitein, De (The Black Captain) — A Flemish opera, music by Joseph Mertens, libretto by Lagye, produced at The Hague in 1877. This opera was very successful and popular.

Zweikampf mit der Geliebten, Der (A Lover's Duel) — German opera, music by Louis Spohr, text by Schink, produced at Hamburg in 1811 with success.

Z'widerwurzen (Crosspatch) — German opera in three acts; music and text by E. Korten: first produced at Elberfeld in 1905. A little village story in which Stasi, a pretty but haughty young girl, harshly rejects her lover. Her heart is kind but her tongue is sharp, and the rest of the village sympathizes with her lover and call her "crosspatch." But he shields her and succeeds in winning her love and makes a splendid woman of her. The text is based on a folk-play by Hermann von Schmid.

Zwillings Brüder, Die (The Twin Brothers) — German comic opera in one act, music by Schubert, words by Hoffmann, produced in Vienna, 1820. The libretto is adapted from the French.

SELECTED BIBLIOGRAPHY

Aldrich, Richard — Guide to the Ring of the Nibelungs.

Alexander, Louis — The Opera-Glass.

Annesley, Charles — Standard Opera-Glass.

Apthorp, W. F.— The Opera, Past and Present.

Barber, Grace E. — Wagner Opera Stories.

Blaze, F. H. J. Castil — The Opera in France. 2 vols.

Buel, J. W., editor — The Great Operas, with introduction by Verdi. 10 parts.

Burney, Charles — The Present State of Music in France and Italy. (1771.)

Carleton, F. E. — Operas, Their Writers and Plots.

Davison, Gladys — Stories from the Operas.

Edwards, H. S. — History of the Opera from its Origin in Italy to the Present Time. 2 vols.

Edwards, H. S. — Rossini and His School.

Edwards, H. S. — The Lyrical Drama, Essays on Subjects, Composers and Executants of Modern Opera. 2 vols.

Elson, Arthur — Critical History of Opera.

Modern Composers of Europe.

Fitzgerald, Percy — The Operas of Gilbert and Sullivan.

Gerard, Frances — Wagner, Bayreuth and the Festival Plays.

Gilman, Lawrence — Phases of Modern Music.

Grove, Sir George — Dictionary of Music and Musicians. (Article on Operas.)

Guerber, Helene A. — Stories of Popular Operas.
Stories of Famous Operas.
Stories of the Wagner Operas.
Henderson, W. J. — How Music Developed.
Hervey, Arthur — French Music in the Nineteenth Century. (Vol. 2 of Music in the Nineteenth Century, edited by R. H. Legge.)
Hervey, Arthur — Masters of French Music.
Hogarth, George — Memoirs of the Opera. 2 vols.
Kobbe, Gustav — Opera Singers.
Krehbiel, H. E.— Studies in the Wagnerian Drama.
Lahee, H. C. — Grand Opera in America.
Lavignac, Albert — The Music Dramas of Richard Wagner and his Festival Theatre in Bayreuth.
Lumley, Benjamin — Reminiscences of the Opera.
Maitland, J. A. Fuller — English Music in the Nineteenth Century. (Vol. 1 of Music in the Nineteenth Century, edited by R. H. Legge.)
Matthew, J. E. — Popular History of Music, Musical Instruments, Ballet and Opera from St. Ambrose to Mozart.
Newman, Ernest — Gluck and the Opera.
Pardon, G. F. — Tales from the Operas.
Parry, Sir C. H. H. — Art of Music.
Riemann, Hugo — Handbook of the Opera.
Ritter, F. L. — Music in America.
Rolland, Romain — History of Opera in Europe before Lully and Scarlatti.
Singleton, Esther — Guide to the Opera.
Streatfield, R. A. — The Opera: A Sketch of the Development of Opera, with full descriptions of every work in the modern repertory.
Upton, G. P.— The Standard Operas.
The Standard Light Operas.
Wagnalls, Mabel — Stars of the Opera.
Weston, Jessie L. — The Legends of the Wagner Drama.

Lightning Source UK Ltd.
Milton Keynes UK
UKHW011556130520
363213UK00008B/1383

9 789354 016004